Revolution and Subjectivity
in Postwar Japan

Revolution and Subjectivity in Postwar Japan

J. Victor Koschmann

THE UNIVERSITY OF CHICAGO PRESS
Chicago & London

J. VICTOR KOSCHMANN is professor of history at Cornell University. He is the author of *The Mito Ideology: Discourse, Reform, and Insurrection in Late Tokugawa Japan, 1790–1864* (1987); coeditor of *International Perspectives on Yanagita Kunio and Japanese Folklore Studies* (1985) and *Conflict in Modern Japanese History: The Neglected Tradition* (1982); and editor of *Authority and the Individual in Japan* (1978).

The University of Chicago Press, Chicago 60637
The University of Chicago Press Ltd., London

© 1996 by The University of Chicago
All rights reserved. Published 1996

Printed in the United States of America

04   03   02   01   00   99   98   97   96   1   2   3   4   5

ISBN 0-226-45121-6 (cloth)
0-226-45122-4 (paper)

The costs of publishing this book have been defrayed in part by the 1996 Hiromi Arisawa Memorial Awards from the Books on Japan Fund won by Marilyn Ivy's *Discourses of the Vanishing: Modernity, Phantasm, Japan* and John Whittier Treat's *Writing Ground Zero: Japanese Literature and the Atomic Bomb*, both published by the University of Chicago Press. The Awards are financed by The Japan Foundation from generous donations contributed by Japanese individuals and companies.

Library of Congress Cataloging-in-Publication Data

Koschmann, J. Victor.
    Revolution and subjectivity in postwar Japan / J. Victor
Koschmann.
        p.   cm.
    Includes bibliographical references and index.
    ISBN 0-226-45121-6 (cloth : alk. paper)
    1. Subjectivity.   2. Revolutions—Philosophy.   3. Philosophy,
Japanese—20th century.   4. Japan—Intellectual life—1945–
I. Title.
B5243.S83K67   1996
126′.0952′09045—dc20

96-21882
CIP

To my parents, Fred and Leona

Contents

Preface

The idea of studying the post–World War II debate on subjectivity in Japan first came to me in the early 1970s in Tokyo during one of many discussions on related issues with Kano Tsutomu, editor of *The Japan Interpreter*. However, I did not act on the idea until after several years of graduate study at the University of Chicago and a Ph.D. dissertation that temporarily redirected my interest in political subjectivity back into the mid-nineteenth century. My first actual writing on the postwar debate was stimulated by an invitation from Conrad Totman and Peter Duus to join their panel on "Postwar Japan as History" at the 1981 Association for Asian Studies convention, but it took a year of research in Japan in 1983–84 to actually launch the larger project that, at long last, has produced this book.

In the course of such an extended and frequently interrupted endeavor, my perspective on the subject has gradually evolved. First, as I have read and attempted to reconstruct the Japanese debate, my conception of political subjectivity has changed from one originally influenced by both liberal modernization theory and Marxism—and thus one quite similar to a number of the postwar theories I analyze below—to one that is postmodernization (if not postmodern) and sympathetic to what Ernesto Laclau and Chantal Mouffe have called post-Marxism. The book no doubt retains traces of the earlier commitments even as it contests them in various ways.

Second, and closely related, a transformation is occurring in my understanding of the early postwar period in Japan. As a result de facto of its exclusions as well as inclusions, this study might be taken to imply that the issue of *shutaisei* (subjective engagement) is intrinsically or uniquely connected with the postwar milieu. Such an implication would be broadly consistent with mainstream historiography until quite recently; it would also reflect the self-consciousness of many early postwar intellectuals themselves, who, like their predecessors among the "enlightenment" ideologues of the late nineteenth century, tended to exaggerate discontinuities with the recent past. Yet I know now that *shutaisei* was problematized repeatedly in the course of wartime mobilization from the 1930s onward, and since completing this book I have been able to explore the wartime connection further as part of a collaborative research project focused on intellectual, social-structural, and institutional continuities between wartime and postwar.[1] The issue of *shutaisei* is not connected intrinsically to either war-

---

[1] On the many continuities between wartime mobilization and postwar democratization, see

time or postwar and can be profitably explored in relation to either, or both. Here, I explore it primarily in the postwar context.

Throughout, I have made liberal use of quotation as well as paraphrase in order to enhance the possibility of a multifacted engagement with the ideas Japanese intellectuals expressed. It should be noted that unless specified otherwise, this study is concerned with the early postwar writings of Japanese intellectuals, not necessarily with what they might have thought, said, or written at a later date.

Japanese names are rendered surname first, in accord with Japanese practice, except where a name has already been reversed by others to fit a non-Japanese publication.

This project has benefited from so much help and goodwill, over so many years, that I hardly know where to begin acknowledging. I apologize to any institutions or individuals I inadvertently leave out. The Japan-U.S. Education Commission (Fulbright) and Social Science Research Council provided generous support for a year of research in Japan, and a summer fellowship from the National Endowment for the Humanities helped me prepare for that year; other research time and travel were provided by the East Asia Program and Society for the Humanities at Cornell University. In Japan, I profited immensely from facilities and staff assistance at the Faculty of Law of Rikkyo University, the Faculty of Literature at Kyoto University, and the Stanford Research Center/Kyoto Center for Japanese Studies.

Invitations to present parts of the argument and receive helpful comments were graciously extended by faculty and programs at many institutions, including Chicago, Columbia, Harvard, Heidelberg, Hokkaidō, McGill, Michigan, Princeton, Rikkyō, Tokyo University of Foreign Studies, Washington, Wisconsin, and the Woodrow Wilson Center. Most important of all were the help, criticism, and encouragement provided wittingly or unwittingly by many friends and colleagues, especially Gary Allinson, Anzai Toshimitsu, Andrew Barshay, Brett de Bary, Jonathan Culler, Norma Field, Carol Gluck, Andrew Gordon, William Haver, Harry Harootunian, Marilyn Ivy, Kamei Hideo, Karatani Kōjin, Ernesto Laclau, Matsumoto Sannosuke, Matsuzawa Hiroaki, Chantal Mouffe, Tetsuo Najita, Narita Ryūichi, Naoki Sakai, Steven Sangren, Irwin Scheiner, Patricia Steinhoff, Takabatake Michitoshi, Alan Wolfe, Yamanouchi Yasushi, and a number of graduate students in History 797–798 and other semi-

---

Yamanouchi Yasushi, J. Victor Koschmann, and Narita Ryūichi, eds., *Sōryokusen to gendaika* (Tokyo: Kashiwa Shobō, 1995).

nars at Cornell. Yoko Miyakawa Mathews and Tomoko Steen provided valu-able research assistance. At the University of Chicago Press, I am indebted to Alan Thomas for his early interest in the project and patient encouragement, Randy Petilos for guiding me and the book through the publication process, and Suzanne Mazurek for handling the editing with accuracy and dispatch.

Thanks are also due to publishers for allowing use of the following mate-rials: Parts of chapters one and two appeared as "The Japan Communist Party and the Debate over Literary Strategy under the Allied Occupation of Japan," in *Legacies and Ambiguities: Postwar Fiction and Culture in West Germany and Japan*, edited by Ernestine C. Schlant and J. Thomas Rimer (The Woodrow Wilson Center Press and the Johns Hopkins University Press, 1991); parts of chapter three appeared as "Sengo shoki ni okeru hihanteki Marukusushugi no unmei: Umemoto Katsumi no shutaiseiron" in *Sengo Nihon no seishinshi: sono saikentō*, edited by Kamishima Jirō, Maeda Ai, and Tetsuo Najita (Iwanami Shoten, 1988), and as "Gijutsu to shutaisei" in *Nihon shakai kagaku no shisō*, edited by Yamanouchi Yasushi et al. (Iwanami Shoten, 1993); parts of chapter four appeared as "Kiritsuteki kihan to shite no shihonshugi no seishin: Ōtsuka Hisao no sengo shisō" in *Sōryokusen to gendaika*, edited by Yamanouchi Yasu-shi, J. Victor Koschmann, and Ryūichi Narita (Kashiwa Shobō, 1995); sections of chapter four also appeared as "Minshushugi kakumei to kokka" in *Gendai shisō* 22/1 (January 1994), and as "Maruyama Masao and the Incomplete Pro-ject of Modernity," in both *South Atlantic Quarterly* 87/3 (July 1988) and *Post-modernism and Japan*, edited by Masao Miyoshi and H. D. Harootunian (Duke University Press, 1989); parts of chapter five appeared as "Mao Zedong and the Postwar Japanese Left," in *Critical Perspectives on Mao Zedong's Thought*, edited by Arif Dirlik, Paul Healy, and Nick Knight (Atlantic Highlands, NJ: Humanities Press, forthcoming), and as "The Debate on Subjectivity in Postwar Japan: Foundations of Modernism as a Political Critique," in *Pacific Affairs* 54/4 (Winter 1981–82). In all cases, these materials are reprinted by permission of the publishers.

Nancy did more than she, or I, will ever know. How does one acknowledge that?

The result of this great avalanche of generosity is merely this book, whose errors, by custom, are mine alone.

Introduction

Subjective is a profoundly difficult word, especially in its conventional contrast with *objective*.

—Raymond Williams[1]

In Japan's early post–World War II period, major prewar discourses—Marxism-Leninism, liberalism, proletarian literature, the naturalist "I-novel," and social science—converged in an articulate concern for human agency, manifested in a debate on active subjectivity. The word for subjectivity in the Japanese context was *shutaisei*: for existentialists it implied the leap of faith associated with the philosopher Sören Kierkegaard, for Marxists the materialist subjectivity posited by Karl Marx in the first of the "Theses on Feuerbach"—or, for Communists, partisanship (*tōhasei*); for students of the sociologist Max Weber it was an individualistic ethos modeled on the Protestant ethic; for behavioral scientists the capacity to make decisions based on either utility or value consistency. The debate is important, not only as a strategic point of entry into postwar Japanese thought, but also as a historical reference point for ongoing discussions of subjectivity and identity in the 1980s and 1990s. Before proceeding in the chapters below to follow the debate on *shutaisei* in some detail, I will focus here on aspects of the concept itself in relation to the postwar Japanese and present-day American contexts.

The unconditional surrender of Japan's armed forces and the nearly total discrediting of the wartime regime and its policies, the new prestige of the Communist party and its historical analysis, and the program of democratization pursued by the Occupation forces combined to create a situation in which the primary front for political struggle could be defined as democracy versus feudalism (or imperial absolutism, the emperor system, etc.). According to the historical-materialist analysis that was prevalent among intellectuals in the postwar period, Japan was at the stage of completing its bourgeois-democratic revolution and top priority had to be given to that task. Why did this analysis of the situation provide the occasion for a debate on subjectivity? Because, put crudely, the accepted Marxian framework prescribed that each stage of historical development would be led by the social subject appropriate to it. The stage of bourgeois-democratic revolution would be no exception. Hence, a series of questions: What social elements will lead? What characteristics will qualify them? How will they be motivated? What if they fail to respond? That is, the success of the postwar Japanese democratic revolution involved an intrinsic connection to a suitable revolutionary social subject, and "subjectivity," or *shutaisei*, was understood to be that subject's normative criterion.

The connotations of "subject" were never limited to the nexus with bourgeois-democratic revolution. Variants seem to have entered the Japanese philosophical vocabulary early in the twentieth century in the process of translating neo-Kantian philosophy, and translators at first employed as an equivalent the Japanese term *shukan*. Japan's most famous modern philosopher, Nishida Kitarō, was the first to introduce the alternative term *shutai* in the course of his reading of the philosopher Immanuel Kant,[2] and it was used increasingly in the wake of World War I in the context of the decline of neo-Kantian thought and rising interest in the "philosophy of life" propounded variously by Arthur Schopenhauer, Friedrich Nietzsche, and Wilhelm Dilthey. Now, for most purposes, *shukan* took on the connotations of contemplative consciousness, while *shutai* referred to the ethical, practical subject theorized by Kierkegaard and Marx.

An account of some of the broader implications of the term *shutaisei* that proliferated in the early postwar period was provided in 1948 by the psychologist Miyagi Otoya. According to Miyagi, postwar writers used the term in seven different ways. First, *shutaisei* referred to human beings' active dimension— their tendency not only to adapt to their environment but to act upon and seek to change it. Miyagi suggests that in postwar Japan this understanding of *shutaisei* arose out of the perception that Japanese Marxism was overly objectivist; therefore, Marxism had to be supplemented with more attention to the active side. Second, the term was used to refer to "behavior unmediated by reflection." This could be understood variously as a certain stance or attitude, a sense of problem or belief, etc. In a related view, *shutaisei* was held to be something uniquely internal, resistant to objectification. Third, some seemed to associate the concept of *shutaisei* with the hermeneutic method of the human sciences, or *Geisteswissenschaften*, as practiced by Wilhelm Dilthey and others. This method consisted in an attempt to grasp subjectively the meaning of another's inner reality. Fourth, and also related to epistemological method, the term referred to the process by which, in quantum mechanics especially, the observation of a phenomenon by the perceiving subject affected the phenomenon itself. Fifth, *shutaisei* often suggested a solipsistic awareness or intuition of existence, a form of self-possession, inner freedom, etc. Sixth, in contrast, ethical *shutaisei* consisted in disciplined conformance to duty of the sort elaborated philosophically by Immanuel Kant. This variety of *shutaisei* was not, of course, solipsistic, but implied the capacity to act within and upon society. Seventh, and last, was logical *shutaisei*, by which Miyagi meant the conception of absolute indeterminacy, or *mu*, in the system formulated by the modern Japanese philosopher Nishida Kitarō.[3] Some of these epistemological, aesthetic, or logical connotations will enter into the discussions recounted in the following chapters, even though the main emphasis will be on political dimensions.

Early Postwar Context

Given its plurivocity and its origins in prewar Marxism-Leninism, the problematic of political *shutaisei* did not depend for persuasiveness on the atmosphere created by Occupation policies. Accordingly, although the time period of this book, 1945 to 1952, is precisely that of the Allied Occupation of Japan following the end of World War II, it is not a study of the Occupation. The debate among Japanese intellectuals on the concept and practice of subjectivity (*shutaisei*) in the context of democratic revolution seems to have responded only indirectly to day-to-day political, economic, and social events. Indeed, because the debate's central issues, which related to the timing, agenda, and subjective dynamics of Japan's bourgeois-democratic revolution, were already more or less in place upon Japan's surrender, they imposed themselves upon postwar intellectuals and activists as components of a shared historical legacy. Of course, as will become clear from the various positions outlined below, it was a complex legacy, whose implications varied according to one's prewar and wartime experience, school of thought, political affiliation, and generational experience.

At the same time, the debate on subjectivity did take place under the Occupation regime and was inevitably affected somewhat by the principles and policies that the Supreme Commander for Allied Powers (SCAP) enunciated, the reforms his offices effected, the political climate they fostered, and the events they brought about. One of the basic conditions for the debate was established by SCAP in October, the second month of Occupation, when MacArthur ordered the release of political prisoners and abolition of the Japanese special police, or Tokkō.[4] Among the several hundred released were leaders of the prewar Communist party, some of whom had spent well over a decade in jail awaiting the opportunity to resume a revolutionary process that had been interrupted by war and intense police suppression in the 1930s.

The party's evolving conception of democratic revolution was contested initially by left-wing literary critics who established a new journal, *Kindai bungaku* (Modern Literature), in early 1946, just as SCAP was ordering full civil and political liberties and beginning to purge wartime leaders. In the meantime, philosophers like Tanabe Hajime, who had helped lend intellectual legitimacy to the wartime policies of total war and Asian dominion, were actively propounding a philosophical interpretation of Japan's postwar situation that was fundamentally continuous with wartime works by several of those identified with the so-called Nishida School of philosophy. Their interpretation of democratic revolution and political subjectivity were vigorously attacked by left-wing philosophers, many of whom were affiliated with the Association of Democratic Scientists (Minshushugi Kagakusha Kyōkai), which began in January 1946. Therefore, between January 1946 and the end of 1947, as SCAP promulgated its major reform legislation—including land reform, zaibatsu dissolution, a new Constitution and Civil Code, a labor union law, etc.—and on through 1948 and early 1949 as SCAP turned to economic rehabilitation, anticommunism, and "reverse course," Japanese philosophers debated the implications of historical materialism and its relation to culture, democracy, and human existence. Also, beginning in early 1946 and extending throughout the Occupation period, liberal to Left social and behavioral scientists engaged each other and Marxists of all types on issues that involved the legacy of the emperor system, philosophies of science and history, the relation of class consciousness to class structure and conflict, and the nature of human subjectivity, nationalism, and democracy.

The debate on subjectivity ended as a result, in part, of the Occupation's gradual turn away from the priorities associated with democratization and toward the goal of insuring Japan's economic and military security as a future bulwark against communism. Sensitive to this changing atmosphere, the Japan-Communist party began to edge away from its earlier policy of support for the Occupation forces. Then, in mid-1948, the party launched a campaign against modernism (kindaishugi). It included under this label not only liberals but Marxists who had criticized the party's tendency to ignore problems related to subjective commitment. The party's reaction against modernism seems to have reflected its growing antagonism toward American imperialism.

In January 1950, when the Cominform criticized the JCP for its postwar policy of support for peaceful democratic revolution, the party moved more decisively toward an anti-imperialist stance and agitated for national independence. Outbreak of the Korean War in June 1950 accelerated preparations for a peace treaty between Japan and most of its former enemies, and also stimulated further nationalist feeling. In the environment of the end of Occupation in the early 1950s, the category of the nation again became a major focal point for subjective identification alongside class and humanity, a process in which the sinologist Takeuchi Yoshimi played an important role. With these events, the early postwar debates on subjectivity came to a close. However, the issues they raised have reappeared throughout Japan's intellectual and political history since World War II.

In its various meanings and guises, the construct of *shutaisei* was fundamental to postwar Japanese thought and to the resurgent ideology of cultural modernization. As the result of a dynamic postwar publishing industry, and despite paper shortages, the debate on *shutaisei* was even followed by a substantial portion of the general public. Explosive postwar growth in the culture industry provided intellectuals with a potential forum for their ideas that included virtually the entire educated stratum of Japanese society. Moreover, the intellectual production analyzed in the following chapters is significant not only as an important dimension of the history of the early postwar period but as a wellspring for the vocabulary and thought structure that has guided important streams of Japanese political discourse down to recent years, especially among those identified with the New Left.

Indeed, in all industrial societies questions of political subjectivity and agency—and democratic revolution as well—have taken on renewed significance in relation to the rise in forms of political activity premised less on identities of class than of race, ethnicity, gender, religion, or sexual orientation. The collapse of the state-socialist economies of Eastern Europe has at the same time raised new questions about historical materialism and caused some "post-Marxist" theorists to declare that socialism ought to be relativized as a stage in the broader process they call democratic revolution.[5] The terminological and conceptual overlap between this present-day political theorizing on democratic revolution and that of the early postwar period in Japan provides an opportunity for dialogical history of a sort that promises both to increase our knowledge of a vital historical era and contribute to our understanding of the political present.

Current Controversy on the Subject

Since the 1970s, much invective has been heaped upon poststructuralist[6] critical approaches, whose exponents have been said to "coincide in a strenuous anti-humanism, and in discrediting or dismantling the interrelated concepts of 'humanity,' 'human,' 'man,' 'the subject,' 'subjectivity,' 'the person,' 'the self.'" The literary critic M. H. Abrams, for example, recently expressed his opposition to these approaches on the grounds that they are "inadequate to the production and constitution of literature that they undertake to explain, and to the process of reading that they expound and recommend." His preferred alternative is a variety of "traditional humanistic criticism."[7]

Others have opposed so-called poststructural or postmodernist theory on grounds less methodological than political. Jürgen Habermas has associated Michel Foucault and Jacques Derrida with "neo-conservatism,"[8] and Perry Anderson charged that "Paris today is the capital of European intellectual reaction."[9] In Japan, Takeuchi Yoshirō echoed Habermas's expressions of unstinting loyalty to the "incomplete project of modernity" by arguing that the poststructuralist critique of subjectivity can only be reactionary in the Japanese political culture where a truly modern political subjectivity has yet to be formed.[10] Some feminists have also taken a negative stance toward deconstruction. They ask: "Why is it, just at the moment in Western history when previously silenced populations have begun to speak for themselves and on behalf of their subjectivities, that the concept of the subject and the possibility of discovering/creating a liberating 'truth' become suspect?"[11]

Others have responded that "the critique of the subject is not a negation or repudiation of the subject, but, rather, a way of interrogating its construction as a pregiven or foundationalist premise."[12] In other words:

> To take the construction of the subject as a political problematic is not the same as doing away with the subject; to deconstruct the subject is not to negate or throw away the concept; on the contrary, deconstruction implies only that we suspend all commitments to that to which the term, "the subject," refers, and that we consider the linguistic functions it serves in the consolidation and concealment of authority. To deconstruct is not to negate or to dismiss, but to call into question and, perhaps most importantly, to open up a term, like the subject, to a reusage or redeployment that previously has not been authorized.[13]

In short, the question of subjectivity and, more broadly, of agency can hardly be sidestepped or ignored, least of all by feminists and others who intend their scholarship to have political impact.

Marxists, whether feminist or not, have responded to the critique of subjectivity by admitting to the latest in a long series of "crises." It is surely true that the most recent intellectual "crisis of Marxism," related closely to the collapse of socialist states in 1989 and after, is focused on the problem that "the original nomination of the revolutionary subject cannot now be sustained." Thus, "the crisis of Marxism is at root a crisis occasioned by the absence of this subject as Marx conceived it."[14] Some Marxists are concluding from this simply that "the crucial task of objectifying the revolutionary subject has to be performed again."[15] Others, who describe their position rather as "post-Marxist," have begun to try to reconceive from the ground up how the subject is formed and activated.[16] For example, contrary to more orthodox Marxist theorists, Ernesto

Laclau begins with the contention that a social totality is, strictly speaking, impossible. Contingency and antagonism are inseparable from society and therefore the social can never be unitary or fully objective. Any system depends on contingent action and therefore is always partially open, never fixed or fully centered. This means that the system is in flux, "as the decisions based upon, but not determined by it" transform and subvert it constantly. Subjects emerge as the agents of those decisions. That is, the subject is not a preexisting essence but is formed situationally and contingently "on the structure's uneven edges." Indeed, Laclau concludes that "the subject is nothing but th[e] distance between the undecidable structure and the decision."[17] Of course, the assumptions regarding subjectivity that were adhered to by early postwar Japanese theorists are often starkly at odds with those animating postmodernist and post-Marxist thinkers. It is precisely this difference, within a political problematic defined in both contexts as democratic revolution, that provides such a fertile opportunity for dialogical critique.

Dimensions of the Study

Chapter 1 lays the foundation for an account of the debate on subjectivity by discussing the democratic revolution in early postwar Japan. It attempts to show that in many contexts throughout Japanese society workers, farmers, students, and others anticipated and often outstripped those reforms by forming themselves into movements to demand food, control of the workplace, an adequate livelihood, and justice. The chapter will also focus critical attention on the policies and practices of the Communist party and other left-wing groups as they struggled to respond to the difficult postwar situation. After placing Japanese Communist policy in the context of fundamental problems in Leninist theory, it will suggest that by late 1946 the party had largely lost its opportunity to support and enhance the autonomy of the movements for equality that had sprung up in the wake of war and thereby to contribute productively to democratic revolution. The purpose of this chapter is not necessarily to imply that the debate reflected or was otherwise derivative of that postwar situation, but rather to suggest that the conflictual processes of change that crisscrossed that situation offered both opportunity and challenge to debaters who sought both to represent and enact a subject for and of democratic revolution.

Chapter 2 will focus on the Communist party's bid to establish hegemony over postwar literary production and the rebellion mounted against that effort by a group of left-wing writers affiliated with the journal called *Kindai bungaku*. The latter group rebelled against Kurahara Korehito's "objectivist" principles and espoused a set of ideals that valorized an egocentric notion of *shutaisei*:

"humanism based on egoism," self-expression rather than self-effacement on the part of "petty-bourgeois" writers, the ultimate primacy of art over politics, and the need for literature to nurture modern subjectivity. The prestigious proletarian writer Nakano Shigeharu counterattacked. In a reassertion of party control, he charged that the *Kindai bungaku* writers were attempting to replace the proletariat with the petty bourgeoisie as the subject of Japan's democratic revolution. The chapter will conclude, in part, that the *shutaisei*-based arguments made by the *Kindai bungaku* writers were vulnerable to Communist party criticism because of their continued reliance upon the Marxist-Leninist metahistorical framework and their tendency to relativize literary subjectivity in relation to that framework.

Chapter 3 is analogous in structure to chapter 2 but it deals with philosophy rather than literary theory. Beginning with the Communist party's attempt to establish hegemony in the realms of philosophy and scientific thought through the Association of Democratic Scientists and journals such as *Riron* (Theory), it will analyze the efforts of "critical Marxists" such as Umemoto Katsumi and Mashita Shin'ichi to orient Marxist philosophy toward problems of subjectivity and revolutionary commitment.

Umemoto Katsumi's early postwar essays on the relationship between historical materialism and human subjectivity touched off what came to be known as the debate on *shutaisei* in the realm of philosophy. Umemoto charged that Marxism lacked an adequate theory of subjectivity and revolutionary action, and argued that materialism could be defended successfully against idealism only if it developed such a theory. Matsumura Kazuto led the reaction against Umemoto from the perspective of the Communist party, which was still largely committed to a mechanistic model of historical development and to reflection theory in epistemology. The chapter contends that Umemoto was vulnerable to Stalinist hegemony because his theory of *shutaisei* was intended only as a theoretical "supplement" to the determinate metahistorical scheme of classical historical materialism which he accepted, and because its notion of commitment had the effect of suppressing desire in a new version of the wartime ideology of selflessness. The chapter will also analyze interventions by other Marxist *shutaisei* theorists, including Mashita Shin'ichi and the Marxist-existentialist Takakuwa Sumio.

Chapter 4 will focus on approaches to political subjectivity from the perspectives of social science, humanism, and the modern ideal. Liberals, social scientists, Christians, and others relied on the notion of *shutaisei* to express their own programs for the postwar era. One of the most articulate non-Marxist *shutaisei* theorists was the intellectual historian and political scientist Maruyama Masao. After an initial section devoted to the economic historian Ōtsuka Hisao's conception of *shutaisei* based on modern social values, the chapter will survey Maruyama's postwar studies in political thought and Japanese intellectual history in order to reconstruct aspects of the conception of modern subjectivity that he embraced in the early postwar period. It will also discuss the positivist critique of *shutaisei* mounted by behavioral scientists such as Shimizu Ikutarō and Miyagi Otoya, and a roundtable discussion that pitted these behaviorists against Maruyama and a group of Marxists.[18]

Chapter 5 will describe the effective end of the early postwar debates on *shutaisei*, in part by analyzing the arguments against "modernism" produced by Communist party loyalists. Coinciding with the party's critique of modernism was a gradual turn in overall party policy away from open support for the Allied Occupation and toward national independence. This newly nationalistic stance was reinforced in the wake of the Cominform's criticism of the party in January 1949, when independence from American imperialism became the main plank in the party platform. The Communist shift was followed by another critique of "modernism" from the non-Communist Left. In a series of essays beginning in 1951, Takeuchi Yoshimi called for renewed emphasis on the Japanese *Volk* in a "national literature" (*kokumin bungaku*). He severely criticized the tendency of *shutaisei* theorists like Maruyama and Ōtsuka Hisao to locate modernity outside Japan, in European and other models, and argued that unless this kind of modernism were overcome, Japan would never be able to achieve genuine modernity, by which he meant becoming "truly itself."

The rehabilitation of a kind of nationalism both within and outside the Communist party coexisted uneasily with the categories of class, humanity, individual, and subjectivity that had provided the framework for early postwar thought. The ideology of *shutaisei* did not entirely disappear but was increasingly displaced by, or incorporated into, new forms of communalist particularism. The chapter will locate these tendencies in relation to the controversy surrounding the impending peace treaty (signed in 1951), the Korean War, and other political events.

The Politics of Democratic Revolution in Postwar Japan

> While recognising the incontestably bourgeois nature of a revolution incapable of *directly* overstepping the bounds of a mere democratic revolution our slogan *advances* this particular revolution and strives to give it forms most advantageous to the proletariat.
>
> —Vladimir Lenin[1]

Although, as noted in the introduction, the problematic of democratic revolution was inherited from prewar Japanese political thought, the Allied Powers of World War II also contributed to postwar Japanese intellectual and political history by beginning long before Japan's defeat to form an ideological framework for reconstruction that emphasized the values of humanism, self-determination, and liberal democracy. The forceful, if in some ways hypocritical, enunciation of such values by the Allies in the Atlantic Charter of 1941 and elsewhere contributed to the construction of a shared realm of discourse for the postwar era. "Democracy," "humanity," and "freedom," along with "class" and "individual," were commonly accepted as the appropriate terms of debate across a rather broad political spectrum during the first few years of Occupation.

From the perspective of the Japanese intellectuals whose views are sampled in this study, the most significant general outline of Allied objectives was probably the July 1945 Potsdam Declaration, which provided the basis for Japan's surrender. Its tough-sounding statements of intent regarding the elimination of Japanese militarism appealed to all those in Japan who had come to feel like the military's victims rather than beneficiaries, and broadly paralleled the analyses prepared in exile and in prison by Japanese Communists. The document also deployed in a powerful way the symbols of democracy and respect for human rights, suggesting that these moments were already latent in the Japanese environment and would emerge if given an opportunity:

> The Japanese Government shall remove all obstacles to the revival and strengthening of democratic tendencies among the Japanese people. Freedom of speech, of religion, and of thought, as well as respect for the fundamental human rights shall be established. (Paragraph 10)

Such statements, and the early pronouncements that in conjunction with tangible institutional reform reiterated and operationalized their generalities, gave new salience and legitimacy to what might be called the "democratic social imaginary," that is, a conception of democracy as a particular mode of instituting society.[2] Fundamental to this conception, according to Claude Lefort, is the

institution of democracy as "a society without a body, as a society which under-
mines the representation of an organic totality."[3] This definition implicitly depends, of course, on a certain understanding of the monarchical regime prior to
the French Revolution.

> The society of the *ancien regime* represented its unity and its identity to
> itself as that of a body—a body which found its figuration in the body
> of the king. . . . The important point is that . . . the king . . . possessed
> the power to incarnate in his body the community of the kingdom, now
> invested with the sacred, a political community, a national community,
> a mystical body. It was a unity which was both organic and mystical, of
> which the monarch was at the same time the body and the head.

One should not equate the prewar Japanese state with the French *ancien ré-
gime*, even though the prewar "emperor system" was fashioned according to
European monarchical models and the concept of "absolutism" did play an important role in Marxist analyses of the prewar sociopolitical system.[4] What is
more directly applicable to Japan from Lefort's analysis is his clear illustration
of the transition from a social imaginary that construes society as a unified, organic totality—indeed, as a "national body" (*kokutai*)—to one that recognizes
the impossibility of such a totality.

> The democratic revolution, for so long subterranean, burst out when the
> body of the king was destroyed, when the body politic was decapitated
> and when, at the same time, the corporeality of the social was dis-
> solved. There then occurred what I would call a "disincorporation" of
> individuals. This was an extraordinary phenomenon, the consequences
> of which seemed, in the first half of the 19th century, absurd, even
> monstrous, not only to conservatives, but to many liberals. For these
> individuals might become entities that would have to be counted in a
> universal suffrage that would take the place of the universal invested in
> the body politic. . . . Number breaks down unity, destroys identity.
>   The modern democratic revolution is best recognized in this muta-
> tion: there is no power linked to a body. Power appears as an empty
> place and those who exercise it are mere mortals who occupy it only
> temporarily or who could install themselves in it only by force or cun-
> ning.[5]

In Japan, in a fateful decision made finally by General Douglas MacArthur,[6]
the "king" (Emperor Hirohito) was not "decapitated" symbolically or actually
by the Occupation forces but was rather reinvested as the "symbol of the State
and of the Unity of the People."[7] As a result, some Japanese philosophers such
as Watsuji Tetsurō could argue in the early postwar period that the "democratic

revolution" in the form of SCAP's reforms would not, in itself, change the "national body" (*kokutai*) at all.[8]

As if to prove Watsuji correct, political scientist Yamaguchi Jirō has recently analyzed the counterdemocratic role of the imperial institution in postwar politics. Drawing on Max Weber's distinction between traditional and legal authority, he shows how the imperial institution suppresses contestation and legitimizes such extralegal forms of power as the bureaucracy's administrative guidance. He also argues that the institution represents and helps maintain hierarchical forms of social integration that act as a brake on protest and the free exercise of rights. Thus, Yamaguchi's interpretation emphasizes the function of what is tantamount, even in the postwar era, to a bureaucratic "emperor system" in maintaining a certain positivity of the social that constrains thought and behavior to move in prescribed channels.[9] The system clearly represents a particular form of social institutionalization that functions to constrain the scope and erode the importance of democratic politics. By evoking a pre-political general will, it trivializes processes for the formation of a practical political will; by evoking a substantial, communal order, it helps suppress the social difference and contingency that alone can guarantee the continued openness of the political.

When elaborated further by Ernesto Laclau, Chantal Mouffe, and others in ways that are outlined below, Lefort's characterization of democratic revolution provides a useful standpoint from which to reconsider the democratization of Japanese society in the early postwar period. Following Lefort, we will understand the democracy that *might have been* instituted in early postwar Japan as a practical "social imaginary" that prevents society from being represented as a whole:

> [T]he important point is that democracy is instituted and sustained by
> the dissolution of the markers of certainty. It inaugurates a history in
> which people experience a fundamental indeterminacy as to the basis of
> power, law and knowledge, and as to the basis of relations between *self*
> and *other*, at every level of social life (at every level where division,
> and especially the division between those who held power and those
> who were subject to them, could once be articulated as a result of a be-
> lief in the nature of things or in a supernatural principle).[10]

By the same token, there can be no "natural" or otherwise ontologically authenticated political subject, no subject that is "both rational and transparent to itself," nor any that can be considered "as origin and basis of social relations."[11] Once the essential unity of the social itself is dispensed with, it must be admitted that social subjects are constructed discursively and their identities can never be more than "precariously and provisionally fixed."[12] This results in a proliferation of groups and movements no longer constrained by nature or tradition.

The Limits of SCAP's "Democratization"

SCAP's pronouncements as well as actions clearly reveal a conception of democratic revolution that goes only part of the way toward a purely conditional, political understanding of society; that is, still implicit in the notations and actions of SCAP authorities is a belief in the prediscursive, natural legitimacy (or illegitimacy) of certain social formations and subjects even as others (e.g., labor unions) are allowed to be conditionally constructed within the social itself.

Early guidelines on reform were hardly comprehensive, and it is difficult to find in SCAP records anything that resembles a philosophical rationale for democracy. The "Basic Initial Post-Surrender Directive" issued in December 1945 expands only minimally on the basic principle of rights and freedoms established by the Potsdam Declaration:

> The United States desires that this government should conform as closely as may be to principles of democratic self-government. . . .

> The Japanese people shall be encouraged to develop a desire for individual liberties and respect for fundamental human rights, particularly the freedoms of religion, assembly, speech, and the press. They shall also be encouraged to form democratic and representative organizations.

> Militarism and ultranationalism, in doctrine and practice, including paramilitary training, shall be eliminated from the educational system. Freedom of religious worship shall be proclaimed promptly. . . . Democratic political parties, with rights of assembly and public discussion, shall be encouraged, subject to the necessity for maintaining the security of the occupying forces.

> Laws, decrees, and regulations which establish discriminations on ground of race, nationality, creed, or political opinion shall be abrogated. . . . Persons unjustly confined by Japanese authority on political grounds shall be released. The judicial, legal, and police systems shall be reformed as soon as practicable to conform to the policies set forth . . . [above] . . . and thereafter shall be progressively influenced, to protect individual liberties and civil rights.

With regard to the economy, the "Directive" seemed to aim at a liberal environment of free competition among many economic units:

> Encouragement shall be given and favor shown to the development of organizations in labor, industry, and agriculture, organized on a democratic basis. Policies shall be favored which permit a wide distribution of income and of the ownership of the means of production and trade.[13]

Overall, the early guiding principles laid down for the Occupation were predominantly negative in the manner of the classically liberal view of democracy, which tasks society with ensuring the freedom and equality of all its members who are understood to be rational, individual agents endowed with formal rights; in the Potsdam Declaration, democratization is presented as a task primarily of "removing obstacles." Of course, in some cases—most notably the Constitution—SCAP did far more than remove impediments to freedom. But it is significant that these minimalist statements of Allied objectives are generally consistent with a liberal notion of democracy defined as guaranteed rights in the private realm plus free competition in the marketplace and representative government. Joe Moore argues that "the Western Allies (U.S. policymakers in particular), meant by Japan's democratization the establishment of popular sovereignty, to be realized through universal suffrage, political parties sharing a liberal philosophy, and a representative form of government."[14] This type of social philosophy leads to emphasis on questions related to "access," both to a free market and to government by way of the vote. That is, "under liberalism, citizenship becomes less a collective, political activity than an individual, economic activity—the right to pursue one's interests, without hindrance, in the marketplace. Likewise, democracy is tied more to representative government and the right to vote than to the idea of the collective, participatory activity of citizens in the public realm."[15]

These initial principles were developed and augmented during the first twenty months or so of reformist activity, and the U.S. government's aggregate approach turned out to be more complex than a simple appeal to classical liberalism would suggest. For one thing, the Occupation clearly went beyond classical individualism in its conception of the legitimacy of labor unions as vehicles for the aggregation and expression of interests. In Moore's interpretation of Occupation economic theory:

> Washington's view was compounded of anachronistic ideas about small-business capitalism reminiscent of the American economy prior to the rise of corporate monopolies, and progressive notions inspired by

the experiences of the New Deal about recognizing labor as a legitimate
interest group in capitalist society. By righting the balance between
capital and labor . . . U.S. planners hoped to embed democracy in postwar Japanese society. At its heart, the American approach to a free
economy for Japan was based on a belief in the fundamental identity
of political democracy and small-scale, free-private enterprise capitalism.[16]

A prominent Japanese student of the Occupation, Hata Ikuhiko, has emphasized the important ideological role among Occupation leaders of what he calls
Midwestern democracy: "Rooted in an independent, self-supporting farming
population, this political ideology has been referred to by Richard Hofstadter as
'conservative while being liberal.'"According to Hata, "An underlying tone of
Midwestern democracy is identifiable in MacArthur's advocacy of the decen-
tralization of power, women's rights, antitrust and educational reform, as well
as in his zeal to break up the former Japanese establishment and to set up large
numbers of independent landowning farmers."[17]

In terms of more recent political theory, it might also be argued that Occupation authorities augmented their classical model of citizenship, which was
focused on the individual "subject of rights" in the context of the democratic
state, with certain assumptions that had been articulated in the pluralist theory
advanced by Harold Laski and others in the 1920s. According to Kirstie
McClure, these theorists realized that "the traditional individualist principle of
geographical numerical representation was inadequate to reflect the political
significance of occupational group concerns and interests." Therefore, they proposed various forms of occupational representation that included "electoral categories specific to labor" and "special forms of interest representation through
boards and commissions with specific points of influence built into the policy
process." By attaching political prerogatives to certain occupational identities,
they "transformed the figure of the 'subject of rights' into something quite other
than the autonomous individual." That subject was now "a creature whose *political* identity was no longer given by virtue of its 'individuality,' but rather was
contingently constituted, *within* the social, by its participation in group processes." In its broader significance, this form of pluralism "initiated a shift in the
interior of Anglo-American liberalism towards the construction of a social subject distant not only from Marxism's ontologically privileged class agency, but
from liberalism's autonomous, rational individual as well." The limitations as
well as the advantages of this early-twentieth-century pluralist theory are all too
clear, in that it authorized some groups as "public/political," while excluding

others. Occupational groups qualified as public because their interests were deemed fundamental to the "welfare of the nation as a whole."[18]

This characterization of nascent Anglo-American pluralism provides a theoretically informed interpretation of the "political philosophy" pursued de facto by the Occupation forces. An excellent example of the weaknesses of this limited pluralism in the context of the Occupation reforms is provided by the question of women's political status in the emerging postwar regime. Largely owing to the efforts of a few female SCAP officials, Occupation reforms with regard to the status of women, and especially Article 24 of the new Japanese Constitution, "went far beyond what the U.S. Congress, the state legislatures, and many Americans are willing to accept in their own country, even today, in the area of legal guarantees for women's equality and rights."[19] Nevertheless, male officials balked when these female SCAP officials and a few Japanese feminists asked them to encourage more positive, assertive actions by women as a group seeking to actualize their equal rights in the form of increased power and status in society. For example, referring to a crucial memo written by Commander Alfred R. Hussey, Jr., Special Assistant to the Chief of Government Section, Susan Pharr observes that

> [i]t reflects the classic liberal democratic view of the rights and prerogatives of oppressed groups. On the one hand, it vigorously opposed the idea that any group should be denied full equality under the law. . . . On the other hand, [it] rejects the right of oppressed groups to organize in support of their objectives and to press their claims against those in relation to whom they are in this "inferior and completely dependent position"—that is, men. . . . Hussey's position on this fundamental issue appears to have been fully shared by General MacArthur. . . . The views of these men predate a pluralist view of democracy, which by the 1960s had gained currency in the United States, that it is legitimate for social groups to form "blocs" to press their "independent special claims" as long as their methods are legitimate.[20]

In sum, "top SCAP policy makers generally saw only the human rights issue inherent in promoting the status of women, and not the controversial redistributive issue it raised."[21]

For these same policy makers and their staff in GHQ's labor division, the case was quite otherwise with respect to workers (indeed, the "working class"!) as a group, whose demands for not only individual rights but the collective right to pursue economic and political interests they not only recognized but applauded. Labor division reports said, for example, that May Day parades in

1946 "demonstrated the new freedom which the Occupation has given to the Japanese people and the political vitality of the working class which, properly guided, can be a potent force in the democratic reconstruction of Japan."[22] Clearly, the concept of pluralism that implicitly determined for SCAP which social interests could legitimately be pursued by groups *as such* was one that— as in the pluralist theory of Laski and others—distinguished clearly between "occupational" groups, whose public/political status it recognized, and others such as women, which it continued to stigmatize as private and nonpolitical. Implicitly, the Occupation tended to believe that workers were properly constituted contingently as a group *"within* the social" and therefore comprised a legitimate interest, whereas women were constituted as a group only by natural endowment or essence, *outside* the social, and therefore were not, as a group, a legitimate political actor.[23]

Robert Ward has argued that the authors of the "Initial Post-Surrender Directive" took a "broad view of democratization," and "had far more than institutional and legal tinkering in mind." In his view, the directive "treats or implies the necessity of supportive reforms of the educational and economic systems, the encouragement of democratic political parties, and the promotion of new attitudes and desires among the Japanese people." He also suggests that one of the methods used with success by the Occupation forces was "the creation of new vested interests," by which "rights that have been sought, or at least aspired to, are now accorded legal status and recognition, and in this sense the group concerned is given a new vested interest in their protection and further expansion."[24] Yet Pharr's analysis goes far toward suggesting the limitations of SCAP's conception of which groups should be encouraged to pursue "vested interests"—that is, to construct an identity as political subject—and by what means. SCAP constituted groups as legitimate political subjects only to the extent deemed necessary to authorize what would have to stand as a "democratic" regime. Workers' organizations were thought to be essential, but a women's movement was not.

Even with regard to the workers and farmers whose collective pursuit of vested interests it considered legitimate, SCAP soon reached the limit of its tolerance. A difficult combination of factors, including the repatriation of millions of soldiers and civilians from abroad, disastrously small harvests, inept government food policy, and a big business sit-down strike in anticipation of gains from runaway inflation caused tremendous suffering in late 1945 and early 1946 on the part especially of the urban population.[25]

Spontaneous actions to secure redress were by no means uncommon. As early as October 8, 1945, prior to the Occupation's October 11 order that

women be granted the right to participate in politics, students at Ueno Women's
High School went on strike to protest the school president's appropriation for
private use of the food they had raised on the school fields. They called for equi-
table distribution of farm produce and dismissal of the authorities responsible.[26]
Nor was protest merely an urban phenomenon. Beginning in October 1945,
farmers formed unions in thousands of local areas. In February 1946 the Nihon
Nōmin Kumiai (Japan Farmers' Union) was formed as a national center and by
late June its branches numbered 2,900 and membership mounted to 600,000.[27]
Moreover, "As early as December [1945] there were instances of farmers' mass
meetings that hauled up Agricultural Association and local-government heads
before the village equivalent of a 'people's court.'"[28] The issue for farmers was
not just land reform but the abolition of the compulsory government system of
crop deliveries, and democratization of distribution. Moreover, early in 1946
farmers' organizations, labor unions, government employees, war victims' associations and other groups joined together in a Kantō Democratic Food Council (Kantō Shokuryō Minshu Kyōgikai), which in March formed a major
element of the national movement to overthrow the Shidehara Cabinet.[29]

Labor struggles broke out almost immediately, beginning among Korean and
Chinese workers, many of whom had been brought forcibly to Japan to work in
the coal mines. On the day of the surrender about six hundred Korean workers
protested their forced servitude at the Seika mine in Hokkaido, and Korean and
Chinese workers organized to secure the release from jail of some two hundred
Korean and Chinese prisoners.[30] Labor unions proliferated explosively in late
1945 and early 1946, going from none in August 1945 to 12,007 unions with
3,681,017 members by June 1946.[31] On 26 October 1945, 130 nurses at Tokyo
Police Hospital formed a union and demanded the expulsion of a hospital executive who had distributed resources unfairly.[32]

In some ways the most militant and certainly the most potentially significant
of the various methods of contestation employed in the early postwar period
was "production control" (*seisan kanri*), in which workers took over and ran
enterprises by themselves in order to maintain their livelihood at a time when
enterprise managers were sitting on their hands either because of uncertainty or
a desire to profit from inflation. Originated at *Yomiuri* newspaper on October 24
and then instantiated at Keisei Electric Railway on December 11, use of this
tactic spread throughout a number of mines and factories until it was "the major
form of labor dispute in April and May [1946]."[33] By some estimates, by
mid-1946, when the incidence of production control struggles decreased markedly, more than a million Japanese workers had participated in such actions.[34]

The significance of production control movements is not fully conveyed by numbers alone. It can be argued that, regardless of the intent of workers in specific cases the tactics of production control by their very nature challenged liberal notions of private property and thus capitalism itself:

> The workers' careful attention to keeping production control legal as a dispute tactic eroded as the employers dug in their heels and labor disputes became increasingly bitter. At this juncture, the anti-capitalist implications of production control surfaced in two ways: the workers' committees began to assume sweeping rights to use company assets and facilities during the dispute for whatever purposes they deemed fit, and demands for permanent extension of workers' control to matters of policy-making and organization began to displace strictly economic demands as the crucial issue.[35]

Some who would have hoped for the actual overthrow of capitalist relations of production have criticized those who employed the tactic for a lack of class consciousness and a readiness to use production control not as a revolutionary weapon but merely as a means to achieve such immediate aims as wage increases and democratic rights. Others have argued that despite ambiguity as to its aims, production control was itself revolutionary in that it greatly advanced workers' authority over matters such as personnel decisions that traditionally were guarded jealously by managers.[36]

In any case, production and other indices often increased precipitously under worker management. At the Mitsubishi Bibai mine, for example, the production of coal more than doubled, and "[i]n the case of Keisei Electric Railway, one witnessed perfect attendance by workers, rapid repair of damaged vehicles, more trains in operation, increases in fare receipts, etc." Writing in the April 1946 issue of the journal *Genron* (Fundamentals), Miyajima Jirō noted that normalization of production control would mean that "[c]apital's just profit would certainly not decrease, so capitalists are also watching with a keen eye." Workers looked beyond their own immediate benefit, even to such goals as ameliorating Japan's financial crisis. This has led some to comment on the "trans-class" quality of the movements, which worried Communists and might have been partly responsible for the party's abandonment of production control in favor of conventional unionization. Most important, however, were the opportunities such movements offered the workers to "empower" themselves as social subjects. As Kan points out, "they were movements for the workers' self-revolution."[37]

Throughout most of the period of widespread use of production control SCAP had maintained a neutral stance toward the propriety of its use. Indeed, in

February 1946 the Occupation authorities nullified a Japanese government attempt to declare the tactic illegal.[38] Nevertheless, as mass demonstrations against the government mounted in April and May, SCAP's view of unconventional and extraparliamentary methods for pressing group demands rapidly soured. On April 7, a broad front of organizations concerned about food, corruption, big-business sabotage of production, and government suppression of production control rallied against the Shidehara government. At the conclusion of the rally, some fifty thousand participants marched to the prime minister's residence, broke through the gate, beat policemen, and were finally dispersed only by the intervention of American military police.[39]

The celebrations on May Day 1946 brought hundreds of thousands of Japanese into the streets to ratify demands such as "the establishment of a democratic people's government, purge of war criminals, food for the working people, people's control of food supplies, a drive to uncover hoarded food, recognition of labor's right to strike and bargain collectively and of workers' control of production."[40] A mass rally at the Imperial Palace Plaza was followed by another march on the prime minister's residence, while a separate group paraded past SCAP headquarters. When, on May 15, a plea for support apparently delivered by demonstrators to SCAP was introduced by the Soviet representative for consideration by the Far Eastern Council, the American chairman of the council, George Atcheson, responded with an anticommunist tirade.[41]

On May 12, more than one hundred participants in a "Give Us Rice" rally broke into the imperial palace kitchens,[42] and on "Food May Day," May 19, there were again massive rallies and demonstrations. The latter culminated in an all-night sit-in at the prime minister's residence by JCP Secretary-General Tokuda Kyūichi and others. Then, the next day, MacArthur issued a stern warning against "the growing tendency toward mass violence,"[43] and in doing so finally made clear SCAP's increasingly sceptical attitude toward the people's movement and support for the conservative government of Yoshida Shigeru. When Yoshida banned production control on June 13, he was backed by SCAP. Furthermore, SCAP reforms soon co-opted some popular demands:

> SCAP had alread been moving with its own solution to the demands for
> food distribution and land reform and had preempted both of these as
> issues for popular mobilization well before the next upsurge in the
> workers' movement in the winter of 1946–1947. Large-scale distribu-
> tion of food imported from the U.S. began almost immediately after the
> May upheavals. The land reform program was passed by the Diet in
> October 1946.[44]

In effect, the revolutionary crisis that had escalated in the course of the Occupation's first nine months was defused by SCAP in May. Unions continued to proliferate and remained militant under the Sanbetsu national federation, but the union movement's effort to overthrow the Yoshida cabinet by means of a February 1, 1947, general strike was frustrated by SCAP at the eleventh hour, and the Occupation moved into the reactionary phase of "reverse course."[45]

In the early stage of the Occupation, SCAP's somewhat conflicted combination of individual rights–oriented liberal democracy on the one hand and limited political pluralism on the other brought significant results, not only in the reform of institutions but also through catalyzing a set of practical, egalitarian expectations throughout society—aspects of a "democratic imaginary"—that encouraged a variety of new antagonisms and conflicts. Yet this upsurge soon exceeded the bounds of the classically liberal bedrock of SCAP's philosophy, leading to a reaction that defused the popular movement and set the stage for "reverse course."

SCAP's intervention alone did not defeat the popular movements, although it must be considered the major factor; nor did the machinations of government bureaucrats in conjunction with the Japanese business elite. Responsibility must also be borne by the left-wing parties, including the Communists, whose own limitations with respect to democratic revolution were part of a broader process of development within Marxism-Leninism.

Hegemony and the Logic of the Supplement in Marxism-Leninism

In Europe, first mention of the "crisis of Marxism" apparently occurred around the turn of the century. The phrase appears to have referred to the discrepancy between historical processes that had been postulated as necessary in the Second-International Marxism of Karl Kautsky and Georgi Plekhanov, on the one hand, and the actual appearance presented by society and the working class on the other. According to an analysis recently proposed by Laclau and Mouffe, orthodox Marxism attempted to account for this discrepancy by resorting to one or another form of dualism, according to which the true reality—the "essence"—revealed in theory was assumed to be hidden beneath or beyond superficial appearances. In other words, orthodoxy instituted an interpretive procedure that Laclau and Mouffe call the "strategy of recognition." This procedure enables one to decode the events of experience in order to read the essential truths they concealed. It postulated, implicitly, that

> [i]n as much as Marxism claims to know the unavoidable course of history in its essential determinations, the understanding of an actual event

can only mean to identify it as a moment in a temporal succession that is fixed a priori. Hence discussions such as: is the revolution of year *x* in country *y the* bourgeois-democratic revolution? Or, what forms should the transition to socialism assume in this or that country?[46]

This strategy took on special importance for Russian Marxists such as Plekhanov who believed that they could properly interpret their situation only by comparing it with the case of Western Europe: "For Russian Marxists, therefore, the social phenomena of their country were symbols of a text which transcended them and was available for a full and explicit reading only in the capitalist West."[47] It was this conviction that led to concern about the comparative immaturity of Russian capitalism. This epistemological orientation also suggested a perspective on practical strategy. That is, Russia's apparent divergence from the Western European model seemed to imply the need to add a logic of political contingency to that of necessity. Specific kinds of political intervention would be necessary to bring appearances in line with economically determined essences.[48]

In Russian Social Democracy, the space of autonomous political intervention came increasingly to be designated by the term "hegemony." The major Russian problems confronting the doctrine of historical necessity were the backwardness of capitalism and the consequent weakness of the bourgeoisie. Since the bourgeois class was incapable of performing the revolutionary tasks assigned to it in doctrine, the working class itself had to assume leadership in the bourgeois-democratic revolution. As early as 1883–84 Plekhanov had originated the idea that the bourgeois-democratic revolution would depend on the working class, and in 1901 Paul Axelrod wrote that "[b]y virtue of the historical position of our proletariat, Russian Social-Democracy can acquire hegemony (*gegemoniya*) in the struggle against absolutism."[49] Lenin picked up the idea in *What Is To Be Done?* and other pamphlets. In 1905, he wrote that because of the weakness and ambivalence of the Russian bourgeoisie, it was the duty of the proletariat "to carry the democratic revolution to completion and to extend and strengthen the forces of the socialist proletariat, which needs freedom in order to carry on a ruthless struggle for the overthrow of the rule of capital."[50] Indeed, Lenin thought of leadership in the democratic revolution less as an onerous task for the proletariat than an opportunity, a means to seize power earlier than would otherwise be the case.[51] Therefore, "To achieve that end *Social Democracy must strive with all its might for hegemony over the democratic masses and for developing revolutionary energy among them.*"[52]

Despite the vital importance he granted to vigorous, immediate intervention by the working class, Lenin wrote in 1905 that "[w]e cannot get out of the bourgeois-democratic boundaries of the Russian revolution."[53] That is, he remained faithful to the metahistorical paradigm codified in orthodox historical materialism—the paradigm which Laclau and Mouffe call the "first narrative." This narrative prescribes not only that democratic revolution must precede socialist revolution but also that the true subject of democratic revolution is the bourgeoisie. However, because they confronted a situation in which the bourgeois class was unable to fulfill its role, Lenin and others pragmatically wove a "second narrative" in terms of which, according to the political logic of hegemony, the bourgeoisie's revolutionary role was to be assumed by the working class. This second narrative of hegemony was to be a "supplement" to the first narrative, but could never replace it.[54]

The image of supplementarity evoked by Laclau and Mouffe reminds us that, for the Leninist party, this second narrative in some ways shares the structure of what Jacques Derrida has called, quoting Rousseau, the "dangerous supplement."[55] Derrida's reading of Rousseau reveals a double sense of the term "supplement" in that, on the one hand, it is a "surplus," something extra added on to what "*should* be self-sufficient."[56] In relation to the problem of Lenin's approach to revolution in Russia, this would imply that the political intervention that forms the second narrative is a mere incidental accretion to a historical necessity that is already full and complete in itself. On the other hand, "supplement" also has the sense of filling a gap or inadequacy, thereby calling attention to the incompleteness of what it augments: "it adds only to replace. It intervenes or insinuates itself in-the-place-of."[57] Indeed, it might said that the supplement "produces that to which it is said to be added on."[58] In the context of Leninism, this would imply that the first narrative, which stipulates that the bourgeoisie is the subject of the bourgeois-democratic revolution, is somehow mistaken or incoherent unless supplemented by the second narrative, which replaces the bourgeoisie with the proletariat. In both these senses the supplement is "presented as exterior, foreign to the 'essential' nature of that to which it is added or in which it is substituted."[59] Yet inevitably the ontological security of that "essence" (in the case of Leninism: the first narrative = orthodox historical materialism) is called into question by the second implication of the "supplement," that it is an essential addition to make up for a deficiency or fill a lacuna. Indeed, it might imply that the first narrative (essence) shares the qualities assumed to be characteristic of the second narrative (supplement), i.e., that it is historically relative and situational, the result not of natural economic necessity but rather of contingent political intervention, and therefore possessed of no special authority. The following chapters will argue that this logic of supplementarity in its various facets pervaded the postwar discourse of subjectivity (*shutaisei*).

The historical materialist logic of the supplement in Leninism might be said to have been "dangerous" in another sense as well, from the perspective of other political actors. It can be argued that it was one source of the authoritarian stance sometimes assumed by the vanguard party in the context of democratic revolution, in Japan as elsewhere. For Lenin the relationship between the task (bourgeois-democratic revolution) and the agent actually carrying it out (proletariat) could not be other than external and conditional. Thus, there could be no question of the proletariat's "identifying" with its democratic task, of *becoming* democratic as one participant, equivalent to others, e.g., in a united front. The proletariat's link to the bourgeois-democratic task and the masses who were involved in it had ultimately to remain entirely detached and instrumental—even manipulative.[60] That is because the proletariat (incarnate in the Leninist party) claimed ontological priority based on the historical role granted it in the first narrative—the role of final liberator, not only of itself but of all mankind. As the ordained subject of the future socialist revolution, it had above all to maintain its integrity and purity as it stepped into the breach to lead the bourgeois-democratic transformation. The proletarian party's pretensions are ironic in that *at the stage of the bourgeois-democratic revolution*, it was the bourgeoisie, not the proletariat, that had been ordained in the first narrative as the primary historical subject. The proletariat's role was supplementary. Nevertheless, by virtue of the tautological chain in which the first narrative confers on the proletariat the metahistorical destiny of universal class, and that destiny, in turn, provides the proletariat with the epistemological privilege to know and interpret metahistory, the vanguard party was able to claim full priority and centrality, even as it took the place of the ordained historical subject.

Following the October revolution, and the party's claim to have moved beyond the bourgeois-democratic stage, the term *hegemony* was no longer employed in the homeland of the revolution. Nevertheless, the concept continued to be used by the Comintern, in theses issued by the first two World Congresses of the Third International, and in documents issued by that body.[61]

Laclau and Mouffe also point to a transformation in the way in which hegemonic tasks were conceived by the Comintern. Broadly speaking, from the early 1920s to the early 1930s, Comintern policy was dominated by a relatively narrow, class-centered economism. Zinoviev's 1924 dictum regarding Bolshevization, and the program inaugurated by the Sixth Congress of 1928, which denounced social democracy as "social fascism," are especially emblematic. However, the rise of Hitler in Germany forced a change of strategy, and in March 1933 the Comintern publicly invited Communist parties to explore with social democratic parties the possibility of joint action against fascism. Then, in 1935, the Seventh Congress formally adopted the policy of popular front.

The transition from Bolshevization to popular front appears to have meant not only a nascent turn away from authoritarianism but also an expansion of the realm of political articulation that is required by the process of hegemony. The transition signified a somewhat more flexible approach to doctrinally defined links between certain tasks (e.g., democratic revolution) and certain subjects (e.g., the bourgeoisie). Moreover, although the relationship between the hegemonic class and other elements remained external, it also became somewhat less narrowly instrumental. United-front strategy, in particular, raised difficult questions for the party regarding the quality of the relationship that should obtain among the elements of a front. In general terms, it confronted Communist parties with a choice. At one extreme, they could see the fronts as merely tactical, and the political relations they entailed as mere machinations to achieve predetermined ends—ends which were grounded in an entelechy of historical interests. At the other extreme, they could renounce whatever ontological privilege they felt entitled to on the basis of metahistorical necessity and accept the front as a process of open political articulation among different forces whose identity and function were not predetermined solely on the basis of class.[62] This articulation

> is not the confirmation of a de facto situation, but has a performative character. The unity of an ensemble of sectors is not a datum: it is a project to be built politically. The hegemonization of such an ensemble does not, therefore, involve a simple conjunctural or momentary agreement; it has to build a structurally new relation, different from class relations. This shows that the concept of "class alliance" is as inadequate to characterize a hegemonic relation as the mere listing of bricks would be to describe a building.[63]

The Comintern first applied the logic of hegemony to Japan through the "Draft Platform of the Japanese Communist Party" of November 1922. This document, which set the basic framework for future Communist policy in Japan, observed that "Japanese capitalism still demonstrates characteristics of former feudal relationships," and characterized state power as "semifeudal." Accordingly, "completion of the bourgeois revolution" (which would "be a direct prelude to proletarian revolution") was the immediate goal, the achievement of which was "dependent upon a powerful proletariat and the mass of

revolutionary peasants." The Communist party was directed to adopt the hegemonic policy of mobilizing "all social forces that are capable of carrying on the
struggle against the existing government." However, the party's relationship to
these forces was to be external and manipulative (it was to "make use of " peasants), and its commitment to bourgeois democracy was to be merely temporary:
"democratic slogans were to mean nothing more . . . than a temporary means of
struggle against the imperial government."[64]

Although the emphasis of Comintern directives fluctuated significantly between the initial Draft Platform of 1922 and the Theses of 1932, their main
thrust remained broadly consistent. The '32 Theses reiterated that "the path to
the dictatorship of the proletariat in present Japanese conditions can only be
through a bourgeois-democratic revolution," and that, in a manner analogous to
the Russian case, the proletariat was to play a supplementary, hegemonic role as
the subject of that revolution in the place of the bourgeoisie: "successful development of the revolution can take place only if there is a close alliance of
workers and peasants under the hegemony of the proletariat." Moreover, this
bourgeois-democratic revolution would have "a tendency to grow rapidly into a
socialist revolution." Bourgeois-democratic revolution was to mean not only
"the overthrow of the monarchy" but "expropriation of the landlords, and the
establishment of the dictatorship of the proletariat and the peasants." That is,
Communists were to begin establishing the basis for socialism at virtually the
same moment they completed the bourgeois-democratic tasks. "The dictatorship of the proletariat and the peasants and the transformation of the bourgeois-
democratic revolution into a socialist revolution will take the form of powerful
soviets of soldiers', workers', and peasants' deputies." Therefore, a major slogan of action was to be "establishment of a workers' and peasants' soviet government."[65] Joe Moore writes of this strategy that

> [t]he two-stage revolution in the Theses was telescoped to the extreme,
> coming down to a rapid and violent seizure of power by soviets under
> the leadership of the JCP. Far from envisaging a more or less lengthy
> period of tactical common fronts with progressive petty bourgeois or
> social democratic groups for completion of the bourgeois-democratic
> revolution, the Theses treated only the workers, peasants, and urban
> poor as revolutionary. The others must be struggled against and re-
> vealed as the false liberals and social fascists they were. . . . The JCP
> intended to forge an alliance of workers and peasant organizations like
> unions, bypassing their opportunistic leaders. The heart of the "closed
> alliance of workers and peasants" would be a "united front from below"
> that would unite the heretofore fragmented working class.[66]

With their narrow definition of the revolutionary subject and confident assessment that "the objective conditions for socialism exist," the '32 Theses comprised the major policy line to which the Japan Communist Party had committed itself prior to the decimation of the party in mass arrests and defections of 1933–34. It was, therefore, also the primary reference point and precedent for postwar Communist strategists.

"Lovable" Communism and the Deferral of Socialist Revolution

Planning for postwar Communist policy had apparently begun months prior to Japan's defeat in several locations, one of which was the Fuchū penitentiary near Tokyo. Fuchū housed a number of prewar Communist party members, including the important leaders Tokuda Kyūichi and Shiga Yoshio, who had been political prisoners for eighteen years. In his memoir of those years, Tokuda says he and Shiga "studied and planned in the greatest possible concreteness and detail," especially after they moved to Fuchū, where "they finally let us read newspapers, and we had more opportunities to meet face to face." According to Tokuda, they also wrote several documents in prison, including "An Appeal to the People," which was issued after their release on October 10, 1945.[67]

"An Appeal" was one of the first postsurrender documents issued by the party, and it is particularly important in retrospect because its principal author, Tokuda Kyūichi, emerged from his prison ordeal to become the party's secretary-general and one of the most powerful Communist leaders in postwar Japan.[68] "An Appeal" outlines a lasting orientation to postwar politics and society, whose major elements are as follows.

First, support for the Allied forces, which had "advanced into Japan for the purpose of liberating the world from fascism and militarism," and acceptance of the July 1945 Allied Potsdam Declaration as the operative program for "democratic liberation and world peace." It appears that even prior to drafting "An Appeal" the jailed Communists had argued over whether to define the Allied forces as a "liberation army," and this issue was to become more contentious later on. For example, Shiga claims to have told Tokuda that "MacArthur will later suppress us, and it would be best, therefore, to omit that point." However, according to another Communist imprisoned in Fuchū, Yamabe Kentarō, "Our reply was yes, we of course realize that. . . . but for the time being we will make use of the Occupation forces. . . . We took the 'Allied' element in the Allied forces very seriously. Since Soviet forces were involved, we considered it an international antifascist front and didn't know yet about the internal contradictions of the Allied forces."[69] Contentiousness and uncertainty among Communist leaders was no doubt responsible in part for the ambiguity that pervaded the party's early postwar policy—an ambiguity that, as I will attempt to show, provided the occasion for wide-ranging debates on democratic revolution and subjectivity (*shutaisei*).

Second, the appeal welcomes Japan's democratic revolution, which had begun as a result of the Allied advance, and warns that it would be necessary to destroy the "emperor system" completely before democratization could be carried out. That "system" consisted in "a union of the emperor and court, the military, administrative bureaucracy, the peerage, parasitic landlords, and monopoly capitalists." Tokuda also mentions as part of democratization the need to "inaugurate a national parliament elected by all men and women over the age of eighteen."

Third, the document calls for establishing a "people's republic government" on the basis of the popular will. The people's republic seems to have been a distinctly postwar innovation, as the '32 Theses had called for a "workers' and peasants' soviet government."[70] "Appeal" includes no explanation of the nature of the people's republic that was envisioned.

Fourth, it calls for the confiscation and distribution to peasants of all land held by idle capitalists and landlords, establishment of workers' freedom to unionize and bargain collectively, and a few other specific provisions such as freedom of religion, an eight-hour workday, and repeal of the Peace Preservation Law and Public Peace Police Law.

Fifth, it lays down the basic guidelines for hegemonic political action by demanding the formation of a "united front with all organizations and forces which share these goals" and construction of the people's republic government on the foundation provided by that front.[71]

Virtually all the main elements this document outlines were to endure as pillars of Communist policy throughout the first few years of Allied Occupation. However, the "action program" adopted at the party's Fourth Party Congress extended the position outlined in "Appeal" somewhat in a leftward direction by providing not only for labor unions but also for "workers' control over essential enterprises."[72] It seems clear that Tokuda had anticipated direct action by workers in order to form a united front from below and eventually something like soviets, in line with the prescription in the '32 Theses. Indeed, in light of the party's later lukewarm attitude toward production control, it is interesting that he and Shiga claimed they had planned for workers' direct action while still incarcerated: "Since we anticipated that the government and capitalists would attempt to sabotage production, it occurred to us that in order for workers to break this sabotage with their own hands and rebuild Japan's industry, we should change the struggle policy of the past which relied only on strikes and pursue the method of management control. We made such plans in prison."[73]

Moore's characterization of party policy at the time of the Fourth Party Congress is again clarifying:

> The question in 1945 was: on what points were the 1932 Theses regarded by Tokuda and the JCP as still valid in the postwar situation. . . . With the caution in mind that it does violence to the complexities and ambiguities of the thinking and activities of JCP leaders, the Tokuda-Shiga position can be described as a two-stage line. It envisaged the attainment of the first *strategic* goal of completing the bourgeois-democratic revolution through two partially complementary and partially contradictory means. On the one hand, the JCP would cooperate to the fullest with SCAP in erecting the institutional framework of bourgeois democracy, and on the other the Party would ensure the reforms' social consolidation by tactics augmenting workers' control over industrial production, city-dwellers' control over food, and farmers' control of the land. More fundamentally, the revolutionary *tactics* of popular control over production, rice, and land (to echo Lenin's call in 1917) would provide the essential preconditions for attaining the second (as yet unstated) *strategic* goal of socialist revolution—soviet-like organizations of people in Japan's workplaces, neighborhoods, and villages. When the time was ripe they would be the social base for establishing dual power, and making the transition to a soviet, socialist government as had been called for in the 1932 Theses.[74]

While still broadly consistent with the '32 Theses the Tokuda-Shiga line had effected a basic modification in accord with the objective circumstances of Allied Occupation. That is, they now recognized "an indeterminate transition phase in the two-stage revolution, a period of progressive democracy before the socialist revolution."[75] During this phase, the JCP would attempt to combine the tactics of revolutionary organization "from below" within a broad, temporary strategy of cooperation with SCAP and other democratic forces "from above." It is not surprising, therefore, that the party's overtures to social democratic parties in pursuit of democratic front were confused and seemingly contradictory.

The first such overture took place on October 19, 1945, when Communist party representatives Shiga Yoshio, Kamiyama Shigeo, and others visited Socialist party headquarters to propose formation of a people's front. Beginning in the early postwar period, the Socialist party had been reorganized under the control of the party's right wing, and these leaders replied that the Communist request was premature because the JCP had not yet published a party program. Again, on December 6, after publicizing its platform following the Fourth Party Congress, the JCP sent Kamiyama Shigeo and Kuroki Shigetoku to ask the Socialist leaders Nishio Suehiro and Kōno Mitsu about the possibility of a united front. The JSP representatives refused a second time; and then a third time on December 26. As Moore points out, these initiatives from the JCP amounted to the practice of united front from above. However, "even while pressing for a popular front in October, the JCP leaders also began attacking the JSP as a pseudo-socialist party, and stigmatized Nishio and Matsuoka Komakichi as war criminals who had collaborated with the fascists and the zaibatsu."[76] Such tactics could only be justified according to the logic of united front from below, which aimed ultimately at overthrowing the right-wing leadership of the Socialist party and its union affiliates.

A democratic front between the Socialists and Communists was also impeded by a fundamental policy difference over the emperor system. As noted above, the "Appeal to the People" issued by Tokuda and Shiga had called for the overthrow of the emperor system as the condition for establishing a people's republic government. Moreover, in a manifesto published along with "Appeal," the party related this policy directly to united front: "At present, the central focus of our people's front must be: 'Overthrow the emperor system, establish a people's republic government.'" "Accordingly," the document went on, "since the Socialist Party's main theme is protection of the emperor system, there is no reason to join it precipitately in a common front." Moreover, the first point of the twenty-five-point action plan adopted by the party at the Fourth Party Congress in December was "overthrow of the emperor system and establishment of a people's republic government." Indeed, Tokuda said at the Fourth Congress that "[o]nly fifty days after our liberation, the better part of the masses already agrees with overthrowing the emperor. In not too many months, every last person will agree."[77] There is little doubt that up to the end of 1945, at least, the JCP anticipated no compromise on the emperor system.

In the meantime, the Socialist party, under right-wing leadership, was clearly moving toward a policy of retaining the imperial household, and on December 4, the party's Standing Executive Committee decided that, "[w]ith regard to constitutional doctrine, the theory of the juridical state in which sovereignty is regarded as lying in the state shall be adopted and the Imperial institution retained; . . . the prerogatives of the Emperor shall be reduced in accordance with the spirit of democracy; . . . democracy and socialism will be advanced under a democratic Imperial institution."[78] Therefore, it is not surprising that the Socialists refused the Communists' proposals of united front on December 6 and 26; Socialists claimed that at least some Communists did not really want a joint struggle at all. As Morito Tatsuo complained in the journal *Kaizō* (Reconstruction) in July 1946,

> The Communists have proposed that the first common target of the two parties should be the abolition of the Emperor system. However, the Communists knew full well at the time they made their proposal that the Socialists had already decided to support the Emperor system and that the Socialists could not possibly accept the Communists' proposal. Furthermore, when the Socialists, quite naturally, rejected the proposal, the Japan Communist Party flaunted the rejection about in an attempt to show that the Socialists are reactionary.[79]

Clearly, as Moore has argued, confusion and contradiction between bourgeois democracy at the level of strategy and united front from below at the level of tactics pervaded party activity throughout the rest of 1945.

A decisive role in not only moderating but also bringing more consistency to Communist policy was played by another Communist leader who had spent the war years in the Soviet Union and China rather than in jail. Nosaka Sanzō had focused his attention at least partly on the Japanese situation ever since arriving in Yenan in 1940 from the Soviet Union, where he had lived since 1931, and he had already formulated a plan for the postwar democratization of Japan which he publicized in China through speeches and writings.[80] He arrived in Japan from China on January 12, 1946, and very quickly became active in Communist party affairs.[81] He seems to have opposed the dimension of Tokuda's program that still called for workers' direct action leading to socialist revolution, and also questioned the bitter denunciations of the Socialist leadership that had filled early editions of the party newspaper, *Akahata*.[82] During his long stay in China, Nosaka seems to have been strongly influenced by Chinese Communism and to have developed ideas about Japan's democratic revolution that diverged in some ways from the '32 Theses.

Moreover, Nosaka had attended the Seventh Congress of the Comintern, where Georgi Dimitrov had introduced the new line of antifascist popular front and, in effect, the "united front from above" with all antifascist elements. Following that congress, Nosaka and Yamamoto Kenzō, who also attended, had written "A Letter to the Japanese Communists," in which they called for a popular front in and through the rightward-leaning Social Masses Party that would ultimately strive to precipitate joint struggle that would include "all the farming population" along with the "petty bourgeoisie and working intelligentsia." The new strategy for Japan was premised on the perceptions that

> [t]he interests not only of tenant farmers but of all peasants are opposed to those of the landlords; the interests of small businessmen are opposed to those of the large industrial enterprises that enslave them; the interests of small merchants are opposed to those of the huge department stores; the interests of the working and intellectual classes are opposed to those of the corrupt bureaucrats and high government officials. And the working class has been enslaved by the capitalists. The workers, who already lack rights and are oppressed by the police, are threatened with even greater tyranny at the hands of the fascists and the military.[83]

Nosaka's support in 1935–36 for the antifascist popular front policy of the Seventh Comintern Congress might have helped predispose him in early postwar Japan toward the use of united front from above and a maximally inclusive definition of the subject of democratic revolution.

According to U.S. Foreign Service officer John Emmerson, who interviewed him in Yenan, "Nosaka . . . placed great emphasis on a Diet. . . . He rejected confiscation of property as impractical, instead proposing purchase by the government of the holdings of absentee landlords as a first step toward liquidating the traditional landlord system. Nosaka said nothing about supporting the Soviet Union. . . . He endorsed wholeheartedly the pronouncements of Mao Tse-tung."[84]

Then, at a gathering with Japanese party members on January 15, 1946, Nosaka was to remark that "we must become a lovable communist party [aisareru kyōsantō]."[85] The phrase caught on among journalists as a shorthand description of the Communist stance in the early postwar years.

A rally in Nosaka's honor in Tokyo on January 26 offered him an opportunity to elaborate further his views on the Japanese situation and what he took to be the appropriate Communist response. Although in many ways consistent with the policies Tokuda had announced in late 1945, Nosaka's approach was fresh in several respects.

First, he placed major emphasis on a democratic people's front, which he described as a union among democratic forces, including especially the Communists and Socialists but also "the Liberal party, democratic forces within other parties, labor unions, farmers' organizations, cultural organizations, associated owners of small and medium-sized enterprises, and all other democratic entities." Moreover, he saw the upcoming election as an opportunity to form such a front because it was an occasion on which the central committees of the Socialist and Communist parties had an incentive to cooperate. Nosaka conceived of the democratic front as a broad alliance from the top down among existing organizations, and foresaw that front's subsequent appropriation of a leadership role in organizing and carrying out measures to stabilize the economy, form a democratic government, purge reactionary forces from positions of power, abolish the emperor system, and achieve other necessary goals. Nosaka's emphasis was clearly on the need for centralized Communist control through top representatives of the various organizations who would join in forming the front. In a plea for unity and centralization, he urged that "all democrats recognize the importance of this front," and that "no matter what their political party affiliation they set aside their own and their party's interests in order to assume an attitude of serving the people."

Second, his conception of the "people," as opposed to the elite, was very broad, as suggested in his contrast between two types of democracy. The first type is "the kind of democracy desired by such entities as the present government, capitalists, and the existing parties. This is the kind in which bureaucrats, capitalists, and big landlords have leadership power. That is, it is a democracy that promotes the interests of the small minority of the privileged classes, the exploitative classes, the upper classes. It is the old democracy."

In contrast, it was essential now to demand "a new democracy, a democracy in which workers, farmers, *the working intellectual class, and small and medium-sized commercial and industrial businessmen* will take the leading role" (emphasis added). Similar to the "New Democracy" Mao Zedong had advocated in early 1940, this conception is noteworthy for its inclusiveness, extending even to certain kinds of small and medium-scale capitalists and, implicitly, small landlords.[86]

Third, Nosaka made a special attempt to allay conservative fears that the Communists might attempt to move rapidly toward socialist revolution. He says, "Just because I have spoken this way does not mean that we intend, today, to overthrow capitalism and establish socialism. We intend merely to use the power of a workers' government to frustrate the rampages of big capital and place certain restrictions on their unbridled exploitation."

Fourth, he presented the antiwar Communists as the "true patriots," in contrast to those who had falsely used patriotism to fan the flames of war and aggression and to promote their own interests.[87]

Overall, Nosaka propagated the image of a mild and unthreatening Communist party that was willing to defer its socialist goals in order to focus on the achievement of a broad democratic front and a "people's government." Through that government, the front would dismantle the "emperor system," achieve national recovery, and stabilize the majority's livelihood. This vision of a "lovable" Communist party was codified in the declaration issued on February 25, 1946, at the party's Fifth National Congress:

> The Japan Communist party has as its present goal the completion of our country's bourgeois-democratic revolution, which is progressing at present by peaceful and democratic methods. Therefore, it is not the case that the party is insisting on abolishing the capitalist system in its entirety and on realizing the socialist system at once.[88]

The declaration's caveats and assurances about the nature of the party's ultimate goal of socialism are tortuous:

> In a manner dependent upon developmental circumstances in our society, with the agreement and support of the vast majority of the people and through their efforts, our party intends after completing the bourgeois democratic revolution to bring about peacefully and through democratic methods a movement toward a social system that is more advanced than the capitalist system, a socialist system in which one person does not exploit another. . . . In realizing this society our party will not use violence, will avoid dictatorship, and will proceed peacefully and by educational methods through the mechanism of a democratic people's republic government of a sort that is appropriate to Japanese social development.

The document is also expansive in its assurances about the fate of private property:

> Our party has never believed in the "complete nonrecognition of private property." That would not be viable in any society. . . . In the future, even when a socialist system is realized, private property will continue to exist in a manner appropriate to society. . . .
>
> The ultimate objective of our party is to abolish the system of exploitation by abolishing the means by which one person exploits another—that is, the private ownership of capital by the capitalist who does not work and the private ownership of land by the landlord who does not work—and transferring those means to public ownership. In so doing, we intend to make the goods consumed by all the people, and also the means of their production, as bountiful as possible, and through them to stabilize the lives of all the people and make them bright, abundant, and ever advancing.

Other political measures would include forming a democratic system that would operate through a people's republic government and unicameral parliament.

The party's demands with respect to labor were similarly moderate and tended toward promoting cooperation, not only among various segments of the "people" but between workers and capital. In place of the "workers' control" called for by the Fourth Party Congress, the declaration proposes "management of industry by a management council system in which workers will participate" (but not seize the lead). Moreover, the declaration envisions these councils as functioning primarily to help achieve increased production rather than industrial democracy: "We anticipate the heightening of the general efficiency of industry by employing a system of management councils."

Finally, the declaration maintains Nosaka's orientation to broad-based centrism. For example, it calls for an inclusive "people's consultative council" that would "bring together labor unions, farmers' committees, and citizens' food administration committees" for the purpose of distributing food. Once this network had "expanded throughout the country," it could eventually be incorporated into the people's republic government.[89]

Moore persuasively concludes from this declaration that, for the Communist party in the early postwar period, "[a] greatly lengthened two-stage revolution became the orthodox line, and committed the party to the gradual attainment of socialism by parliamentary means. The new policy foreclosed the possibilities implicit in the Tokuda-Shiga approach, which had left the way open for an early and to some extent violent socialist revolution."[90] Implicitly, that is, the party seemed now to have moved backward toward a policy appropriate to a slightly earlier historical stage—a stage closer to the classic bourgeois revolution than that of a "bourgeois-democratic revolution with a tendency to grow rapidly into a socialist revolution" that had been prescribed by the '32 Theses. It is perhaps suggestive that even in his conversations with Emmerson in Yenan, Nosaka had reportedly said that the democratic revolution might take longer than his own lifetime.[91]

Roughly coinciding with events related to Nosaka's return there appeared in the journal *Kaizō* a call for a democratic front by Yamakawa Hitoshi, the prewar socialist leader and theoretician of the Rōnō, or Labor-Farmer, stream of Japanese Marxism. Yamakawa observed that

> [t]he present stage of the democratic revolution is extremely odd: political authority has slipped from the hands of the old ruling class, but it hangs suspended in mid-air because the new forces which must come to grips with it have yet to make their appearance. . . . The revolution through which we are now passing is a democratic revolution whose

aim it is to liberate, from the fetters of the imperialistic *bourgeoisie*, the laboring proletariat and a wide spectrum of the people. The new democratic forces which are yet to emerge to fill the present political vacuum will have to represent this wide spectrum of the people and must be composed of all of Japan's democratic political parties, labor unions, farm groups, cultural organizations, and individuals. Such a united democratic front, or, if you prefer, such a united popular front, is the only device capable of rescuing our country from its present confusion and chaos.[92]

In spirit, Yamakawa's proposal was well timed to coincide with Nosaka's broadly inclusive conception of the subject of democratic revolution and flexible attitude toward interparty cooperation. Concerning the policy of such a united front, Yamakawa mentions only a few items, including that war responsibility should be thoroughly investigated, that the state should be completely democratized according to the principles of popular sovereignty, and that the people should take it upon themselves to solve the problems of food and restoration of production. Beyond making these few suggestions, he basically feels that the question of popular front is fundamentally one of "'organization' rather than 'philosophy,'" and that a platform should be hammered out "carefully and democratically by the participating groups." The most significant omission from Yamakawa's plan is that he does not once mention the issue of the imperial household or emperor system. This no doubt illustrates a difference between the Rōnō and Kōza interpretations of the development of Japanese capitalism and, by extension, the differing degrees of importance granted to the emperor system as an obstacle to progress. But it also most likely reflects the delicate immediate circumstances, in which Nosaka was apparently exerting a moderating influence on JCP policy with regard to the emperor issue.

It is important to note that in Yenan prior to his return Nosaka had been much more flexible on the emperor issue than was the JCP under Tokuda and Shiga. Concerning Nosaka's views, John Emmerson reported:

> The Comintern theses had called for the destruction of the emperor system as the starting point for the Communist program, but Nosaka modified this position to permit the existence of an emperor should the Japanese people so desire. . . . Nosaka's ideas were later spelled out in a report that he delivered to the Seventh National Congress of the Chinese Communist party, held in Yenan in May 1945. In that speech he stated, "If the majority of our people fervently demand the perpetuation of the emperor, we must concede to them."[93]

Moreover, a press release issued following an informal meeting of the JCP central committee soon after Nosaka's return had said:

> Our views are entirely in accord with respect to confirming the correctness of the policy of overthrowing the emperor system. By overthrowing the emperor system we mean abolishing it as a state system. As to what should happen after that with regard to perpetuation of the imperial household that is a separate question. That should be decided according to the will of the Japanese nation in the future, after the democratization of Japan has succeeded.[94]

On January 14, Socialist party spokesman Mizutani Chōsaburō responded favorably to what appeared to be a modification of JCP policy on the emperor system, but the Socialist party's right-wing leadership still demurred from a final decision to cooperate with the Communists. When the JCP emphasized the urgency of a breakthrough on the food issue, clarified the point that people's republic government did not mean a soviet government, and announced its acceptance of Yamakawa's proposal to convene a preparatory committee for the formation of a united front, Mizutani also accepted the Yamakawa proposal but continued to express his party's doubts about Communist policy.[95]

When Nosaka gave his speech at the welcoming celebration on January 26, he hardly mentioned the issue of the emperor, and did not include it in a draft program for a united front. Then, in the Declaration issued following the Fifth Party Congress on February 25, 1946, the party basically reiterated the view agreed upon among Nosaka, Tokuda, and Shiga except that in this declaration the term "overthrow" is replaced by "abolition":

> The party will seek to realize the following:
> 1. Abolition of the feudal absolutist military police political system that is the emperor system. Concerning the retention or abolition of the imperial household, it will be decided by a vote of the people after the formation of a democratic people's republic government. We will pursue the war responsibility of the present emperor.[96]

However, in the meantime, at MacArthur's order the Government Section of SCAP had drafted a Constitution and pressed it upon the Japanese government, which had been unable on its own to come up with a draft deemed acceptable. Since the new Constitution unambiguously provided for popular sovereignty and retained the emperor as only a "symbol of the nation and the unity of the people," the document was more radical in this respect than the policy of any Japanese party other than the Communists. Thus, the effect of SCAP's action was to render the emperor system a dead issue, at least until Japan regained its sovereignty. Ironically, the Declaration of the Fifth Congress differed most markedly from that of the Fourth Congress in that it said nothing at all about the need for a united front.[97] For the time being, hopes for a united front were fading. Moreover, the Fifth Congress called for cooperation not only among various segments of the "people" but between workers and capital. In place of the "workers' control" called for by the Fourth Party Congress, the new declaration proposed "management of industry by a management council system in which workers will participate." Moreover, the declaration envisions these councils as functioning primarily to help achieve increased production rather than industrial democracy: "We anticipate heightening the general efficiency of industry by employing a system of management councils."[98]

Considering that production control movements were mushrooming at the time, it is difficult not to see the party's conservatism as potentially in contradiction with the democratic emphasis latent in its proposal for united front. Democratic front could have meant a broad expansion of the political space in which a plurality of different entities could become active, form alliances, and establish lines of antagonism against common enemies. It might have implied new possibilities for exercising political initiative, free from the rigid definitions based on class and metahistorical stage. Moreover, such a policy of democratic front could have been entirely consistent with the encouragement of spontaneous movements for workers' control. Instead, the party now seemed willing to adopt a kind of political quietism.

The party's conception of bourgeois-democratic revolution provided only an ambiguous framework for political action and cultural production. In some aspects, it seemed consistent with a policy of democratic hegemony, while in others it retained the authoritarian tendencies that in the past had accompanied the presumption of metahistorical privilege. In any case, the postwar writers and activists who appealed in various ways to theories and concepts of subjectivity, or *shutaisei*, attempted both to work within this broad framework and to expand the scope it allowed for free, independent action. That is, they sought in varying degrees to focus attention beyond metaphysical "necessity" toward the moment of contingent political action. As they did so they, too, were often led inexorably to unanticipated forms of essentialism, historicism, and supplementarity.

To some extent, therefore, the direction and ambiguities of Communist policy and, to a lesser degree, the policies and actions of the other left-wing parties and SCAP, opened the space for contention among intellectuals and activists regarding the subject of democratic revolution. Also of considerable potential importance was the obviously widespread willingness among workers, farmers, students, women, and others to resist inequities and fight oppression as they perceived it. This grass-roots democratic revolution, whose dimensions far exceeded the few examples mentioned above, provided both challenge and opportunity not only to political activists and the progressive parties but to theorists of *shutaisei* and democratic revolution. Would the latter succeed in conceptualizing the political moment and the forms of political agency appropriate to it in such a way as to include rather than exclude those who were already engaged in struggle? Would their blueprints for action be sufficiently compelling to contribute to rather than detract from the process of articulating democratically-engaged forces into powerful chains of equivalence, whether or not those chains were encompassed within one or another form of united front? Such questions need to be addressed at various levels, from the "bottom" as well as the "top." From the "bottom," we need to know more about how student, feminist, worker, and other activists viewed the policies of the Communists and other parties, and how they interpreted and responded to revolutionary theory and strategy, including the voluminous discussions of democratic revolution and *shutaisei*. This book can only scratch the surface of such knowledge. Rather, beginning with chapter 2, it delves directly into the topic of revolutionary theory with the aim of better understanding the strengths and weaknesses of postwar theory in terms of its logic, coherence, *and* practical relevance to ongoing social processes of democratic revolution. To the extent that this study attempts to suggest the dimensions of those social processes themselves, it does so only briefly, in order to suggest that revolutionary theorizing did not take place in a vacuum but rather in a historical context that was in many ways ready to accept, respond to, and contribute to the "myth" that the theorists produced.[99]

Literature and the Bourgeois Subject

In order to ascend to heaven, we must pass through the gates of hell.

—Sakaguchi Ango[1]

In January 1946 a group of seven young literary figures produced the first issue of a new journal that, like *Bungakukai* (Literary Society) of the Meiji period and *Shirakaba* (White Birch) of Taishō, was "to determine the direction of literary history."[2] The issue's lead essay, by Honda Shūgo, introduces many of the major debating points which the *Kindai bungaku* group has been credited with broaching in the postwar environment: the problem of subjectivity (*shutaisei*), the importance of generational difference, the war responsibility of writers, literary issues related to ideological conversion (*tenkō*), the relationship between politics and literature, the problem of base and superstructure in cultural analysis, the role of the petty bourgeoisie, the question of the intellectuals, and the importance of the "ego."[3] All these related in one way or another to questions of consciousness in relation to history and society, and thus as they pursued these issues the *Kindai bungaku* partisans laid the foundations for the debate on *shutaisei*.

"For the artist," Honda writes, "that is art which most perfectly satisfies 'the promptings of the heart.'"[4] Therefore, "it is nonsensical to adhere to the dictates of *messhi hōkō* ['obliterate the self, serve public authority']. Artists must never suppress the self." *Messhi hōkō* had been a favorite prewar and wartime slogan, implying that people should deny their personal needs and desires in order better to serve the higher good of the "public" or, in other words, the emperor, the imperial state, and the war effort. For Honda, the slogan was anathema not only because it evoked the authoritarianism of the imperial state but because in his mind it also described the mind-set typical of the Communist party.[5] For Honda and others of the *Kindai bungaku* group, it was not "selfless devotion" but precisely the self's full extension and engagement that would produce great art and, ultimately, contribute to democratization: "Where joy and fascination do not burst forth from within the artist, where passion does not flow outward from the self—the individual self—of the artist, all art will die. Literature died during the war."[6] This preoccupation with writers' subjective involvement formed the basis for the *Kindai bungaku* group's understanding of *shutaisei*.

Honda's life trajectory is in many ways typical of all seven of the new journal's founders. Born in 1908, he graduated from the faculty of literature, Tokyo Imperial University, in 1932 and then joined the Proletarian Science Research

Institute (Puroretaria Kagaku Kenkyūjo), where he began a career as a critic and theorist of proletarian literature. By 1933 he had published (under the pseudonym Takase Tarō) essays on the methodology of criticism and the historical novel; he had also paid homage to the critical theory of one of the leading Communist literary theorists of the time, Kurahara Korehito, to whom we will return below.

Before Honda had a chance to publish his next work, a study of Mori Ōgai, he was arrested in November 1933 and held until March 1934. His release from prison happened to coincide with the liberation of a number of other prominent proletarian writers who had been arrested in 1932, including Nakano Shigeharu, Kubokawa Tsurujirō, Murayama Tomoyoshi, and Chūjō Yuriko. Thus, when Nakano and Murayama subsequently published accounts of their so-called "ideological conversion" (tenkō),[7] Honda read them with great interest because of his similar experience.[8] While working at the Ministry of Post and Telecommunications in 1937, he published a study of Murayama Tomoyoshi in the journal Hihyō (Criticism), which he had founded with Yamamuro Shizuo and Hirano Ken.

In 1941, Honda resigned from the ministry and immersed himself in a study of Tolstoy's War and Peace—a project that in the course of the wartime years would transform his approach to literature and prepare him for cultural activism in the postwar era. He describes it as "the product of an all-out effort to escape from Kurahara's theory and bring about a rebirth of the self."[9] Accordingly, it is ironic that the postwar era should immediately test the changes Honda and his friends had gone through by throwing them directly into confrontation with their former leaders, Kurahara Korehito and, somewhat later, Nakano Shigeharu. These encounters will be detailed below.

Kurahara had majored in Russian as a student at the Tokyo School of Foreign Language Studies (later Tokyo University of Foreign Studies), and had traveled to the Soviet Union for the first time as a newspaper correspondent in 1925. He became an organizer and activist in the Japanese proletarian literature movement almost from its inception, joining and later organizing a number of groups, including the All-Japan Federation of Proletarian arts (NAPF). In 1929 he joined the Communist party, and when the police issued an order for his arrest in April 1930, he went underground. Soon, however, as a result of a party decision that he should work for an extended period in the Comintern, he left for the Soviet Union. After the Fifth Comintern Congress, he changed plans again and returned to Japan.

In Moscow, Kurahara had attended the Agit-Prop Council at the Fifth General Meeting of the Profintern in August 1930, and upon his return had carried out a reorganization of the proletarian literary movement that brought the new Japan Proletarian Culture Federation (KOPF) and the Japan Proletarian Writers' League into direct affiliation with such transnational groups as the International Union of Revolutionary Writers.[10] These moves were part of the Bolshevization of literature, by which was meant increased contact with and organization of the masses and the imposition of firm political standards for writing. The effect of the policy was "to make the art movement essentially a movement for agitation and a didactic instrument for the political indoctrination of the masses."[11] For writers, the major criterion of literary value was to be faithful adherence to Marxist-Leninist epistemology.[12] He was also instrumental in imposing on proletarian writers a strict historical-materialist framework that included rigid forms of base-superstructure analysis and reflection theory, by which thought (or literature) was believed to mirror objective reality. In one essay he argued that "[n]ot only does a work of art reflect the ideology of its era and class, it also in some manner or other reflects its era's *objective reality* (nature, human life). Therefore, in assessing a work's value we have to make clear *how accurately the work reflects the objectivity of reality at the time.* That is what comprises the *objective value of art.*"[13]

When KOPF was suppressed in 1932 Kurahara was arrested, and because he stubbornly refused "ideological conversion" he remained incarcerated until 1940 when, sick with tuberculosis, he was finally released and hospitalized. He spent the rest of the war recuperating and studying.

In the postwar era, he emerged immediately as a Central Committee member of the newly legalized Communist party and leader in the formation of the Shin-Nihon Bungakukai (New Japan Literary Society). In November 1945, a mere two months after the onset of the Occupation, he wrote a short, two-part piece for a major newspaper, *Tokyo Shinbun.* Although inconspicuous, the article was to become well known as the initial announcement of a Communist literary agenda for postwar Japan. It had been primarily this article, moreover, that stimulated Honda to write his manifesto in the inaugural issue of *Kindai bungaku.*

Kurahara's article focuses on a topic familiar to Marxist literary historians, the history and fortunes of literary realism.[14] He mentions that in Japan the major early forms of realism were Meiji-era naturalism and late Taishō and early Shōwa proletarian literature, and then argues that the incipient realism of these movements was aborted, first in the years following the Manchurian Incident of 1932, when writers under government pressure turned away from social objectivity toward the portrayal of a "subjective," entirely mental, form of reality, and again after the attack on China in 1937, when the government clamped down even more severely on culture, causing writers either to retreat into the reactionary pursuit of "art for art's sake" or to enlist opportunistically as propagandists for Japan's continental military adventures.

Kurahara's second installment begins:

> Now, however, on the occasion of the decisive defeat of the "imperial
> army," the regime of cultural oppression has been overthrown, the
> army, bureaucracy and financial cliques which supported it confront
> imminent dissolution, and the culture they had suppressed is rising
> again. In the present era it is finally possible to construct a culture for
> the people. So what is the task of our writers in the realm of literature?

Clearly evident are the hyperbole regarding Japan's defeat by the Allied Powers, which was typical in the postwar period among not only Communists but a broad spectrum of the resurgent Japanese Left, and also a hint of real confidence that the Allied military occupation would carry out its promises to demilitarize and democratize Japanese society. At least on the surface, these factors were very important considerations in the formation of Communist literary policy in the early months after Japan's surrender.

Also obvious is the didactic tone Kurahara and other Communist leaders had been accustomed to employing before the war. When situated against the background of his prominence in the prewar proletarian literature movement and his high status in the postwar Communist party, Kurahara's short article was clearly designed to preempt a position of authority in the literary milieu. It announced the beginning of the party's bid to set forth and control the terms of postwar literary discourse.

> First of all, writers must recover the element of reality that has been
> missing from literature, and reproduce within literary works the true
> circumstances and voice of the people. They must restore to literature
> its artistic value by accurately and vividly portraying the reality that has
> been distorted in the past. Of course, portraying the true form of reality
> and, what is more, portraying it artistically, are hardly easy tasks. To
> accomplish them, it is first necessary that our writers should know real-
> ity, and in order to know reality they must live and fight with, and share
> the happiness and misery of the people.[15]

According to Kurahara, moreover, it was time not only for writers to describe the people "without deceit or contrivance" but also to show them "the way out of their predicament"—that is, to "instruct" them in "life." The individuality and identity of the writer was not entirely irrelevant to such a task, but had to be considered secondary to the need for objective "research on social life" and the literary reconstruction of that life.

By drawing a simple, hierarchical distinction between "objective" and "subjective" in literary production, Kurahara's brief essay established the basic framework for the postwar debate on subjectivity, or *shutaisei*, in literature. Moreover, to the extent that in the early postwar period there was a tendency for the party increasingly to conceive democratic revolution as a matter of party control over other progressive groups rather than of encouraging workers and others to act autonomously, one can easily see the resonance with a literary policy that, according to Kurahara, directed the artist to study and then to portray the objective realities of daily life rather than to give expression to the artist's autonomous perspective of the world; and to serve, moreover, by means of this objective literature, as an instructor to the people in order both to give voice to their standpoint and to show them the way to a new life.

Kurahara's postwar emphasis on realism in literature and insistence on the need for writers to adopt the popular standpoint would not have surprised anyone familiar with the programmatic essays he had written in the context of the prewar proletarian literature movement. For Kurahara, the end of the war and the onset of democratic revolution signified an opportunity to take up with new vigor and optimism an agenda that had been suspended prematurely through the interference of militaristic state power. Social realism in literature had been aborted along with Japan's bourgeois-democratic revolution in the early 1930s, but now Kurahara anticipated that they could reach full fruition concurrently. He assumed that as the Allied Occupation went about transforming the social base, writers and other artists could devote themselves to the construction of a cultural superstructure appropriate to the transition to socialism.

And yet, despite—or, rather, because of—the respect Kurahara and other prewar Communists had paid to reductive models of economic determinism, in the early postwar era they put culture in the van and assigned it a revolutionary function that to some extent seemed to go beyond party political policy as it was developing under Nosaka's influence. Kurahara seems to have placed such confidence in the radicality and thoroughness of SCAP's socioeconomic reforms that he believed culture could now pass rapidly through the bourgeois-democratic stage and even begin actively to prepare the way for the construction of socialism. He described the reforms in exaggerated terms in an essay he wrote from his sickbed in January and February 1946:

> Japan is now entering a period of unprecedented change. Of course,
> we have been brought to the present day by a series of past transforma-
> tions—the Taika Reforms [645], establishment of the Kamakura
> bakufu [1185], the Meiji Restoration [1868]—but the changes now un-
> derway promise to be much broader and more fundamental than any of

these. Primitive, ancient and feudal elements which have survived all
those past transformations will now finally be subjected to unsparing
criticism and judgment, and even the emperor system, which has ex-
isted for over a thousand years, will be called into question.

In principle, literary development had to follow social development:

> A new society demands a new literature. But that new literature cannot
> be conceived independently, in a manner that separates it from social
> construction. . . . It is only by cooperating in the construction of a demo-
> cratic society that literature can itself become democratic.[16]

Yet he expects the social development brought about by the reforms to be so
rapid and fundamental that immediate literary advances would not be unduly
inhibited. The expected transformation in social institutions would clear the
way for a "cultural revolution" that might be more radical and thorough even
than Nosaka's political transformation. Kurahara's language clearly suggests
that with respect to literature the postwar democratic revolution should indeed
manifest the "tendency to grow rapidly into a socialist revolution" that had been
anticipated in the '32 Theses:

> As a result of Japan's defeat, the feudal forces are being pulled down
> and their feudal social base will not be spared. Of course, they are not
> yet decisively overthrown, but the way has been opened and the objec-
> tive conditions for the construction of a democratic society are in
> place. . . .
>
>   Our situation calls to mind the European Renaissance which
> brought a temporary flowering of the art of the bourgeoisie (*citoyens*),
> the peasants and handicraft workers. However, there is a fundamental
> difference: That democratic cultural movement occurred when capital-
> ism was on the rise, while this one will occur in an era when capitalism
> is being transformed.
>
>   Clearly, the democratic society we are constructing should not be
> the type that seems to have been built in Europe and America in the era
> of capitalism's development, nor should it be the sort that Japanese lib-
> erals tried to construct following the Meiji Restoration. It should not be
> a society devoted to free and unrestrained activity and exploitation by
> capitalists, but rather a society dedicated to uplifting the lives and cul-
> ture of the working masses. Only a democratic society will make
> possible the transition from capitalism to socialism.
>
>   Therefore, the democratic literature of the near future must corre-
> spond to this kind of society and contribute to it. Needless to say,
> among [the three types that comprise democratic literature—i.e.,] the

literature of the bourgeois, of the peasant, and of the worker—the bourgeois component cannot consist merely in the reproduction of the so-called bourgeois literature of the past. The [new] bourgeois literature must encompass the transfer of the class base from the wealthy and idle upper bourgeoisie to the working elements of the middle and lower bourgeoisie, and should make the transition from a consumption and pleasure-oriented literature to a literature directed toward production and labor.[17]

Despite the party's apparent move in early 1946 toward a political strategy of parliamentary gradualism and indefinite deferral of the socialist revolution, its cultural policy under Kurahara seems to have been geared toward preparing for an early transition to socialist revolution. Rather than indicating a belief on Kurahara's part that culture could advance beyond the institutional base, this suggests rather that both Nosaka and Kurahara were quite hopeful regarding the burgeoning labor and popular movements and the SCAP reforms. For Nosaka, the radical political reforms promised by SCAP provided an opportunity for the party to present a "lovable" image and attract broad-based support while leaving the Occupation to grapple with the difficult and controversial measures that were necessary in order to revolutionize institutions. Conversely, for Kurahara, SCAP's reform of the economic base promised to fulfill the objective conditions for a type of cultural production that could move with greater speed than ever toward the promotion of socialist consciousness and the world outlook of the laboring masses.

During the early postwar era, therefore, in a manner paralleling the ambivalence between support for institutional democracy and construction of workers' soviets in the early policies of Tokuda and Shiga, the meaning of democracy in politics and culture shifted unstably between associations with the institutions and processes of liberal parliamentarism that were being established by the Occupation, on the one hand, and on the other echoes of the pejorative associations that the concept of bourgeois democratic revolution evoked in the Leninist tradition.

A Petty Bourgeois Response: *Kindai bungaku*

The differences in nuance between Nosaka's relatively open espousal of democratic revolution and Kurahara's focus on the cultural transition to socialism seem to have created a double bind for writers whose difficult experiences with the prewar proletarian literature movement predisposed them to question party control over literature. As "petty bourgeois intellectuals," these writers were surely encouraged by the party's postwar political emphasis on a broad democratic front and its support for parliamentary democracy to think that they could play a progressive cultural as well as political role *as* petty bourgeois. Yet Kurahara's opening salvos on culture had admonished them to dedicate themselves to "living and fighting with the people" and writing with the "true voice of the people."

Kurahara's injunction to writers reflected an ideological process through which, under conditions of bourgeois-democratic revolution, the primacy that orthodox historical materialism had granted the proletariat was now extended for practical purposes to the "people" (*minshū*) as a whole. Moreover, Kurahara clearly posited a correlation between a conception of revolution that focused on the working masses and presumed a rapid transition to socialism, on the one hand, and on the other an "objectivist" literary strategy that encouraged writers to abandon their own perspectives and adopt the standpoint of working people. A younger generation of left-wing writers reacted negatively.

Manifesto for a Modern Literature

In responding to Kurahara in the remainder of his lead essay, Honda makes quite clear the differences that during the war and after defeat had separated him from his former leader. Kurahara was still asking for an objectivist approach to literature that would require writers to abandon their own subject positions and adopt that of the "people." For a "petty bourgeois" author like Honda, however, there seemed to be no honest way to contribute to democratic revolution "other than to be true to the inner necessity of our bourgeois selves." To Kurahara's directive to writers that they should "live and fight with the people," Honda retorts, "Except by being the best petty bourgeois writers they can be, there is no literary way for them to live and fight with the people."[18] Honda also argues that, in criticizing other authors and their works, the most important criteria were integrity and authenticity. One had to focus on the work as a whole, and see it as an integral expression of the mind and worldview of the writer. For example, those Marxist critics who tried to separate the progressive Tolstoy from the reactionary Tolstoy succeeded only in "killing" Tolstoy as a writer and human being.

In sum, Honda argues that the standards of art should be primarily aesthetic. Scientific standards, as represented by the canons of historical materialism, were not entirely irrelevant but had to be flexible enough to allow even an irrational or reactionary work to be judged a good piece of art. Honda cites Max Weber's point that the object of scientific investigation—unitary,self-consistent nature—differs fundamentally from the shifting historical world portrayed in literature. Science is cumulative, in the sense that new discoveries always both build upon and supersede past ones, but art cannot be. A work of art represents a unique moment in time and space and therefore can be neither replicated nor superseded. As Weber had put it, "A work of art which is genuine 'fulfillment' is never surpassed; it will never be antiquated."[19] Therefore, Honda suggests, it is not very meaningful to talk about the "development" of literary realism from Homer through Dostoyevski (or, in Japan, from the naturalists through proletarian social realists). "Realist" writers of the past had written in different eras, about different objects, with different concerns. Therefore, their individual works of artistic sensibility should not be subjected to the kind of homogeneous standard that was appropriate only to science.

This distinction between art and science also called into question Kurahara's demand that progressive writers should aim at "portraying the true form of reality and, what is more, portraying it artistically." Why, Honda asks, should there be a difference between portraying reality and portraying it artistically? Since good art would always be true in an artistic sense, scientific criteria of truth were irrelevant. In Honda's view, Kurahara's admonition was fundamentally misleading. For art, life is reality—"the source, origin and basis of everything else"—and (in implicit contrast to science, which emphasizes systematic perception) this reality "emerges precisely when art grasps intuitively, without any other mediation." Honda was concerned that any acceptance by artists of scientific standards of reality would encourage the party to demand that progressive artists "study historical materialism and materialist dialectics" in order to know reality better. Indeed, this is precisely what Kurahara had argued in 1931.[20]

Honda also differentiates art fundamentally from "politics," which for him means the class partisanship the party demanded from proletarian writers—that is, the politics of external, manipulative relations between the proletarian party and others who participate in the democratic revolutionary task. Politics of this sort was materialistic and provided "discipline from without," while art was spiritualistic and "persuades from within." According to Honda, although both forms of endeavor address problems of meaning and are oriented to value judgments, the range of such judgments in politics is relatively narrow in comparison to art. Art raises such questions as "why people die and why they were born; and what is the meaning of humanity"—questions that are not the business of politics understood in this manner. Therefore, he is saying in effect that the external demands of Leninist control should not be allowed to replace artistic standards.

Honda also objects to Kurahara's views on recent history. He takes issue with the statement that during the war believers in the primacy of art (or "art for art's sake") had first opposed proletarian literature then become "connected to the most vulgar form of politics" in service to the state. Honda offers not only Masamune Hakuchō and Shiga Naoya but Kobayashi Hideo, Katayama Tamihiko, and Hori Fusao as exceptions to this generalization. He adds, in an admonition no doubt inspired by his own study of Murayama Tomoyoshi's *tenkō*, that Kurahara seemed unable to understand "how the literary spirit had survived the collapse of the leftwing movement." Moreover, according to Honda, even prior to the intense police repression of 1931, the proletarian literary movement had already become "both narrow and shallow, so rigid as to be incapable of further development."

Honda recalls Kurahara's statement that, after the collapse of the left-wing literary movement,

> the writers who remained were ruled by anxiety and unrest, and the literary world was in confusion. Indeed, soon these writers made that anxiety itself the focal point of their literature, and took its faithful portrayal to be their primary mission. In other words, writers who had lost the freedom to portray objective reality turned instead to the elucidation of subjective reality. But this turn also signified their abandonment of any attempt to be with the people or to defend their lives.

Honda replies:

> When the world descends into chaos, it is natural for literary eyes which had once looked outward to turn inward, and for a realism of depth to replace a realism of breadth. In times of adversity or illness, people who have seen only the surface of human life sometimes learn to regard it in a more layered, three-dimensional perspective and experience great personal growth as a result. How can he say with certainty that our shift from breadth to depth is incapable of dredging a new channel for literature?[21]

Finally, Honda introduces the issue of generational difference in relation to the experience of war and the collapse of the proletarian literary movement. All but one of the seven founding members of *Kindai bungaku* were in their thirties at the end of the war: Yamamuro Shizuka (39), Honda Shūgo (37), Hirano Ken (37), Haniya Yutaka (35), Ara Masato (35), Sasaki Kiichi (31), and Odagiri Hideo (29).[22] Whereas the leaders of the prewar socialist movement had been at least twenty-five years of age (Kurahara had been twenty-nine) at the time of the Manchurian Incident, and thus were generally in their forties as they reemerged to take charge of the postwar Left, members of the *Kindai bungaku* generation had not, on average, turned twenty-five until about the time of the Marco Polo Bridge Incident of 1937, and thus had been able to serve only as the "rear guard" of the prewar movement. According to Honda, they had naively witnessed a complete historical cycle from the era of democracy and further Westernization after World War I, to the insular militarism and oppression of the 1930s, and back again to the reauthorization of democracy and infatuation with the West that were occurring in the early postwar era. They had been beset by nagging doubts about the validity of unilinear historical materialism. They had also watched with dismay in 1933 as top party leaders such as Nabeyama Sadachika and Sano Manabu recanted (*tenkō*) and became supporters of Japanese expansionism.[23] Thus, it is not surprising that most of these younger men also eventually became disillusioned and followed their elders in various forms of *tenkō*.

In the postwar era, the *Kindai bungaku* generation was often self-consciously emotional, suspicious of the party line on culture, and preoccupied with the inner need to confront and articulate artistically the meaning of their own prewar and wartime experiences. This time, they refused to suppress the "egoistic" forces that welled up from inside. They felt that the party's prewar policy on art, particularly in its final form as articulated by Kurahara in 1931, had been too preoccupied with dialectical materialism and insufficiently sensitive to the human, subjective dimensions of history and creativity. The party had attended to "external necessity" without paying sufficient attention to the "irrepressible necessity within." Now, in the postwar era of democratic revolution, that "lack" would have to be made up and the "self" (*watakushi*) of the writer given its due.[24]

Dialogue: Kurahara versus Kindai bungaku

Most of the issues broached by Honda were explored further in a question-and-answer session between Kurahara and five of the *Kindai bungaku* members, also published in the journal's first issue. This encounter dramatizes more directly than had Honda's own essay the newly adversarial relationship between the younger writers and their former leaders in the prewar movement. In the course of his introduction to the discussion, Honda recalls an incident of around 1933 in which he and the Marxist philosopher Matsumura Kazuto had discussed writing a letter to Kurahara, who was then in prison. He then remarks, "At that time I had never met Mr. Kurahara, but for me—for all of us—he was like a god."[25]

Sasaki Kiichi begins the discussion by raising the question of Kurahara's distinction between "objective" and "subjective" approaches to literature and charging that Kurahara seemed to be adhering to an outmoded form of reflection theory. Were not the subjective and objective dimensions of literature always unified in the circuitous process of literary construction? Kurahara replies that if reality were conceived as dynamic process, and the writer successfully oriented his work in the direction of objective historical movement, then his literature would reflect objective reality correctly and a kind of unity would result. For Sasaki, however, this is still too objectivistic: "It is not just a matter of objective reality, even when understood fluidly and historically, but of the human spirit which confronts that reality; I think there is a problem of the spirit here, a problem of humanity (*ningensei*) in the midst of objective reality." Kurahara responds that since "there is no pure subject, separate from experience and science," one should not essentialize subjectivity or the spirit, that is, one should remain sensitive to its historical relativity. Moreover, writers should not hesitate to avail themselves of scientific method: "I do not mean to imply that it is impossible to portray reality correctly without becoming a scientist, but if one rejects science and just views reality through subjectivity or intuition, one will often not see that reality correctly."[26]

As the conversation progresses, Haniya Yutaka redirects attention to the friction between politics and literature. Might not even the "new politics" of the postwar era soon make unreasonable demands upon literature? According to Haniya, "Politics is always concerned about the present. . . . Moreover, its priorities are extremely limited in terms of time and content. Literature, however, is very broad, spatially and temporally, and its concerns are more fundamental than those of politics. . . . Therefore, as political demands get stronger, they tend increasingly to reduce literature to a political tool."

Kurahara replies that politics in the postwar period should be able to transcend such immediate demands and focus on the broad, long-range goal of realizing the kind of truly human society called for in the Potsdam Declaration. However, "a socially-involved writer should not ignore reality" by attempting subjectively to transcend political and social conditions. Therefore, "I cannot agree with writers who cut their literature off from social development. . . . If a writer stands on the belief that the actualization of the Potsdam Declaration is a necessary process in the development of reality, he will be unable to write literature that conflicts with that."[27]

Ara Masato then moves the discussion toward a topic that he would explore further in a series of essays: the relationship between a writer and the people, or the masses. Kurahara had said that a writer must "strive always to make the people's standpoint his own, try to be close to the people, and be aware of their suffering and joy." But to Ara, this was likely to imply, as it had in the prewar literary movement, that the writer would be expected to "live with ordinary people by engaging in organizational activities in circles and neighborhoods, running settlement houses," and performing other purely political functions that detracted from his major vocation as a writer and, indeed, seemed to trivialize the importance of writing itself as a form of political intervention. Moreover, most writers were not of working-class or peasant backgrounds. For such writers, the political injunction to "be with" the people seemed to imply an artificial, even hypocritical, quest for the people "from somewhere outside them." Wasn't it possible to be with the people in a strictly literary sense without actually trying to enter among them physically?

Kurahara, however, continued to insist that, "there is nothing better than for a writer to go regularly to farms or factories and work together with the people. By working with them . . . one comes to understand them better, and therefore is no longer just looking at them from outside." Of course, if a writer found that form of activity impossible, he could still make a contribution either by writing about other segments of society such as capitalists, or by observing the people from a distance and getting to know them that way. The latter method was likely to fail, however, as had the aristocratic Tolstoy's sincere but ultimately unsuccessful attempt to write from the perspective of peasants.

For Ara, this was unconvincing: "As petty bourgeois intelligentsia, we [can only] portray ourselves. To thoroughly investigate oneself, not as an observer, but with attention to various elements of one's inner self—this should be the starting point of literature from this moment forward, and ultimately it is this endeavor which will connect us in a literary sense with the people."

To begin from one's own position and one's own outlook on life did not necessarily mean abandoning all social relevance or concern. Ara argued that the self provided a literary route to the people; and Honda added the minimalist argument that "[n]o human being entirely lacks a social concern, so, [as writers,] if we do what we are able to do most seriously and avidly, and develop ourselves through that activity, it would be strange indeed if social concern did not naturally result."

Kurahara remained skeptical, cautioning the younger generation that "[i]t will not do to write as if one's own subjectivity as a petty bourgeois intellectual were absolute. It is necessary to align one's subjectivity with real historical development, and in order to do that a writer has to move as closely as possible to the standpoint of the people."[28]

It is clear from Kurahara's argumentation that the party's program of democratic revolution created problems in the realm of culture. Although Nosaka's "new democracy" and the logic of democratic reform demanded that bourgeois and petty bourgeois elements should play an active, often leading, role in reconstruction, Kurahara and other Communist writers of his generation, whose ideas were formed in the prewar proletarian movement, found it very difficult to admit to the legitimacy of a petty bourgeois writer's own perspective of the world as the starting point for artistic engagement. Where Kurahara demanded that writers present a relatively direct and unmediated literary representation from the viewpoint of working people, the *Kindai bungaku* writers insisted on the priority of their own mediating presence.

From Egoism to Humanism

Ara, Hirano Ken, Odagiri Hideo, and other writers affiliated with *Kindai bungaku* proceeded to fill its pages with a variety of polemical essays that elaborated and made more precise the arguments suggested in their initial exchanges with Kurahara. Among the first to publish was Ara Masato.

Born in Fukushima prefecture in 1913, Ara entered Yamaguchi Higher School in 1930 and soon became active politically as editor of the school newspaper. As a result of his precocious political leftism he was detained by the police for nearly a month and suspended from school until 1933, when he finally was able to resume his studies. In 1935 he entered the literature faculty of Tokyo Imperial University and soon formed a literary study group together with Sasaki Kiichi, Odagiri Hideo, and others. Indeed, it was because of this study group that Ara was eventually jailed between April and December 1944. After graduation in 1938, he had become a middle-school teacher, first in Fujisawa and then in Tokyo, where he joined Sasaki and Odagiri in publishing *Bungeigaku shiryō geppō* (Monthly Arts Documentary), became acquainted with Haniya Yutaka through the magazine *Kōsō* (Concept), and met Hirano Ken and Honda Shūgo through *Gendai bungaku* (Contemporary Literature). Between 1942 and 1944 he concentrated on translation.

Upon the end of the war, Ara's association with the several friends mentioned above led to his involvement in the formation not only of *Kindai bungaku* but also, with Odagiri and Sasaki, of the periodical *Bungaku jihyō*. In the meantime, apparently in March or April 1946, Ara joined the Communist party.[29] He died in 1979.

His "Daini no seishun" (Second Youth) was a long and laboriously crafted piece that gave full vent to its author's often dramatic, flamboyant style. The essay begins with an evocation of the end of war:

> Soon after I began reading literature I learned of Dostoyevski's rare experience in which, having been implicated in the Petrashevsky Incident, he was condemned to death; and then, just before the sentence was to be carried out, was miraculously pardoned by a new directive. Rather than executed, he was now merely to be exiled to Siberia. As I read of this incident, I could hardly suppress a feeling of envy that approached

despair—envy not of his genius but of a life experience of the sort that
visits only one person in a million. My feelings probably stemmed from
a romantic longing to plumb the depths of human existence.

But when we reflect on our recent defeat and compare it to the momentous experience of the nineteenth-century Russian writer, we find
that our own ordeal is in no way inferior. Good men and women, who
were impelled by desperate strategies (!) like the "decisive battle for the
main islands" and "one hundred million honorable deaths," had committed themselves to collective suicide right up to the moment when
unconditional surrender was announced. They had consecrated their
precious lives during the air raids, in the corners of bomb shelters that
were less inviting than garbage pits.[30]

Ara's is perhaps the most powerful and evocative statement of a theme that
appears very frequently in early postwar writing, the theme of a sublime experience of negativity—death, pain, degradation—that leads to heightened subjective awareness and vitality.[31] For Ara, as for Dostoyevski, the sentence of death
provided a necessary, dialectical prelude to meaningful life. But the new negativity in postwar Japanese literature emerges not only in dialectical process but
also in the tense immobility of irony, or oxymoron, as suggested by the title of
Ara's essay. This variant of negativity evokes the existentialist Dostoyevski, for
whom individuality, for instance, is "wretched and revolting, and yet, for all its
misery, the highest good."[32] Ara fills his essay with ironic twists linking naiveté
with cynicism, illusions with disillusionment, youth with maturity, humanism
with egoism, heaven with hell:

> In passing through the era of left-wing movements, by way of fas-
> cism and war and democratic revolution to reach yesterday and today,
> through hopes, despair, and hopes again, in the eras of brightness, dark,
> and light again, if I have discovered anything it is the beautifully ign-
> oble—ignobly beautiful—human being. I learned to expect pettiness
> in the midst of greatness, and to find greatness in the midst of squalor.

Grounding his polemic squarely in an autobiographical context, Ara recalls
the bittersweet purity of his "first youth." His memory is of friends with whom
he had

> shared the consciousness that we were fighting for humanism under the
> flag of the left-wing movement. More concretely, it is the memory of a
> youthful attraction to the philosophy of liberty, equality and fraternity,
> whose currents generously filled the cup of our youthful desire. Indeed,
> this philosophy provided a broad spillway for all the psychological ten-

dencies of youth—pursuit of ideals, abhorence of hypocrisy, discovery
of the spirit of struggle, satisfaction in self sacrifice, hero worship.[33]

He and his schoolmates had been taken temporarily with Christianity, but eventually turned to "a new kind of humanism called comradely love. . . . This love had none of the false nobility of what the Christians called brotherly love." But even the purity and naiveté of this youthful humanism was tinged with inhumanity:

> We judged human beings solely by the standard of how fervent was
> their ideological commitment and how courageous their practice. We
> paid no attention to personal qualities, such as depth or shallowness,
> wisdom or stupidity, warmth or coolness. Our human landscape, which
> portrayed a simple, constricted spirit capable of classifying people only
> as allies or enemies, was entirely monochromatic.

The party's lynching of spies, both real and imagined,[34] and the other irregularities that plagued the proletarian movement in the early 1930s—finally culminating in the *tenkō* incidents of 1933 and after—shook the youths' highminded humanism: "Before, one would often hear, 'Say, he's a pretty good guy,' but now it was just 'He's no good,' and backbiting, slander, distrust, jealousy—this is what had become of comradely love. I soon resigned myself to the egoism that was exposed once the mask of humanism had been peeled away."[35]

Not even in the context of the postwar liberation could there be a return to simple humanism. On the contrary, "in this second youth we can by no means resurrect the innocent feelings of the first."[36] Ara now recognized that true humanism could only emerge dialectically from utter negativity. Those "who don't know despair, haven't felt the abyss, and have never seen hell" were "false humanists," hypocritical, or worse. The postwar world was full of bad actors who covered their real faces with the masks of hypocrisy. But the only way to achieve artistic vitality and authenticity was to admit to egoism and follow its lead:

> We don't need the kind of arithmetical thought that sees egoism as the
> psychological reflection of social contradictions, or that represents it as
> something pretty that will never dirty one's hands. Let's pursue the
> thought of our own flesh; let's extend it over the abyss—through the
> limitless realm of negation that wells up from that abyss—all the way
> to the cosmological limit! And what will we find there? Infinite progress and development, or Nietzschean eternal repetition? Whichever it
> is, we can then return to the cares of daily life girded with a thorough

sense of negativity. Human beings are egoistic, ugly, despicable, and human conduct is submerged in nothingness—Let us feel this keenly, and all else will follow![37]

This attitude led to a new skepticism toward the party's authority: "We once made the mistake of enshrining the party leaders as gods, but this kind of behavior is no less primitive than that of the emperor system's slaves, who blindly worshipped the child of the sun." In terms of the new skepticism, political activity could occur only as an extension of self-centeredness rather than at its expense: "Instead of those humanist gladiators who expected no reward for their selfless service, it is rather the greedy, ambitious disciples of egoism who are the purest followers of humanism."[38]

Negativity and the Body

Ara's theme of negation and paradox was common to a broad cross-section of early postwar writing, and perhaps at some level intersected with the wartime experience of a broad range of his countrymen. As Tsurumi Shunsuke has observed, the postwar generation "witnessed the values they had believed in fade to the point of transparency." They became convinced of the "meaninglessness of all values," and concluded that "only when the self hurls forth passion will the world respond with meaning."[39] This loss of faith in values, philosophies, and ideologies often correlated with new concern about defining and differentiating humanity from other forms of life. For many writers, it was only in the lowest common denominator of human existence that some glimmer of hope for the future could be perceived, and this often meant emphasizing the flesh rather than the spirit. For example, just as for Ara humanism could be based only in the ego, for Tamura Taijirō the only possible bedrock was physical desire.

Tamura was demobilized in 1946 following six years as a soldier in China, and almost immediately began to produce a form of literature that came to be known as *nikutai bungaku*, or "carnal literature." In a rare essay, published in 1947, he argued that philosophy (*shisō*) of all kinds had to remain intimately bound to flesh and blood if it was to be potent enough to respond to problems of war, poverty, and dislocation: "During the war I learned that no 'philosophy' that ignored the flesh could offer any resistance against national actions that overran normal boundaries. Moreover, after a long time in the field I saw Japanese who claimed to revere high-sounding philosophy become transformed into beasts. I myself was among them."[40]

But since the war, philosophy had lost its persuasiveness:

The flesh is now an outlaw, rebelling against everything. Isn't it true
that today the flesh is raising up banners and placards, beating the gong,
and waging a frontal attack on "philosophy"? Starving widows sell
themselves on the streets to feed their children. Somewhere a young
man is working as a burglar so he can run off to Atami with a dancer.
A "gentleman" rapes and strangles one woman after another. A student
sells wheat flour as opium for ¥50,000 and then kills his customer
rather than be exposed. The streets are filled with homeless waifs and
wild dogs who pilfer and collect garbage. The flesh is pained, and cries
out; bodies collide, blood flows, and sparks fly. Docsn't this suggest
that the flesh is now totally distrustful of "philosophy"?

In the postwar world, therefore, where "only the flesh is true," it was impossible to conceive of a humanism that was not deeply rooted there: "What power
could there be in a form of humanity that is not grounded in the flesh? To know
the meaning of the flesh is to know the meaning of the human being."[41] If there
is to be any meaning at all, it must be materially constructed and always conditional rather than absolute; never cut off from sensuous needs, it is rather their
extension.

Tamura's fiction aptly followed his prescription. One of his stories, in particular, was to become a landmark in postwar popular culture. Entitled "Nikutai no
mon" (Gateway to the Flesh), the work deals with a group of teenage women
surviving as prostitutes in the rubble of bombed-out Tokyo. The narrator describes them as more like beasts of prey than human beings:

They are like mountain lions or panthers, those fairly small, but nimble
and fierce, beasts that chase down their prey in the dark of the jungle.
Driven by the desperate urge to survive, the women stalk the pitchblack
streets. . . . They obey neither laws nor the morality preached in society. Such things had all disappeared, along with days spent in the war
production factories, bathed in sweat and machine oil; along with the
bombs—and along with their homes and families. All that had van-
ished, and they had now turned back into beasts.[42]

The work seems to illustrate three principles: First, survival is the ultimate
value and goal of human life. Questions of meaning inevitably appear specious
in light of constant threats to human survival. Suppression of problems relating
to meaning is dramatized in a scene where Ibuki and the girls are feasting on
vodka and beef:

Ibuki said, "You can't buy this kind of beef even for ¥40." And then
Sen [another of the women] leapt up as if she had discovered something
momentous, and announced, "Hey, 100 momme of beef is ¥40 and so
are our bodies. It's the same! Isn't it strange for human bodies and beef
to be the same? Don't you think so? What's the point of eating beef at
¥40 and selling your body for ¥40? Do you sell to eat, or eat to sell?
What meaning does life have then?" Ibuki laughed, "Don't think so
hard. You are living this way and you can eat like this, so that is
enough, isn't it?"[43]

Second, behavior is governed by instinct rather than conceptual reasoning,
and animal life provides the most compelling similes with which to describe it.
Social order is merely the tenuous product of instinctive, unarticulated attrac-
tions and repulsions. Tamura portrays human life without a guiding Logos.

Third, the motif of *nikutai* (flesh) emphasizes surface, texture, and opacity.
This is well exemplified in a discussion of the tatoo that Sen is getting on her
shoulder:

For Sen it was fascinating that all kinds of pictures and writing could be
sculpted into the human skin. . . . But that was not all. Just as primi-
tives have to turn themselves into something superhuman in order to
stand up against tigers, alligators or bears, in Sen's life of daily struggle
she had an instinctual desire for a mystical, robust power beyond her
natural strength. When she thought about the fancy pan-pans from
Yamanote who sometimes invaded her turf, and how she would now be
able to pull one into an alley and startle her by baring the . . . tatoo in
the light of the moon and neon signs, Sen's breast tingled with fighting
spirit.[44]

Here the flesh generates a form of subjectivity as the will to fight, but only as
a dependent variable, an extension of the biological need to survive. Indeed, it
seems that the source of vitality is not in the will per se, but in the material
marks—the writing itself. Thus, the human logos, the voice, and therefore the
subject, is elided: power resides in the inscription, which, when etched onto the
body's surface, gives it the capacity to signify a magical threat quite alien to
human will and understanding. Ultimately, the story allows for transcendence
only if that is defined as a transition from numbness to sensation: it consists
entirely in a higher form of carnal knowledge.

Of course, resort to the flesh as a potentially reliable essence capable of
grounding values was not limited to Tamura's work. Among other explorations

of the body as the basis for life and struggle in early postwar literature is that provided by Dazai Osamu's *Shayō* (Setting Sun, 1946), a work more familiar to English-language readers than Tamura's. There, from his drug-induced delirium, one of the main characters assures us that all manifestations of the spirit are unreliable. He writes in his journal, "Philosophy? Lies. Principles? Lies. Ideals? Lies. Order? Lies. Sincerity? Truth? Purity? All lies."[45]

A problem the novel addresses is whether it is possible for former aristocrats to go on living after the war at a very basic, biological level. Naoji decides that it is not, and chooses death by suicide, while his sister Kazuko perseveres. In order to survive, however, she must confront the selfishness of life: "I can't escape the feeling that it is by sucking the lifebreath out of Mother that I am fattening." Also inescapable is life's ugliness: "The dying are beautiful, but to live, to survive—those things somehow seem hideous and contaminated with blood." Yet once negated as a means to any external ideal or purpose, life can be reaffirmed as an end in itself and thus, paradoxically, provide the basis for a form of engagement: "There was something to which I could not resign myself. Call it low-minded of me, if you will, I must survive and struggle with the world in order to accomplish my desires."[46] Then, in a letter to her former lover, she discovers the final rationale for life in the biological capacity to give new life: "Recently I have come to understand why such things as war, peace, unions, trade, politics exist in the world. I'll tell you why—it is so that women will give birth to healthy babies."[47]

Here, meaning in life and active engagement with the world do not result automatically from the removal of feudal or fascist constraints. They are neither the natural outgrowth of liberation nor the inevitable counterparts of historical development, but rather the children of renunciation, desperation, and pain.

As these examples suggest, Ara's critical thematic of irony and oxymoron was by no means an isolated phenomenon. In the early postwar period truth, sincerity, and humanity were all called into question, and meaning, like existence itself, always seemed very tenuous. In light of the decadent, often nihilistic, atmosphere these literary figures represented, it is not surprising that the party's call for self-abnegating homage to the people was sometimes greeted with rebellious derision.

Authorial Subjectivity and the People

In the April 1946 issue of *Kindai bungaku*, Ara followed "Daini no seishun" with an essay entitled "Minshū to wa tare ka" (Who Are the People?). Here, irony and skepticism are transformed into biting sarcasm, as Ara extends a thematic focus on the Russian populists and their slogan, "V narode" (To the people), into a scathing attack on what he interpreted as the orthodox leftists' hypocritical preoccupation with "the people." To dramatize his points, he fills the essay with wry reminiscences:

> As I try to go to sleep at night, my mind is visited by vivid scenes:
>
> *Wife*: Luck has finally come your way, hasn't it? Isn't the Communist party organizing openly? When do you think we'll have a democratic- front cabinet?
>
> *Husband*: We'll definitely take over in one or two years. Like France, you see? I'm going write up a storm this year.
>
> *Wife*: Really? Oh, good! Will you earn lots of money? There are lots of things we could buy if we only had the cash.
>
> *Husband*: I'll get the first royalties on the translation by the 23rd. Hmmm . . . , I'd like to go out right now and buy about ten cigarettes.
>
> *Wife*: It is bad for your health to smoke so much. I'd get some rice from the black marketeer next door, and that olive oil—it's a little expensive, but I'd buy it. Oh, but now I'm likely to get used to having money so you will have to work fast. I'll help by rewriting your drafts and doing anything else I can. I really want to get an all-wave radio, an electric washer, and an astrakhan overcoat. But I suppose when you have money it all goes for taxes, huh?
>
> *Husband*: Umm, but I'm thinking about buying a house anyway.

This happy couple's sweet-as-candy conversation is hardly over, but a short selection is all we need to get the gist. Whenever this fighter for humanism opens his mouth, it is to stir up the people and attack reactionary politics; when he shows up in round-table discussions, on the radio and in the news, rushing here and there, he hardly warms his seat before he dashes off. But we must remember that he speaks and writes on behalf of the people, from the bottom of his heart.[48]

Integral to Ara's rhetorical strategy is an implicit comparison between the Japanese party leaders and the naive, upper-class *narodniki* of nineteenth-century Russia, with whom they shared a paternalistic, objectified image of the people. Yet he also makes it clear that in sincerity and self-sacrifice, the rationalistic Japanese Communists could never measure up:

> The literary intelligentsia appoint themselves as teachers and enlighteners. But are more than a few of them able to see, like Herzen, that their own lives are evil? And do they have enough love in their hearts to view the peasants as sacred? Like Tolstoy, do they feel drawn to the ex-

tremes of humanism, choking off their own egos in order to set right
their relationship to the people? Do any of them even have the consci-
entiousness of an Arishima Takeo? . . . They think they can just squat
contentedly atop a stack of manuals and pamphlets.[49]

The Japanese Communist party narodniks are more petty and superficial, taking
their pedagogical mission for granted:

A dormitory song at a bourgeois school [in Japan] goes like this, "Under the moon of Heidelberg, we recall the fervor of the *narodniki* . . . "
Well, we know what generally happens to the fervor of these young
Japanese narodniks once they finish college and go into society, but
the few who are not suited to becoming officials or businessmen or politicians turn instead to culture and the arts. So long as they remain in
their ivory towers, ensconced in a world of aesthetics, they are quite
harmless, but whenever they venture into the broad field of humanist
endeavor they become more difficult. And the ones who enter the liberation movement are most troublesome of all. These petty bourgeois
intellectuals, raised in a hothouse, begin to talk endlessly about the
workers, the peasants, the people. Their slogan is scholarship and art
for the people. They are the people's teachers, their leaders, their en-
lighteners, and I suppose that is benign enough. But if given a chance,
I would like to put one of them a question: "Teacher, are 'the people'
them, or are they *you*, or *us*? Could you just calmly give us your own
opinion?" And then he would say, "Wha . . . wha . . . what do you
mean, them, you or us? Of course *they* are the people. . . . Well, hold
on, now. No, they are *you*. Wait a minute! The people are *us*!" . . . The
artless performance of this former school-boy narodnik, progressive,
rationalist, and humanist, makes for a sorry scene in the comedie hu-
maine.[50]

Intellectuals delude themselves when they allow their paternalistic pretensions to draw them toward factories, farms, and settlement houses.

They sometimes get so excited when supporting workers in a labor
struggle that they forget they are not workers themselves and start hal-
lucinating that a five-fold increase in wages would actually connect
somehow to their own petty bourgeois lives. Eventually, they can be
heard to say things like, "We workers . . . ," etc.[51]

But no honest writer can find the people anywhere except in his own heart:

In short, the people are not they, you or us. They are myself, the solitary
I. . . . The people are me, no matter how much it might serve to authorize my petty bourgeois intellectual nature, with its mean, dirty, ugly

egoism. Nay, it is that nature itself that shows the paved road to Parnassus. . . . To be oneself, that is the way to the people. And because we have that belief as a foundation, all will flow from ourselves, with nothing borrowed. Petty bourgeois egoism itself shows love for the people and amounts to the highest humanism.[52]

As Ara had argued in "Daini no seishun," writers had utterly to deny naive humanism. The new, tougher humanism could only be an "affirmation through negation, the plenitude at the very extremity of nothingness, and the pristine humanism that is the extension of our egoism."[53] The ego marked the unavoidable, and irreducible, pole of a dialectical process, a topos that had to be fully occupied before humanism would emerge as a possibility. Only when one could rest comfortably in the negative state of egocentrism could one reach out tentatively in a gesture of humanistic affirmation.

To many, against the background of wartime devastation and postwar deprivation, Ara's evocation of the darkness that encloses (and makes possible) light, and of the descent into nothingness that must precede or accompany the affirmation of meaning, made logical and compelling sense. So did his argument that any authentic, productive, and artistically valuable portrayal of the plight of others must be premised on an honest, searching look into the self.

However, the assumptions that the ego, or the body, was capable of providing a ground for subject-formation that was somehow more substantial and reliable than "philosophy," and that egoism was a viable foundation for humanism, also seemed questionable to some critics in the early postwar period. One of these was French literature specialist Katō Shūichi, who attacked (without naming them) Ara and the others who espoused egoism.

Katō agrees with the *Kindai bungaku* writers' perception that high priority had to be given to establishing a "literary subject" and consolidating "the subjectivity of the individual in the process of democratic revolution." However, the conviction embraced by those writers that the content of that subjectivity should be egoism betrayed "a misunderstanding of humanism and a logical and emotional poverty with respect to aesthetics." In their belief that petty bourgeois writers should feel free to express their own egocentric feelings and worldview, Ara and the others had been led to glorify the "substantially feudal as well as petty bourgeois" family life that comprised those writers' favorite topic. More specifically, advocates of the authorial ego were placed in the position of defending the confessional I-novels (*shishōsetsu*) produced in the Taishō period by the likes of Kasai Zenzō and Kamura Isoda.[54] Yet the direct transcription of events in the writer's personal life that was typical of these novels could never add up to a satisfactory account of true human reality, which always lay "beneath the facts," like original sin in the novels of François Mauriac. Never merely objective and narratable as such, authentic human reality had always to include the dimensions of subjective depth and perspective. Speaking of literary realism, Katō writes: "Here, as in Balzac as well, the Latin term realismus is Platonic. The artless record of the daily life of the writer that constitutes the I-novel can never be called 'realistic' in this Platonic sense. Hegel, who was an eminent aestheticist, would never call something in history 'realistic' that was not rational." In other words, a truly "real" human being had to be apprehended at the intersection of the historical and the transhistorical:

> The literary image of man must be located historically and socially, and at the same time be a transcendental, existential reality. Thus in a double sense, it takes shape only upon the negation of petty bourgeois, everyday life. Only through the mediation of that negation can the novelist's creativity become possible. . . .
>
> "For Whom the Bell Tolls"? The reality of people abandoning their wives and children and throwing themselves into the Spanish Civil War—for whom, and by whom, will it be portrayed? Not by petty-bourgeois intellectuals, egoists, but by humanists from among the intelligentsia who act alongside the people. Revolutionary literature emerges from revolutionary consciousness, and revolutionary consciousness is sustained by revolutionary action.

In Katō's view, "human reality is none other than the tension between metaphysical experience and political concern that supports our existence." Therefore, a genuinely new humanist/literary subject could appear only through an active process of mediation and conflict: "the reality of the soul should not be subjected to logical unification, but rather authenticated through action; rather than abstractly regulated, it should be expressed in the novel." By the same token, egoism could never lead to humanism no matter how those terms might be defined because "there exists between them not a quantitative difference that could be filled by expansion [of the ego] but a qualitative difference that could be crossed only via a leap."[55]

With its strong Kantian overtones, Katō's elitist critique of the directly expressed, unmediated subjectivity valorized by Ara parallels the perspective developed by the intellectual historian and political scientist Maruyama Masao in an essay entitled "From Carnal Literature to Carnal Politics" that he published two years later (see chapter 4).

War Responsibility and the European Ego

Kindai bungaku's insistence on the priority of self-expression ramified in a variety of directions. In a roundtable discussion early in 1946, the emperor system and writers' war responsibility were the issues that led the journal's members back to a focus on the self. Odagiri Hideo suggested that writers should see the emperor system not as an external structure but as a set of unconscious emotions that predisposed them toward feudal behavior: "Feudalism penetrates even the small corners of our sensibility in daily life. Therefore, we can fight against it only by conquering what is feudalistic within ourselves." Ara responds:

> The emperor system must share responsibility for the war, but the emperor has not admitted that. When confronted with this [anomaly], writers tend either to put up a front of ignorance, on the pretext that as writers they know nothing of politics, or just leave the pursuit of the emperor's war guilt to the Communist party. But these evasions leave them impotent to take up the war responsibility of writers. If, as writers, we are to pursue the emperor's war responsibility in a literary way, we will have to struggle with the semi-feudal sensibilities, emotions and desires that are rooted in our own internal "emperor systems." That is the only way we can negate the emperor system per se, and the only way that is conducive to the formation of a modern person. . . .
>
> We were unable to oppose the war. . . . Why . . . ? Because we did not have within us a modern ego.

Notions of a "modern person" and a "modern ego" were often premised on an Orientalist dichotomy between (premodern) Asia and (modern) Europe. Europeans had achieved a universalistic, "human" belief system and a sense of equality before God, whereas in Japan people still defined themselves according to hierarchical social roles with no autonomous identity as human beings. Such notions were based ultimately on Japanese readings of modern European philosophers and social scientists who frequently employed a notion of the static and despotic "Orient" as the defining contrast to modern Europe's transcendent faith and supposed subjective depth. According to Haniya Yutaka, "If we think of Europe, there has always been a kind of authority—for example, until the last century there was God . . . the God of all mankind. Europeans were always standing before a kind of court. . . . And even when this God was transformed, to be replaced by society, or humankind, people always faced a judge, and harbored the internal imperative of a 'should' (*sollen*), a notion of how the individual should be as a human being." In Japan, on the other hand, the private individual was virtually absent, subsisting merely as a dependent locus of needs and desires that required the encompassing support of communal bonds:

> We [Japanese] have been able to gain self-awareness as human beings only as a result of passive evasion. Our awareness is so pervaded by the Eastern way of thinking, that only by escaping or retreating can we ever hope to occupy a purely human standpoint. We know how to be Japanese nationals (*kokumin*) but not how to be human beings. Humanism has been nothing but an empty word.

It was logical, therefore, that if there was to be a renaissance in the postwar era, it would occur only when the Japanese self was transformed in a modern, which is to say European, direction:

> *Ara*: We have to liberate the Japanese ego. It should become like European individualism.
>
> *Hirano*: Can it be elevated to the level of the European ego? I wonder. It's just not possible to wipe out a tradition overnight, and although one might prefer to replace it with another tradition, that is impossible.
>
> *Ara*: Not necessarily. You are free to determine whether your own ego will be elevated or not. That is the freedom of our generation. We have to give life to that freedom. I feel a powerful sense of urgency in that regard. Isn't that why we are struggling to publish *Kindai bungaku*?

And yet, their commitments to the West and to the panacea of modernity were not entirely unambivalent:

> *Ara*: We have had no feeling of equality. As a result, we were not modern enough to oppose the war. . . .
>
> *Honda*: If you mean the reason that we were unable to resist effectively was that modernity was not established within us, I think in the broad sense you are right. But I really don't quite understand the meaning of modernity. . . .
>
> *Sasaki*: Yes, because the Europeans themselves were unable to avoid the war. But I think you can say this: In Japan where the modern ego has not been established people do not keenly feel war responsibility as their own personal problem. Writers just say, "It couldn't be helped." . . .
>
> *Honda*: I think it is true that the lack of consciousness regarding war responsibility is the result of our failure to establish a modern ego. But now that we are at the stage of wondering how to think about war

responsibility and what to do about it, it doesn't help much to say
that the remedy is to establish a modern ego and a modern literature. . . .[56]

Although they could reach no consensus on how to rectify the situation, the
Kindai bungaku writers seemed to agree that tasks such as rooting out the emperor system through democratic revolution and fully airing the problem of war
responsibility had to be carried out internally, in the minds of individuals, as
well as externally in the political arena. This conviction led them to the ideal of
modernity, which was intimately associated with the development of autonomous subjectivity, and also to a conception of European culture as the exemplar
of that modernity. Yet their preoccupation as writers with self-clarification and
expression set them at odds with the Communist party's literary ideals of objectivity and realism, and its traditional assumption that politics (the party) should
lead culture.

Although couched in a literary language and problematic, *Kindai bungaku*'s
demands are all thoroughly understandable as reactions to the Leninist privileg-
ing of the working class (glossed as "the people" [*minshū*] in the postwar era of
united front) as the uniquely qualified revolutionary subject. Ara and his comrades were anxious to write and act for themselves rather than for the working
class. As writers, they wanted to be inside the democratic revolution, as its subjects, rather than outside it in the supplementary role of well-meaning inter-
lopers.

Elsewhere, Ara returned repeatedly to the controversial question of how to
define and constitute the subject of democratic revolution. For example, in his
"Nakano Shigeharu-ron" (On Nakano Shigeharu), Ara had written:

> To be sure, the proletariat is ultimately in charge, but surely liberation
> in a democratic revolution is achieved through the self-assertion of the
> petty bourgeoisie. . . . Rather than disinterested humanism, shouldn't
> we be attempting to mobilize self-interested egoism? Shouldn't the
> petty bourgeoisie be connected to the revolution through the urge to
> provide for themselves rather than for the people and, indeed, the urge
> to feel that they themselves are the people?[57]

The purport of Ara's complaint is that against the background of the "first narrative" view of bourgeois-democratic revolution, which Leninism had long since
revised, the petty bourgeoisie should play at least as important a role as the proletarian masses. Intellectuals should therefore shed their supplementary function and freely identify *themselves* with the transition that was under way.

In "Tetsugakusha Q e no tegami" (Letter to Philosopher "Q"):

Virtually any intellectual can respond clearly when asked to identify the
main actor in today's historical transformation. . . . At the same time,
in their hearts a secret aspiration is quickening. That is the aspiration,
not to see the gap between themselves and that main actor suddenly
smoothed over, but rather to overcome it step by step while remaining
true to themselves. Although I am courting misunderstanding, I should
say it is a desire for self-realization. It is precisely because they are well
aware of the fissure between themselves and the people that they hope
they can securely fill it in. . . . Isn't it time to start thinking about a reality in which the intelligentsia as such are able to participate in political
praxis? . . . In any case, in order to be true to themselves, to cultivate
personal growth, and to liberate themselves—that is, in pursuit of
their own happiness—I think it is necessary that in complex ways they
should merge with the subject of historical change and eventually construct a social subject. There is no room for doubt that, owing to both
internal and external causes, today's political climate is conducive to
the actualization of this process.[58]

And in "Sanjūdai no me" (In the eyes of the generation in its thirties):

The proletarian movement has always demanded that intellectuals
should liquidate their petty bourgeois natures, take the standpoint of the
people, and move to their side. This requirement has been connected to
the philosophy of proletarian hegemony, and amounts to a tendency to
disparage the intelligentsia. . . . But the political demand of the moment is for democratic revolution. Leaders of this revolution should
include the petty bourgeois intelligentsia as a matter of course, along
with small capitalists, medium and small-scale landlords, and others, so
as to create the broadest and deepest democratic front. The philosophy
of hegemony has a broad range of nuance. The petty bourgeois intelligentsia will participate in this revolution, not through self-liquidation
but through self-assertion, that is, for themselves above all. Self-
liberation is connected directly to liberation of the people as a whole. I
am the people—this perception is not a defensive reaction, or anything
of the sort, but the expression of raw feelings. Those in the forty-year-
old generation who are raising a ruckus over this will ultimately be left
behind by history.[59]

Ara appeals directly to the vocabulary of hegemony, which in Marxist-
Leninist discourse had traditionally referred to the supplementary moment
of contingent political action. He suggests that in the Japanese party and else-

where, proletarian hegemony had been taken to mean role differentiation according to a rigid class hierarchy and suppression of other standpoints. However, he correctly points out that "the philosophy of hegemony has a broad range of nuance" and can also be interpreted as the product of a more open process of articulation among all elements of the people, including the petty bourgeois intelligentsia. Further, in "Shōshimin no tachiba" (The standpoint of the petty bourgeoisie), Ara had written:

> The revolutionary process is peaceful and democratic. Not only workers and farmers, but small and medium landlords and small capitalists as well, belong to the democratic front and are liberating the people. Democratic revolution is the actual situation of society. It is not a question of who has to sacrifice for whom; all who participate in this revolution will enjoy freedom and happiness together. That is the standpoint of the petty bourgeois intelligentsia.[60]

In pointing to democratic front and the policy of peaceful and democratic revolution, of course, Ara was merely taking the party leaders at their word. These were fundamental elements of the party's political program as originally outlined by Nosaka Sanzō and the Fifth Party Congress. And yet, although they opposed the Leninist politics of necessity—and the paternally manipulative form of control that was its external supplement—the *Kindai bungaku* writers were unable on the whole to counter with a coherent politics of contingency and free subjectivity. Indeed, at times they claimed to want to abandon politics and to expend their efforts on the elaboration of a supposedly nonpolitical, subjective vision of literature. That is, for them, politics had to do primarily with the party's demands for compliance.

Politics and Literature

The *Kindai bungaku* writers were preoccupied with the relationship between literature and what they called politics—that is, the demands of class loyalty and partisanship. As noted above, both Haniya Yutaka and Honda Shūgo raised the issue in roundtable discussions, opining that politics was relatively narrow in content and values and was concerned solely with present exigencies, while literature was broader, more spiritual, and more fundamental in its substance. It is particularly suggestive of the kind of politics they are referring to that Honda is convinced that politics "disciplines from without" while literature "persuades from within." But the question of "politics and literature" in this framework was pursued most intensively by Hirano Ken.

Hirano was born in Kyoto in 1907, attended Eighth Higher School along

with his classmate Honda Shūgo, and went on to the faculty of literature at
Tokyo Imperial University. There he began to participate in an illegal reading
group, involved himself in union activities, and joined the proletarian literature
movement. He became a member of the Proletarian Science Research Institute
on Honda's recommendation while still a student; upon graduation he was connected to the secretariat of KOPF and helped edit *Puroretaria bunka* (Proletarian Culture). However, in 1933 he was shocked by the Communist party's
"lynch" incident, in which a Central Committee member was killed while being
interrogated by other party leaders on suspicion of being a police spy, and became disillusioned with the party and the movement that surrounded it.

In the late 1930s, while working at editorial jobs, he joined Yamamuro Shizuo
and Honda Shūgo in founding the journal *Hihyō*, and came to know Haniya
Yutaka through their common affiliation with *Kōsō*. Upon the outbreak of war
with the U.S. in 1941, he entered the government's Intelligence Bureau, where
he worked until 1943, and became a member of the Society for Patriotism
through Literature (Bungaku Hōkokukai). In 1944 he joined the Mishima Field
Artillery unit, but was ejected ten days later for medical reasons.

In the early postwar era Hirano was a founding member not only of *Kindai
bungaku* but also of the Central Committee of the New Japan Literary Society.
After teaching here and there, he became professor of literature at Meiji University in 1958, and taught there until his death in 1978.

In two famous essays published in April and May 1946, Hirano focused on
events in the history of the prewar communist movement in order to illustrate
the "inhumane" effects of external political demands. He says, "It has always
been the special characteristic of politics to sanction employment of any means
to reach a desired end." Politics detaches means from ends, relating them only
instrumentally—that is, externally—rather than intrinsically, while in literature "all detachment of means from ends is illegitimate . . . that is, [in literature]
we have to look closely at the ends that are implicit in the means themselves."
Seemingly mindful of the Kantian precept that a human being "is never to be
used merely as a means for someone (even for God) without at the same time
being himself an end,"[61] Hirano relates two incidents that he believes illustrate
the tendency of the prewar movement to manipulate human beings in inhumane
ways.

The first case is only indirectly related to literature, having to do with a Communist dramatic actor and director, Sugimoto Ryōkichi, whom Hirano suspects
of having cynically persuaded an innocent film actress, Okada Yoshiko, to accompany him as a diversion in a dash across the border from the northern island

of Sakhalin into the Soviet Union. If one accepts Hirano's construction of the incident—that Sugimoto "used a living woman as a stepping stone" in order to achieve his own ends—it aptly illustrates the point he wishes to make about the prewar proletarian movement: that it so sanctified its own goals as to be willing to sacrifice the private lives of countless individuals. On the other hand, in the process of making his point, Hirano manifests an aspect of his notion of *shutaisei* that might characterize the *Kindai bungaku* approach more broadly and, perhaps, that of postwar Japanese theories of *shutaisei* in general: Hirano's conception of subjective intentionality is thoroughly male and patriarchal. Hirano portrays the actress, Okada, as devoid of ideological or, indeed, rational intent, attributing all instrumentality in the incident to Sugimoto:

> I just could not fathom how this beautiful, vivacious actress would be intrepid enough to run across to the Soviet Union. . . . I have no way of connecting Okada with any philosophy or ideology. She most likely was in love with Sugimoto. Perhaps the heart of this small, aging actress was ablaze with a flame of adventure and martyrdom similar to the one that consumed the bar hostess played by Marlene Dietrich in *Morocco,* who at the end of the film kicks off her sandals and follows her man into the desert. . . .
>
> I don't know if Sugimoto also loved Okada. Perhaps in his heart of hearts it was in order to develop further the god-given artistic talents of the woman he loved that he took her across the Soviet border. That is the most charitable way of interpreting the incident. . . .
>
> Of course, I don't know what kind of ideals Sugimoto Ryōkichi was possessed of, or what sort of dead end he might have confronted that would make him decide to flee to the Soviet Union. All I know is that in order to achieve his end, Sugimoto used a lovely, middle-aged actress. And it is this small fact that is most significant.[62]

In Hirano's imagination, only Sugimoto might have been motivated by political or other instrumental goals; Okada is driven by emotions, especially those of love for and devotion to a man. Sugimoto "uses," "develops," and "persuades" Okada, while she never acts, but is a passive object, acted upon. An equation between the male and activity, the female and passivity, is of course pervasive in modern European ideology. One can turn to Hegel, for example, or to a number of other philosophers in the "Western" tradition.[63] Rather than a peculiarly Japanese aberration, therefore, what we confront here is tantamount to a staple element of the modern philosophy of subjectivity. Unfortunately, texts associated with the debate on subjectivity do not often bear directly upon gender relations—except in that they are virtually all by males—and therefore generally offer few grounds for a more thorough exploration of this aspect of modern theories of subjectivity.

The case of the "housekeeper," which Hirano mentions only in passing, struck to the heart of the prewar literary movement in that it involved the Japanese proletarian writer who was most revered by the Left, Kobayashi Takiji. In Kobayashi's unfinished novel, "Tōseikatsusha" (Life of a Party Member), which was probably autobiographical, the protagonist marries a "petty bourgeois" typist largely for convenience and to provide him with a place to stay as he devotes himself to party activity. The protagonist explains to his wife that she is performing an important task by helping him work for the liberation of the proletariat, but she feels like she is being exploited.

Hirano argues that "housekeeper" arrangements such as this one in the proletarian movement provided the precedent for Sugimoto's treatment of Okada.[64] In other words, because the Communist party as well the emperor system oppressed human beings in pursuit of political goals, both should be criticized:

> If asked why I raise these questions now I would have to reply that the theme of writers' war responsibility and the issues of the Marxist literary movement's mistakes and ideological conversions (tenkō) are in fact inseparable. . . .
>
> I cannot but be a little skeptical about the current movement [led by Kurahara and others] to revive the past Marxist literary movement just as it was. The faults of that movement, with its policy that could only result in ideological apostasy, and the complex set of internal and external circumstances that constituted an inexorable tendency, must be surgically removed from inside the movement itself. In the course of that effort, tendencies and mistakes such as those typified in the "border incident" will reveal the need for a spirit of self-criticism.

Hirano's most inflammatory gambit was to compare the Communist martyr, Kobayashi, who was tortured and beaten to death by police in 1933, to Hino Ashihei, a popular writer who was caught up in Japan's expansionist policies and wrote voluminously about Japanese soldiers at the front:

> The exposure of Hino Ashihei's war crimes is probably inescapable, but the naive and tender feelings he embraced when, as a youthful author, he wrote *Mugi to heitai* [Barley and Soldiers] are clearly revealed in . . . his letters. . . . In just the same way as Kobayashi Takiji's life represented the sacrifice to contemporary expediency of the truest ac-

tivist of the mistake-ridden proletarian movement, the literary activities
of Hino Ashihei which began with *Mugi to heitai* were also caught in
the terrible waves of Japan's aggressive war and sacrificed to the era.
To put it boldly, the presently confused literary world demands the kind
of mature literary eye that is able to see Kobayashi Takiji and Hino
Ashihei as two sides of the same coin.[65]

In his second article, Hirano continues his argument concerning the "inhumanity" of political efforts to control literature. He suggests that the literature of
the Shōwa period (from 1926) had been dominated by the problem of "politics
and literature" through an early period up to 1936, during which political dominance over the movement had been exercised by the Left, and a later period
when control had been taken by the "military cliques, the bureaucracy, and the
'renovationist' (*kakushinteki*) writers who surrounded them." He goes on:

> The content of "politics" in the early period is the complete opposite of
> what it became in the later period. But precisely because the two pe-
> riods emerge as positive and negative sides, together they form a
> whole. Does not such a realization broaden the outlook for our consid-
> eration of the problem of "politics and literature"? I have previously
> written that Kobayashi Takiji and Hino Ashihei should be seen as two
> sides of the same coin; in terms of the schema introduced here these
> two writers can be treated, respectively, as representative of the early
> and late stages of Shōwa literature. Of course, Shōwa literature is not
> over yet, so isn't a spirit of bold self-criticism indispensable in order
> that it might reach its full potential?[66]

Hirano proceeds to recount aspects of the complex history of proletarian literature from its beginnings in the early 1920s to the authoritative doctrinal
statements published by Kurahara in the early 1930s. Concerning this final
stage of consolidation, he says:

> The question [of the relationship between the vanguard party and
> literary organizations] was carried forward by Kurahara Korehito's pro-
> posals regarding the establishment of communist literature, the
> Bolshevization of literature, the dialectical materialist method of cre-
> ativity, and so on. [As a result] the orthodox development of Marxist
> literature was consolidated in a systematic institutional pattern, with the
> formation of a cultural league and circle organizations in the form of a
> pyramid. This marked the completion of the problem of "politics and
> literature." And the feature that persisted throughout that historical de-
> velopment was the unshakeable ideal of the "primacy of politics."[67]

The "primacy of politics," in turn, was connected to the Communist party's long-standing emphasis on proletarian leadership and ultimately dictatorship, despite the short-range focus on bourgeois-democratic revolution mandated by the Comintern directives. According to Hirano, the party's orientation to proletarian socialist revolution was responsible for the rigid control exercised by the party over cultural organizations such as the—aptly named—*proletarian* literary associations, despite the fact that the preponderance of their membership was petty bourgeois. Within these organizations, "politics" referred to external party dictates. As party control of the cultural movement intensified around 1931–33 in accord with the Bolshevization movement led by Kurahara and others, the result was pathological spy incidents and lynchings,[68] and also the torture and death at the hands of the police of the movement's martyr, Kobayashi Takiji. Hirano even suggests that the party's responsibility was equal to that of the police, who had accelerated their repression under the impetus of the Manchurian Incident.[69]

Although one can understand Hirano's demand for a more flexible and tolerant party attitude toward culture, his analogy between state repression of the Left via the Special Higher Police, or Tokkō, and the party's rigid and authoritarian control of proletarian literature can only be considered farfetched and gratuitous. Implicitly legitimated by the Peace Preservation Law of 1925, torture and murder by the Tokkō had gone on at least since the roundup of Communists on March 15, 1928, and despite what might well have been the party's application of unreasonable pressure for conformity on loyal writers such as Kobayashi, the agents of his torture and murder were Tokkō officers, not Communists.[70]

In conclusion, Hirano demands that, rather than seeking in the postwar era to dominate literary production—through a movement now called the *democratic literary movement*—according to the same principles and modus operandi that had been established in the prewar era, the party should engage in serious self-criticism concerning its prewar mistakes and adopt a new policy more appropriate to the postwar era's democratic politics of equal participation in united front.

> The best translations of the adjective *revolutionaire* are "radical" (*kyū-shinteki*) or "progressive" (*shinpoteki*). The International Union of Revolutionary Writers is named correctly, in this sense. The major figures in Japanese proletarian literature are undoubtedly radical, petty-bourgeois intellectuals. This movement, and these groups, are and should be anti-feudal, anti-capitalist and anti-fascist entities *revolutionaire*. Although, of course, they are not trans-partisan organizations,

they should in fact be non-partisan. . . . They should not arbitrarily demand that artistic works manifest the Communist—which should be strictly differentiated from the socialist—viewpoint. There should be no question of a "vanguard viewpoint" according to which the political program of a single faction is expected to be duplicated in artistic activities. In a word, it is a mistake to make the "primacy of politics" into a principled demand.[71]

Hirano does not expand upon the kind of democratic-front politics the party should pursue in the postwar era. From the perspective of literature, he quite accurately identifies the undemocratic practices and structures that might be justified by appealing to ontological authority. It would seem that the party's rigidly hierarchical authority structure and essentialist claims to infallibility did mirror those of the "emperor system," as anti-Communist party student radicals were to point out in the 1950s and 1960s.[72] Nevertheless, it was disingenuous to imply on the basis of such an analogy that the party's responsibility for politically motivated oppression in the prewar era was equivalent to that of the state. Moreover, Hirano's extremely political essays about literary works clearly contradicted his professed belief in the insularity of "literature" from "politics."

The Party Counterattacks: Nakano Shigeharu

Although he appears to have gone too far in equating party authoritarianism with that of the prewar state, Hirano's strategy of recounting the failings of the prewar movement in order to develop a critical angle on left-wing politics and literature in the postwar era was apt in the sense that the major literary organization sanctioned by the Communist party in the early postwar period, the New Japan Literary Society, was "essentially at first a straight-line restoration of the former proletarian literary movement." This was true organizationally as well as philosophically, as "the pattern of organizational control used by the former Proletarian Writers' League was in every major detail duplicated."[73] The first regular issue of the organization's major journal, *Shin-Nihon bungaku* (New Japan Literary Review), was published in April 1946 and included Kurahara's programmatic essay, referred to above.

It was not long, however, before the pages of *Shin-Nihon bungaku* came increasingly to be devoted to counterattacks on the *Kindai bungaku* group. The centerpiece of this genre was a three-part series by Nakano Shigeharu, who, along with Kurahara, Miyamoto Yuriko, and a few others, was a leading figure in both the prewar and postwar proletarian literature movements.

Nakano had left the rural area of his birth in Fukui prefecture to attend

Fourth Higher School and then Tokyo Imperial University, where he belonged
to the radical student organization Shinjinkai. He became a published poet
while still a student, but also had begun to write essays and critical pieces by the
time he graduated in 1927. As a participant in the proletarian literature movement beginning in 1928, he wrote regularly for and edited the journal *Senki*
(Battle Flag). His first arrest also came in 1928 while campaigning for the
Labor-Farmer party. He joined the underground Communist party in 1931, and
in April 1932 was imprisoned for two years, toward the end of which he admitted that he had belonged to an illegal organization (the Communist party) and
promised to desist from such activity in the future. After publishing "Mura no
ie" and other famous *tenkō shōsetsu* (stories of ideological conversion), he was
again placed under surveillance, and soon was denied the right to publish for a
year.[74]

Nakano spent the war in near silence, but in 1945 he returned to the party and
to active participation in political and literary activities.[75] He published the first
of his three critical essays, all of which came to be titled "Hihyō no ningensei"
(The humanity of criticism), in the fourth issue of *Shin-Nihon bungaku*. It consisted largely in a series of long quotations from major early postwar essays by
Ara Masato and Hirano Ken, interspersed with commentary. Nakano's strategy
is basically to turn the arguments advanced by Ara and Hirano back onto their
own position. He does this by presenting Ara's call for humanity in literature as
itself "inhumane," and by arguing that the relation between means and ends in
Hirano's own criticism is less consistent than in the politics Hirano attacks. He
parodies Hirano's equation between Kobayashi Takiji and Hino Ashihei, and
ridicules Ara and Hirano for presuming to retire from the fray of politics in order to pursue art for art's sake.

Nakano says, "[T]hey want to be the kind of critics who will nurture humanistic literature. But . . . is their criticism . . . itself humane? It appears to me as
the opposite."[76] In order to slander the proletarian literary movement, Ara had
"fabricated" incidents and conversations, such as the dialogue between husband
and wife in "Minshū to wa tare ka," recounted above.

> This is the kind of thing Ara bases his argument on. We do not know
> who these people are or where these things took place, things he and
> Hirano conjure up in their own minds, accidental things, pathological
> things. . . . They verbally kick around as "sentimental blow-hards"
> those artists who have sincerely tried to enter among the people. But
> they praise the petty bourgeois intelligentsia's "small, mean, ugly ego-
> ism" as showing the "paved road to Parnassus."
> Critics are free to build castles in the air, and construct make-believe

people. But illusions and notional personalities do not themselves constitute a basis for criticism. To rely on such stratagems reveals the weakness of the critics themselves and their own theoretical anxiety.

By indulging in such fabrication, Ara and Hirano had used inhumane means to attain what they claimed to be humane ends, thus indulging in precisely the sort of separation of means from ends Hirano had critically associated with politics rather than literature.

Hirano himself illustrates the separation of means from ends. Naturally, a critic who cannot think humanely about politics . . . will use any means to achieve his ends. Ara and Hirano are not discriminating in that respect. They are hoping to attain their ends by using their vulgar imaginations and making reference to those who are dead or in exile. This reveals their quality as human beings.

With regard to Hirano, Nakano quotes his suggestion that "the present literary world demands the kind of mature literary eye that is able to see Kobayashi Takiji and Hino Ashihei as two sides of the same coin," and comments pointedly:

This is the same as saying, with respect to the war, that the emperor and the corporal both sacrificed. The emperor starts the war and sends the corporal into it, thus making a "sacrifice." The corporal is ordered to go to war and is sent to his death, thus making a sacrifice. Kobayashi was slaughtered by his enemy because of his involvement in revolutionary literature and democracy thereby making a sacrifice. Hino helped the enemy along by opening the way, thereby making a "sacrifice." Hirano is certainly free to retire from the fray and rely on his "mature literary eye." But it is a shameful error if he becomes so detached that he blurs the differences among these so-called "sacrifices."[77]

The *Kindai bungaku* writers' attempt to "retire" from political engagement in order to devote themselves to literature is "childish, immature, naive," because "[i]t is not detachment but fighting that will nurture literature."[78]

Nakano concludes by contextualizing the Ara and Hirano essays in relation to the political program of democratic revolution, charging that these writers "are exerting themselves in order to turn back a democratic literary movement that is striving to expand under unfavorable conditions."[79]

Neither Hirano nor Ara wasted much time in responding to Nakano's riposte. Regarding the issue of the dramatist's use of the actress to facilitate his border crossing, Hirano wrote:

After all, Sugimoto should have made the difficult decision to enter the
Soviet Union alone. Wouldn't that have been the best means to attain
his end? It seems so to me. But instead, Sugimoto Ryōkichi took the
easy way of using Okada Yoshiko as a spring board to crash the border
from Karafuto. I could not help but see there an unfortunate precedent
whose significance transcended any question of ease or difficulty. It
only confirmed for me that the disease pervaded the Marxist artistic
movement as a whole.

And on the topic of Kobayashi Takiji:

> Consider the treatment of the woman character named "Kasahara" who
> is portrayed in Kobayashi Takiji's classic, *Tōseikatsusha* [Life of a
> Party Member]. This work blithely condones in the name of the move-
> ment a contempt for humanity . . . and a willingness to use any means
> to attain an end. And not the slightest bit of authorial anguish is ex-
> pended in connection with it. . . . However, this tendency toward
> contempt for humanity is not Kobayashi's individual problem. It is the
> responsibility of the entire Marxist art movement of that time.

As further evidence that the prewar movement systematically subordinated
ethics to the demands of partisanship, Hirano recalled Kurahara's comments
on a related problem in one of his 1931 Bolshevization essays, entitled "
Geijutsuteki hōhō ni tsuite no kansō" (Thoughts concerning artistic method).
Kurahara had raised the issue only to set it aside as a "petty bourgeois devia-
tion" rather than bringing it to bear in a reassessment of the movement as a
whole.

> Kurahara based his argument on the postulates of proletarian leadership
> and the primacy of politics. But principled demands cannot solve an ac-
> tual malignancy. Therefore, in line with Kurahara's brilliant analysis,
> the most faithful follower of that theory, Kobayashi Takiji, was able to
> dispose inhumanely of a woman in *Tōseikatsusha* without a glimmer of
> remorse.

Hirano also had suggested that the highly politicized way in which Nakano
responded to his arguments was itself indicative of the continued problem of the
"primacy of politics"—that is, the detachment from democratic articulation—
that plagued the Communist party.

> All in all, Nakano's criticism itself very aptly demonstrates the urgency
> of the very problem that I felt obliged to raise clumsily as "a certain
> counter-supposition." Should I be thankful to him for unwittingly re-

confirming in my mind that it is necessary to look at the problem of "politics and literature" in a "literary" manner, and that to look at it in such a manner is the only "humane" way to proceed?

For his part, Ara contests Nakano's charge that he "fabricated" people and incidents to make up his reminiscences in "Minshū to wa tare ka," replying, "If he wants, I would be happy to present my list of the models for the essay's 'cast of characters,' but if possible I would like to avoid that kind of mud-slinging."[80]

Nakano's second installment of "Hihyō no ningensei" was originally written in the form of reports to the annual convention of the New Japan Literary Society. It is entirely different in style from the first essay, substituting a broad political perspective for the close scrutiny of a few essays, and an impersonal focus on social forces for the earlier attacks *ad hominem*. In it, Nakano warns that reactionary forces are mounting a cultural counteroffensive against the democratic revolution. Indeed, culture was the main arena in which counterrevolutionary forces were waging their struggle: "Now that the military has been seized, the police weakened, and the emperor divested of his divine charisma, these ruling forces have no choice but to appeal primarily to culture." Moreover, "literature is the most powerful means employed by these reactionary forces."[81]

Nakano enumerates three reactionary trends in literature. First, "propaganda designed to induce amnesia concerning the war"; second, carnal literature. With respect to the latter, he says:

> Liberation from war also meant the liberation among the people of a torrent of love problems, which had long been suppressed. Reactionary forces are taking advantage of this to separate love, now reduced to eroticism, from the problem of humanity as a whole. . . . It was not primarily lust that the war of aggression trampled down but love. It trampled love in order to crush the totality of humane conduct. Therefore, erotic literature as a reactionary tendency is doubly criminal in that it continues and intensifies the trampling down of love which was begun by war.

Third, and most important with respect to *Kindai bungaku*, "certain reactionary tendencies in literature are designed to demolish the popular spirit that had already been disrupted by war and to maintain it in a weakened state." Although Nakano does not mention Ara, Hirano, and their comrades in this connection, his reference to their belief in the primacy over political partisanship of freedom, self-expression, and humanism is unmistakable: "Conservative liberalism and capitalist democracy under the name of humanity are the theoretical pillars of this literature. . . . It seeks to substitute an abstract human being for the actual people. . . . it propounds as the true humanism an individualism which turns its back on the reconstruction of the Japanese nation (*minzoku*)."

Here Nakano implicitly makes the argument, put much more explicitly by Kurahara, that Japan's democratic revolution is not the classic variety that establishes the power of the elite bourgeoisie but a "new" democratic revolution that will be led by and establish the power of the workers, peasants, and lower bourgeoisie. "Liberalism and individualism were always the spearheads of the capitalistic in opposition to the feudalistic and the absolutistic. But now, the same tendencies have turned their backs on the democratic construction of the nation that is occurring in the midst of historical changes of capital."[82] In other words, particularly with respect to literature, Japan's democratic revolution was moving rapidly beyond the stage of bourgeois-democratic revolution per se to the process of socialist construction.

Nakano also indirectly criticizes Hirano and others via an attack on the separation of politics and literature. Literature could not be separated from politics because it "stands on the entirety of human conduct . . . and is aimed at the holistically humane nurturance of human life." Those who "advance a notion of the cultural that is free from the political and social" were merely attempting, by means of that rationale, "to be free from the ongoing revolution." With unassailable logic, Nakano insists that no one, and especially no writer, could ever be free from politics, "even if he refuses to pay taxes and never votes."[83]

In March 1947, Nakano published the third installment, which dialectically subsumes the earlier two. The essay singles out for pointed criticism a variety of writings which Ara published in 1946 and early 1947, and brings the Communist party standpoint concerning the errant members of *Kindai bungaku* to a familiar conclusion: They were to be seen as the "literary spokesmen of the political forces seeking to transfer from the proletariat to the petty bourgeoisie the power to lead Japan's revolution, its democratic revolution." This was their "class essence."[84]

Nakano objects most vehemently to Ara's implication, in several essays, that the democratic front should include virtually all classes and groups on an equal footing, even though that had been Nosaka's definition of the "new democracy" in January 1946. Nakano charges that, inasmuch as it implied an attitude of "welcome, welcome, everybody's equal," this view of democratic revolution was "tantamount to the desire that the class nature of the leading forces of the revolution should be changed." It is in the "fire-thief" nature of the petty bourgeois intellectuals like Ara to want to participate in the revolution only for short-term advantage, even as they attempt to rationalize their position through high-sounding literary ideals. They are, in fact, only trying to "escape" the real revolution of the proletariat, whose leadership ought to be honored.

> In opposition to the historical progress of the revolution and the working class which is actively promoting this revolution, and which is liberating for all time the petty bourgeoisie . . . (and therefore even Ara himself) from the shackles of their own petty ownership, he comes forward out of a desire to protect his freedom to try to escape the revolution on those points that satisfy his egoism.[85]

This not only impedes the progress of revolution as a whole, but might "interfere with the growth of [other] petty bourgeois intellectuals who are participating actively in revolution and are attempting to liquidate their petty bourgeois nature."

The narrow, classist interpretation of proletarian hegemony is presented here with its full moral force. On behalf of all classes, the working class was unilaterally and singlehandedly carrying out the historical mission which the bourgeoisie had shirked. Petty bourgeois writers who sought to participate were mere "fire thieves," grabbing spoils (freedom!) without being at risk. Only by liquidating their class identity could they play any constructive role at all.

Although Nakano concentrates his attack on Ara, he does not neglect Hirano, to whom he devotes a substantial portion of his rejoinder. In Nakano's view, Hirano is using false humility to his own advantage. He quotes passages from Hirano in which the latter had continued, in a more pointed and detailed manner than in his earlier essays, to press charges against the prewar Communist party and proletarian literary movement for elevating partisanship over humanity.

Nakano's response to Hirano's more detailed and tenacious argumentation was cleverly evasive. In response to Hirano's questions concerning the humanity of Sugimoto's treatment of Okada, and of the Communist party's use of the "housekeeper" arrangement, Nakano says:

> It is Hirano, not I, who has written that the Japan Communist party "used the housekeeper system," and that Sugimoto "lured" Okada with "monstrous" stratagems. Before Hirano asks this stiff-necked old writer to demonstrate to him that an event which never occurred "was actually 'humane,'" Hirano should offer proof that it actually happened. But Hirano just calmly says, "It was not for me to know the circumstances of the party at that time."[86]

Nakano appears to have argued in an uncharacteristically personal and vindictive manner during these exchanges, but he had been provoked by the excesses of Hirano and Ara. Despite that, his overall stance can be taken to

represent not only the party's line on cultural production but also its widely recognized authority to interpret history and to set revolutionary policy.

The Limits of Critique

The *Kindai bungaku* writers found an opening for their critical initiative in the
Communist party's policy of democratic revolution. In Nosaka's definition of
"new democracy," the revolutionary subject was to include not only the
workers and farmers but petty bourgeois as well, and this seemed to clear the
way for a progressive literature of subjective involvement, an art that would
apprehend an objective, historical world by way of subjective presence rather
than at its expense. At the same time, however, the party's literary spokesper-
sons, such as Kurahara and Nakano, seemed often to demand that literature be
oriented not toward bourgeois reform in anything like the classical sense but
rather toward the socialist revolution which they believed already to be immi-
nent in the democratic stage and which demanded that the leadership of the
proletariat be immediate and unambiguous. The conflict between the older generation of proletarian artists and the generation in its thirties as represented in
Kindai bungaku was of genuine importance; the issues it raised were fundamental to the emergence of a postwar style and orientation in culture and, more specifically, the debate on *shutaisei*. Nevertheless, *Kindai bungaku*'s rebellion
against the party's cultural paternalism was still ambivalent and ultimately in-
conclusive.

First, the *Kindai bungaku* writers failed to substitute for the party's politics
of unilateral control an alternative form of cultural politics, one that would
premise hegemony on egalitarian equivalence and articulation among independent elements. Instead, they often claimed to want to abandon politics alto-
gether in favor of a supposedly "non-political" conception of literary art. It
appears that Ara went further than the others toward raising and defining the
problem of political subjectivity—that is, the problem of who or what groups
would form the subject of democratic revolution and by what political process.
Hirano persuasively debated the issue of the role of political partisanship in literature and literary movements, but it was Ara who most carefully related literary priorities to postwar political issues, such as how a people's front should be
constituted and how in other ways the Left could best operationalize the theoretical and historical concept of democratic revolution. All the *Kindai bungaku*
writers were to a greater or lesser extent opposed to external party control of
literary priorities and production, but Ara was most outspoken in arguing that
different elements of the democratic front should interact horizontally, on the
basis of equality, rather than vertically under party authority.[87]

Ara's perspective was vital in that it avoided the party's paternalistic tendency to treat the "people" as the objects rather than the subjects of revolution. Ara's conviction that even petty bourgeois intellectuals *are* the people and should concentrate on transforming themselves rather than others implied that working people should be, and perhaps were, transforming themselves into active subjects as well. Yet Ara's perspective on subject-formation among the working class as well as the bourgeoisie remained implicit. Neither Ara nor the other *Kindai bungaku* writers drew meaningful connections between their own drive for self-determination and that of workers embroiled in production control or other postwar social movements.

Partly at fault would seem to be their overly narrow conception of "politics," which they interpreted as party domination expressed through the demand for unconditional partisanship rather than as the conflictual, social process of subject-formation itself. That is, they failed to note that the "politics" of party control was in fact antipolitical, in that it claimed to be the manifestation of historical necessity and thus rendered secondary or epiphenomenal people's willful actions under conditions of uncertainty. If the politics of hegemony is not "an external relation between preconstituted social agents, but the very process of discursive construction of those agents,"[88] then not only the *Kindai bungaku* intellectuals but the workers who were embroiled in production control and other struggles had been engaged in politics from the start. Yet the *Kindai bungaku* writers' *concept* of politics remained undeveloped, so they were unable to theorize productively the politicality of their interventions in culture. They continued to couch their activities in a rhetoric of unpoliticality.

Second, and related to their inadequate grasp of politics, was their failure to direct any sustained critique at the postwar state. One is reminded in this connection of political activist Oda Makoto's later recollection of the early postwar era:

> Neither nationalism nor the state and its institutions that had been imposed upon us as our sole source of support could begin to compensate us adequately [for wartime suffering]. So rather than appeal to the state, we embraced the universal principles of democracy, freedom, and human rights imported from America and the system of institutions that went with them. . . . We adopted democracy . . . as if it were not in reality just another system of state power.[89]

In the background, of course, as Oda points out, was a powerful victim complex that focused attention on the evils of the wartime state but had in the immediate postwar the parallel result of deflecting criticism away from the Occupation, the censorship and other forms of oppression it engaged in, and the powerful state structure it was erecting.[90] Was it also, in part, such a complex—directed in his case more heavily toward the prewar Communist party than toward the state—that allowed Hirano Ken to portray the party as more or less equivalent to the Tokkō in its victimization of writers?

Third, although they removed historical materialist science and the metaphysics of necessity to the far horizon of concern, they were unable to free themselves from it entirely. At the time, the very notion of "democratic revolution" was intelligible only against the background of a historicist orthodoxy, increasingly codified during the Stalinist period, which located *the* bourgeois-democratic revolution at a stage of transition between feudalism and capitalism, and implied—although this had been challenged as far back as Lenin's analyses of the Russian revolutionary situation—that this transition had somehow to be accounted for prior to moving on to socialist revolution. In the early postwar era in Japan, the authority of this metahistorical framework was greatly augmented by the defeat of the Axis forces (as Japanese Communists claimed to have predicted) and the initiation by the Allied Occupation of a policy of demilitarization and democratization.[91] It was further reinforced by the victorious return to political life from jail and exile of such postwar party leaders as Tokuda, Nosaka, and Shiga, and the publicizing of their record of stubborn refusal to recant for periods of up to eighteen years. In short, in the postwar era the validity of the Marxist-Leninist science of dialectical materialism and its metanarrative of revolutionary progression toward socialism through certain stages was virtually incontestable. It is not surprising, therefore, that both sides in the *Kindai bungaku* debates on literature, class, and subjectivity tacitly accepted the authority of that science, and that the arguments of both sides tended to presume its truth. As one writer pointed out in the midst of a searching reevaluation of postwar thought in the 1970s, the debate on subjectivity demonstrated the degree to which postwar intellectuals were "obedient to the myth of 'Marxism.'"[92] By this view, *Kindai bungaku* was "an approach to '*shutaisei*' constructed along the axis of 'the God of history.'"[93]

Even as they bitterly contested central aspects of the party's cultural line, the *Kindai bungaku* writers very often paid homage to Marxist historicism and the science of dialectical materialism. For example, in his programmatic essay, "Geijutsu, rekishi, ningen" (Art, history, human being), Honda appeals to historical determinism in order to legitimize the ego:

> The way of thinking which makes of the human being a mere pawn of history does not necessarily void all effort. . . . If reality is necessity,

then the ego is also necessity. If I am but a tool, then I will be a good tool—this, too, must be the will of the unseen god. . . . You who only recognize external necessity and set aside the irrepressible necessity within, you are but a broken, ruined tool. It is human to rebel against necessity and achieve freedom.

They also tended to justify their criticism of the party's postwar literary policy by arguing that it was excessively narrow and rigid *in the context of democratic revolution*. By doing so, of course, they announced their acceptance of the metahistorical scheme that prescribed "(bourgeois-) democratic revolution" as the appropriate designation for the postwar stage. For example, to a caricature of conventional proletarian literary method Odagiri adds the caveat: "We do believe that, as a philosophical world view, dialectical materialism is correct, and that realism is the most effective literary method. Nor do we doubt that we are at the stage of democratic revolution."[94] Moreover, the strategy of opposing the party's literary policy on the basis of the peculiar historical character of the postwar era often led him and his comrades to grant that the policy *had* been appropriate for the prewar stage. Honda again:

The proletarian literary movement of the past inspired and channeled us into local activities. We did not resent it, nor did we think at the time that it was a bad policy. Indeed, the literary theory of that time penetrated to the center of our being and motivated us. No other was more correct for the time. It was appropriate to our own youth and to that of the movement. However, from this point forward, there must by all means be compensation for the insufficiencies that the maturity of history has now revealed.[95]

Here, Honda clearly betrays the modest scope of his critique. He praises the prewar line on literature, and even in the postwar context demands only that it be *supplemented* by more attention to the ego in compensation for a lack that had been clarified by "the maturity of history." The party's policy had been appropriate before the war but now, owing to the advance of history to a new stage, it had to be modified to accommodate increased attention to self-expression. However, since the party was the undisputed custodian and interpreter of "historical necessity," to accept necessity was implicitly to accept the authority of the party, not only in the prewar context but in the postwar context as well. Therefore, what at first reading might have sounded like a radical critique of the historical-materialist position amounted in the end to a much more limited, and in some ways self-contradictory, form of contentiousness occasioned largely by ambiguity in the party's own definition of democratic revolution.

A similar desire to stop short of any radical critique of the party as the custodian of historical necessity is evident in part of Ara's response to Nakano's attack.

> All I was trying to express in "Minshū to wa tare ka" was the subjective pathos that I, myself, am the people. I recalled that the people had always strictly excluded the petty bourgeois intelligentsia, and that the latter had always been required to shift to the former (taking the side of the proletariat). *I merely wanted to reexamine that principle in light of our new circumstances.* These circumstances demand a revolution not through military power and dictatorship but by way of peace and democracy. To the extent that the democratic front is to be broad enough to include not only the proletariat and poor farmers but also the petty bourgeois intelligentsia, ordinary farmers, and even small and medium-scale capitalists, was it not advisable to revise somewhat the previous way of evaluating the proletariat and the intelligentsia? *At this new stage*, everyone from the proletariat to the small and medium-scale capitalists would be struggling against reactionary forces, and cultivating democracy, not for others but for themselves. I, who had given up on humanism on behalf of the people, wanted rather to approach humanism and the people by way of an egoism for myself. That is where I found my second youth. That is how I discovered the people, the people within myself. And that is where I unearthed subjective pathos.[96] (emphasis added)

Here, too, only a new historical stage whose political mode of action was to be the democratic front had made it possible for intellectuals and even small capitalists to participate in history on their own account rather than on behalf of the proletariat. Only the subjective involvement that democratic revolution demanded of the petty bourgeoisie could bestow legitimacy on their egocentrism. Implicitly, therefore, Ara admits that at a different historical stage, egocentrism would be unacceptable.

Hirano attacked not only the postwar but the prewar policy of the proletarian literary movement, charging that it was thoroughly penetrated by an ethic of political expediency. He was therefore less vulnerable than Honda and Ara to a reassertion of party authority on the basis of the science of historical necessity. Yet a writer in the 1970s has argued that Hirano, too, was evidently dominated by a kind of guilt complex over his own prewar abandonment of the party and participation in government and private organs in support of the war. This caused him to react defensively to any suggestion of disloyalty or apostasy. That is, to a greater or lesser degree all the *Kindai bungaku* members continued to manifest a Stalinist belief in the ideal of rigid commitment, and this belief allowed the party to reassert its authority and control over them despite their disaffection with its literary theories. That is why Hirano reacted with such remorse to Nakano's charge that he was now among the "counter-revolutionary forces" that were attempting to turn back the democratic revolution.[97] Hirano wrote:

> Nakano Shigeharu criticizes Ara Masato and me in the lead article of the fourth issue of *Shin-Nihon bungaku*. He says we are among those "counter-revolutionary forces in literature" who are "exerting themselves to turn back" a "democratic literary movement that is striving to expand under unfavorable conditions." Nakano Shigeharu is a poet whom I have quietly loved and trusted for a long time. . . . Now, that very same person has stamped me as a demagogue of "counter-revolutionary" forces. I feel wretched.[98]

Overall, the *Kindai bungaku* writers played a very important role in the postwar cultural revolution by exposing party policy and procedures to new scrutiny and opening the discourse on politics and literature to new forms of contestation. Their criticisms of the party for what they believed to be its facile reestablishment in the postwar milieu of all the principles and assumptions of the prewar proletarian literary movement seem even today to be persuasive in some respects. Moreover, in their ironical skepticism toward established brands of humanism and partisanship, insistence on the legitimacy of ego-centered subjectivity and desire, and self-critical confrontation with war responsibility, they answered directly to the iconoclastic atmosphere of the early postwar period.

And yet, their rebellion against the metahistorical claims of the vanguard party, which premised itself on the "infallible" science of dialectical materialism, was ultimately incomplete. They remained under the spell of "historical necessity" and in the end merely attempted to supplement, and thus, in effect, to complete and vindicate, what in principle was a closed metahistorical system.

THREE

Philosophy and the Lacuna in Marxism

Hence it happened that the active side, in contradistinction to materialism, was developed by idealism—but only abstractly, since, of course, idealism does not know real, sensuous activity as such.

—Karl Marx[1]

Not only in modern Europe had the philosophy of action been developed largely by idealists. In twentieth-century Japan, the so-called Kyoto School of philosophy led by Nishida Kitarō and Tanabe Hajime had been the most attentive to issues of subjective agency. Perhaps, in part, for that reason, in the postwar milieu—often recalled as an "age of philosophy"—people lined up in the street to purchase copies of Nishida's prewar works, and Tanabe's *Zangedō no tetsugaku* (Philosophy of Repentance) of 1946 was perpetually sold out. However, from the dialectical materialist perspective, Tanabe's philosophy purveyed "only love between the ruling class and the working masses in place of the struggle for thorough democratization; religion and idealist philosophy in place of scientific observation; criticism by intellectuals instead of leadership by the working class; and in place of class confrontation, a process of conciliation." Indeed, Tanabe had argued, in effect, for the "complete elimination of class conflict in the name of the nation."[2] It is not surprising, therefore, that in the early postwar period the Communist-led Association of Democratic Scientists (commonly called Minka) assigned top priority to the need to criticize Nishida, Tanabe, and other Kyoto philosophers.

Minka had been formed in January 1946 on the initiative of the Communist party, but included among its members a variety of prominent non-Communist scholars and writers. It was intended as a "united front body for scientific activities," and initially proposed a set of objectives that included such elements as establishing the scientific spirit and building democratic science; struggling against antidemocratic educational institutions, policies, and ideologies; mobilizing science and technology for the welfare of the masses; and demanding complete freedom for scientific activities.[3] These were appealing objectives in a time of democratic "enlightenment," when most everyone believed that all the dark corners of wartime obscurantism and mysticism had to be flooded with the light of scientific reason. In the philosophical realm, Minka's major voice was the monthly *Riron* (Theory), whose first issue in February 1946 was devoted to the critique of Kyoto School idealism.

Both the leadership and the scientific orientation of Minka had roots in prewar Marxism. Its organizers represented two major streams: one was heir to the Proletarian Science Research Institute, which had been formed in 1929 by Kurahara Korehito, Miki Kiyoshi, and others, and which in early 1933 was dissolved into the Puroretaria Kagaku Dōmei (Proletarian Science League); the other descended from the Yuibutsuron Kenkyūkai (Materialist Study Group), which Tosaka Jun, Hattori Shisō, Nagata Hiroshi, and others had formed under repressive conditions in October 1932 and continued until 1938.[4]

Philosophy and Politics in Postwar Japan

In 1946 Tanabe Hajime began to adapt his philosophical logic to questions of postwar political action. In a long essay entitled "Seiji tetsugaku no kyūmu" (The urgent need for political philosophy), he apparently intended to provide for reformed Japan a political philosophy that would take full account of the social, political, and economic changes that were being pressed forward by SCAP. In response to the postwar atmosphere of democratic revolution, he focused on problems of equality and freedom and called for a new form of "social democracy" that would be constituted through the dialectical transcendence of both freedom and equality, mediated in the state.

Tanabe was born in Tokyo in 1885 and attended First Higher School; he went on to graduate from Tokyo Imperial University in philosophy in 1908. His first work, *Saikin no shizen kagaku* (Recent Natural Science), was published in 1915 while he was teaching at Tōhoku University, and in 1919 it earned him the degree of Doctor of Letters and a position as associate professor in the Faculty of Literature of Kyoto Imperial University. His early orientation was toward German neo-Kantianism, but he was powerfully influenced by Heidegger while studying in Germany from 1922 to 1924. In 1928, he succeeded to Nishida Kitarō's chair in philosophy, becoming the second leader of what came to be known as the Kyoto School of philosophy. Upon retirement in March 1945, he was first evacuated to, and then took up permanent residence in, the mountain village of Karuizawa. He died in 1962.

In the preface to the postwar essay he writes, "Philosophy has a very important duty to perform in relation to the problem of rebuilding the fatherland. . . . New times require new philosophies."[5] But in approach and thought structure, his "new" political philosophy was in fact thoroughly recognizable as an extension of the old. His definition of politics, for example, continued to assign an essential role to the state as totality, in direct continuity with his earlier "logic of species," in which he had argued that coercion by the state was converted to freedom at the level of the individual.[6] He writes: "Politics is essentially the action system of transformative mediation through which the individual accepts as the basis of his own existence the communal social control exercised by his racial group [or 'tribe'—*shuzoku*] and converts it, as something that can be freely chosen, into the mediation of his own self-autonomy; as a result the individual is, in his own existence, positively subjectivized as a member of the totality."[7]

There could be no freedom without the negative mediation of the state: "The freedom of the individual cannot exist without mediation." The individual can actualize freedom only in opposition to coercion exercised from without. Therefore, the freedom and autonomy of the individual are always dependent upon, or "equated" with, the control exercised by the political totality. In Tanabe's terms, "Freedom takes as mediation the moment of totalistic necessity which negatively opposes it, and establishes itself with absolute negativity in the totality which is the defining substance of dominance and control." This was as true for democracy as for any other political system. What was special about democracy was only that it elevated to the level of first principle the dialectical process between freedom and totality that was latent in any political community: "Democracy . . . proclaims as a norm the very principle by which [government in general] is formed, that is, of mediation and conversion among domination qua freedom, control qua self-determination, and totality qua individual."[8]

Democracy, therefore, had to be conceived not as a set of institutions or a system, but as an active dialectic between freedom and equality. Indeed, it would appear that Tanabe's overall objective in this essay was to vindicate such a dialectic and the controlling totality it implied:

> Today, freedom of the individual will be unrealizable if it is not combined with equality, which can arise only from social control at the level of the totality. When it comes to guaranteeing in a just manner that the proletariat's right to exist is equal to that of the propertied classes, freedom alone is an empty term. . . . That is why it can no longer be concealed that yesterday's liberals are today's conservatives, nay reactionaries. We cannot put new wine in old bottles. If the old philosophy of liberalism is not dialectically overcome—mediated by new socialism in order to become a philosophy of social-democracy—it will be impossible to unite freedom and equality as the two essential moments of democracy. Only in a philosophy of social democracy can democracy as liberalism, and communism as the most thorough form of socialism, both be negated and at once resurrected as moments in a concrete, comprehensive standpoint as the philosophy for a new age.[9]

As might be expected, the emperor plays a central role in Tanabe's philosophical prescription for postwar politics.[10] Clearly the Japanese people were emotionally in favor of retaining the emperor; the problem was how to provide the emperor with a "rational" role in relation to a democratic politics. As the first step toward a solution, he notes that, in contrast to what had been the case in England, the Japanese people had never fought against the emperor in a struggle for sovereignty; rather, they had "revered and trusted him as the unifying center of the Japanese *minzoku* (Volk; race)." Here, then, was a basis for the emperor's continuing role. Citing Carl Schmidt's dictum that the essence of the political is confrontation between friend and enemy—a confrontation that was ultimately destined to split the nation itself—Tanabe finds the role of the postwar imperial institution in its ability to "transcend the confrontation between political parties and thus ideally express the unity of the national totality."[11] He recalls that such a rationale had sometimes been offered to justify the British sovereign as well, but argues that in practice the British principle of "the king in parliament" resulted in the complete absorption of monarchical sovereignty into popular sovereignty, thus preventing the monarch from transcending the people to provide a higher principle of unity. As a result, the British monarch's role was not really political at all but merely ceremonial.

But how was it possible to maintain a thoroughly democratic polity while at the same time allowing the emperor to transcend the conflictual essence of the democratic system? Tanabe's answer inevitably descends into the sort of mystification that Marxists and modernists found so typical of the "Kyoto School":

> So long as we have democratic politics in a system of constitutional monarchy, it is absolutely necessary that there be no transgression of popular sovereignty. It must be fully respected, so monarchical sovereignty can only be exercised through the mediation of the gratitude [*on'i*] of the people. . . . Concretely, the imminent dimension must exist in mediated unity with its opposite, the transcendent dimension. The principle of their unity must be the active mediation of nothingness [*mu*] through transcendence-in-imminence and imminence-in-transcendence. In the politics of constitutional monarchy, the monarch is both inside parliament and at the same time outside and above it. Here, in a manner that overcomes the fiction [*gisei*] of the English constitution, reverence for the emperor as the unifying nucleus of the national totality gives rational content to our imperial ideal. The emperor is the embodiment of the ideal of a unified national totality and therefore is also the point of unity in parliament.[12]

But did not the emperor's transcendence of parliament—even through the mediation of *mu*—compromise the principle of popular sovereignty? Tanabe goes on:

Sovereignty lies with the people while at the same time devolving toward [*kikō suru*] the emperor. The emperor is not merely an organ of
the democratic state under popular sovereignty; he transcends it by rati-
fying its legislation and by being the subject of absolute unity that mili-
tates against disunity. . . . Thus, the emperor must be understood as a
being that symbolizes nothingness [*mu*]. It is not being but rather *mu*
alone that is capable of unifying things that are in contradictory opposition. The absolute inviolability of the emperor arises from this
transcendent quality of *mu*. It is precisely the symbolic existence of the
emperor understood in this manner that both allows democracy and
provides the principle for the absolutely negative unification of the
oppositions that democracy entails.[13]

Interestingly, Tanabe found that he could not logically oppose the assign-
ment of war responsibility to the emperor, and even argued that rather than
waiting for the Occupation's intervention, the assets of the imperial household
should have been offered out of the emperor's benevolence as the means of alle-
viating the people's misery and starvation.[14] Yet, when combined with the
philosophical interventions of Watsuji Tetsurō and other conservative ideologues, Tanabe's formulation of the postwar role of a democratic emperor went
far toward legitimizing the postwar emperor system that SCAP had imposed by
fiat.

Japan's first postwar election, held only eight months into the Occupation on
April 10, 1946, stimulated Tanabe to also take account of electoral politics. The
result was "Shakaitō to Kyōsantō no aida" (Between the Socialist and Communist parties), which he published in July 1946. The turnout of voters had been
72.1 percent, and they had elected 140 Liberals, 94 Progressives, 92 Socialists,
14 Cooperative party representatives, 5 Communists, 38 minor party candi-
dates, and 81 independents.[15] These results, which might on the surface seem to
indicate solid support for conservative political forces (some 325 of those elected could be associated with the "old guard"[16]), must in fact be interpreted cau-
tiously because of the "overall ineffectiveness of the purge" prior to the election
and the Occupation's "failure to destroy the strongholds of authoritarian influence represented by such agencies as the neighborhood units, the labor bosses,
and the Agricultural Association." As T. A. Bisson concluded in the late 1940s,
"Any claim that the April 1946 election gave the Japanese people a free chance
to express their views concerning the new constitution and the retention of the
emperor system was transparent pretense."[17]

In any case, following the election there ensued a forty-day period of confusion in which leaders of the Liberal, Progressive, and Socialist parties bargained and manipulated in an attempt to form a cabinet headed by the Liberal party. When it looked as if Liberal party president Hatoyama Ichirō would succeed in forming a government, he was promptly purged by SCAP. The final result was the formation on May 22 of the first of several cabinets to be headed by Yoshida Shigeru. In the meantime, food shortages led the list of problems facing Japanese authorities, and on "Food May Day," hundreds of thousands of people had gathered to protest in front of the Imperial Palace and elsewhere.

In response to this political impasse, Tanabe blames the preceding Shidehara cabinet for the food crisis and inflation, and the Liberal and Progressive parties for unseemly power hunger. He also criticizes the Socialist party, which, instead of aligning itself firmly with the Communists in a democratic front, had compromised with the conservatives in an effort to enter the government and in the process had lost the confidence of the people.[18] At the same time, he notes that those voters whose suspicions were aroused by the JSP's maneuvers did not necessarily gravitate to the Communists as an alternative, and he attributes this to their nervousness concerning the Communist theory of proletarian dictatorship. Therefore, it was by offering a critique of this theory that Tanabe sought to promote his own political position, which he described as "between the Socialist and Communist parties."

Tanabe grants that, according to historical materialism, proletarian dictatorship occurs at the "final stage of class confrontation" and "the point of conversion to a classless society." Therefore, from a purely scientific standpoint, an interim period of dictatorship ought to be capable of smoothly bridging the transition to communism. However, objective science alone was an inadequate basis for political strategy. It was necessary also to take into account the subjective dimension of human nature and psychology. In parallel appeals to the logic of the master-slave dialectic which Hegel had elaborated in *The Phenomenology of Spirit*, and to a fundamental postulate regarding human nature, viz., "the desire to support oneself in idleness by coercing and employing others, bending them to one's will," Tanabe argues that the dictatorship of the proletariat as envisioned by the Communists would lead only to "perpetual hostility" and eventual rebellion: "Even if a classless society were to be achieved, those with more ability would coerce and use those with less; they would disrupt the equal distribution of materials, and revive inequality and unfreedom. The individual's rebellion against the totality would never disappear and the result would be a split in the totality." The "propertied classes" refuse to recognize the truth of materialist science, and it is precisely for that reason that Marxists believed the mechanism of proletarian dictatorship to be necessary; however, by the same logic, so long as the "propertied classes" remained intransigent and sought revenge, dictatorship in itself could never lead to a classless society.

Conflict should not necessarily be avoided, however. On the contrary, Tanabe professes that "conflicts, which are difficult for mere mortals to avoid, must by all means be fought out." Moreover, conflict should never be viewed as a means to love and reconciliation. Conflict could never lead directly to peace, nor could domination lead to freedom. Rather, it was only as "negative mediation" that conflict could open the way to harmony. Only after they had thoroughly fought out their differences could human beings "keenly experience their mortality and become painfully aware of their sin, so through repentance they would convert to love." Once this occurred, the conflict could be transcended toward a higher plane of unity. However, an essential role in this dialectical approach to conflict was played by an attitude of self-sacrifice on the part of the winners. Conflict implied "a burden" which had to be borne "by the winner as well as the loser." This burden was the need for self-denying love, without which there could be no end to conflict:

> As class struggle is pressed forward and proletarian dictatorship is
> pushed to an extreme, it is inevitable that the winner's self-satisfaction
> in victory will lead to a perpetually armed peace fraught with tension.
> Such an outcome can be overcome only through an attitude of self-
> sacrifice on behalf of the totality, the winner's incorporation of the
> loser through self-denying love, and a tendency on each side toward ap-
> peasement and consensus in the totality.

Unless the winner adopted an attitude of self-negation and sacrifice, "victory itself would mean defeat, and domination of the other would constrain one's own freedom." Only when mediated by self-negation could "struggle be mediation for love, and conflict the negative moment of peace" in a dialectic of "struggle qua reconciliation."[19]

Based on his rationale of "love as nothingness," Tanabe advanced a view of contemporary politics that called for a dialectical standpoint of "renovation" between the opposing poles of "revolution," as represented in the Communist party, and "reform," as propounded by the Socialist party. In a manner that recalls the logic of dialectical conflict between freedom and equality which he had outlined in "Seiji tetsugaku no kyūmu," and the negative tension at the level of species between universal and individual, Tanabe explains:

> In general . . . although we opt for a socialism that is thorough enough
> to be close to communism, we should stop short of the extreme at

which a struggle based on violence becomes unavoidable, and do everything possible to maintain a democracy of consensus based on persuasion. The imposition of socialism based on class struggle and the democratic freedom of agreement based on persuasion should be mediated in mutual negation leading to unity in social democracy. What might at first glance seem to be a mid-point between the Socialist and Communist parties is not merely the result of syncretism. Rather, it should be understood as the mutual negation and conversion of what appear in extreme form to be contradictory demands, and their elevation—through practice arising out of the absolute nothingness which underlies their joint negation—to a standpoint of creativity that transcends both.[20]

More concretely, he suggests that this might mean support for a new renovationist party based on the "democratic people's league" proposed by Yamakawa Hitoshi.

Umemoto Katsumi's Critical Marxism

Even as Minka and other left-wing groups were working desperately to isolate and discredit Nishida School philosophy, intellectuals who before and during the war had been schooled intensively in the works of Nishida, Tanabe, Watsuji Tetsurō, and others were now struggling to reorient themselves toward Marxism. They responded to Minka's call for a critique of idealism, but as they struggled through their own reorientations from the perspective of the Nishida School's concern with problems of subjectivity and practice, they became keenly sensitive to what seemed to be serious inadequacies in the Japanese tradition of Marxism-Leninism.

The representative case of a postwar intellectual who approached Marxism initially from the perspective of Nishida, Tanabe, and Watsuji, and in the process sought to revive the critical humanism of the young Marx, was Umemoto Katsumi. Born in Tochigi prefecture in 1912, Umemoto attended Mito Higher School, where he was exposed not only to Nishida but to neo-Kantianism; he then studied ethics at Tokyo Imperial University under the direction of the philosopher and cultural historian Watsuji Tetsurō. After his graduation in 1937, with a thesis on the thirteenth-century Pure Land Buddhist leader Shinran, he went briefly on to graduate study. He soon dropped out, however, and after several years of working for the Ministry of Education and then the Kokusai Bunka Shinkōkai (Society for the Promotion of International Culture), he eventually ended up back at Mito Higher School, where, for the rest of the Pacific War, he taught ethics and began to read Marxian economics. Indeed, he remained there

until that school was dissolved into Ibaraki University in 1950, so it was in Mito
that he wrote the seminal postwar essays that would touch off the so-called "debate on *shutaisei*" among philosophers and force Japanese Marxists to reassess
their philosophical foundations.[21]

Umemoto joined the Communist party in late 1947, but his membership was
not made public until January 1949. After leaving Mito Higher School, he lectured at several universities and worked briefly for the National Personnel Authority. He was named professor in the Faculty of Literature of Ritsumeikan
University in 1954, but was unable to accept on account of illness, which kept
him hospitalized until April 1958. He left the party in 1959, and was broadly
associated with the Japanese New Left until his death in 1974.

According to Umemoto, it was in order to contribute to the critique of
Tanabe's political interventions that, in August 1946, he wrote "Ningenteki jiyū
no genkai" (The Limits of Human Freedom) and eventually published it in
Tenbō (Outlook) in February 1947. His references to Tanabe are not explicit,
and initially he avoids political polemics in favor of a highly speculative, eclec-
tic form of philosophical argumentation. In addition to outlining a materialist
perspective, the essay tentatively introduces Umemoto's own critique of scientific materialism by forcefully raising the question of freedom. While he does
not mention Tanabe by name, Umemoto begins his essay with an unmistakable
reference to "Shakaitō to kyōsantō no aida":

> It appears that social democracy is being provided with a philosophical
> foundation and is being praised by the intellectuals. They say that in the
> course of its development liberalism alienated equality and thus placed
> its guarantees of freedom in jeopardy; and while they celebrate commu-
> nism for its equality, they see it as having again alienated freedom.
> Thus, on that basis, they now propose the unification of liberalism and
> communism [in social democracy].[22]

Umemoto's contribution to the critique of Tanabe's philosophy might have
had organizational as well as personal motive. In June 1946, a few months before he completed "Ningenteki jiyū no genkai," he had joined in organizing the
Mito branch of Minka,[23] and most likely adopted its priorities as his own. At the
same time, his early essays were also the products of a serious effort to purge his
mind of vestiges of wartime ideology and to establish a secure grasp of Marxism. He later wrote, of this "period of transition" from idealism to historical
materialism, that he was "forced into a confrontation with my line of thought up

to that time." Like most intellectuals, he was racked with war guilt: "I was in the situation of recognizing the bankruptcy of my own philosophy, which in the end had been unable to loose a single arrow in opposition to fascism; at the same time I was unable to free myself from it entirely." Therefore, in the postwar environment in which, as a result of Tanabe's essays, "the problem of political commitment had hurdled the stage of concrete social-science and, willy-nilly, become the object not merely of philosophical but densely metaphysical conceptions," Umemoto's effort to criticize Tanabe's position "between the Socialist and Communist parties" inevitably lured him into a certain methodological complicity with the object of his critique.[24]

In attempting to respond to Tanabe from a Marxist perspective and at the same time satisfy himself regarding the Communist commitment to human freedom, Umemoto retrieves Marx's own early writings on the topic of freedom and humanism. He recalls the statement in "On the Jewish Question" that "[e]very emancipation is a *restoration* of the human world and of human relationships to *man himself*."[25] In *The German Ideology* and elsewhere, Marx had argued that such an emancipation could only be achieved "in a communal society where bourgeois production had been dialectically overcome." Umemoto freely paraphrases the former essay in order to sketch in the historical background to human emancipation:

> Liberalism set the modern citizen free *politically* from the fetters of feudalism. But this consisted essentially in an emancipation of the modern bourgeois from all that constrained his spirit of self-interest. As a result, feudal society disintegrated into an aggregate of selfish, isolated individuals, while the moral personality was left hanging in the air. Modern capitalist society is composed of such selfish individuals, who gradually commodify all the elements of society. This signals the complete bifurcation of humanity [*ningensei*]. . . . Even now, we must seek to bring into the real person that *true* person that hangs there abstractly.

When capitalist society is transcended humanity will gain, for the first time, the "means of cultivating its gifts in all directions," thus making "personal freedom possible."[26] Early in his essay, therefore, Umemoto appropriates from Marx a teleological—even utopian—view of the unalienated, "true" individual that, in the postrevolutionary realm of freedom, is destined to replace the "real" individual of the capitalist world.[27] Only this new individual can truly be the "real *conscious* lord of Nature."[28] Of course, against Tanabe's "idealist" approach, Umemoto follows Marx in insisting that a full recovery of humanity can occur only after a transformation of the economic base, until "even the memory of class domination has receded."[29]

Nevertheless, this article of faith does not entirely satisfy Umemoto, and his hesitancy implies that he is willing within limits to accept some aspects of Tanabe's definition of the problem. There was still "the issue of how, in the final analysis, the philosophical standpoint that underlies communism is able to deal with the possibility of human freedom." How aware of the problem were those who spoke for Marxist philosophy? How much attention did they devote to problems of individuality and personality? In other words, having accepted the basic tenets of historical materialism, Umemoto now challenged it to explain more fully what was meant by the ultimate goal of human freedom.

He argues that although it was certainly necessary to differentiate scientific socialism from moral demands, surely one could not generate a viable conception of humanity and its emancipation on the basis of Kautsky's dictum that morality was merely a "weapon of class conflict." And although one could not deny that history was the history of class conflict, "a presupposition about man that reduced everything to a single condition" risked turning human liberation into an abstraction—an abstraction that would be "expressed in the illegitimate oppression of any form of humanity that departed from that condition." Therefore, it was necessary to avoid dogmatism and to "broaden our perspective on what the human being is."[30]

Referring to Engels's *Anti-Duhring*, Umemoto recounts how nature first, and then society, "rule humanity as an unfeeling destiny." Gradually, however, as human beings learn the laws of nature and society they develop the ability to use them in consciously controlling their own history and expanding their freedom. As Engels had written, "Freedom does not consist in the dream of independence from natural laws, but in the knowledge of these laws, and in the possibility this gives of making them work towards definite ends."[31]

Umemoto finds this view profoundly true but ultimately inadequate, since it explains only the objective conditions for freedom rather than its subjective sources.[32] It fails to explain the human "ability to decide":

> By saying that people make history Marx already separates himself
> from all forms of mechanistic materialism. No matter how it is con-
> strued, Marxism can have no connection with any theory of automatic
> functioning or destiny based on the natural development of objective
> reality. The demand for revolution itself testifies to this most elo-
> quently. History does not take place as people stand by with folded
> arms.[33]

vention. Yet, instead of celebrating the
hich would necessitate conditional hu-
in theory, by providing an authentically

ask of providing a materialist theory of
objective, or "ideal," of Marxism is. He
mmunism is for us not a *state of affairs*
which reality [will] have to adjust itself
bolishes the present state of things."44
all, as had Marx, for a "total redemption
he human world and of human relation-
ain definition of the true human being—
then, were the "attributes of the human
of communal society in which 'the free
development of all'"? Umemoto's tenta-
manity in which "individual interest and
hus, a "restoration" of that true humanity
of capitalism, the system that had origi-

d that the authentic human being was in
s well as social.

d out, that . . . the further back we go
that ties the individual to the more
of the individual as part of the whole
then, since there have always been
themselves against the whole. . . . It
ve society where no taboo has ever
notion of a taboo without any expecta-
tory.48

atsuji Tetsurō, had made the same point,49
eing was always both individual and social
uman being that he attributed to "contem-
ntical to that proposed by Watsuji. Watsuji
is 'the group' (*yo no naka*) and also the
man being is, therefore, *not* only the 'per-
Here we can see the dual quality of the hu-
e essentially human, in this view, is to be
ual nor in the social group, but rather in the

Umemoto clearly registers the insight that—especially in Marxism—his-
tory/society could never be constituted as completely objective. This implies
that society is open, never free of undecidability; never itself completely determinate, it could therefore never be fully determining in relation to human
beings. Umemoto admits that the economic dimension of society probably
showed the way to an understanding of everything else, but even the economy
already presupposed the free, creative activity of human beings. Rather than
inhibiting freedom, therefore, history moves ahead through the continuous
"conversion of freedom into necessity." Human beings act, and thereby initiate
predictable chains of cause and effect. Thus, freedom always underlies inevitability. Science relies upon human creativity—indeed, takes it for granted—
but cannot explain it. Therefore, an exploration of subjective choice lies beyond
the bounds of science per se.34 Employing the vocabulary of the Kyoto School,
Umemoto observes that "[h]istory presupposes the emergence of creativity
from nothingness."35

Having briefly raised the problem of subjectivity in relation to agency,
Umemoto then moves toward epistemology via the question of how subjective
freedom of any kind could be conceivable under the "reflection," or "copy,"
theory of knowledge, according to which objects are believed to be more or less
passively reflected in the mind of the perceiving subject. He also considers at
the same time the theory that the economic base directly determines the political
and ideological superstructure. In other words, Umemoto attempts to confront
the major philosophical weakness of Marxist theory in the twentieth century: its
attachment in both political strategy and epistemology to theories of historical
necessity and unilinear determination.36 To counter these theories, which he associates with "mechanistic materialism," Umemoto argues—in a manner reminiscent of Georg Lukács—that the dialectic must be understood to apply not
only to relations among objects themselves but to the interaction between subject and object, or "individual and totality." Only then would the dialectic provide an active role for the subject of perception and action and thus preserve
human freedom.37

In the last few pages of the essay, Umemoto draws upon his own youthful
study of Buddhism to reengage, albeit indirectly, Tanabe's religious theory of
action. In a highly figurative reference to the "abyss" of nothingness that must
underlie the freedom of the acting subject in the historical world, Umemoto
meditates on sin and morality, which he says will continue to be necessary so
long as man is neither perfectly free like a god nor perfectly unfree like an animal. He also evokes Shinran and the Tokugawa-period Zen master Hakuin in
order to draw a parallel between science and what Hakuin had called the "talis-

man to prevent an escape from life" (*datsumyō no shinpu*).[38] Umemoto concludes, therefore, with a reaffirmation of the liberating role of science: So long as historical materialism remained subjectively self-aware, it would be capable of constituting a unity of freedom and necessity that would bring people ultimately to the full recovery of their humanity.

Umemoto sought in his first postwar essay to rescue Marxist science from what he believed to be a largely contemplative stance toward nature and society. If dialectical materialism continued to rely on theories of unmediated reflection in the realms of perception and social determination, it would be in danger of reaffirming a closed system that would leave no opening for subjective commitment or voluntary action. Umemoto tried to show that, in any case, materialist science presupposed subjective freedom since it employed categories not given in nature and an experimental method that itself was a form of subjective intervention. Nevertheless, qua science, it could never fully explain that freedom. Therefore, in his next essay, he was to suggest that Marxism had to provide a theory not only of epistemology but of ethical commitment.

In sum, Umemoto's initial polemic was situated ambivalently between Japanese idealism, represented most immediately by Tanabe, and mechanistic historical materialism. Although he apparently set out to offer a materialist critique of Tanabe's religiously saturated proposal for a new "social democracy," the logic of his argument led him to challenge contemporary Marxism's reliance on a contemplative approach to science and relative neglect of the moment of subjective intervention. Here Umemoto was on firm ground. It seems quite clear that a preoccupation with scientific epistemology was part of Japanese Marxism's legacy from before the war. As Maruyama Masao later observed, prewar Japanese scholars had adopted Marxism not only as a theory of ideology but as "an integrating, systematic science." Especially as their society became increasingly militaristic in the 1930s, and "ideologues of the 'Japanese spirit' " gained the ascendancy, Japanese Marxists had adhered with increasing stubbornness to what they believed to be the scientific, objective premises of historical materialism: "The tighter thought control became the more they had to stress the scientific requirements of universalism and objectivity, rather than the partisan (*parteilich*) character of any study."[39]

Yet Umemoto draws some of his critical concepts, such as "nothingness" and "dialectical relations between individual and totality," from Kyoto School philosophy and the ethics of Watsuji Tetsurō, and in a limited way he initially works within the problematic of freedom versus determinism that Tanabe had posed. Moreover, the existentialist angst exuded by his characterizations of the abyss of nothingness—"the self has within it something that cannot be fath-

to be the point of free, subjective inter
inevitable existence of such a fissure, w
man action, he seeks to "fill" it, at least
Marxist account of subjectivity.

Umemoto begins to approach the t
subjectivity by asking what the ultimate
is mindful of Marx's insistence that "C
which is to be established, an *ideal* to
. . . [but] the *real* movement which a
Nevertheless, in Umemoto's view, to c
of humanity"[45] and a "restoration of t
ships to man himself"[46] implied a cer
that is, a Marxist anthropology. What,
being that is presupposed by the sort
development of each becomes the free
tive answer is that it presupposes a hu
social interest are perfectly fused."[47] T
could occur only after the overthrow
nally torn those interests apart.

Umemoto's definition also implie
some manner essentially individual a

It is certainly true, as Marx pointe
in history the stronger is the bond
powerful whole. Yet the existence
was nevertheless recognized even
instances in which individuals set
is impossible to imagine a primiti
been broken, and in fact the very
tion of infraction is self-contradic

Umemoto's erstwhile teacher, W
and indeed, the idea that the human b
led Umemoto to a definition of the h
porary ethics" but that is virtually id
had written that "[t]he human bein
'person' (*hito*) in the group. The hu
son' nor simply 'society' (*shakai*).
man being's dialectical unity."[50] T
found neither in the isolated individ

Umemoto clearly registers the insight that—especially in Marxism—history/society could never be constituted as completely objective. This implies that society is open, never free of undecidability; never itself completely determinate, it could therefore never be fully determining in relation to human beings. Umemoto admits that the economic dimension of society probably showed the way to an understanding of everything else, but even the economy already presupposed the free, creative activity of human beings. Rather than inhibiting freedom, therefore, history moves ahead through the continuous "conversion of freedom into necessity." Human beings act, and thereby initiate predictable chains of cause and effect. Thus, freedom always underlies inevitability. Science relies upon human creativity—indeed, takes it for granted—but cannot explain it. Therefore, an exploration of subjective choice lies beyond the bounds of science per se.[34] Employing the vocabulary of the Kyoto School, Umemoto observes that "[h]istory presupposes the emergence of creativity from nothingness."[35]

Having briefly raised the problem of subjectivity in relation to agency, Umemoto then moves toward epistemology via the question of how subjective freedom of any kind could be conceivable under the "reflection," or "copy," theory of knowledge, according to which objects are believed to be more or less passively reflected in the mind of the perceiving subject. He also considers at the same time the theory that the economic base directly determines the political and ideological superstructure. In other words, Umemoto attempts to confront the major philosophical weakness of Marxist theory in the twentieth century: its attachment in both political strategy and epistemology to theories of historical necessity and unilinear determination.[36] To counter these theories, which he associates with "mechanistic materialism," Umemoto argues—in a manner reminiscent of Georg Lukács—that the dialectic must be understood to apply not only to relations among objects themselves but to the interaction between subject and object, or "individual and totality." Only then would the dialectic provide an active role for the subject of perception and action and thus preserve human freedom.[37]

In the last few pages of the essay, Umemoto draws upon his own youthful study of Buddhism to reengage, albeit indirectly, Tanabe's religious theory of action. In a highly figurative reference to the "abyss" of nothingness that must underlie the freedom of the acting subject in the historical world, Umemoto meditates on sin and morality, which he says will continue to be necessary so long as man is neither perfectly free like a god nor perfectly unfree like an animal. He also evokes Shinran and the Tokugawa-period Zen master Hakuin in order to draw a parallel between science and what Hakuin had called the "talisman to prevent an escape from life" (*datsumyō no shinpu*).[38] Umemoto concludes, therefore, with a reaffirmation of the liberating role of science: So long as historical materialism remained subjectively self-aware, it would be capable of constituting a unity of freedom and necessity that would bring people ultimately to the full recovery of their humanity.

Umemoto sought in his first postwar essay to rescue Marxist science from what he believed to be a largely contemplative stance toward nature and society. If dialectical materialism continued to rely on theories of unmediated reflection in the realms of perception and social determination, it would be in danger of reaffirming a closed system that would leave no opening for subjective commitment or voluntary action. Umemoto tried to show that, in any case, materialist science presupposed subjective freedom since it employed categories not given in nature and an experimental method that itself was a form of subjective intervention. Nevertheless, qua science, it could never fully explain that freedom. Therefore, in his next essay, he was to suggest that Marxism had to provide a theory not only of epistemology but of ethical commitment.

In sum, Umemoto's initial polemic was situated ambivalently between Japanese idealism, represented most immediately by Tanabe, and mechanistic historical materialism. Although he apparently set out to offer a materialist critique of Tanabe's religiously saturated proposal for a new "social democracy," the logic of his argument led him to challenge contemporary Marxism's reliance on a contemplative approach to science and relative neglect of the moment of subjective intervention. Here Umemoto was on firm ground. It seems quite clear that a preoccupation with scientific epistemology was part of Japanese Marxism's legacy from before the war. As Maruyama Masao later observed, prewar Japanese scholars had adopted Marxism not only as a theory of ideology but as "an integrating, systematic science." Especially as their society became increasingly militaristic in the 1930s, and "ideologues of the 'Japanese spirit' " gained the ascendancy, Japanese Marxists had adhered with increasing stubbornness to what they believed to be the scientific, objective premises of historical materialism: "The tighter thought control became the more they had to stress the scientific requirements of universalism and objectivity, rather than the partisan (*parteilich*) character of any study."[39]

Yet Umemoto draws some of his critical concepts, such as "nothingness" and "dialectical relations between individual and totality," from Kyoto School philosophy and the ethics of Watsuji Tetsurō, and in a limited way he initially works within the problematic of freedom versus determinism that Tanabe had posed. Moreover, the existentialist angst exuded by his characterizations of the abyss of nothingness—"the self has within it something that cannot be fathomed; there is no greater anxiety than this"—suggested to some that he was in danger of descending into mysticism. Given the high priority Minka and the party were devoting to all-out attacks on the Nishida School, this was dangerous ground for a would-be Communist.

Umemoto wrote his second major essay in August of 1947 and published it in *Tenbō* in October of the same year. Rather than diffuse and speculatively suggestive in the mode of his first effort, it was tightly argued and polemical. The second essay at least nominally confronted the borderland, which Tanabe had been anxious to preempt, between religion and historical materialism. Umemoto begins by quoting the prewar Marxist pioneer Kawakami Hajime, who had reflected toward the end of his life that "the religious truth of absolute selflessness and the scientific truth of Marxism are firmly bound in dialectical unity within my heart."[10] By recalling this testimonial, Umemoto is able to focus the problem of freedom versus determinism, which he had raised in his first essay, on the specific issue of Marxism's supposedly inadequate theoretical grasp of the subjectively engaged human being. Just as Kawakami found that he needed both scientific truth and religious truth, in Umemoto's view any revolutionary Marxism had to have not only objective historical movement but human commitment: "In the course of the liberation process, there is constant contact between the scientific truth by which we are able to identify the material conditions for human liberation and the existential fulcrum of the human being who is thereby liberated. If that were not the case, the objective conditions for liberation would have no way of asserting their rights as conditions."[41]

Without human action, "objective" historical laws are impotent. The problem, not only for Umemoto but for many Western European and American Marxists since, has been that Marxist theory on the whole has neglected the problem of "what happens 'in people's heads,' or in the psychical structures of the human beings who are subjected to [social] processes."[42] In Umemoto's words, although the subjective commitment of Marxist leaders was obvious, the problematic of subjectivity as such had been "omitted" (*shōryaku*) from theory. This "lacuna" in Marxism invited revisionism because, "[t]o the extent that we are unable to fill this lacuna from the standpoint of Marxism, efforts will inevitably be made to satisfy it in some other way. The experiment of the neo-Kantians in attempting to augment Marxism with Kant's moral laws is such an attempt. . . . Yet such efforts were invited by the existence of a genuine lacuna, and by the conviction that for humanism there was nothing more important than filling that lacuna."[43] In effect, Umemoto questions the ability of the objective, historical structure identified in historical materialism to fully constitute itself as a closed system. He finds a fissure at the center of structure, which he believes to be the point of free, subjective intervention. Yet, instead of celebrating the inevitable existence of such a fissure, which would necessitate conditional human action, he seeks to "fill" it, at least in theory, by providing an authentically Marxist account of subjectivity.

Umemoto begins to approach the task of providing a materialist theory of subjectivity by asking what the ultimate objective, or "ideal," of Marxism is. He is mindful of Marx's insistence that "Communism is for us not a *state of affairs* which is to be established, an *ideal* to which reality [will] have to adjust itself . . . [but] the *real* movement which abolishes the present state of things."[44] Nevertheless, in Umemoto's view, to call, as had Marx, for a "total redemption of humanity"[45] and a "restoration of the human world and of human relationships to man himself "[46] implied a certain definition of the true human being— that is, a Marxist anthropology. What, then, were the "attributes of the human being that is presupposed by the sort of communal society in which 'the free development of each becomes the free development of all'"? Umemoto's tentative answer is that it presupposes a humanity in which "individual interest and social interest are perfectly fused."[47] Thus, a "restoration" of that true humanity could occur only after the overthrow of capitalism, the system that had originally torn those interests apart.

Umemoto's definition also implied that the authentic human being was in some manner essentially individual as well as social.

> It is certainly true, as Marx pointed out, that . . . the further back we go in history the stronger is the bond that ties the individual to the more powerful whole. Yet the existence of the individual as part of the whole was nevertheless recognized even then, since there have always been instances in which individuals set themselves against the whole. . . . It is impossible to imagine a primitive society where no taboo has ever been broken, and in fact the very notion of a taboo without any expectation of infraction is self-contradictory.[48]

Umemoto's erstwhile teacher, Watsuji Tetsurō, had made the same point,[49] and indeed, the idea that the human being was always both individual and social led Umemoto to a definition of the human being that he attributed to "contemporary ethics" but that is virtually identical to that proposed by Watsuji. Watsuji had written that "[t]he human being is 'the group' (*yo no naka*) and also the 'person' (*hito*) in the group. The human being is, therefore, *not* only the 'person' nor simply 'society' (*shakai*). Here we can see the dual quality of the human being's dialectical unity."[50] The essentially human, in this view, is to be found neither in the isolated individual nor in the social group, but rather in the tension between them: the human being exists as "a dialectic between individuality and sociality."[51] One is always socialized, but always also capable of rebellious individuation. Indeed, it was probably Watsuji who led Umemoto back to ethics in relation to the problematic of revolutionary subjectivity in Marxism, since for Watsuji "the study of ethics is the study . . . of the subject as a practical, active connection (*jissenteki kōiteki renkan*)."[52]

The core of Umemoto's essay consists in an effort to synthesize this ethical definition of the human being as potential rebel with historical materialism. First, he has to deal with Marx's own references to "man as such." The most important of these is the proposition in *The German Ideology* that "[m]en can be distinguished from animals by consciousness, by religion or anything you like. They themselves begin to distinguish themselves from animals as soon as they begin to produce their means of subsistence."[53] Yet for Marx, too, of course, this production was from the beginning social. Thus, he says, "the production of life, both of one's own in labour and of fresh life in procreation, now appears as a double relationship: on the one hand as a natural, on the other as a social relationship."[54] Umemoto adds that "if social relations are omitted from this double relationship, one is left with reproduction in the same fashion as animals." That is because, according to Marx (as well as Watsuji), "the animal does not enter into relations with anything, it does not enter into any relation at all."[55]

Umemoto concludes that human beings begin to be ethical just as soon as they begin to produce the means of their subsistence. The productive social relationship, therefore, is the genesis not only of the human being as a producer, whose activity provides the basis for the science of historical materialism, but also as an ethical being, whose essential qualities are capable of forming the basis for a Marxist humanism.

He goes on to argue that the human being defined ethically, as a field of tension between individuality and sociality, and the human being defined economically, that is, as producer of the means of subsistence, are each equally necessary to the philosophy of historical materialism. In doing so, he again seems to draw upon points made earlier by Watsuji, who also distinguished "relationships" per se from the productive relations valorized by Marx. Watsuji had written:

> The works of Marx seek to grasp human existence principally from the perspective of "society" and to pursue its dissection as *economics*. The problem is whether or not human existence is solely an economic entity, and whether or not human existence viewed exclusively from the economic perspective suffices as the basis of law and morality. The most important element in social structure is that in order to satisfy

their desires people work cooperatively and therefore enter into relations of production. Yet, are these *relations among people* solely for the
purpose of satisfying desires, without any other foundation? Marx very
significantly clarified the difference between people and animals by
means of the notion of "relations." Animals, too, act in order to satisfy
their desires. But they do not assume an attitude appropriate to the construction of relations with others. Human beings, on the other hand,
forge relationships and develop language and consciousness. Moreover,
on that basis their material production is *social*, and they can form *productive relations*. Thus, the most basic criterion of human existence is
the formation of relationships between self and others, and the assumption of a certain attitude or posture in order to accomplish that. . . .
Marx's view of society as relations of production in fact implicitly assumes such "relations."[56]

Based on this distinction, which he draws from Watsuji, Umemoto attempts to
make two arguments: First, without a theory of the person's "sensuous," material connection to the world through labour and procreation, it is impossible to
explain scientifically the real historical stages through which human liberation
in communism will be achieved. Second, and conversely, without a theory of
the ethical possibility of individual rebellion against the old totality and of self-
dedication to the new one, it is impossible to explain how history passes from
one stage to the next.

First, Umemoto seeks to show that the purely ethical definition of the human
being is in itself inadequate because it fails to recognize the material and historical conditions for that being's recovery of his true humanity. Umemoto says, "If
we were to focus abstractly on social relations alone, and attempt to find there
the laws of historical development, we would be able to find the motive force for
that development only in relations of negation between individual and totality."
The best example of such an approach was Tanabe Hajime's notion of species.
Umemoto summarizes Tanabe's position:

The unity of individual and totality appears concretely as the unifying
principle of a historically specific society. This principle is called *shu*
(species). . . . Species is pregnant with the tendency to split as a result
of the activity occasioned by the incessant operations of the negativity
of nothingness [*mu*], and from the depths of its negative destruction a
new species is born. This is the origin also of the logic that the death-
and-resurrection of the individual is mediated by the negative transformation of species in response to absolute nothingness. The movement
from one social relationship to another is dependent upon the contradic-

tion and splitting of the previous relationship, but the ultimate motive force providing the occasion for that is nothingness. Using species as its channel, or mediation, in the realm of existence, nothingness impregnates species with contradictoriness, and through the development of such contradictions nothingness determines and develops itself as history.

Thus, when the logic of that standpoint is followed through, Umemoto says, the motive force of historical change turns out to be "nothingness" (*mu*), and when used in this way nothingness is "little more than a logical deception. . . . No matter whether, or to what extent, nothingness is experienced in the death-and-resurrection of the individual, it cannot immediately become the motive force of history." The real motive forces of history are those that had been identified by Marx and Engels: "The so-called economic factor—this is the realistic motive force of history which even Hegel, for all his genius, turned to more than once when other forms of explanation failed."[57] In sum, an ethical anthropology that omitted economic determination could lead only to an unhistorical form of idealism.

In order to illustrate further the inadequacy of an exclusively ethical definition, Umemoto turns his attention to the sensuous dimension of human life. Here he focuses on Feuerbach. Feuerbach was a materialist, but he tended to see the "sensuous" human relationship between "I" and "Thou" as fundamentally different from that of animals. That is because he rooted those relations in a universal essence, a "species being," that was inherent in each individual. Thus, Feuerbach's humans were already equipped with the basis for a truly human community, without the need for a historical progression. Moreover, by setting the human essence apart from the sensuous, material processes of production and procreation, he left out of his recipe for human beings precisely that ingredient that makes them historical—their productivity. Feuerbach's so-called materialism left humans contemplative and unhistorical. In the first of his "Theses on Feuerbach," therefore, Marx insisted that sensuous contact with the world had to be conceived as active and subjective rather than contemplative. Only then would it be possible to explain the historical process that would allow humans to regain true humanity.

Umemoto tries to demonstrate in the manner described above that the ethical notion of humanity as a dialectic of negation between individuality and sociality is, in itself, insufficient to explain how humanity will find liberation. He then proceeds, in effect, to argue that Watsuji's insufficient definition is, nevertheless, a necessary supplement to the Marxist idea of mankind as producers. It is necessary because, while scientific Marxism could predict and explain the structural contradictions that would arise when, as Marx put it, "the material productive forces of society come in conflict with the existing relations of production,"[58] it did not adequately explain how or why people would take radical action in the "age of revolution" that would be brought about by that contradiction. This was what Umemoto had called the lacuna (*kūgeki*) in Marxism: its lack of a theory of subjective commitment to action. "We must not overlook the fact that the contradiction between the relations of production and the forces of production that occurs when the forces develop is at the same time the occasion for the possibility of rebellion on the part of the individual who forms an aspect of the social relations among human beings."[59]

In other words, if people are not innately capable of rebelling as individuals, as stipulated in the ethical definition of humankind, then no mere contradiction between forces and relations of production would be sufficient to bring about a historical transformation. Thus, Umemoto explains the need for an ethical understanding:

> The individual possesses, in the moment of its formation, a negative relation to the social whole. At the same time as human beings become such through production, they also enter into a relation between the rebellious individual and unity with the totality. Indeed, if we assumed, to the contrary, that social relations consisted in a natural, organic totality that did not include individuals as such, no development of the productive forces could ever bring about a contradiction with such "relations."[60]

Umemoto fails to distinguish clearly between contradiction and antagonism, but his point is clear: contradiction does not logically imply open conflict.[61] Action by individuals is necessary to make revolution. Therefore, Watsuji's human being, who is innately equipped with the ethical capacity to rebel, is a necessary adjunct to Marx's, who produces socially until the productive forces come into conflict with the productive relations and thereby give rise to a revolutionary situation.

In any case, according to Umemoto, while the existing mode of production is dynamically expanding, even the subordinate classes are able to identify with it and accept its ideas and morality. When it moves into the stage of collapse, however, the old social ethic loses its foundations and the "non-ruling classes are no longer able to find themselves in the existing totality." One would think that the only remedy for this estrangement would be to throw oneself into the new totality—that formed by the proletariat as the "class that bears the historical duty of overcoming contradiction."[62] But given the intrinsic split in the human being between individuality and social totality, even identification with the new totality does not immediately repair that self-alienation.

According to Umemoto, even at such a time of crisis there can be no "organic" unity: "By the time the class that has been in a subordinate position becomes conscious of a social totality peculiarly suited to it, that new society will already contain its own contradictory unity between individuals and the totality. It might appear that when the awareness of struggle is intense, there would be no room for divisions. Yet in reality the very reverse is true."[63]

Therefore, partisans of the new totality will not always rise up "naturally" and throw themselves into the struggle against the old order. They may not be able, psychologically or existentially, to "decide" to support the new society. Indeed, why should they, since those who carry out the revolution are often not the ones who ultimately will enjoy its benefits? If they are to become partisans, therefore, they must be able to devote themselves to liberation without any expectation of personal reward. That is, they must adopt a posture of "absolute selflessness."

How, Umemoto asks, is this possible? He finds the key in the objective, historical role of the proletariat as a "special class." Materialist science had demonstrated that by liberating itself the proletariat would, indeed must, liberate all mankind. Therefore, devotion to the cause of that class "is at the same time the conscious expression of devotion to the emancipation of all humanity. There is in this consciousness a dialectical unity of love and struggle."[64] In the combination of subjective, selfless commitment, on the one hand, and the objective destiny of the proletariat to finally bring an end to human alienation, on the other, there was the possibility of a "restoration" of true humanity along the lines suggested by the early Marx.

Although Umemoto continues to insist that the possibility of individual rebellion that lies at the bottom of the difficulty many experience in committing themselves to the new totality is not an attribute of human nature as such but rather the result of social relations formed in the context of labor, his concern with the problem of how to define the human being leads him back to the soteriological humanism of the young Marx. He observes that "[w]hile the human being contains original self-interest, it is only through the denial of that selfish interest that the self can regain its original nature." Again apparently following Watsuji, Umemoto suggests that this denial involved a leap, or discontinuity (*danzetsu*), which was also the moment of "nothingness."[65] Accordingly, a "religious" element was unavoidable: "if people are to regain their original nature and secure true freedom, they must ultimately appeal to the absolute unity of individual and totality. What is called religious in that unity is its absolute denial of egoism—the aspect related to the experience of death." What was different about the materialist view, however, was that rather than seeing human alienation as an aspect of "human nature," it realized that alienation was the result of development in the relations of production and could therefore be overcome in a real, historical transformation. In sum, "The death-and-resurrection of the individual that occurs in the absolutely negative unity of individual and totality gains its actual basis only when it is located in the new totality that is able dialectically to overcome the actual split in humanity. Through devotion to an actual historical object, selflessness achieves the liberation of all humankind and in the process is conscious of itself as love."[66] And this liberation is also to be the human "restoration" anticipated by the young Marx.

Once Umemoto extends his analysis to the point of calling for selfless devotion to the proletariat as the concrete universal, it becomes evident that underlying his vision is not only the Lukácsian interpretation of Leninism but the prewar ethics of Watsuji Tetsurō larded with vocabulary from Nishida and Tanabe. In addition to defining the human being as a negative dialectic between individual and the social totality (one in which individuality was defined as the negation of totality, totality as the negation of individuality), Watsuji had completed his ethical prescription with the injunction that incumbent upon the ethical subject was a negation of the negation leading to the dissolution of self in a moral totality.[67] He took this moral totality to be the nation as a spatial, cultural entity, and the selfless commitment as exactly a *return* of the individual to the authentic self latent in national community.[68] During the war this conception had led Watsuji into statements supportive of the militarist regime.

When one considers Naoki Sakai's probing analysis of the construction of Watsuji's ethics,[69] it seems fairly clear that Umemoto has substituted a Lukácsian understanding of the proletariat for Watsuji's conception of national community. Although Umemoto wanted at one level to open historical materialism to the actual contingency and historicity of subjective praxis, he seems at another level to have come close to providing it with an equally totalizing, deterministic *theory* of subjectivity. That is, for Watsuji rebellion could be understood only as a temporary diremption inasmuch as one's subjective position was already fixed in the communal totality and immanent in the individual; by the same token, for Umemoto the Marxist's subjective decision, which seems at one level to be so contingent and precarious, is at another level preordained in the proletariat's historical destiny and thus is precisely a restoration of what is already immanent. Umemoto comes dangerously close to Watsuji, for whom the "negation of the negation brings a person back to what totality inside that person dictates."[70]

Sakai remarks that "[t]he call of totality to urge a person to return to his or her authentic self in Watsuji's anthropology can be explained as a detailed exposition of Althusser's famous definition of ideology that ideology "hails or interpellates concrete individuals as concrete subjects."[71] This would seem to be equally true for Umemoto's anthropology, where, indeed, the humanist totalizing of Lukács seems to meet the antihumanist totalizing of Althusser, for whom "ideology interpellates only whole human entities, forming them as 'subjects.'"[72]

No doubt the structural similarity between Watsuji and Umemoto in terms of this ideological interpellation should not be allowed to obscure the very real difference. Umemoto calls for a decision, which may be interpreted as the valid constitution of subjectivity in historical time (rather than space, as for Watsuji), thus preserving contingency at the moment of action. Nevertheless, for Umemoto as well, totality was always in the background, providing a presumptive guarantee.

Another problem in Umemoto's critique of contemplative Marxism is latent in certain caveats he interjects in the course of his second essay. Early in that essay he had argued explicitly that there was a lacuna in Marxist theory with respect to the ethics of human action. However, at the same time, he had insisted that this lacuna was only in theory, and that in practice Communists, especially the leaders, were always already subjectively engaged:

> In the course of the liberation process, there is constant contact between the scientific truth by which we are able to identify the material conditions for human liberation, on the one hand, and the existential standpoint of the human being who is thereby liberated, on the other. This contact, or unity, has generally been assured among our great leaders. Although omitted from theory, it has occupied an essential position in praxis as, for example, when one commits oneself to liberation without expectation of reward, or absolutely renounces selfishness. Nevertheless, we have for the most part neglected the task of consciously reflecting on that unity and thereby providing it a legitimate place in our theory.[73]

He goes on to argue that if Marxism is unable to provide a theory of human subjectivity, revisionists will inevitably try to "fill the gap" with some kind of non-Marxist thought, such as neo-Kantianism. But here Umemoto's argument takes a fateful turn in the direction of the same cycle of supplementarity that had limited the effectiveness of the *Kindai bungaku* writers' contentions. Building upon his earlier remark to the effect that existential awareness is "assured among our great leaders," he reminds his readers that in practice Marxists *are*

able to commit themselves and *do* gain ample "existential support" for that
practice. Apparently, his plea is merely that Marxist philosophers should expli-
cate the mechanisms involved in that process and thus complete in theory what
had already been secured in practice. This Umemoto proceeds to do, as outlined
above. But in relation to the issue of how to avoid a benign, contemplative
stance in Marxism, it is crucial to note that rather than calling for a renewed
ethical commitment to action, Umemoto seems to limit the problem of *shutaisei*
to a purely explanatory, and thus ultimately contemplative, role. Umemoto
seems to have sought from the beginning of his argument only to "understand
the world"—if, in this case, the "world" is taken to mean Marxist practice—not
to "change it." Accordingly, he scrupulously denied any prescriptive or normative intent, and set out merely to provide a theory of *shutaisei* that would adequately account for the way Communists already behaved. Moreover, the
theory he proposed was intended only to supplement the historical science of
Marxism—merely to fill a small gap or oversight—never fundamentally to
contest that science. Therefore, one might argue that Umemoto's theory of subjective action functioned not so much to open new possibilities for action as to
achieve theoretical closure.

The Party Responds: Matsumura Kazuto

The spectre of revisionism raised by Umemoto's suggestion that Marxism was
incomplete and therefore had to be further developed or, indeed, supplemented
was bound to antagonize the Communist guardians of philosophical orthodoxy.
Several philosophers rose to counter this apparent revisionism in minor ways,
but just as Nakano Shigeharu had played the grand inquisitor in literature, in
philosophy that mantle was assumed principally by Matsumura Kazuto.[74]

Matsumura's attacks on Umemoto were comradely, in general, and were
sprinkled with caveats to the effect that Umemoto's position was not "reactionary or without significance," that he was "attempting to avoid falling into idealism," and that he showed "honesty and theoretical ability."[75] Nevertheless,
Matsumura was uncompromising in his excoriation, first, of Umemoto's
"ethical revisionism."[76] He charged that, like Hermann Cohen, Rudolf Stam-
mler, and Karl Vorländer in Germany, Umemoto seemed to be trying to reconstruct Marxism on the basis of ethics rather than economics and class struggle.[77]
Matsumura observed that while ethical revisionism from within Marxism had
been very unusual in Japan, in the postwar period it had suddenly become a
major force to be reckoned with in the form of theories of *shutaisei*.[78]

Such theories were not in themselves insidious: "To the extent that they aim at encouraging the masses who have been deprived of the freedom of thought and action to struggle on behalf of their own interests; to the extent that they encourage struggle based on social and class consciousness and aim at satisfying the demands of the masses, they are certainly essential and do not necessarily constitute a revision of Marxism."[79]

Umemoto, however, had based his argument on the premise that "interests" alone could not explain struggle. He had argued that Marxists lacked a theoretical awareness of their own motivations, and that this lack constituted a theoretical "lacuna" in Marxism. Therefore, he had proceeded to try to fill it with a new "definition of humanity" that emphasized not only self-interest but self-sacrifice. In Umemoto's own words, "While human beings contain original self-interest, it is only through the denial of that selfish interest that they can regain their original nature."According to Umemoto, therefore, in effect "It is precisely in the active meaning of 'killing the self and acting humanely' that we can find the source of the Marxists' practice, and it is precisely the values based on this elevated 'original humanity' that give the Marxists' practice its meaning and motivate them from within."[80]

But to Matsumura, this "definition of mankind" smacked of a false universality. His second major criticism had to do, therefore, with Umemoto's apparent resort to a hypothesis concerning the characteristics of human beings and society as such and his parallel neglect of class standpoint. According to the mistaken notions of the German neo-Kantian revisionists and Umemoto as well,

> the main inner element that drives the Marxist toward practice is the individual's return to original humanity, his overcoming of "rebellion against the totality." To Umemoto, therefore, the "subjective" basis of a socialist movement is to be found not in demands based on a correct perception of the position of the working class in capitalist society but in the original nature of human beings in general. . . . [Therefore] he agrees in his most fundamental method of thought with the bourgeois thinkers who presented the demands of the capitalist class as the demands of people in general and sought to derive them from "human nature."

Despite his caveats against transclass ideals, apparently Umemoto was attempting in Matsumura's view to "affirm partisanship from a standpoint that is not partisan," to "sacralize class from a transclass position."[81] Marxism recognized only real classes in conflict; it was the practical theory of the liberation of the proletariat by the proletariat, not "a transclass theory but the theory of the proletariat itself."[82] Marxism did not reach out to the proletariat from some transcendental standpoint but remained immanent within that class's own subjective, practical consciousness. Therefore, it did not need to borrow a universalistic theory of subjective motivation, or *shutaisei*, from the Kyoto School of idealist philosophy. As the organic expression of class interests, Marxism was always already engaged practically and subjectively on the side of the proletariat. Umemoto had forgotten this, so his argument "completely lacks the standpoint of class."

> When actual society is composed of classes whose interests are fundamentally opposed—that is, exploiters and exploited, those who have an interest in preserving the present social system and those who have an interest in revolutionizing it—to argue solely in terms of social and individual interests leads to unwarranted abstraction and an obfuscation of the main issue. In class society, and particularly in a class society which has progressed to the stage of forming revolutionary and anti-revolutionary camps, the starting point should not be society and the individual but the problem of opposing forces with fundamentally divergent interests.[83]

In his third major criticism, Matsumura pointed to Umemoto's failure to recognize that an accurate understanding of objective class interests provided an adequate basis for explaining revolutionary commitment. Once one located Marxism in the standpoint of the proletariat rather than that of humanity in general, it would become clear that "the subjective (*shutaiteki*) dimension of Marxism inheres in the interest of the proletariat, the necessity of its liberation, and the consciousness of class and class solidarity that are formed through joint struggle." It was neither necessary nor desirable to develop another theory of *shutaisei*. Members of the working class "suffer under exploitation and harbor resentment against their exploiters, desire a happier society and are defiant against the power of the exploiters to inhibit change. They feel solidarity with those whose interests they share, and dedicate themselves to them. There is plenty of "*shutaisei*" and action here. There is no need for an ethical baptism drawn from "humanity" in general or society at large." Indeed, inasmuch as Umemoto's notion of *shutaisei* as self-sacrifice "neglects the inner relationship to the interest of each individual, it is in some ways analogous to the spirit of Japan's wartime suicide pilots (*tokkō seishin*)."[84]

Although here he seems to subscribe to a mechanistic theory of *shutaisei* as an automatic reflection of the social base, in other contexts Matsumura seems to have recognized that subjective commitment and action would not necessarily follow directly from "objective" contradiction. Referring to Marx's statement in the "Preface to *A Contribution to the Critique of Political Economy*" that "[a]t a certain stage of their development, the material productive forces of society come in conflict with the existing relations of production. . . . Then begins an epoch of social revolution," Matsumura commented as follows in February 1948:

> Note the degree to which this selection appears to rely on a conception of objective law. No doubt it does. In reality, however, it is simplistic to assume that once the forces of production fall into contradiction with the relations of production a revolution will take place by itself. There are objective laws, but they are not objective in the same sense as the laws of nature. Indeed, even when the forces of production are objectively in contradiction with the relations of production, if that contradiction is not clearly recognized, and, moreover, if the way out of the contradiction is not clearly understood among the masses, there will be no revolution. Unless the masses have the requisite consciousness themselves, or follow leaders who are conscious and therefore become themselves a self-conscious subject of sorts—without the actions of such a subject, revolution will never occur. Therefore, Lenin said that for capitalism there is no such thing as a road with absolutely no exit. This means that Marxism is not simply objectivistic.[85]

Nevertheless, as noted above, Matsumura also argued that once one located Marxism in the standpoint of the proletariat rather than in that of man in general, it would become clear that subjectivity was always already present in the consciousness of class and class solidarity that are formed through joint struggle."[86] He was able to argue in this manner, not necessarily because he believed that antagonism was intrinsic to the exploitative relation between capitalist and workers, but apparently because he felt that the overall life situation of the workers would eventually cause them to develop antagonistic feelings toward capitalist relations of production. According to Matsumura, "no mystical '*shutaisei-ron*' is necessary to make people dedicate themselves to the true happiness of the people. *The subjective dimension already exists in the whole concrete reality of the people.*"[87]

Because contradiction between the forces and relations of production does not necessarily entail antagonism, Matsumura resorts to a hypothesis concerning the effect on consciousness of circumstances external to those relations, that is, the "whole concrete reality" of the workers' lives, as the source of antagonistic motivation. He also argues that consciousness is conditioned by situational factors and can be raised only through contingent political intervention: "if left alone, people will not raise the level of their demands."[88]

From the vantage of the 1990s, it seems that a reasonable way of acting on this awareness in the early postwar context would have been a strategy of democratic hegemony that renounced all pretense of deterministic necessity and therefore also of any political priority or privilege that might have been claimed by the "vanguard" party. Rather than jockeying for political control at the center, the vanguard party could have devoted maximum effort to the discursive task of constructing equivalences between and articulating the demands of the diverse movements and groups that were becoming active politically, including farmer's unions, shop floor movements to seize control over production, women's groups protesting the Occupation's venereal disease countermeasures, and consumer groups demanding distribution of food and other commodities. That is, on the basis of his apparent belief that the "social agent is constituted *outside the relations of production*," Matsumura might have concluded that the political process was unlikely to have a central point of coherence or control. Indeed, writing in 1990, Laclau suggests that

> the workers' expectations are bound up with a certain perception of
> their place in the world. This perception depends on the participation
> of workers in a variety of spheres and on a certain awareness of their
> rights; the further democratic-egalitarian discourses have penetrated
> into society, the less will workers accept as natural a limitation of their
> access to a set of social and cultural goods. Thus, the possibility of
> deepening the anti-capitalist struggle itself depends on the extension of
> the democratic revolution.[89]

Shutaisei could be expected to form among workers and others in response to a variety of contingencies arising in unpredictable ways. Therefore, the working class as such might not emerge as the determining point of leadership. This was essentially what Ara Masato was arguing through his insistence that, *at least at the stage of democratic revolution*, the proletariat need not monopolize the subjective role.

To the contrary, however, Matsumura makes it clear that in his mind political intervention is tied securely to the working class, even though "at the present time the bourgeoisie is politically, economically and culturally dominant. . . . All the proletariat's means of collecting information on its own have been snatched away." Only the vanguard party, as the representative and tutor of the working class, was capable of rectifying the situation: "No matter what the circumstances, without a vanguard leadership's clear perceptions and consciousness, even revolutionary situations will fail to develop into revolution."[90]

Matsumura is very much aware that, rather than determined socioeconomically, consciousness is conditioned by situational factors and can be "raised" only through contingent political action. Yet at the same time he retains essentialist conceptions of the proletariat as *the* privileged class subject (whose class consciousness would naturally be high if not for bourgeois domination) and of the Communist party as the uniquely qualified vanguard of not only the socialist revolution but the democratic one as well.

Matsumura concludes that the reason Umemoto has to emphasize such an embarrassing degree of selfless dedication is that he has situated himself at the standpoint not of the proletariat but of the middle class, particularly the intellectuals, who, as Umemoto says, have "lost their social foundation" and can only regain it by committing themselves to the new "totality" (e.g., the proletariat). Matsumura admits that the question of how to gain the loyalty of intellectuals is an important issue. However, "the wavering of the intelligentsia results from the fact that part of their interests lie with the ruling class. . . . [and] an empty ethical term like 'totality' is not going to help in fighting against this."[91] Like Kurahara Korehito and Nakano Shigeharu in their injunctions to the *Kindai bungaku* writers, Matsumura here insists that Umemoto abandon the position of petty bourgeois intellectual and adopt the standpoint of the proletariat. But, of course, that is just what Umemoto wanted to do.

Materialism and Nothingness

In a series of other essays, Umemoto delved more deeply into the actual dynamics of freedom in relation to materialism by making more explicit his critique of the so-called philosophy of nothingness (*mu*) espoused by Nishida Kitarō and, especially, Tanabe Hajime. Along the way, he further elucidated the extent to which he believed that their philosophy could contribute to a materialist understanding of subjective commitment. It is important to recognize that Umemoto was less concerned than were more orthodox Marxists about keeping a safe distance from Nishida and Tanabe. Umemoto dared to engage in the kind of immanent critique that, he hoped, would allow him to employ his understanding of Nishida, Tanabe, and Watsuji in advancing the effort to overcome them.

In an essay written at the end of 1947 and published in the spring of 1948, Umemoto posed the question of how the philosophy of nothingness could be put to use by materialists. This question was relevant and important, he argued, if it would help answer the more fundamental question of how we can return to our authentic selves in the midst of objective historical necessity. Put another way: How can humanity's subjective freedom be guaranteed in the midst of objective necessity?

Before attempting to work through Nishida and Tanabe's philosophies in pursuit of an answer, however, Umemoto insists that the philosophy of nothingness had first to be cleansed of the reactionary political distortions—such as the harmonization of classes and use of the emperor as the symbol of nothingness—that the ruling-class partisanship of its formulators had imbued in it from the beginning. Tanabe had also mixed into his philosophical system a variety of psychological and religious elements, and these were all too prominent even in his postwar effort to combine the Buddhist philosophy of nothingness with Marxism through the mediation of Christianity, an operation he hailed as the "second religious reformation."[92]

Once a thorough purge was complete, however, Umemoto believed it would be possible to "consider the moment of materialist dialectics to which the remainder corresponds," and thus effectively to criticize the philosophy of nothingness while also, perhaps, raising productive questions regarding the contemporary issue of Marxism's relationship to humanism—that is, the problematic of human emancipation. More specifically, the proper place for the logic of nothingness was in the fissure between materialist dialectics and the standpoint of the subject. Whereas conventional dialectical materialism relied on the assumption that everything could be objectified, Umemoto espoused a standpoint that, "while having no quarrel with dialectical materialism as a logic of being in the dimension of objectification, nevertheless sees at the base of the subject something unobjectifiable." Only a logic of nothingness could resolve the contradiction between the two viewpoints.[93]

Umemoto traces the question of freedom versus necessity from the medieval theological issue of how sin was possible in light of God's omnipotence, down through Luther's "internalization of God" and, eventually, to Kant's struggle to reconcile a now secularized natural law with human freedom. In the course of the latter struggle, and especially in his engagement in the *Critique of Pure Reason* with the third antinomy—that between freedom and necessity—Kant had "found in the ego as practical subject an entity that just could not be objectified, that is, something that could only be understood objectively as absolute nothingness (*mu*)." He had found that pure reason could not give an account of the acting subject. This led him to the problematic of practical reason, which he developed in the second critique. There he attempted to resolve the third antinomy by means of the distinction between what Umemoto calls "phenomena" and "essence," or between the standpoint of the empirical, sensible world, which was governed by cause and effect, and that of the intelligible world of the "thing in itself," which was governed by reason. Kant proceeded to ground freedom and the moral will in the latter dimension, leading Umemoto to observe that through Kant's innovation, "existence in itself, in the strictest sense, was taken away from nature and installed behind the practical subject." This abyss of "existence in itself," the source of elemental, self-determining subjectivity expressed in moral practice, could not be objectively grasped, hence objectively it was *mu*. Therefore, it was clear that the philosophy of nothingness "originates in German idealism against the background of Christianity."

However, the dual nature of Kant's human being gave to the element of nothingness a troublesome tendency toward mystification and substantialization, and this tendency was exploited by F. W. J. Schelling, Schopenhauer, and eventually Hegel, for whom "the source of freedom became a world spirit that transcended individual consciousness." It was left to Marx to bring that "source of freedom" back into the social-historical world through the principle that existence determined consciousness.[94]

Yet Marxism also had a problem with the subject. Even if one adhered, like Engels, to the notion that freedom is the "appreciation of necessity," one would still have to account for the subject of that appreciation, which implicitly lay outside of necessity and was therefore a tempting foundation for hypostatization and mystification. Therefore, according to Umemoto, since "historical materialism has driven all theological teleology from the world of history," the only way to avoid a reification of *mu*, theological or otherwise, while still vindicating human freedom was to follow the "logic by which necessity totally negates human freedom until nothing is left." When subjective freedom is completely negated (or denies itself), necessity assumes the content of freedom and in the process ceases to be necessity at all: "when the appreciating subject is negated by necessity, necessity itself becomes the foundation of the ego." That is, the absolutely negative mediation of nothingness negates not only freedom but being itself as the object of appreciation.[95]

The logic of emptiness informing this transformation was based on the "experience of death-and-resurrection," an experience whose nature and implications could be understood only with reference to Buddhism, especially the teachings of the medieval sage Shinran. According to Shinran, people commonly went through despair and self-denial as a result of the impossibility of achieving salvation through moral action. Yet, precisely in this self-denial, or resolution toward death, there was the possibility of transcendence through a release from karma, where karma, according to Umemoto, was to be understood as "a kind of necessity in the face of which all moral effort is ineffective." The encounter with the absolute that accompanies this release from karma—i.e., release from necessity—is experienced as the death of one's former self and simultaneously as the resurrection to a new life. Umemoto refers to this as the "uncanny experience of the formation of absolute self-negation merging without interval into absolute affirmation," and speculates that it forms the basis of "all religious paradoxes." However, in Buddhism, and in the Kyoto School philosophy of nothingness that was in some manner connected to it, it was usual to ask such questions as, How is it possible for the self to negate the self? When pursued, such questions led to the conclusion that the origin of negation was negativity itself. According to this view, there was "no alternative but to understand as the machination of the absolute the inexorable progression through the moral stages that leads one to despair, and the resolve toward death as the summons of that absolute." That is, "desire is the summons of Amida."[96]

Whether or not it was described in terms of the religious metaphor of the bodhisattva, according to Umemoto, nothingness came to be understood against the background of this religious tradition as the basis of existence itself: "Particularly when it is rationalized as topological intuition abstracted from the historical basis of reality, it becomes Nishida's logic of absolutely self-contradictory identity through which the mutual negation between thing and thing amounts to the self-determination of nothingness."

With his logic of species Tanabe had begun the process of bringing this notion of determination down to earth. In his new formulation, "Nothingness does not appear in itself but only through its real channel which is historical being. . . . What determines the individual is always species as an historical, relative, particular form of being. It is not some absolute negativity of nothingness apart from the movement of this relative negativity." Tanabe had added, "This is the point of contact between the philosophy of nothingness and Marxism." Of course, before that could be true, species had to be reinterpreted to refer to class rather than "race" or "nation."[97]

In his late wartime and early postwar writings, however, Tanabe had brought the logic of death-and-resurrection back to an explicitly religious level. Umemoto undoubtedly had in the back of his mind the experience of conversion Tanabe had recorded in his *Zangedō toshite no tetsugaku* (Philosophy as Metanoetics), written in the final stages of the Pacific War and published in 1946. Tanabe had claimed that he was "tormented by . . . indecision" regarding whether or not to speak out against the war and in what form, and finally,

in my despair concluded that I was not fit to engage in the sublime task
of philosophy.

At that moment something astonishing happened. In the midst of
my distress I let go and surrendered myself humbly to my own inability. I was suddenly brought to new insight! My penitent confession—
metanoesis (*zange*)—unexpectedly threw me back on my own interi-
ority and away from things external. There was no longer any question
of my teaching and correcting others under the circumstances—I who
could not deliver myself to do the correct thing. The only thing for me
to do in the situation was to resign myself honestly to my weakness, to
examine my own inner self with humility, and to explore the depths of
my powerlessness and lack of freedom. Would not this mean a new task
to take the place of the philosophical task that had previously engaged
me? Little matter whether it be called "philosophy" or not: I had already come to realize my own incompetence as a philosopher. What
mattered was that I was being confronted at the moment with an intellectual task and ought to do my best to pursue it.

Tanabe's account also exemplified the tendency, referred to above, of attributing the conversion to an external agent:

To be sure, this [new task] is not . . . to be undertaken on my own
power (*jiriki*). That power has already been abandoned in despair. It is
rather a philosophy to be practiced by Other-power (*tariki*), which has
turned me in a completely new direction through metanoesis, and has
induced me to make a fresh start from the realization of my utter help-
lessness. . . . Yet insofar as this entails an act of self-denial, it points to
a paradox: even though it is my own act, it cannot be my own act. It has
been prompted by a Power outside of myself. This Other-power brings
about a conversion in me that heads me in a new direction along a path
hitherto unknown to me.[98]

Despite Tanabe's overtly religious turn at the end of the war, for Umemoto
the logic of species (as class conflict) provided a way to begin reconciling the
determinism of historical materialism with a conception of human freedom. In
this formulation, the demise of an order dominated by a particular class (e.g.,
the bourgeoisie) casts adrift those who depended on and identified with it. They
experience a "loss of foundations" and "to the extent that they fail to cast themselves into the abyss and go through negative conversion they will become isolated in an empty existence." That is, "What negates the individual and what
gives it life is in actuality species, so the splitting of species and the overcoming

of that split in a new species are the actual bases for the death-and-resurrection of the individual. . . . Species produces the death-and-resurrection of the individual through the individual's own negative conversion, and thus provides nothingness with existential mediation."[99]

The element of nothingness (*mu*) causes an experience of discontinuity "between the ego that is destroyed and the new ego," and "to be a materialist subjectively implies a leap toward that discontinuity."[100] Put another way, "*Mu* is a reality of consciousness that is born when the negative conversion of historical reality is grasped subjectively." The clash of species creates a loss of foundations for the individual, who despairs entirely regarding the possibility of meaning and historical efficacy. In that despair, however, is the possibility of a subjective, self-negating conversion, a death-and-resurrection, in which the individual is able to transcend himself toward newly emerging historical reality. This is the meaning of subjectivity, and *mu*, for the Marxist.[101]

Umemoto's formulation contained the clear insight that subjects are formed when decisions are necessitated by the failure or incompleteness of structural determination (the "old order"). Subjects emerge from absence rather than presence, and are therefore penetrated by lack (Umemoto's "loss of foundations," resulting in *mu*). Yet, in a manner perfectly understandable in relation to the historical context of his thought, Umemoto ultimately fails to escape the grasp of humanist assumptions: Decision arises from the individual's "experience of discontinuity,"[102] and the result of "negative conversion" is the "death-and-resurrection of the individual" resulting in self-transcendence. That is, from lack and fragmentation Umemoto succeeds in recuperating a unified, self-possessed individual.

At about the same time as he wrote the above essay, Umemoto attempted more systematically to contrast the worldview of historical materialism with that of the philosophy of nothingness, suggesting how the latter might in a limited fashion be suggestive in regard to a Marxist approach to subjectivity. First, he established the basic legitimacy of his focus on consciousness by quoting Engels:

> We simply cannot get away from the fact that everything that sets men acting must find its way through their brains. . . . The influences of the external world upon man express themselves in his brain, are reflected therein as feelings, thoughts, impulses, volitions—in short, as "ideal tendencies," and in this form become "ideal powers." If, then, a man is to be deemed an idealist because he follows "ideal tendencies" and admits that "ideal powers" have an influence over him, then every person who is at all normally developed is a born idealist and how, in that case, can there still be any materialists?[103]

Umemoto's point regarding Marxists, of course, is still that they have not adequately theorized this dimension of consciousness, not because they make light of it but, on the contrary, because revolutionary consciousness is so fundamental a part of their worldview that they take it for granted.[104] Umemoto himself is concerned to elaborate such a theory, through an immanent critique of the works of Nishida and Tanabe in relation to materialism.

His discussion can be divided into two parts: first, he dwells again on the issue of freedom versus necessity, contrasting the standpoints of materialism and the Kyoto School; then he moves toward limited appropriation of the philosophy of nothingness in a new conceptualization of class conflict. Umemoto refers, in fact, more to Nishida's work, especially the *Tetsugaku no konpon mondai* (Fundamental Problems of Philosophy),[105] than to Tanabe's in arguing that the worldview of the philosophy of nothingness differs fundamentally from its materialist counterpart, virtually from the beginning.

According to Umemoto, Marxism presupposes a genetic, evolutionary dialectic of man-in-nature in which consciousness can never be in more than *relative*, temporary contradiction with the natural, material world. Nishida's philosophy of nothingness, in contrast, began with the realm of consciousness and then tried to go from there to an understanding of the material world. The latter strategy resulted in a tendency to see consciousness and matter in the abstract, cut off from their generative, historical context, and also, therefore, to conceive of the need for an absolute mediation between them. This mediation was provided by the notion of "emptiness," which developed, eventually, into a nonhistorical but nonetheless genetic, or emanationist, construct that Nishida called *mu*, or nothingness. Thus, in this philosophy dialectics is understood as "absolute dialectics," occurring between absolutely contradictory terms that remained equivalent and mutually defining. Such a dialectic did not necessarily involve movement or development, and therefore was unhistorical and supportive of the status quo.

The intent of Umemoto's review of the philosophy of nothingness is to show, in a manner of speaking, that this philosophy offered a form of subjective freedom without history. Although conservative and idealist, Nishida's philosophy had focused attention precisely on those issues related to subjectivity that dialectical materialism seemed to take for granted. Therefore, Umemoto was anxious to explore the possibility of reappropriating for materialism an analogue of Kyoto philosophy's theory of choice and action.

Turning to historical materialism, he observes that if the generative dialectic were understood from the outset to be unilaterally determined by existence, there would be no possibility of action in the true sense of the term. That is, Marxism's commitment to a relative dialectic—i.e., continuity—between consciousness and the material world would effectively exclude freedom. This exclusion could be overcome only if it were possible to conceive of the juncture between consciousness and matter in such a way as to preserve freedom of decision. Since human action presumed free choice, it required that there be a break or rupture in the web of determination, or, in other words, that the individual be capable of destroying the existing universal. If it were true in principle that the individual-that-destroys could never itself be free entirely of social-historical determination, and that therefore a determining totality, or universal, could never be absent, it had also to be true that free activity on the part of the individual was capable of destroying or rending that totality. Therefore, it had to be the case that intrinsic to the act of destruction was the simultaneous instantiation of a new totality. Indeed, this is what occurred at the macrosocial level in the form of class conflict:

> It is the viewpoint of materialist dialectics that the individual who is capable of destroying the old universal does so at the leading edge of the new universal, and that the actual process of the maturation of that new universal must be grasped as an aspect of the material base. Here, the relationship between universal and individual is clearly understood as class conflict, and the old unity is destroyed at the extremity of this opposition. . . . The dynamism capable of incessantly destroying the world from its foundations is not, in this view, a floating, topical determination. It is to be understood as an historical, material movement that gives rise to opposition.[106]

Umemoto had now added a structural schematization of revolutionary change to the more subject-centered viewpoint of his earlier essay on *mu*. Rather than nothingness, it was now to be ultimately material, historical forces that provided the energy by which the "old universal" was replaced with the new through class conflict. Individuals who suffered a "loss of foundations" in that historical transition could become historical subjects through self-denial and the "death-and-resurrection" of conversion. Through that process they would recover their "original humanity," and join forces with history by throwing themselves behind the "new universal." In the context of the materialist dialectic of man-in-nature, this moment of "destruction" and "rebirth" would be experienced as a sublime unity of determining and being determined, and it would be possible to grasp historical necessity rather as opportunity.

Umemoto's reconsiderations of both Kyoto philosophy and historical materialism were bound to attract criticism from orthodox Marxists, and again Mat-

sumura Kazuto rose to the challenge. In a June 1948 rebuttal, Matsumura takes
note of Umemoto's caveat that the philosophy of nothingness had to be "puri-
fied" prior to any rethinking in relation to Marxism, but he begins, nevertheless,
by making sure that his readers realize the important role the philosophies of
Nishida and Tanabe had played in supporting fascist ideology. In order to stamp
out Marxism and individualism, Japan's totalitarian prewar leaders had found it
necessary to engage in domestic ideological warfare. They had initially employed for this purpose a mythical and unsystematic form of "Japanism," which
placed major emphasis on state Shinto and emperor worship. However, "its
mythical content was old-fashioned and it failed entirely to satisfy the intelligentsia." Therefore, the state sought out an ideology that was capable of providing "a more internal affirmation of 'absolute obedience.'" They found it in
Nishida, and also in Tanabe's philosophy as propounded especially in his *Tetsugaku tsūron* (Introduction to Philosophy) of 1937. According to Matsumura,

> In contrast to Japanist philosophy, which viewed the emperor as a liv-
> ing god, Nishida and Tanabe's philosophy sacralized Japan's "national
> essence" [*kokutai*] as the reflection of a deistic structure; and whereas
> Japanist philosophy was relatively authoritarian, their philosophy
> advocated "obedience" of a more internally-generated sort and there-
> fore included elements of individualism and existentialism. We were
> told incessantly to convert to an ethic of "self denial" toward the single
> totality [*zentaiteki ichi*] and the absolute [*zettaisha*]. . . . [The philoso-
> phers of totalism] felt they had to make it seem that the mystical
> purpose of the "totality," the "unintentional intentionality" [*mokuteki
> naki mokutekisei*], was actually the true purpose of the various individ-
> uals, and that killing oneself was actually the true way to bring oneself
> to life. They did this by splitting the "self" of each individual in two.
> That is, they split each individual into a true self that embodied the
> mystical, transcendental "totality" and listened to the "voiceless voice,"
> and the other self that was consumed by selfishness and had to be de-
> nied. Thus, according to Tanabe, "the personality as moral subject
> denies its limitations and particularity as merely a separate being that
> satisfies desires in a selfish manner. Then, in the standpoint of absolute
> negation, it is resurrected and elevated to the level of a true individual,
> self-determined in absolute nothingness." (Matsumura quotes from
> Tanabe, *Tetsugaku tsūron*, pp. 73–4)[107]

Behind this unconscionable imposition of a "mystified totality" that blurred
people's own interests and forced them to think "from the perspective of serving
the totality" were, of course, the interests of the "military cliques, the bureau-

cracy, big capitalists, and big landlords." Therefore, it was above all essential that Japanese working people should now be encouraged to reconsider these totalistic ethical precepts "which they had imbibed with their mothers' milk" and to reformulate a "new morality" based on their own common interests.

> In other words, what has to be pointed out first concerning Nishida and Tanabe's theory of "historical reality," which Umemoto wants to use in order to fill the "lacuna" in Marxism, is that when it propounds unity between historical movement and the inner individual it entirely excludes the problem of the common interests and happiness of the people. It pays no attention to the people's combining of forces in support of their clear, common interests, and no attention to the construction of the discipline and devotion that a mass movement on the basis of those interests would demand. It merely says that people should obey the will of a mystical "transcendental totality," and "absolute nothingness," and that true spontaneity will result from the perspective of "absolute nothingness."[108]

Having clarified his view of Kyoto philosophy and its exclusion of the interests and desires of the people, Matsumura turns to what he considers to be Umemoto's attempt to use the Kyoto philosophy of subjectivity to "fill the lacuna" in Marxism. Here Matsumura observes that Umemoto "differs from Nishida and Tanabe in the fundamental direction of his intention and practice, but he shares with them an inability to discover a true reason to assent to the overall movement of history and to participate in it." Umemoto thinks it is necessary to have a special reason to participate in history because he does not recognize the subjective dimension that is intrinsic to historical processes. Like many bourgeois scholars, he thinks of "historical necessity" merely as a material process, cut off from living human beings. But concerning the "subjective development" of the forces of production, Marx had written that

> [l]arge-scale industry concentrates in one place a crowd of people unknown to one another. Competition divides their interests. But the maintenance of wages, this common interest which they have against their boss, unites them in a common thought of resistance—*combination*. This combination always has a double aim, that of stopping competition among the workers, so that they can carry on general competition with the capitalist. If the first aim of resistance was merely the maintenance of wages, combinations, at first isolated, constitute themselves into groups as the capitalists in their turn unite for the purpose of repression, and in the face of always united capital the

maintenance of the association becomes more necessary to them than that of wages. . . . In this struggle . . . all the elements necessary for a coming battle unite and develop.[109]

As an intellectual, Umemoto is charged with failing to recognize the naturally generated "subjectivity of the proletarian subject's class interest," and of speaking of historical forces as if they were purely objective. This leads Umemoto to try to bring in a subjective supplement from outside. For example, Umemoto had admitted that concern about historical *shutaisei* was "a phenomenon peculiar to the intellectual class," while members of the working class were able to "connect the basis of subjectivity to historical necessity without any logical mediation at all." However, he had also argued that it is precisely because of its consciousness of loss that the intellectual class is able to pose the question of the "possibility of decision," one that ultimately affects not only intellectuals but everyone.

From Matsumura's perspective, of course, this was merely further evidence that Umemoto shared "the standpoint of bourgeois and petty bourgeois intellectuals who are responding to the new movement of history led by the proletariat, but at the same time have no deep solidarity of interest with it." The lacuna, therefore, was in Umemoto's own outlook, not in Marxism.[110]

Matsumura turns in conclusion to the "logical mediation" Umemoto thinks can be appropriated from the philosophy of nothingness. He takes note of Umemoto's argument about the need for a "logic through which necessity totally denies human freedom until nothing is left" but responds, "How can he talk about 'human freedom' without including the desires and interests of all the people, particularly the proletariat?" Surely it was necessary to consider "the will of the class for whom revolution was a life or death matter." That Umemoto did not, revealed that "there are no common interests or solidarity between the new movement of the people led by the proletariat and Umemoto, who contemplates that movement." Therefore, instead of practical interests as the engine of revolutionary commitment he focused only on "self-denial and devotion."[111]

The Historical Destiny of the Proletariat

Umemoto replied to certain of Matsumura's criticisms in the November 1948 issue of *Risō* (Ideals), focusing on the problem of class interest in relation to *shutaisei*. Matsumura had argued that the natural solidarity that arises among workers and their feelings of resentment against their exploiters provided a fully adequate basis on which to explain the emergence of revolutionary *shutaisei*. In this essay, Umemoto seeks to argue that, to the contrary, although workers' "naturally-generated" feelings are adequate motivators for economistic wage struggles, they cannot provide a sufficient basis for explaining the "subjectivity of a Marxist." Matsumura had sought to trivialize the question of *shutaisei* by saying that any individuals whose oppression originates in a common source have the "social ability" to protect each other and rise up against the source of their misery. But Umemoto counters with charges that are analogous to those of ahistoricity and bourgeois universalism that Matsumura had earlier leveled at him. Was not Matsumura appealing to an ahistorical dimension of "human nature" as the basis for revolutionary action by the proletariat? If so, was this not tantamount to ignoring class standpoint? What Umemoto proposed instead was that the subjective commitment of revolutionaries must originate in keen self-awareness of their status as representatives of the class uniquely destined to liberate not only itself but all mankind. Their consciousness is thus not universal, as an attribute of abstract humanity, but specifically historical and partisan.

For the revolutionary, who has to "separate himself entirely from all objectivism and economism," true subjectivity could be located only "in the awareness of an internal connection between the class-oriented individual and history." Therefore, for Umemoto the problem of revolutionary subjectivity had to do most fundamentally with how an individual "transcends the finite self and connects with history."[112] Of course, Umemoto did not imagine that this subjective awareness was independent of the materialist science that had succeeded in demonstrating the world-historical destiny of the proletariat. To the contrary, it is precisely this objectively proven destiny which undergirds and authenticates class hatred and solidarity, giving it the status of a profoundly ethical duty. That is, in the course of revolution, the proletariat's "instinctual hatred is organized into a duty to the class totality, and is also undergirded by the entire history of mankind."[113]

At the same time, Umemoto argues on the basis of the young Marx that to find ethicality in the revolutionary self-awareness of a Marxist does not necessarily constitute "ethical revisionism," as charged by Matsumura. Contrary to Matsumura's assumptions about the "organic" relationship between Marxism and the proletarian class, Umemoto points out that Marxism did not orginate in the proletariat itself but was brought to it by intellectuals—most notably Marx and Engels themselves—who initially adhered to the ideals of bourgeois humanism. In "On the Jewish Question," for example, Marx had premised his value judgments on the doctrine put forward in the French Revolution that human beings are naturally free and equal, and in his "Contribution to a Critique of Hegel's *Philosophy of Right*" he had defined the problem as the "total loss of humanity." Marx was also in the process of discovering the proletariat as the only possible agent for the achievement of those ideals and was coming to realize that only class conflict leading to the revolutionary victory of that class could bring about the abolition of all classes and thus establish humans as "species" beings. In other words, "what distinguished the consciousness of the new intelligentsia . . . from the old humanism was their awareness that the proletariat itself is the subject of history, an originary material force, and that their own liberation could be secured only in conjunction with that subject." Then, of course, once they attached themselves to that material subject, they became involved in a historical dialectic that precipitated a fundamental transformation in the original bourgeois standards themselves, converting them into something quite different from what the bourgeoisie had intended. In sum, an essential role in the revolutionary process had to be played by self-conscious revolutionary awareness, a worldview that can be characterized as "faith in history."[114]

It followed, moreover, that this "faith" had to imply selfless devotion. Umemoto contends that people under capitalist domination—if not people in all eras—are consumed by selfishness and are unlikely to pursue more than narrow self-interest if left alone. Therefore, when "natural" solidarity and anger are inadequate, as they inevitably will be, the revolutionary process can be moved forward only by those whose awareness of historical destiny has caused them to renounce selfishness and devote themselves to the cause without hope of personal reward. Ergo, the fundamental correctness of his earlier premise (in some ways analogous to the ethical return to the totality in Watsuji's ethics) of a "human essence revealed as one's own original nature which fundamentally includes selfishness but can be discovered only on the basis of the denial of selfishness."[115] The historical subject could only be fully effective when (in a process mediated by the objective historical destiny of the proletariat) individuals "returned" to their original essence of selflessness and there discovered the ability to die for a cause. Only scientific prediction *plus* denial of self-interest could justify optimism regarding the revolutionary project.

Umemoto's response to Matsumura clarified further the role of class partisanship in his theory of *shutaisei*, but it did not significantly alter his original argument, which might be summarized as follows: Umemoto challenged the naturalistic assumptions of scientific Marxism and reflection theory in epistemology and practice. He argued that, while scientific Marxism could explain the contradictions that arose when the material productive forces of society came in conflict with the existing relations of production, it had not yet accounted theoretically for how or why people converted those latent contradictions into actual conflict by engaging in revolutionary action. Thus, Umemoto contended that the absence of a properly Marxist theory of subjectivity constituted a "lacuna" in Marxism that had to be filled in theory even though he had no doubt that, in practice, Communist revolutionaries acted resolutely on behalf of revolution.

In order to develop a theory that could account for what he saw as sacrificial subjectivity, Umemoto reverted back to the ethical view espoused by his erstwhile mentor, Watsuji Tetsurō—that of the human being as "a negative unity between individuality and sociality." This philosophical anthropology posited that human beings as individuals have an innate propensity to rebel against the totality and, by extension, to act against those who seek to maintain outmoded relations of production. Umemoto certainly did not deny the more orthodox, materialist anthropology Marx and Engels had outlined in "The German Ideology"—that of man as producer—but suggested that the Marxian revolutionary paradigm would be complete only when a theory of the ethical person was developed as a supplement to the human being as producer.

Ultimately Umemoto concluded that revolutionaries acted out of devotion to the metahistorical destiny of the working class to liberate not only itself but all humanity. Thus, his was virtually the same solution that had been adopted by the Hegelian Marxist Georg Lukács, who had posited the proletariat as the "identical subject-object"[116] of history and the Communist party as the "organized form" of the "correct class consciousness of the proletariat."[117]

Moreover, despite the cogency of his challenge to a narrowly scientific, objectivist Marxism, Umemoto's own strategy also led him to parallel Lukács in adopting an essentialist perspective that apotheosized the proletariat as savior. Through a Hegelian recuperation, he attempted to reduce both historical necessity and contingent subjectivity to moments of a totality that was capable of overcoming their dangerous supplementarity. As a result, it can be argued from the perspective of the 1990s that, rather than helping to open up the process of hegemony to an emergent, egalitarian process of articulation among contending forces and demands, his theoretical intervention had the paradoxical effect of reinforcing the rationale offered by those who sought to impose unilateral control on behalf of the working class.

Umemoto's confrontation with Matsumura suggests that to a significant degree the logic of the supplement pervaded the postwar Japanese discourse on democratic revolution, in philosophy as well as in literary criticism. Indeed, it might be argued that (bourgeois-) democratic revolution itself, at least as it had been defined in the Comintern Theses, functioned in a supplementary fashion in relation to a metahistorical paradigm that validated the proletariat as the universal class and gave highest priority to that class's own revolution. Although it was considered to be an essential component of the revolutionary process (indeed, in the early postwar era, arguably the *entire* revolutionary process, since the socialist stage was for some purposes indefinitely deferred), the democratic revolution was nonetheless implicitly stigmatized as merely a kind of house-keeping—a mopping up of feudal remnants—which the proletariat had to complete as expeditiously as possible before moving on to its true calling of socialist revolution.

Yet it is suggestive that the recent attempt by Laclau and Mouffe—in, admittedly, a global situation quite different from that of early postwar Japan—to reconsider socialist strategy in relation to a radical democratic politics led them to reverse this hierarchy. In their view, "socialist demands" should comprise a "moment internal to the democratic revolution" rather than the other way around.[118] In a deconstructive reconsideration of Marxism-Leninism, they seek to complete the effort to de-essentialize and demythologize the stages, classes, and subjects that in the past have claimed metahistorical primacy. Contrary to Leninist practice, they assume that united fronts form and reform subjects just as subjects form united fronts; that the composition of a front is determined primarily by external lines of antagonism rather than internal essence; and that revolutionary practice is a matter of forging hegemonic relationships in an environment of political contingency. This suggests that only an ongoing process of democratization is capable of reproducing such an environment, without which the socialist project would degenerate. Thus, they conclude—in a manner appropriate to a critique of postwar Japanese discourse on bourgeois-democratic revolution—that "the task of the Left . . . cannot be to renounce liberal-democratic ideology, but on the contrary, to deepen and expand it in the direction of a radical and plural democracy."[119]

Postwar Philosophy and *Shutaisei*

Umemoto Katsumi was the boldest and most provocative of the early postwar philosophers of *shutaisei*, but he was not the only one. Although they did not all attempt, like Umemoto, to construct a new materialist theory of political subjectivity, several did criticize what they felt to be the excessively objectivist view of society and history that had been held by Japanese proponents of historical and dialectical materialism. They also took issue, implicitly or explicitly, with aspects of Umemoto's synthesis and also with the "existentialist" position they identified with Ara and the other *Kindai bungaku* writers.

Objectivism, Existentialism, Death

Amakasu Sekisuke (Mita Sekisuke) had joined the Materialism Study Group in 1932 after graduating from Kyoto Imperial University, and in 1940 he was arrested on suspicion of violating the Peace Preservation Law. In the same year,

he began teaching in the preparatory course of Nihon University, a position he
held until 1947. After the war, he was a member of the Association of Democratic Scientists and sat on the editorial board of its journal, *Riron* (Theory). He
joined the faculty of Osaka Municipal University in 1951 and taught there almost until his death in 1975.

In a 1948 essay, Amakasu complained that Japanese Marxists had been
warned away from "subjectivism" (*shukanshugi*), and had received the impression that society functions like nature, independently of human consciousness.
To the extent that any consideration at all was devoted to subjectivity in the
education of Japanese Marxists, it was that only of the epistemological, theoretical subject, not the practical subject of history. In effect, Japanese materialism
was not really practical, and had "forgotten the human being."[120]

However, it is not the human being as revolutionary that Amakasu sets out to
discuss but rather the human being as "subject" of planned change in the context
of the postwar "human revolution." That is, from a materialist perspective conditioned by the debate on *shutaisei*, he addresses the question of how the task of
reform should be approached. What degree of credence should be given to the
transformation of mentality and culture?

Because they were convinced of the causal efficacy of socioeconomic relations in determining human consciousness, Japanese materialists had argued
that in the absence of social revolution the human revolution—transformation
of consciousness, in the sense of overcoming feudal attitudes, etc.—would
be completely impossible; conversely, they contended that once social revolution had been achieved, human revolution would follow without much effort.
Amakasu argues, however, that "social revolution and human revolution interact under the overall primacy of the former, and rather than being completely
derivative of the social, human revolution is relatively independent." Therefore,
human consciousness sometimes had to be transformed before social change
could become feasible.[121]

Individual human beings could be transformed, according to Amakasu, because rather than simple and homogeneous, their minds were complex and
sometimes contained inner conflict. Not entirely self-affirming, they manifested
an aspect of dissatisfaction with the self; whereas the self-affirming aspect
of the human mind tended toward the conservatism of unconscious habit and
emotion, the latter aspect was conscious and action-oriented, seeking progress.
These aspects correlated, in turn, with a public dimension that was theoretical,
political, and moral on the one hand and, on the other, a personal, private dimension that was sentient and emotional; a temporal aspect opposed a synchronic

aspect; and so on. Because human beings were split in this way, they were always changing, and this was especially true in the transitional era of the postwar.[122]

Therefore, human revolution of a certain type was a valid and indispensable goal. It was indeed a mistake, according to Amakasu, to believe that it was possible and desirable to construct a free, independent, modern person within the existing Japanese social order.[123] Nevertheless, democratic revolution did demand the employment of cognitive means—not necessarily theoretical but experiential—to raise consciousness among not only the proletariat but the people as a whole. Participation in struggles related to their daily livelihood was essential, but such experiences could be augmented or simulated if necessary using literature and art. Only when it was received sensually would cognition become secure and take on the power to change people.[124] In sum, it was important for materialists to learn to deal with human beings not only in their external, social dimension but internally, in relation to their consciousness and desire.

Funayama Shin'ichi, who during the war had been a member of Prime Minister Konoe's intellectual advisory group, the Shōwa Kenkyūkai (Shōwa Research Association), also turned from his own perspective to the question Umemoto had raised concerning the persuasiveness of Marxism in the postwar milieu. Criticizing Japanese dialectical materialism as "regressive,"[125] Funayama argued that unless it could be presented in such as way as to seem relevant to the life of each individual, it could never be broadly convincing.[126] Of course, the problems of Japanese Marxism were to some degree a result of the kind of conditions that had confronted Marxists during the war. At the same time, the roots of objectivism were already there in the work of Marx, Engels, and Lenin. Marx—especially in "Theses on Feuerbach"—had sought to render sensuousness practical and practice sensuous. At the same time, Marx—and later Engels and Lenin—had understood the subject more idealistically than had Feuerbach. Materialism had in common with idealism the tendency to treat thought and existence as if they were related extrinsically, while Feuerbach had thought of the subject as a unity between thought and existence, flesh and spirit. For him, the subject (*shutai*) referred neither to materiality nor to consciousness but rather to the human being as a whole.[127] After criticizing both existentialism and Nishida philosophy for failing fully to grasp the subject in relation to objective reality, Funayama briefly evokes technology as representing the subjective unity between the transcendent and the real, and suggests that democracy itself could be thought of as a technological unity of thought and practice.[128] In attempting to bring into the postwar milieu the problematic of

technology that had been raised in the Shōwa Research Association by Miki-
Kiyoshi, Funayama's approach paralleled that of Taketani Mitsuo, to whom we
will turn below.

Mashita Shin'ichi also criticized materialism for excessive objectivism in
the wake of World War II. A prominent figure in the prewar antifascist front
movement, Mashita had witnessed as a student the transition from Nishida to
Tanabe in the philosophy department of Kyoto Imperial University from 1926
to 1929 and had become very familiar with the "philosophy of nothingness."
Upon graduation, he formed a historical-materialist study group whose leading
member was the Marxist philosopher Tosaka Jun. Mashita also became a participant in the Materialism Study Group when it was formed in 1932. After teaching for a few years, he returned to Kyoto University as a graduate student and
was actively involved in the student protests that opposed the rightist-inspired
dismissal from Kyoto's Law Faculty of the liberal legal scholar Takigawa
Yukitoki. In 1933 Mashita took up a position at Dōshisha University in Kyoto;
he also joined with Nakai Masakazu and Niimura Takeshi in publishing the antifascist journal *Bi/hihyō* (Aesthetics/Criticism). In 1935 this group began to
publish *Sekai bunka* (World Culture) and became, in effect, part of the world-
wide antifascist front that the Comintern had called for at its Seventh Congress.
As a result, Mashita was arrested in the so-called Kyoto Popular Front Incident
of November 1937, and in September 1939 he was sentenced to five years in
prison, three of which were suspended. After the war, he taught at Nagoya University and eventually became president of Tama Bijutsu University.

In his speech before the students and faculty of Meiji University in October
1947, Mashita was especially critical of those Marxists who during the war had
reduced dialectical materialism to a method of objective analysis and put it at
the disposal of fascism. But in his view, Marxism in general was still excessively objectivist even after the war, and one of the regrettable effects of this
tendency was to force intellectuals to turn away from Marxism toward existentialism or Kyoto School philosophy in order to quench their thirst for subjective
engagement. Marxism could satisfy the total desires of humanity only by grasping materialism subjectively and practically, as a worldview rather than as
merely a system of necessary laws. More specifically, he argued, it was necessary to demonstrate that what in existentialism remained merely an abstract
concept of *shutaisei* could become truly concrete only in materialism.[129]

The "most primitive stage," at which *shutaisei* remained most solipsistic
and passive, was that of reliance on immediate sensation, or *jikkan*. Mashita
observes that certain literary figures (without mentioning Ara Masato and his
comrades by name!) had argued that truth and authenticity lay in the subjective

immediacy of intuition. But such intuition recognized no objective standard for resolving conflicts between one intuition and another.

Existence (*jitsuzon*) was the next stage in Mashita's proto-Hegelian typology of subjectivity, a stage at which *shutaisei* is understood as the individual's search for transcendence. This gives rise to the existentialists' grasp of *shutaisei*, in which Mashita distinguishes two types: the lowest level is occupied by the "classical" mode, which is Kierkegaard's notion of negative transcendence toward the totality on the part of the "nobly exceptional" individual. But this kind of existentialism was incapable of being activated by social reality; it had no internal connection to society or history.[130]

The higher stage of existentialism included such philosophers as Jean-Paul Sartre and Tanabe Hajime, who had concentrated their efforts on opening a road to historical, social existence. Mashita proposes that there were more similarities than differences between the philosophies of Sartre and Tanabe, and suggests that such divergences as did exist could be attributed to the disparity in development between Japan and Europe with respect especially to religion. More specifically, he argues that the underlying disparity was really between "France, which has already passed through the establishment of civil society, and Japan, where the establishment of modern civil society has been retarded and in which both feudal and bourgeois elements coexisted under the umbrella of absolutism." He also argues that "the political-economic meaning of the existentialism of Sartre and others is anarchism," and that although anarchism or anarcho-syndicalism was not entirely dissimilar to Marxism, it was politically ambiguous enough to be capable of moving to the extreme right as well as the extreme left.[131]

In the context of his discussion of Tanabe's effort to connect individual existence to history, Mashita cannot resist a detour in which he criticizes Tanabe's "absolute dialectics" in a manner very similar to Umemoto. Mashita points out that Tanabe had written his *Tetsugaku tsūron* at the time of the Takigawa incident, in what was probably Tanabe's "most progressive period," but that its logic of "absolute dialectics," which sought to avoid being caught up in either Hegelian idealism or Marxian materialism, ended up as pure mediation, "spinning around in thin air" with no connection to the immediacy of the natural, material world. According to Mashita, "dialectics has to be a logic of mediation and also, at the same time, a logic of immediacy." Hegel had realized this clearly, as had Marx: "What keeps materialist dialectics and Hegel's dialectics of the spirit from being thin-air dialectics is that they have a subject and a basis in either material or spirit. If one thinks of dialectics as only a logic of mediation, it ceases to be the dialectics of anything and therefore spins freely as just the dialectics of *mu*." In sum, despite Tanabe's attempt to historicize Kyoto philosophy, in his hands, "the dialectics of nothingness are reduced to the nothingness of dialectics."[132]

Mashita seems to consider the higher level of the existentialist stage, especially as represented in the species theory of Tanabe, to constitute in effect a third stage, after *jikkan* and *jitsuzon*, which he calls *jissen*, or practice. Once it reaches this stage, *shutaisei* becomes much more concrete and begins to relate to social and historical practice. However,

> [I]t is insufficient to think of the materialist concept of *shutaisei* merely as social and historical practice. If it were just a matter of understanding practice as social and historical, the philosophies of Nishida and Tanabe would do. The problem is to go one step further, toward a deeper understanding of this concept of historico-social practice. In respect to the materialistic concept of *shutaisei*, this is the most important point. A really concrete concept of practice is that of partisan practice [*tōhasei*], which is the subjective, political expression of class. For the subjective grasp of materialism, this concept is the most fundamental.[133]

Only *shutaisei* as class partisanship, understood concretely as commitment to the vanguard party, could offer the trenchant connection to social-historical context that the Marxist required. Class partisanship was, in that sense, postexistentialist in that it included the sense of "either/or" that had been elaborated by Kierkegaard and related to society in different ways by Sartre and Tanabe. Mashita told his listeners that they had to choose: "we are pressed for a responsible decision toward history." In the political context of 1947, *shutaisei* as partisan praxis required that people "take as their own the struggles for freedom and peace, the defeat of fascism, and the thorough establishment of democracy." *Shutaisei* required that "we stand clearly on the side of democratic revolution, and exert ourselves on its behalf."[134]

Mashita's resolution of the question of *shutaisei* in terms of partisanship broadly paralleled Umemoto's analysis, but without the ambiguous hint of complacency one detects in Umemoto's conviction that Marxists and their sympathizers were *already* actively committed so that there remained only the task of explaining that commitment. Mashita appears to make no such assumption and accordingly issued passionate calls for "decision" and "struggle."

Existentialism also provided the basis for Komatsu Setsurō's critique, from a more orthodox, materialist perspective. He argued that existential philosophy, as espoused by Kierkegaard, Nietszche, Martin Heidegger, and Karl

Jaspers, had historically been the product of periods of violent social change—suggesting why it had again achieved such popularity in postwar Japan—and was pervaded by a tendency to reject society and seek peace of mind through resort to a solipsistic subjectivity. Japanese existentialism consisted largely in imports from the works of these European thinkers, but its peculiarity was a tendency to try more assiduously than had they to socially engage the concept of existence, that is, to connect individual existence with society and history.[135] Nevertheless, Komatsu argues, Japanese existentialism should be understood as a manifestation of late capitalism that would disappear once the contradictions constitutive of that period of transition to socialism were clarified and, ultimately, solved through socialist revolution.[136]

Komatsu notes that Tanabe Hajime had begun the process of trying to relate existentialism to historical materialism by suggesting that Kierkegaardian Christianity could mediate a rapprochement between Buddhism and Marxism. An analogous but more worrisome move was the effort by would-be Marxists such as Umemoto Katsumi to make up for the deficiencies of Marxism by supplementing it with existentialism. According to Komatsu, Umemoto's dialectics as outlined in his "Yuibutsuron to ningen" were Kierkegaardian in the sense that they seemed to presume absolute discontinuity between the individual and social aspects of humanity—that is, between "existence" and "social relations"—thereby creating an opening for Tanabe's notions of "death-and-resurrection" and "conversion of being and nothingness."[137] It was this conviction of absolute discontinuity that marked Umemoto's understanding of materialism as revisionist.

Komatsu also attacks Umemoto's apparent desire to dilute materialism with religious existentialism by arguing that "the fervor of materialists is sustained by the pillar of rationality. It was not religion but rationality—passion based on rationality—that supported *Gokuchū jūhachinen* (Eighteen years in prison)."[138] He refers, of course, to the book written by Communist party leader Tokuda Kyūichi concerning the eighteen years of resistance Tokuda had waged in prison against mistreatment and intense pressures to recant.

Komatsu concludes by evoking Hegel's "cunning of reason" as an appropriate model for the relationship between human subjectivity and history. That is,

Human beings make human society and move it forward, but social laws are independent of the concerns, feelings and desires of individuals. . . . It is historical materialism that is able to understand those necessary laws. Indeed, it is by grasping those laws that we can understand how the individual passions and desires of human beings arise. Historical materialism does not deny the subjective realm. Rather, without separating subject and object, it clarifies the sort of objective base that supports that realm.[139]

In sum, "existentialist philosophy and historical materialism do not have equal rights as antagonists. Historical materialism can explain how existentialism emerged and grew."[140]

Umemoto responded to Komatsu's reading of "Yuibutsuron to ningen" by repeating the caveat he had included there, to the effect that he did not support any revision of Marxism through the addition of supplementary elements from Kierkegaard or Tanabe. Indeed, Umemoto was trying to prevent such moves by arguing that it was incumbent upon Marxists themselves to provide a historical-materialist theory of subjectivity: "To the extent we are unable to fill this lacuna from the standpoint of Marxism, efforts will inevitably be made to satisfy it in some other way. The experiment of the neo-Kantians in attempting to augment Marxism with Kant's moral laws is such an attempt."[141]

In response to Komatsu's appeal to the "fervor based on rationality" of Tokuda, Umemoto agrees that Tokuda's impetus was rational, but argues that it was the kind of rationality that led him to say, "I might die, but the outlook for history is bright." Tokuda's rationality was not contemplative but subjectively engaged: "In this correspondence between 'I' and 'history' . . . is the realm of subjective dialectics to which materialist dialectics should lead us."[142]

It is impossible to discuss fully the postwar critique of existentialism from the perspective of *shutaisei* without including the contribution of philosopher Takakuwa Sumio. Born in Nara in 1903, he graduated from the philosophy department of Jōchi University in 1927 with a concentration on Spinoza and medieval scholasticism. After teaching at Meiji Gakuin University and his alma mater, he became professor at the Army Officer Training School in 1940. In the meantime, his philosophical position apparently gravitated toward that of Miki Kiyoshi. After defeat, he shifted his research focus from medieval European philosophy to materialist thought, and as a professor at Aichi University from 1947 became very active in the postwar peace movement. In 1960 he visited China with a delegation sent by the Kokumin Kyōkai (National Association), the major umbrella organization opposing ratification of the revised U.S.-Japan Security Treaty. He died in 1979.

Like Komatsu, Takakuwa saw the great popularity in Japan of existentialist thought, especially that of Kierkegaard, as a symptom of specifically postwar conditions of rapid social change and disruption. On the other hand, for Takakuwa the popularity of other sorts of existentialism, especially that of Jean-Paul Sartre, in Japan signified not existential agony but rather a kind of perversion of the European tendency. That is, in Japan the genuine nihilism of Sartre had been replaced by a pale, petty bourgeois angst whose representatives merely perceived in the postwar situation a threat to their own personal life situation. Indeed, postwar theories of *shutaisei*, especially those that emphasized the solipsistic ego, were themselves products of the era of disintegration.[143]

For Takakuwa, however, the postwar milieu could not be described merely in terms of change, collapse, and disorientation. To describe the Japanese situation throughout the roughly fifteen years preceding 1945, he prefers to use the term "socialization" (*shakaika*), meaning the intentional elevation of social priorities over individual ones. Individual personality had been suppressed in favor of the rote performance of public obligations. "Thus, the ego (*jiga*) that survived the war was no more than the emaciated, physical ego."[144] After defeat, desire was widespread for the restoration of *shutaisei*, now understood as equivalent to *jishusei*, or autonomy. However, from the perspective of the individual, the wave of democratization that swept through postwar society amounted to merely another version of the "socialization" that had occurred before and during the war. That is, initially at least, postwar democratization was concentrated in the state structure and therefore passed over the heads of individuals.[145] Public priorities were dominant, and politics was so pervasive as to submerge the individual. As a result, the desperate urge to maintain personal integrity in opposition to social forces was expressed in the desire for *shutaisei*. People so intensely distrusted all social norms and authority that they tended to accept as normal a self-construct that was impervious to social concerns.[146] They had come to hate all social forces and institutions, and this hatred became the basis for a negative concept of individuality. Here, then, was the social-psychological origin of the postwar move toward existentialism and the ideals of subjective freedom and autonomy.

The problem, of course, was that *shutaisei* in this form was destined to remain negative and antisocial in its underlying impetus, and various expressions as well. It subsisted in a circumscribed inner world where the illusion of freedom was maintained in the face of all kinds of social pressures and determinations. Takakuwa calls this an "abstract" conception because it was isolated from the broader human context of history, society, and nature. He admits that under certain circumstances, this abstract autonomy could be turned into something quite admirable. Kierkegaard, for example, had developed this solitary form of existence to an advanced level.

> Postwar believers in individuality are adopting none other than the thought of Kierkegaard. . . . However, the difference between them

and the pious Kierkegaard is that he had the courage to reject everything and leap toward God, while their resoluteness emerges only in
the form of discontent and resistance against socialization. . . .
Kierkegaard's solitary individual was premised upon the necessary
dissolution of everything social and could exist only on the basis of that
sacrifice, but their exaggerated individuality . . . appears only in their
fear of being submerged in society and in their attempt to expand autonomy slightly in order to ride out the dangers of socialization. Here,
there is no leap [of faith].[147]

In conceptualizing the limitations of Kierkegaardian freedom, Takakuwa
turns to Hegel's notion of "subjective freedom," which implied that all ethical
and religious appeals were external and unworthy of obedience and which
based itself solely on the subject's inner heart, feelings, and conscience. Self-
consciousness was, of course, essential to subjective freedom in the Hegelian
model but not sufficient. As Takakuwa points out, Hegel also insisted that subjective freedom be transcended toward the objective world. That is, one could
actualize freedom only when one moved beyond the purely formal, "subjective" stage to enter into practical negotiation with the social-historical world.[148]

Yet, Takakuwa argues, many Japanese who waved the banners of subjectivity and so-called autonomy feared that too much sociohistorical engagement
would lead to objectification and, eventually, to the obliteration of subjective
freedom. One such ideologue was Tanabe Hajime, who wrote in 1948 that
"[w]hether or not nature and society are ruled by freedom, one can have virtually complete freedom so long as one is free in oneself. That is how, in both
East and West, the religious leaders and wisemen of old, who lived at a time
when control over nature and society was largely impossible owing to the lack
of science, were able to have freedom virtually without impediment."[149] Elsewhere Takakuwa pointed to Tanabe's "excess zeal for salvation solely of the
self" and commented that "with respect to widespread poverty and misery he
has only sympathy to offer."[150]

Takakuwa observes that, in any case, Tanabe's type of subjective freedom
would soon collapse in the context of an unfree society. How could people be
free and active participants in the society to which they were, in any case, bound
inextricably? For Takakuwa that was possible only once they credited the social
necessity that impinged upon them. Once they recognized necessity, they could
work dialectically to sublate it, internally as well as externally, and by that
means become truly subjective (*shutaiteki*) in the social and historical sense.[151]

This required, of course, that theorists of *shutaisei* should themselves be
subjectively engaged in their attitude toward thought and life. For Takakuwa,

this meant close identification with and participation in the democratic movements of the masses, but it also meant "wagering their whole existence," life or death, on the philosophical and political enterprise that was *shutaisei*. In making his point, Takakuwa quotes from a January 1948 essay by the Marxist historian Hani Gorō, to the effect that "[p]hilosophy is something by which we live and die. Whether it is idealism or materialism is only secondary." Hani had also written, "A philosophy espoused by scholars who are not sure whether they themselves are willing to live, or die by it, will find it difficult to move people."[152] Elsewhere, Takakuwa himself remarks, "For present-day philosophers who make an issue of subjectivity but are not at all subjectively engaged themselves, these words must have seemed painfully accurate. They have studied *shutaisei* objectively but have found nothing there they can die for."[153] Indeed, the question of death formed a major component of Takakuwa's approach to the question.

In his postwar polemical writing, Takakuwa frequently used a discussion of philosophical understandings of death as the medium through which to illuminate essential aspects of *shutaisei*. As a specialist in European thought of the medieval and Renaissance eras, he often drew his examples from that milieu. In several of his essays, Takakuwa constructed a hierarchical framework of thanatologies, beginning with the naturalistic philosophy he associated with the Renaissance. Lucretius, for example, had argued that death is objective nihility—an extinguishing of the spirit as well as the body—and, as such, was nothing to fear. Montaigne's view was comparable. Takakuwa comments, however, that this amounted to a strategy of dissolving one's own death into the universality of death in general, and therefore contained not an ounce of *shutaisei*.[154]

With Pascal, the understanding of death changed from naturalistic-ethical to religious-subjective. According to Takakuwa, there were two great traditions in European ideas of death: the Greek, which included Lucretius and Montaigne, and the Christian, which included Pascal. It was the Christian view that implied a subjective (*shutaiteki*) approach to death. For example, Pascal admitted that he felt no personal connection to the death of the Spartans, but he did feel strongly linked to the martyrs' deaths. That is, he belonged to their same body, and thus felt that "their resolve (*ketsui*) is our resolve."[155] As Takakuwa explained in other essays, the religious subjectivity of Christianity was premised on common membership in a "sacred society," understandable as the body of Christ. This body was bound by love, and it was this love that moved Pascal subjectively, causing him to adopt the martyrs' deaths as his own and to feel their pain.

It was an "invisible society," but only as a member of it could each
Christian gain subjectivity [*shutaisei*] in all his or her praxis. That is
because Christ is the social subject of this invisible society, and the
Christians' belief in that subject, or rather, their sharing of his torment,
comprises the practical impetus of their daily lives. Each individual is
connected to this society via Christ as the social subject. By taking
Christ's death upon themselves, that is, by denying their individual
subjectivity, they connect to the social subject and that connection pre-
cipitates an objective subjectivity that transcends all arbitrariness and
selfishness. Objective subjectivity is an oxymoron. However, if
we can use such an expression to refer to a form of unity with the social
subject that avoids the *shutaisei* theorists' reification of the so-called inner self, then can we not find there the highest and most humane
shutaisei?[156]

Here Takakuwa brings to a high point of perceptiveness his conviction that
shutaisei had to be social rather than individual. Although, like them, he begins
with individuals, he then insists that it is only by becoming a believer and thus
by "denying their individual subjectivity" that "individuals" are able to become
part of a social subject that has a certain objective existence. In the process, they
"avoid the [*shutaisei* theorists'] reification of the so-called inner self."

However, Takakuwa is not content to stop with Christian *shutaisei*, precisely
because the "body of Christ" is an invisible, that is to say ideal, society rather
than a "real" one. Therefore, his third philosophical approach to death and, by
extension, to *shutaisei* is formed from the materialists' recognition of real connections between "individual subjects" and the social subject in the form of
class consciousness and common interests. Here the social subject is a collec-
tivity that has been determined by historical and social laws to be the subject of
history.[157] Where such connections are manifest in solidarity toward a common
destiny, they can comprise a real social body analogous to the idealized body of
Christ, such that the deaths of members of that body will be felt as if they were
one's own. Takakuwa cites the early postwar prison deaths of Tosaka Jun and
Miki Kiyoshi as events that evoked among like-minded partisans precisely this
sort of pain and sense of common destiny.[158] Therefore, it is only by renouncing
all arbitrariness and acting in concert with the actual social subject that one
could achieve "objective subjectivity" in the social-historical world.

In fact, Takakuwa's argument for the fundamentally social existence of *shutaisei* recalls the prewar work of Miki Kiyoshi, who explicated that quality in
conjunction with a theory of technology. The line of reasoning begun by Miki
was in some degree taken up after the war by a physicist, Taketani Mitsuo.

Subjectivity and Technology

Miki Kiyoshi was born in 1897 and read Nishida's *Zen no kenkyū* (A Study of the Good) while still a student at First Higher School. In 1917 he entered the University of Kyoto in order to study philosophy under Nishida, and after graduation he was sent to study for three years in Europe. Upon his return to Kyoto he found that a position would not be available at the university there, so he moved to Tokyo, where he studied and wrote voluminously as a private scholar. A member of the Proletarian Science Research Institute, he established his reputation as a philosopher through such works as *Shakai kagaku no yobigainen* (Preliminary concepts for a social science) and *Shiteki gainenron no shomondai* (Problems in the formulation of historical concepts); he also teamed up with Hani Gorō in editing the journal *Shinkō kagaku no hata no moto ni* (Under the flag of the new science). In 1930 he was arrested by the special police for allegedly contributing money to the illegal Communist party; virtually at the same time he was also expelled from the Proletarian Science Research Institute for his unorthodox approach. These experiences seem to have affected him profoundly, turning him away from the Marxist sympathies of his youth. In the early 1930s he turned to a focus on the philosophy of history, and began work that culminated in his famous study entitled *Kōsōryoku no ronri* (The logic of creativity). Ironically, he was jailed again in early 1945, and died there in September 1945, before the Occupation forces commanded the release of all political prisoners.

In 1939, under the auspices of the Shōwa Research Association, Miki had labored to produce a philosophical account of Japan's New Order, both domestically and throughout East Asia. It was clear to Miki that "[w]hether we are talking about the construction of a new political organization, the expansion of productive power, or the creation of a new culture, all of these things must be based on practice." Practice, therefore, had to be the basis of the new philosophy of cooperativism that would undergird the New Order. Practice was a matter of making things, "whether a political system, the material objects of economic life, or a cultural asset." Therefore, it subsumed the activity of cognition but was not, of course, just a matter of consciousness apprehending external objects. Accordingly, the practical subject had to be embodied in "a human being as concrete life consisting of both body and mind."[159]

The making of things could also be termed the practice of technology, which "seeks to synthesize the laws of nature and human will"; technology, in turn, had to be considered social: "the practical subject (*shutai*) in its original sense is not the individual, but rather society." Moreover, "society as the practical subject cannot be abstract and universal; it is concrete and universal like the ethnic group (*minzoku*) and the state." Unless mediated by the (ethnically defined) nation and the state, the individual remained "merely abstract." When understood in this socially and nationally mediated sense, technological practice was always historical: "We are made by history, and conversely, we make history."[160] Miki's pronoun "we" has to be understood as referring to the ethnic nation, or Volk, which was the locus of historical subjectivity: "all world-historical movements are initiated by a certain ethnic group/nation." It was appropriate, therefore, that Japan should initiate the New Order in East Asia.[161] Yet in doing so, "the will of the Japanese nation must be moral to the greatest extent."[162]

Miki's insistence on the nation as the locus of practical subjectivity was echoed by several of his philosophical contemporaries, such as Kōyama Iwao, Nishitani Keiji, and Kōsaka Masaaki, in a variety of contexts at around the same time. In a roundtable discussion published in the journal *Chūō kōron* (Central Review) in January 1942, however, Kōyama and Kōsaka distinguished between the ethnic folk (*minzoku*) and the nation (*kokumin*) or state with respect to historical subjectivity.[163] As Sakai points out,

> For Kōyama as well as for Kōsaka, the unity of the subject of history, of pluralistic history, is unequivocally equated to that of the nation-state. Yet they stress that the nation-state does not immediately correspond to a race (*jinshu*) or folk (*minzoku*). The state for them is a being-for-itself which is opposed to other states, and, in this regard, it exists in the "world." The state . . . has to be mediated by its relationships with other states and consequently be self-reflective—that is, a subject.

The "*moralische Energie*" of the communal folk (*minzoku*) had to be mediated through the rational state to become a true historical subject. Sakai adds, significantly, "One can hardly discern any difference between this understanding of modern subjectivity and that of the Hegelian dialectic."[164]

Precisely because, during wartime, historical subjectivity was conceived to reside primarily in the nation-state as symbolized in the throne, in the era of democratic revolution following defeat most philosophers and political theorists obeyed a powerful urge to transfer the locus of meaningful agency to the individual and to class, especially the proletariat, and to reformulate fundamental concepts such as technology in a manner consistent with empirical science. One who seems to have been stimulated by a critical reading of Miki's prewar work was the physicist Taketani Mitsuo.

In February 1946, the same month in which Ara Masato published "Daini no seishun" in *Kindai bungaku*, there appeared in another new journal, *Shinsei* (New Life), a two-part essay by Taketani Mitsuo, a physicist who had collaborated at Osaka Imperial University with others such as Sakata Shōichi and the future Nobel prize winner, Yukawa Hideki. The essay was unusual because the second part consisted in a reprint, with minor additions, of a report entitled "Gijutsuron," which Taketani had submitted in response to interrogation by the Special Higher Police while imprisoned in 1944.

Taketani was raised in Taiwan but attended Kyoto Imperial University. By 1938 he was becoming actively involved in the journal *Sekai bunka*, which Nakai Masakazu, Niimura Takeshi, and Kuno Osamu had begun in late 1934. Also, around this time, he threw himself into the study of Marxism. Because, as noted above, the editors were sympathetic with the antifascist popular-front movement, the magazine and its partisans attracted special attention from the Japanese police. As a result of his participation, Taketani was arrested and jailed from September 1938 to April 1939.

Upon his release, he continued his scientific work at Osaka University and became increasingly interested in philosophical and methodological questions related to technology. He also led a study group that touched on not only the theory of technology but such sensitive topics as the war in Europe and the Japanese military. These circle activities provided the pretext for his second arrest in 1944. It was during his interrogation on this occasion that he provided the authorities with a report of his current thinking on the proper definition of technology, and it was this document that he published with minor additions in February 1946.[165]

The report is framed as a critique of the definition of technology ostensibly espoused by Aikawa Haruki and others who in the 1930s had been affiliated with the journal *Yuibutsuron kenkyū* (Studies in Materialism) and, in the postwar period, with the monthly *Riron*, official organ of Minka. Referring to Marx's discussion in the first volume of *Capital*, Aikawa had proposed as the definition of technology the "organization of the means of labor" (*Organisation der Arbeitsmittel*). In 1933 he had written, "Thus, we call technology the organization of the means employed in productive labor in human society at a certain developmental stage. Accordingly, in the productive process technology is the objective element in contrast to human labor power."[166]

According to Taketani, Aikawa and others in this group were theoretically naive enough to believe that it would be insufficiently "materialist" to posit anything other than a solid substance as the locus of technology. That is why they adopted a definition that focused on the "means of labor," taking as part of their rationale the fundamental tenet of historical materialism that self-alienation under capitalism resulted from private ownership of the means of labor, and that therefore the aim of Marxism was to return those means of labor to the social control of the workers. In effect, this definition tended to limit technology to industrial machinery. Taketani responds that the tenet is unexceptionable but that did not mean that the means of labor could be equated with technology. Despite his own insistence that technology should be viewed as fundamentally objective rather than subjective,[167] he was clearly concerned to include in the definition of technology itself a powerful moment of practical subjectivity (*shutaisei*). From his perspective, the "objectivist" Marxists who edited the monthly *Riron*, including Matsumura Kazuto, Yamada Sakaji, Amakasu Sekisuke, and Kozai Yoshishige, were engaged in nothing more than "hermeneutics" (*kaishaku tetsugaku*).[168]

Taketani finally defines technology as "the conscious application of objective rule-governedness in human (productive) praxis."[169] For authority, he quotes Marx's *Capital* to the effect that "[i]n the labour-process, therefore, man's activity, with the help of the instruments of labour, effects an alteration, designed from the commencement, in the material worked upon. The process disappears in the product."[170] In Taketani's interpretation, this means that "technical praxis finds its essence in being planned (*keikakuteki*) and instrumental."[171]

In explicating the distinction between his definition and Aikawa's, Taketani cites with approval Ernst Cassirer's argument that technology had to be grasped functionally rather than substantially. Yet Cassirer had not gone far enough in that direction to satisfy Taketani, who, through his prewar scientific work, had developed a practical epistemology that included three dialectical stages: the immediate phenomenal, the substantialist, and the essentialist. Whereas Cassirer had separated the substantial from the functional, and proposed that as perception develops the former dissolves into the latter, Taketani argued that at the essentialist level praxis is included but at the same time "negated," with the result that "both the functional and the substantial are unified and transcended." In other words, it appears that in Taketani's self-professed "advanced logic of dialectical mediation," the subjective dimension of praxis is ultimately negated and recuperated in a Hegelian form of logocentrism. Indeed, this absorption into objectivity of subjective praxis is prefigured in the quote from Marx above in which "the process disappears in the product."

The dissolution of subjective into objective occurs also in his distinction between skill and technology. He argues that skill is subjective, psychological, and instilled through apprentice-type training, while technology is objective, social, intellectual, and communicable between individuals. Work, moreover, should be understood as the unification of skill and technology, in the sense that in work subjective, individual skills are perpetually dissolved into objective, social technology. When skills are objectified in technology, there are "constant gains not only in productivity but in quality."

Once Taketani links the objectification of praxis with gains in production, it becomes quite clear that the effect of his definition of technology is to infuse subjectivity into the productive forces themselves, thereby safely reabsorbing the negativity and undecidability of the subjective dimension into a positive totality.[172] His emphasis on development of the productive forces hints strongly at a conceptual link to the wartime theories of productive forces (*seisanryoku riron*) advanced by Ōkōchi Kazuo and Kazahaya Yasuji and flirted with by Ōtsuka Hisao.[173] In any case, his argument tends toward imbuing the productive forces not only with subjectivity but with Reason itself as a transhistorical entelechy. This was perceived by Ōi Tadashi, who writes concerning Taketani's definition of technology that "[o]riginally, what can be said to have as its 'essence' the qualities of being 'planning oriented' and 'instrumental' is, needless to say, 'reason,' not the 'labor process' or 'technical praxis.' To attribute to the 'labor process,' which is fundamentally natural and material, and also to some kind of 'praxis' an 'essence' that has the qualities of reason is, of course, idealist."[174] Further contributing to the impression of a pervasive rationality in Taketani's conception of the productive forces is his assertion that technicians themselves are "by nature rationalistic and essentially humanistic."[175]

Taketani's theory of subjectivity—as manifested most succinctly in his definition of technology—emphasizes the "rule-governedness" of both nature and society, and thus postulates that society/history is objectifiable and forms a unified totality. In so presuming, his theory takes its place within a certain Marxist tradition initiated in effect by Marx himself—for example, in the "Preface to *A Contribution to the Critique of Political Economy*" and in *Capital*—that emphasizes the coherence and rationality of history as an autonomous system. It might be argued that Taketani's approaches to epistemology and technology are more sophisticated than those presented by Engels in the *Anti-Duhring* and *Dialectics of Nature*, but he nevertheless adheres to the principle of essential continuity between nature and society, and his definition of technology remains consistent with Engels's famous statement that "[f]reedom does not consist in the dream of independence from natural laws, but in the knowledge of these laws, and in the possibility this gives of making them work towards definite ends."[176] Indeed, Taketani cites as the "guide" to his thought the aphorism from

Hegel—quoted approvingly by Engels and then by Lenin in *Materialism and Empirio-Criticism*[177]—to the effect that "freedom is the appreciation of necessity."[178]

Lacking in Taketani's account is a serious attempt to think through the role of the relations of production, especially class struggle. Clearly, "economic determinism, on the one hand, and the class struggle, on the other, propose two modes of explanation which are irreducible one to the other."[179] That is, class struggle implies antagonism, which, if genuine in the sense that its outcome is never decided beforehand, can never be encompassed within a fully objectified, fully understood system that operates according to internal laws. But there is little antagonism, class or otherwise, in Taketani's account, where subjectivity is always "subjected" in an objective totality.

Overall, Taketani's technological theory of subjectivity evokes an image of the smooth absorption of practical subjectivity through the objective development of the productive forces, amounting in the long run to the advance of instrumental reason. Presumably, Taketani also believed that steady development of the productive forces would at some point conflict with outmoded relations of production, which, as so many "fetters," would eventually "be burst asunder."[180] However, would not the opposite effect be equally possible? What, in Taketani's conception of technology, would prevent steady increases in productivity from playing an apologetic rather than critical role vis-à-vis the existing relations of production and the political regime? Might not that regime succeed in presenting itself and its productive relations as the "technically necessary organizational form of a rationalized society"?[181] The result would then be something like the industrial world as perceived by Marcuse in the 1960s:

> Today, domination perpetuates and extends itself not only through technology but *as* technology, and the latter provides the great legitimation of the expanding political power, which absorbs all spheres of culture.
>
> In this universe, technology also provides the great rationalization of the unfreedom of man and demonstrates the "technical" impossibility of being autonomous, of determining one's own life. For this unfreedom appears neither as irrational nor as political, but rather as submission to the technical apparatus which enlarges the comforts of life and increases the productivity of labor.[182]

Of course, such an outcome could not have been confidently anticipated in 1946. What, then, did Taketani's position as set forth in the report on the theory of technology and in later, related essays mean in the context of the postwar

Japanese democratic revolution and the active debate on *shutaisei*? What did his technological theory of *shutaisei* have to offer with respect to the politics of institutional transformation, united front, and the swiftly gathering popular movements that made themselves known through mass demonstrations, strikes, and production control? What were the "objective laws" that could be "consciously applied" in the drive to extend social and political equality through democratic revolution?

The postwar addendum to Taketani's report calls upon engineers and technicians to do their duty by throwing themselves into the nascent effort to democratize society. Whereas in the past, technical professionals had comprised a kind of worker aristocracy, a "free-floating" class that had served the capitalists by suggesting more efficient ways to exploit workers, now, at the moment of revolution, they should demonstrate their true *raison d'être* by joining the workers rather than helping exploit them. Through their own channels they could form horizontal connections among firms and cooperate with labor unions in advancing democratization of the economy.[183]

Taketani concludes that in order to promote solidarity and self-awareness among technical workers it was necessary to develop a precise and sophisticated understanding of their activities and the roles proper to them. This observation, in turn, leads him to propose the need for a prescriptive definition of technology that would help practitioners not only locate themselves correctly in relation to society but contribute to the development of technology itself. Although Taketani expressed his own views on politics, including support for a democratic front,[184] he did not show how these views followed from his theory of praxis. His early postwar call for self-consciousness and solidarity among technical professionals is potentially important, especially insofar as it could be interpreted to include intellectuals in general, but his technological theory of subjectivity per se fails to intersect meaningfully with the specifically political problematic of democratic revolution. That is, to the extent that politics—especially the politics of democratic revolution—is intrinsically a matter of choices in the midst of uncertainty,[185] and if (as present-day theorists of democracy have argued) the subject only emerges negatively through a break in the line of determinacy at precisely the point where society/history fails to maintain its autonomy and internal consistency,[186] Taketani's conception of a subject that is always dialectically sublated in the structure can only, from our present perspective, be considered counterproductive in relation to the process of democratic revolution.

That Taketani's persistent adherence to a technological concept of *shutaisei*—one that in some ways echoed Miki Kiyoshi's prodigious prewar and

wartime theorizing—did not seem especially anachronistic in the postwar milieu suggests both the range and limitations of the philosophical debate on subjectivity. Just as Umemoto's theory of the revolutionary's return to true humanity through sacrificial devotion to the proletariat recalled in structure if not
content Watsuji Tetsurō's prewar notion of the inevitable return to one's ethnic,
communal essence, Taketani's assimilation of *shutaisei* to the rational process
of expanding society's productive forces evokes the strongly Hegelian cast of
Miki's prewar philosophy of cooperativism. To put it somewhat crudely, the
thread connecting the prewar philosophers with their postwar counterparts is
their common conviction that, in the final instance, totality will prevail over
partiality and all particularity will be reabsorbed in the universal. In the postwar
instance, that totality is usually represented less in explicitly Hegelian than in
historical-materialist terms, but in function it is broadly analogous to the communal or idealist prewar versions.

   That is not to say that the debates between Umemoto and Matsumura or between Mashita Shin'ichi and his critical comrades were derivative or meaningless. Umemoto argued consistently that revolution could not occur without
conscious decision, and thus at the level of the subject reconfirmed the indeterminacy and historicity that are latent in Marxism. He tried to confront the political as well as the logical consequences of his convictions and defended them
against Matsumura Kazuto, an established philosophical spokesman for orthodox elements in the very Communist party Umemoto was in the process of joining. Nevertheless, for Umemoto, and for most other theorists of *shutaisei*, the
subjective decision had ultimately to be guaranteed by metahistorical necessity.

   Postwar Marxist theories of *shutaisei* introduced a potentially liberating
form of contestation into a left-wing political culture otherwise dominated by
mechanistic forms of determinism. Nevertheless, to a greater or lesser degree,
these theories were themselves trapped by the logic of supplementarity in that
each attempt to make a place for *shutaisei* seemed to require a renewed appeal
to the plenitude of metahistory as an external, determinate process that alone
could provide *shutaisei* with its necessity and meaning. But each time *shutaisei*
was reconnected to the supplement of an external history, its claim to free subjectivity was subverted by its own supplementary function as the completion of
a closed metahistorical system. Thus, subjectivity was repeatedly displaced by
contemplation, and active commitment to radical social change was often deferred.

$\mathcal{T}he\ \mathcal{M}odern\ \mathcal{E}thos$

> The principle of modern states has prodigious strength and depth because it allows the
> principle of subjectivity to progress to its culmination in the extreme of self-subsistent
> personal particularity, and yet at the same time brings it back to the substantive unity
> and maintains this unity in the principle of subjectivity itself.
>
> —G. W. F. Hegel[1]

Subjectivity was also an issue for postwar specialists in the behavioral and social sciences, including economic history, political science, sociology, and psychology. Historical materialism was extremely important in these disciplines as
well, albeit usually in admixture with such elements as American pragmatism,
the sociology of Max Weber, the psychology of Sigmund Freud, and European
and American political theory.[2] Practitioners often applied their knowledge and
analytical powers to questions that arose in relation to the politics of democratic
revolution. Moreover, along with a commitment not only to Marxism but to
positivist behavioral and social theory often went a preoccupation with one
or more conceptions of modernity or modernization, understood variously as
world-historical process, program for reform, or criterion of value. Therefore,
interpretations of the historical experience of Western Europe and the United
States figured importantly in social scientific approaches to subjectivity and
democratic revolution.

Forces of Production and the Modern Subject

> [T]he individual is interpellated as a (free) subject in order that he shall submit freely
> to the commandments of the Subject, i.e. in order that he shall (freely) accept his sub-
> jection. . . . There are no subjects except by and for their subjection. That is why they
> "work all by themselves."
>
> —Louis Althusser[3]

As an economic historian whose major research was focused on Western
Europe, Ōtsuka Hisao devoted major attention to the transition to capitalism,
with emphasis on the question of the historical motive force, or subject, that
leads society into that revolutionary mode of production. Moreover, as a Christian who was deeply impressed with Max Weber's emphasis on the economic
role of culture and religious ethics in the development of patterns of economic
life, he was also vitally concerned with the quality of subjectivity (*shutaisei*)
that had characterized that historical subject. Therefore, his early postwar essays formed a major component of the Japanese debate on subjectivity and
democratic revolution.

Ōtsuka was born in 1907 and brought up in Kyoto. In 1927 he matriculated at Tokyo Imperial University and six months later began attending the Sunday bible classes led by the Japanese Christian leader, Uchimura Kanzō, a habit Ōtsuka continued until Uchimura's death in 1930. Indeed, Ōtsuka remained a committed adherent of the Japanese Christian Mukyōkai, or Non-Church movement, throughout his adult life. After postgraduate study, he lectured at Rikkyō and Hōsei universities. Then in 1939 he was invited back to Tokyo Imperial University, where he taught European economic history until his retirement in 1968.

By the end of the war, Ōtsuka had published several major works, including *Iwayuru zenkiteki shihon naru hanchū ni tsuite* (On the Category of So-Called Early Capital [1935]), *Nōson no orimoto to toshi no orimoto* (Rural and Urban Varieties of Textile Manufacture [1938]), and *Kindai Ōshū keizaishi josetsu* (Introduction to the Economic History of Modern Europe [1944]). Upon Japan's surrender, he brought his background in European economic history directly to bear on the urgent questions of agenda and method that were intrinsic to the process of democratic revolution in postwar Japan.

Productive Forces: East and West

Ōtsuka believed that postwar social and economic reconstruction had to be based on a correct understanding of how modernization had occurred endogenously in Western Europe. This was especially the case in view of the common belief that Japanese rural society was still in a feudal absolutist state comparable to Europe two or three centuries earlier.[4] In one of his first postwar essays, he compared contemporary Japanese farmers with those in England in the sixteenth and seventeenth centuries and drew certain conclusions regarding the proper priorities for democratic revolution in the economy. The very idea that English agriculture in the sixteenth and seventeenth centuries could provide a useful comparison to Japanese counterparts in the mid-twentieth century might seem implausible in retrospect. Yet the worldview that made such comparisons seem reasonable—that is, the vision of a basically unilinear, world-historical march of progress through more or less prescribed stages—was reinforced from different angles in the early postwar period by both Marxist and bourgeois theories of history. Ōtsuka's essay introduced a number of the themes that would characterize his early postwar line of argument.

According to Ōtsuka, a major objective factor differentiating English farmers "under the feudal-absolutist monarchy of the sixteenth and seventeenth centuries" from Japanese farmers at the end of World War II was the much larger scale of English agriculture. English yeoman cultivators, who were called "full villein," typically occupied and tilled about thirty acres with draft animals and a heavy plow, and even lower-class "cotters" often farmed from two to six acres. However, from a Japanese perspective, the English farmers' product seemed extremely small in proportion to the land area they had cultivated and the amount of seed they had sowed. In other words, the productivity of English farmland was comparatively low in the sixteenth and seventeenth centuries, whereas in Japan it was very high. Nevertheless, this did not seem to mean that the English farmers had been poor, at least not in comparison with Japanese farmers. Indeed, one was able to find plausible, contemporary accounts that commented evocatively on the prosperity of English farmers, especially in the yeoman stratum. If their land had been so unproductive, why had they been prosperous? Ōtsuka's answer is that even though the productivity of land had been very low, that of the English farmers' labor had been very high. This ratio was the result primarily of objective factors such as geography: In Western Europe, climate and soil quality had dictated livestock husbandry and extensive farming, while in monsoon Asia, intensive, wet-rice agriculture demanded only simple tools but was able to support a large population. Thus, in the former case the productivity of the individual farmer had been enhanced, while in the latter it stagnated. English yeoman farmers were able to see a relationship between effort and prosperity, and this encouraged their development of a work ethic. The result, in direct contrast to the Japanese case, was the productive ethos of diligence and frugality Ōtsuka associated with the "modern type" of human being, and it was this ethos that prepared the English "upper-level farmers and small to medium landlords" for their role as the social subject—or motive force—of modernization. When tempered by the religious atmosphere of Puritanism, the English yeomanry "gave birth from among their number to the stratum of modern industrial capitalists"[5] as well as to the industrial worker class.

Yet Ōtsuka rejected the conclusion that this difference between Japanese and English conditions constituted a geographic or climatic destiny that was incontrovertible. The legacy of objective conditions could be overcome, not only by means of land reform directed to the creation of a stratum of free, independent Japanese farmers, but also through emphasis on the cultivation of a modern ethos among the ordinary people who would have to form the "subjects" of any viable liberal democracy. Therefore, a program of democratic reconstruction of the economy would have to include not only a reform of actual, "objective" ownership but also a comprehensive program of education aimed at reforming the subjective mentality of the people.

Ōtsuka's essay raised a number of points which he developed further in other works, written both before and after 1945. These included an elaboration of the contention that the leading forces in the formation of modern capitalism were not to be found among the premodern merchant scions but rather among lower-level producers such as the English yeoman farmers; that not only objective factors, such as climate and technology, but such subjective factors as value orientation and ethos were essential to that formation; and, perhaps most important, that the transition to capitalism was a world-historical process whose fundamental pattern had been established in the Western European countries and the United States.

The Subject of Capitalism

The upper stratum of the peasantry—yeomanry and small- or medium-scale landlords—played a central role in Ōtsuka's theory regarding the indigenous origins of capitalism in Europe, especially in England. That is, his prewar studies had led him to side with Max Weber rather than Lujo Brentano, Werner Sombart, or R. H. Tawney with respect to capitalism's human subject: rather than by the merchant class and merchant capital, the transition to industrial capitalism had been led by the petty bourgeois producers. Ōtsuka's theory had immediate implications for the early postwar program of democratic revolution because it bore upon the subjective dimension—the ethos—of capitalism and, by extension, of liberal democracy as well. That is, he held up the petty-bourgeois ethos of the seventeenth-century English yeomanry as the authoritative model of the kind of modern *shutaisei* that should be propagated in postwar Japan.

The basic coordinates for Ōtsuka's approach had been established by Marx:

> The transition out of the feudal mode of production (toward the modern one) takes two different forms. The producers rebel against the natural economy of the farm or the guild-like medieval urban industry, and become merchants and then capitalists. This is the way that actually results in a revolutionary transformation. In the other, merchants directly take up production. Historically speaking, this latter way actually functions as a transition, but . . . in and of itself this method does not lead to a transformation of the mode of production, but rather preserves it, and maintains it as a prerequisite to its own survival. (*Capital*, vol. 3, chap. 20)

Marx himself had not directly addressed the question of values or ethics in this connection. The issue for him was one of social class: which class had been the subject, or agent, of early capitalism. Of course, Marx resisted any suggestion that a particular entity or social group, especially the "capitalists," *created* capitalism. Rather, "The historic process is not the result of capital, but its prerequisite. By means of this process the capitalist then inserts himself as a (historical) middleman between landed property, or between any kind of property, and labour. History ignores the sentimental illusions about capitalist and labourer forming an association, etc.; nor is there a trace of such illusions in the development of the concept of capital."[6]

For Marx, capitalists as well as free laborers were the products of impersonal social forces. Nevertheless, he clearly implies that the social carriers of capitalism in its early stages should be understood to be, not the early merchant class, but rather ascendant elements of the producing class, that is, artisans and agriculturalists who dirtied their hands in the material formation of goods.

Ōtsuka agreed but was not content to rely on Marx's authority in this respect. His own research in European economic development had convinced him that the "early-merchant" road to capitalism was ultimately incomplete, indeed "false"; it did not have thoroughly revolutionary implications for the social structure. Therefore, the latter, "producer-type" road was the true way to an entirely new form of society:

> Take late-fifteenth-century England, for example. The old, feudal landholding system (landlord system) was already prematurely breaking up and a stratum of free, independent, self-managing farmers (especially the yeomanry) was appearing. At the new stage, they were to become the agents of new productive forces, and in a corresponding manner were also emerging as commodity producers and accumulating monetary wealth. Thus the producing stratum—I will call it the middle-producer stratum—became prosperous and out of its midst gradually emerged industrial capital. . . . This is none other than the origin of the actual revolutionary transformation of modernization, and is the orthodox road to the historical formation of a modern social structure.[7]

In his earlier works on European economic history, Ōtsuka had argued, more precisely, that *both* capitalists and modern workers had emerged from this predominantly rural, "middle-producer stratum," and this insight was later confirmed independently by the English historian Maurice Dobb.[8]

Ōtsuka's approach to European and Japanese economic history was to become extremely influential in the postwar era, to the point of generating a so-called Ōtsuka-school of history, related more or less to the Kōza-ha, or Lectures Faction, as it had formed in the course of the prewar Marxist debate on Japanese capitalism. Indeed, one major figure in the Kōza-ha, Takahashi Kōhachirō, carried the analysis associated with Ōtsuka into the postwar era and brought it to international attention. According to Takahashi, the Prussian and Japanese forms of feudalism had been able to generate capitalism only via the incomplete merchant route, whereas France and England had followed the producer route.

This meant that in Japan and Germany there had emerged an alliance between capital and feudal absolutism that was inimical to the establishment of modern democracy.[9] Ōtsuka shared this view.

However, Ōtsuka was never entirely satisfied with purely economic analysis. In order to get at the question not only of the social subject of capitalism but of the particular mentality, or quality of subjectivity, that had to characterize that subject, Ōtsuka turned to Max Weber in search of a supplementary account of the superstructural dimension of capitalist development. In his *Protestant Ethic and the Spirit of Capitalism*, Weber had intimated that Protestant faith and practice were conducive to a work ethic among employees as well as employers. Ōtsuka seized upon this consistency between Marx's conception of the authentic road to capitalism—that in which petty producers become merchants and eventually capitalists—and the Weberian account of the spread of the "spirit of capitalism" among petty producers and workers. Just as Marx's revolutionary route out of feudalism implied that the social agents of capitalism were to be found not among rich merchants but primarily among the petty bourgeoisie, Weber had given evidence for the spirit of capitalism among not only capitalists but those who worked with their hands.[10]

The "Spirit" of Capitalism

In a series of essays written between 1943 and 1946, Ōtsuka distinguished meticulously between Weber's concept of the "spirit of capitalism" and the similar term, "capitalist spirit," that was used by Lujo Brentano. Directed primarily against those who had criticized Weber from the perspective developed by Brentano, Tawney and Sombart, Ōtsuka's essays sought to show that such criticisms were premised on a fundamental misunderstanding of Weber's argument. According to Ōtsuka, Brentano had defined the "capitalist spirit" as "nothing but the '*Streben nach grösstmöglichen Gewinn*' ('aspiration for the greatest possible gain'), or in one word '*Erwerbsgier*' ('acquisitive-greed'), an expression used over and over again in [Brentano's] writings." Similarly, Tawney had described the bourgeois ethic as the "temper of single-minded concentration on pecuniary gain."[11] These definitions as such could not be considered wrong, but in Ōtsuka's view they had little in common with Weber's concept of the "spirit of capitalism."

First, these notions of capitalist spirit differed from Weber's in that they applied only to capitalist entrepreneurs and thus excluded wage earners, whose work ethic and calculation of wages Weber's concept of the "spirit of capitalism" had been designed to encompass. Here, of course, a parallel is strongly implied between the abortive, merchant-centered route from feudalism to capitalism mentioned by Marx and the merchant-capitalist—centered "spirit" defined by Brentano, Tawney, and others.

> Weber *basically* denies [the] allegedly continuous relationship between the commercial-financial capitalism "as old as man's history itself" and the industrial capitalism which characterizes the modern age. Rather, Weber contends that, speaking in the historical context, the two had a mutually repulsive, *conflicting* relationship at least in Western Europe during the early phase of modern capitalism, as can be supported by undisputable historical data. . . . Where, then was the movement born which was to develop into industrial capitalism—or, in Weberian terminology, the utilization of capital in industry based on a rational organization of labor? . . . The dominant, or rather decisive force for the formation of industrial capitalism *as a social system* . . . was no other than the activities of the *"gewerblicher Mittelstand"* ("industrial middle stratum"), which developed out of late feudal society (or *"ständischer Patrimonialstaat"* to comply with Weber's terminology strictly). They were, further, in *direct* confrontation with the old *merchant* capitalism. The richer upper part of this industrial middle stratum transformed themselves to the core of modern industrial entrepreneurs, while the poorer lower part formed the core of wage laborers. The "ethos" born by this stratum, as long as its activities served progressive causes in historical context, was what Weber termed the "spirit" of capitalism.[12]

Second, Weber's spirit included an element of ethics, or ethos, while theirs did not. That is, for Weber, "profit-motivation *per se* becomes an 'ethical obligation' and assumes the 'character of an *ethically* colored maxim for the conduct of life.' . . . Weber takes the stand that, while the '"spirit" of capitalism' certainly contains elements of profit-motivation, the structural element which acts upon that motivation to direct its impact toward the formation of *modern* capitalism, particularly rational *industrial organization (Betrieb)* supported by wage labor, is neither profit-motivation *per se* nor acquisitive-*greed*, but a particular '*Ethos*' which embraces and gives direction to the profit-motivation."[13]

Ōtsuka does not neglect to cite Weber's ironic caveat that, in effect, the "'spirit' of capitalism" reaches maturity "just as the ethos of worldly asceticism (*die innerweltliche Askese*), having originally been formed in the ascetic Protestantism, begins gradually to lose its religious enthusiasm with 'acquisition' taking its place as the rallying force."[14] That is, in what amounted to an "inversion of values," mature capitalism had superseded the Protestant ethic and was now driven by pursuit of profit for its own sake. But why had Ōtsuka been so concerned to differentiate between Brentano's purely profit-oriented "capitalist spirit" and Weber's ethical "spirit of capitalism" if, in the end, the latter was also to end up as merely a variety of "acquisitive greed"? Ōtsuka addresses this issue by arguing that Weber's own focus of concern went beyond the explanation of capitalism in the narrow sense. That is, in Ōtsuka's view, Weber's object of investigation is not merely capitalist economic relations but the "inner roles" played by the spirit of capitalism,[15] especially in catalyzing an *"ethos* which looks upon work in a worldly calling as a duty and prompts rational and organizational devotion, in short the 'ethic of a calling' (*Berufsethik*)."[16] That is, the kind of capitalist mentality that developed among producers through the mediation of the Protestant ethic was an "inverted ethical order" in which externally people are devoted entirely to private acquisition while inwardly they firmly believe that by turning a profit they are "making a great contribution to the 'whole' (society, nation, and world)."[17] Only such an ethic would contribute to the "task of building a '*Betrieb*' ('industrial organization') . . . or, a business enterprise based upon rational organization of labor."[18] Rather than "undisciplined *liberum arbitrium*"—an "attitude which sees and judges the world consciously in terms of the worldly interests of the *individual ego*"—Weber (and Ōtsuka) believed that rational *Betrieb* could emerge only from disciplined individualism, forged through the ethos of worldly asceticism, and devoted to the social whole.[19] It was precisely the latter form of individualism that Ōtsuka designated as the "modern human type" and recommended as the ethical model appropriate to postwar Japan's era of democratic revolution.

Weber concludes his essay on a strikingly pessimistic note, evoking a contemporary situation in which "the technical and economic conditions of machine production" had come to dominate like an "iron cage" the lives of all who inhabited them. For his part, in a situation in which he was in effect prescribing an ethos of worldly asceticism as a fundamental component of Japan's postwar democratic revolution, Ōtsuka apparently felt constrained to suggest the possibility of a brighter future, in which that productive ethic that was part of the spirit of capitalism "may be called up again and may, under an entirely new guise, effect a great impact on the course of history."[20]

It is worth noting here that, despite his indebtedness to Marxian concepts and assumptions, Ōtsuka portrays capitalism in terms not of "exploitation" in the manner of Marx, but rather of "the 'smooth' and 'rapid' formation of 'a bright and abundant modern society (= modern productive forces).'"[21] Indeed, he seemed to look forward to a transition from capitalism to socialism that would be equally "smooth," by virtue of being mediated (as will be discussed below) by a new economic ethic that would deemphasize the profit motive and cause people to work directly on behalf of the social whole.

"Objectivist" Response

Ōtsuka's colleague at the University of Tokyo, historian Hayashi Kentarō, was one of those who took issue with what he felt was Ōtsuka's overemphasis on the "spirit" or ethos of historical subjects. Hayashi was born in Tokyo in 1913 and first came in contact with Marxism as a student at the First Higher School. He studied European history at Tokyo Imperial University, and while there was a leader of student protests against dismissal of the liberal professor Takigawa Yukitoki. After graduating in 1935 he remained at the University of Tokyo as an assistant before returning to First Higher School as lecturer and then professor from 1936 until the end of the war. During this time, he participated in editing the Marxist historical journal *Rekishigaku kenkyū* (Historical Research), and in 1942 he published an essay in *Chūō kōron* criticizing the "philosophy of world history" espoused at the time by Kōyama Iwao. He was drafted in December 1944 and spent the remaining eight months of war in uniform.

In 1947 Hayashi was made assistant professor and then professor of history at the University of Tokyo. In the early postwar period he belonged to the Rekishi Kagaku Kenkyūjo (Historical Science Research Institute) led by the Labor-Farmer school (Rōnō-ha) theorist Sakisaka Itsurō, but in the 1950s he turned toward what came to be called neoconservatism.[22] He was appointed president of the University of Tokyo in 1973, and in 1983 began representing the conservative Liberal-Democratic Party as a legislator in the House of Councillors.

In early postwar debates Hayashi generally sought to adhere to the sort of universalistic, social scientific position on Japanese capitalism that was often typical of the Labor-Farmer school of Marxists, and therefore reacted against Ōtsuka's exceptionalist preoccupation with Japan's premodernity. Hayashi introduces his essay as follows:

> Among the issues most frequently discussed by historians and, indeed, scholars in general in Japan today is the problem of how to define the essence of so-called modern society. The starting point for consideration of this problem is the perception that Japanese society is retarded in comparison to Western societies, and can be characterized as premodern or "feudal" in nature. Therefore, attention tends to be focused on those Western societies against which Japan is contrasted, and also on the nature of the capitalism that informs the basic social structure of

those societies. Of course, it is indisputable that a capitalist system also holds sway over contemporary Japan. Thus, the key objective is to locate the defining features of the Western, so-called pure, capitalism from which the peculiar capitalism of our country diverges.

A single, powerful perspective dominates this issue in Japan. That is the perspective developed by our country's preeminent economic historian, Ōtsuka Hisao.[23]

First, Hayashi takes issue with Ōtsuka's interpretation of Marx on the transition from feudalism to capitalism, criticizing the "undialectical" manner in which he believes Ōtsuka reifies Marx's distinction between the merchant and producer "roads." Ōtsuka had turned them into separate types, or categories, in order to disparage one as "false," the other "true," whereas, according to Hayashi, Marx had treated them more subtly. Just to show that Marx had not entirely rejected the potential importance of the merchant route, Hayashi quotes selections including the following:

> There is no doubt—and it is precisely this fact which has led to wholly erroneous conceptions—that in the 16th and 17th centuries the great revolutions that took place in commerce in conjunction with the geographical discoveries, and which speeded the development of merchant's capital, constituted principal elements in the transition from feudal to capitalist mode of production.[24]

According to Hayashi, "the difference between Marx and Ōtsuka is that whereas Marx sees the history of capitalism as centering on capitalist relations of production, the emergence of free labor, and the divestiture of the means of production from the direct producers, Ōtsuka consistently focuses his narrative on a distinction between the *categories* of commercial capital and industrial capital."[25] Rather than hypostatizing them as categories and seeking to vindicate one rather than the other, Ōtsuka should rather ask how these tendencies interacted in real historical circumstances:

> The problem is how products are transformed into commodities and how the formation of domestic markets tends to commodify labor power. In other words, why does commercial capital, which is originally unrelated entirely to the relations of production, become at a certain juncture bound up with changes in the relations of production— this is what we must investigate. Therefore, the issue has to do entirely with the development of the objective forces of production.[26]

But instead, Ōtsuka had isolated his "types" and treated them in an either/or manner. He had understood "the dialectic of the transition from commercial capital to industrial capital in an extremely mechanistic manner."[27]

Hayashi's main point relates to the identity and ethos of the "real entities" which Ōtsuka found to be the subjects of early capitalism, especially the agricultural producers represented by the English yeomanry. According to Hayashi, as Ōtsuka focused increasingly on the subjective qualities of these entities, he was ultimately led to argue that the "human type" determined society while being itself determined by ethos (i.e., "Protestant, particularly Calvinist, religious belief ").

> As the basis for this argument Ōtsuka refers repeatedly to Max Weber's *The Protestant Ethic and the Spirit of Capitalism*. These essays undoubtedly constitute a classical study of the role played by Calvinism in the era of the English bourgeois revolution, and the relationship that Calvinist ethical teachings bore to capitalism. But we must always be aware when reading Weber of the philosophical standpoint presupposed by his theories. As is well known, that standpoint is Rickert's neo-Kantianism. . . . [Moreover] in this work Weber is merely discussing the relationship between the Protestant ethic and capitalism, and does not claim any cause-effect link. Nor does he propose that any sort of spirit defines society's essence. Weber himself is careful to include caveats to that effect, but it seems that wittingly or unwittingly Ōtsuka has proceeded right down the road that Weber warns against. Ōtsuka does indeed take this Protestant ethic as the determinant of European capitalism.[28]

For Hayashi, on the contrary, "The fundamental impetus for the transition from the feudal to the capitalist mode of production must always be sought in the forces of production understood as objective material conditions."[29]

Hayashi's conclusion emphasizes science, materialism, and the historian's craft: "[H]istorians . . . must give primacy to objective reality, and to that extent they must be materialists. Only then can they make a contribution to the solution of the question most pregnant with 'spirit,' that of the 'subject.'" [30] In a manner analogous to Matsumura Kazuto's in response to Umemoto, Hayashi seems concerned to vindicate a more "orthodox" form of economic reductionism than he finds in Ōtsuka's work. From Hayashi's perspective, any attention to the subject or subjectivity had to be carefully subordinated to an account of "objective" economic forces and structure.

The Modern Ethos as Shutaisei

Ōtsuka devoted a number of his early postwar essays to the task of illustrating what he believed to be the essential aspects of a normative model of *shutaisei*. As he did so, he often seemed to go beyond his earlier, supplementary appropriation of Weber to place primary emphasis on the formation of subjectivity through ideology: What was the most important element in the expansion of productivity in society? What qualities distinguished the subject of liberal, capitalist development, and in what sense was that subject equipped to lead the democratic revolution?

In one essay, he contrasted the "modern human type," as illustrated in the life and writings of Benjamin Franklin, against the prevailing social tendency in Japan, which appeared to him to be dominated by "*oyagokoro*," or paternalistic concern. Quoting Franklin's reflections at the beginning of his autobiography, to the effect that "[h]aving emerged from the poverty and obscurity in which I was born and bred, to a state of affluence and some degree of reputation in the world . . . ," Ōtsuka comments, "From the time he was a poor youth [Franklin] seems to have known no servility and to have been equipped with an air of independence and freedom unaffected by established convention." However, when Japanese read his works they thought Franklin to be "strange and eccentric." That was because of the Japanese ethos of *oyagokoro*, which Ōtsuka describes as follows:

> Those above us in a leadership capacity are supposed to have the au-
> thority of parents. The people, or those "below," must be obedient to
> this authority. The leaders who have this authority as parents show
> "love and mercy" toward those below, who obey them. In any case, ac-
> cording to this pattern the people are treated as immature. Indeed . . . to
> be immature is considered a virtue. . . . [Therefore] it can be said that
> the people of our country have no inner originality (*jihatsusei*).[31]

In Ōtsuka's view, such an ethos would seriously impede democratic revolution. In England, where, Ōtsuka believed, modern values had emerged quite smoothly and naturally, "a decisive segment of the people was forged into the modern human type, and as that segment destroyed the old, feudal order it began at the same time to build a new, modern and democratic regime." The background for this natural emergence had been religious as well as economic:

> It was none other than Puritanism (ascetic Protestantism) that began to
> spread like wildfire among the yeoman stratum and eventually forged
> them into the modern human type. The Reformation had instilled a
> deep modesty and thorough obedience toward God. Along with this,

however, came the rejection of all servility and unreasonable, blind
obedience to other human beings. The Reformation taught brotherly
love of infinite depth—not sensual love, but rather the type of love
made possible only by the thorough denial of sensuality—and at the
same time, nay, for that reason, disseminated among the people a tendency to hold one's head high and always face others with powerful
independence and freedom, thereby transforming their character.[32]

In the United States, the ethos of the modern human type had been best articulated by Benjamin Franklin, who showed that "[i]nner originality (*jihatsusei*),
rationality, consciousness of social solidarity and, pervading them, a realistic
attitude of emphasizing economic life—if these are viewed very abstractly, they
manifest the various attributes of the modern human type."[33]

In Japan, on the other hand, democratization was being imposed from outside rather than discovered from within. Far from a "decisive segment of the
people becoming able to objectify its own views as a 'will of the people,'" in
contemporary Japan there were virtually no "modern human types" who were
possessed of democratic *shutaisei*. Therefore, it was essential to initiate a broad
program of education designed to instill the virtues associated with the "modern
human type": diligence and frugality, along with personal autonomy, reason-
ableness, social consciousness, and a consummate devotion to economic values.
When a "decisive portion of the people is molded into this modern human type,
the results will be modern productivity and a potential for managerial construction, along with the endogenous formation of a democratic regime."[34]

Ōtsuka often portrayed the subjective *mentalité* of this capitalist subject by
means of another sort of contrastive strategy, one based on Marx's distinction
between the two roads to capitalism, "early-merchant" and "producer." Ōtsuka
took each road to imply a particular subjective type, or ethos, and in his early
postwar essays made it clear that the development of capitalism in Japan had not
followed the "producer road" and therefore was in the thrall of values directly
inimical to the truly modern ethos that the producer road had historically entailed.

Ōtsuka drew an illustration from seventeenth-century Holland. He tells the
story of the Dutch merchant Bijland, who in 1638 openly supplied weapons and
ammunition to his country's enemies because he felt morally justified in doing
whatever would bring a profit. This merchant espoused an "ethos of naked egoism" that, according to Ōtsuka, was by no means unusual in the European environment of the time. Such individuals ignored the welfare of the commonweal
in pursuit of selfish gain.[35]

In order to relate this egoistic mentality to liberalism, he points out that occurring at about the same time in Holland was a religious dispute between the Libertines and the Calvinists. Ōtsuka points out that, although religious in essence, this dispute had ramifications that touched on various aspects of political, social, and economic life. The Libertines, who were closely connected with the "rich, feudal—that is, aristocratic—merchant stratum that had its base in Amsterdam," believed in toleration with respect to the ethos of "naked egoism" and spoke out only weakly against its excesses. On the other hand, the Calvinists, who indirectly represented the "middle class of producers" including farmers and small to medium industrialists, openly and vigorously criticized the unimpeded competition for profit, and instead "professed strict self-control according to 'conscience.'"[36] Indeed, according to Ōtsuka, the "Calvin-type" people

> have within them true "freedom," a "freedom of conscience" that moves them from inside, and they discipline their thought, speech and behavior in accord with that free conscience. Also within the Calvin-type individual is always "original sin," and "thoughts of the flesh," that is, sensuous desires which incessantly tempt and draw them toward antisocial behavior. Nevertheless, such individuals "exhaust their heart, spirit and thoughts," and "chastise the body," in order to suppress those desires, striving to follow "conscience" and the inner voice of "freedom.". . . In any case, only when a decisive segment of the people is forged into this human type, which possesses "freedom of conscience" and goes through a social "new creation," can liberalism of the true sort take shape.[37]

Clearly, in Ōtsuka's view, the liberalism of the Libertines and urban merchants (a liberalism he attributed to "Renaissance-type freedom") corresponded to what he had described in his historical theory as the "early-merchant road" to capitalism, while the ascetic Calvinist liberalism (based on "Puritan-type freedom"), embraced by the "middle class of producers" and equivalent to the Puritanism of the English yeomanry, corresponded to the "producer road."[38] In his view, only the latter could lead to the overthrow of the old regime and the establishment of an authentic modernity. Therefore, rather than the "freedom for egoism" of the Libertines, Ōtsuka sought to foster among the Japanese people (a secularized form of) the Calvinist ethos of individual autonomy based on freedom of conscience and suppression of selfish desire. The means was to be "education," in the broad sense, which would impact on "all sectors of social life." Such an education should not be limited narrowly to secular affairs, but should ideally result in "something deeper, like the attainment of the *broadest possible religiosity or faith.*"[39]

Daniel Defoe's *Robinson Crusoe* also provided a model of modern ethos, in this case illustrated with reference to the English early industrial bourgeoisie. Delving into the plot of the novel, Ōtsuka recalls Crusoe's father's injunctions that Crusoe should give up his life as a wanderer and settle down in the social stratum in which he was brought up, a stratum he described as "that middle State, or what might be called the upper Station of Low Life,"[40] which was the status "most conducive to human happiness." In Ōtsuka's view, Defoe believed throughout his life that the members of this stratum "carried on their shoulders the prosperity and welfare of their countrymen," and portrayed characters like Crusoe on the model of that stratum's values. This was also precisely the group that had become the historical subject of the English industrial revolution. "In my view," Ōtsuka says,

> the way of life followed by Defoe's Crusoe on that island was none other than that of the English early industrial bourgeoisie (the petty bourgeois stratum). That is, it could be said that once Robinson drifted to the island, he repented socially as well as religiously, and in accord with his father's admonitions returned to the lifeways of the English petty bourgeoisie. As I have said, this was the early industrial bourgeoisie that had already in Defoe's time emerged at the forefront of world history and had become the backbone of English civil society; it would eventually become the leading subjective force in the construction of the enormous, modern productive forces . . . in the industrial revolution, and in the process would split clearly to become both the great industrial bourgeoisie and the proletariat.[41]

What values and way of life did this stratum (as represented in Crusoe) espouse? According to Ōtsuka, Crusoe "formed his life in an extremely rational, planned manner."[42] He showed "diligence, frugality, meticulousness; a consistently autonomous, rational organization of life . . . and a remarkably 'strong' and vigorous constructive ability." Ōtsuka goes on: "To borrow an expression from Max Weber, these comprised the very 'spirit of capitalism' that constituted the subjective motive force in the formation of expansive, modern production."[43] In the aggregate these values also represented major aspects of the modern "human type" (*seishinteki ningen ruikei*) Ōtsuka wished to instill in the Japanese people.

Self-Discipline and the Social Whole

The modernist perspective outlined by Ōtsuka must be admired in some ways. It showed itself able to sustain a critical standpoint in relation to the direction of change in postwar Japan down to the 1950s and 1960s. It was also capable of winning and retaining support for such a standpoint among Christians and other liberals. Nevertheless, its limitations as an approach to democratic revolution are perhaps clearer now than ever before.

First, Ōtsuka considered democratization to be derivative of socioeconomic development. Therefore, he failed to perceive the need for a distinctly political space in democratic society where free decisions—and political subjects of those decisions—take shape precisely because of the failure of the social to function fully as a determining totality. In the early postwar period Ōtsuka considered the subject of democratic revolution to be more or less synonymous with the subject of modern economic (capitalist) development, and the central role he granted to the petty bourgeois ethos in the composition of that subject offers an ironic contrast to the contemporary tendency of other Marxists more closely affiliated to the Party, such as Matsumura Kazuto and Nakano Shigeharu, to disparage the petty bourgeois identity. Yet it should be emphasized that Ōtsuka is not necessarily suggesting, in the manner of the first narrative of historical materialism conceived by Marx, that the bourgeoisie itself should lead Japan's democratic revolution. Despite the importance he gives to the ascetic work ethic associated with the petty bourgeois class in England and Holland, he believes that the subject of the ongoing Japanese revolution could not be the middle class in the narrow sense but rather had to be the nation—the "people" as a whole, especially industrial and agricultural workers and other producers. In Ōtsuka's theory of the development of industrial capitalism in Europe it was the small producer stratum—e.g., yeomanry, then early industrial bourgeoisie—that had been animated by the "spirit of capitalism" and had given rise to both capitalists and wage workers.[44] The "spirit of capitalism" was not just the property of the capitalists. Accordingly, in discussing the importance of the modern ethos in postwar Japan, Ōtsuka consistently demanded that such an ethos be embraced by the majority of the people, or at least its "critical segment," and especially the "laboring masses" (*kinrō taishū*).[45] He wrote, "The people [*minshū*]—and it is essential that it *be* the people—must be formed into a broadly modern, democratic pattern."[46] Accordingly, in his proposal for a "broad" educational program he consistently emphasized the importance of labor unions and farmers' cooperatives as the vehicles for this education.[47] In that regard, Ōtsuka's focus on a conception of "the people" that emphasized the workers and farmers is at least superficially consistent with the call in the '32, Theses for a bourgeois-democratic revolution on the cusp of transition to a socialist revolution led by the working class.

Given Ōtsuka's theory of the endogenous development of capitalism in Europe through the subjective agency of the agricultural and small industrial producers, and the important role played in that development by ascetic Protestant values, it was natural that he should connect early capitalist subjectivity with a liberal ethos of emphasis on individual autonomy, religious and other freedoms, and civil rights. In Ōtsuka's view, this ethos would itself be conducive to the establishment of democratic institutions.

In one of his earliest postwar essays he seems to argue the need for a subject specifically of democratic revolution. He says, "[Japan's reconstruction] can only happen through the formation of a political subject," and he emphasizes "the subjective, instrumental significance of politics in the process of achieving economic reconstruction." However, although he pays lip service to the central-ity of the political in the process of democratic revolution, he generally ap-proaches that dimension in terms of the *pre*political need to "educate the people to fit the modern, democratic human type" and also to create "a material basis for this type of person."[48] Indeed, he very often conflates the socioeconomic subject of production with the political subject of democratic revolution:

> The people must develop an internal consciousness of respect for the human being. Rather than having it bestowed upon them in the manner of premodern natural law, they must themselves become "a free people" who, in a self-disciplined manner, will maintain a forward-looking social order and enhance the common welfare. Only such a "free people" can construct democracy from the bottom up and at the same time autonomously develop the productive forces which will pro-vide the material foundation for democratic reconstruction of the economy. Such a "free people" is itself the decisive element in the for-mation of modern forces of production. Indeed, it *is* those forces.[49]

The implication is clear: in a manner broadly comparable to Taketani Mitsuo's submersion of subjectivity in technology and, by a different route, the orthodox Marxists' reliance on the natural extension of socioeconomic class interests to form a subject for the democratic revolution, Ōtsuka conceives of the genera-tion of political subjectivity as intrinsic to the maturation of the productive forces themselves, implying that development via the producer road will auto-matically reproduce the modern human type and thus provide a subject fit to lead the democratic revolution. It was, therefore, a subject *for* democratic revo-lution, not *of* it.

Second, an unfortunate by-product of Ōtsuka's reliance on European models and analyses of modernization is his uncritical adoption of the German Orientalist view of "Asiatic" society and mentality. Focusing for the most part on China and India, a line of German thinkers who were of central importance to early postwar Japanese thought, including Hegel, Marx, and Weber, had perpetuated a view of "Asia" as not only stagnant but devoid of the inner subjectivity that in their view was the hallmark of the modern. Hegel posited that China represented the "childhood of history," a land where "nothing subjective in the shape of disposition, Conscience, formal Freedom, is recognized";[50] Marx tried to account for the apparent absence of historical change in India by developing the model of an "Asiatic mode of production";[51] and Max Weber searched in vain through Chinese religion and ethics for an adequate analogue to the inner goad to achievement provided in Europe by the Protestant ethic.[52] Ōtsuka borrows the Weberian version of this German Orientalism as a way of summing up the backward Japanese social atmosphere:

> I have often pointed out that at the center of the problem of human types is the matter of ethos, or ethical pattern. In comparing the modern Western European ethos against the Asiatic ethos, Weber characterized the former as an "ethic of inner values" [*innerliche Würde*] and the latter as an "ethic of outer values" [*äusserliche Würde*]. According to him, in the Asiatic ethic, "saving face" and otherwise preserving appearances takes priority. What matters most is procedure. Inner values are of little concern; rather, the level of external refinement, one's rank and position, ceremonials of propriety and etiquette, fine clothing and hauteur—these consume the energies of Asian societies. There is no place here for the concept of original sin. Therefore, the problem of ethical "evil" gets transformed somehow into a matter of aesthetics. Actions are censured only for being "impolite," "vulgar," "filthy," or "unmannerly."
>
> In contrast to this, the ethics of modern European society are deeply rooted in the internality of the individual. No matter how respectable something might appear on the outside, it is not thought necessarily to be high in value. Conversely, regardless of how lacking in outer respectability—or how shabby and abhorrent—something might be, there are times when it should be ethically evaluated all the more highly for that.[53]

Despite its sophistication, this is a view of the Orient whose function was to justify European domination—the "East" as the "West" seen "backward," in both senses of that term. No doubt Ōtsuka's Orientalism needs to be seen in the context of the postwar "Enlightenment," in which disillusionment with Japan's old regime lent plausibility to extravagant claims on behalf of the "civilization" that had brought that regime to its knees.

A third, and even more significant, basis for criticism is evident in Ōtsuka's overriding concern for national economic development and the kind of values and commitments he believes such a process would require among the working population. As we have seen, his early postwar work is suffused with references to the need to develop the productive forces on a national scale, as well as with his contention that rather than merely material these forces should be understood primarily in terms of human resources driven by ethos. In order to clarify the nature of this relationship between subjective ethos and national productivity, it is useful to recall Ōtsuka's anecdote regarding the dispute between the Dutch Libertines and the Calvinists, in which he favored the Calvinists on account of their profession of "strict self-control," their "ascetic and self-disciplined" outlook, "suppression of selfish desire," etc. Productivity, as well as true freedom, could only come through self-denial. In other words, Crusoe clearly represented for Ōtsuka something like those subjects of classical capitalist ideology, as described by Louis Althusser, who "work by themselves"— that is, without external sanctions—because they have internalized and identified with the Absolute Subject (God; the Father).[54] Thus, Asada Akira is correct to characterize Ōtsuka's ideal capitalist subject as having "learned to supervise and motivate itself through discipline and training." He concludes that "if we call this subject the adult, modernization is precisely the process of maturation."[55]

But there is more to it than that. In Ōtsuka's conception of national productivity, self-discipline is linked securely to the demands of the state. In order to illuminate this dimension of his approach, it is necessary to step from the early postwar era back into the midst of the Pacific War. If we look at Ōtsuka's publications during wartime, we notice a clear link between his conviction of the importance of self-discipline on the one hand and, on the other, the significance he grants to the level of "totality," that is, the state and its demands for expansion of productivity. Ōtsuka argued in 1944, for example, that Japan was on the brink of realizing a "new economic ethic," one that would transcend the "spirit of capitalism" as Weber described it. Basically, Ōtsuka argued that the element of profit making in the "spirit of capitalism" was in the process of being eliminated completely so that the Japanese people would soon work entirely on behalf of the social whole, i.e., the state.

Here, too, Ōtsuka's argument follows Weber's. Recall that Weber had emphasized the "'ethic of a calling' (*Berufsethik*)," which meant an "ethos which looks upon work in a worldly calling as a duty and prompts rational and organizational devotion." Moreover, he had pointed out that the kind of capitalist mentality that developed among producers through the mediation of the Protestant ethic was an "inverted ethical order" in which externally people were devoted entirely to private acquisition while inwardly they firmly believed that by turning a profit they were "making a great contribution to the 'whole' (society, nation, and world)." Therefore, even Weber had seen the importance of contribution to the whole, and it is in this inner commitment to the "totality" that we find the importance of the nation-state for Ōtsuka. Nevertheless, according to him, the classical "spirit of capitalism" had still been mediated by the profit motive. This was true despite the important role played in that "spirit" by the totality (state) and the need to make a contribution to the welfare of that totality. More precisely, he says that in Weber's "spirit of capitalism" the individual bore responsibility for enhancing production on behalf of the social whole, but the measure and criterion of that contribution continued to be profit. High profit meant, ipso facto, that a sufficient contribution was being made.

In the new economic ethics that Ōtsuka saw emerging, however, the mediation of profit was being rapidly overcome so that soon people would work directly on behalf of the state, accepting full responsibility for expanding the productive forces. Institutionally, this would facilitate the process of bringing all management under central control and allow it to be fully planned. Ōtsuka clearly links an emphasis on ascetic self-discipline directly to the national task of expanding production.

> World-historical reality now criticizes the supremely historical "spirit of capitalism" and overcomes its limitations, as a new "economic ethic" (ethos) gradually reveals itself. . . . Contrary to the "spirit of capitalism," the new form of "economic ethics" (ethos) transcends the mediation of "profit-making" and is now clearly conscious of the individual's "responsibility for production" in relation to the demand for expansion of productive forces that originates in the "totality" (state). . . . A new "economic control" ("economic plan") is expanding through transcendence of the "free" economics of old capitalism; moreover, management of specific enterprises—along with the "individuals" that carry out that management—is no longer mediated by "profit-making" but is rather brought directly within the "control" ("plan") of the "totality" and by virtue of that takes on sociality and a state character. . . . When viewed from the historical perspective, the meaning of "responsibility for production" can be understood fully only as the consciousness of this kind of "totality" (state) in the new "economic ethic."[56]

Self-discipline was necessary in order to expand the productive forces on behalf of the state. Yet Ōtsuka was not arguing for blind obedience. He emphasized that in order to be supremely *productive* in orientation and impact, the new economic ethic must contain within it the "structural moments" of "inner originality" (*jihatsusei*) and "instrumental rationality." In other words, even during the war, Ōtsuka was clearly talking about a kind of *shutaisei* that was to be self-disciplining, self-motivating, and rational.

It is also important to note that Ōtsuka was not alone in this emphasis. Although differing from Ōtsuka on several points, Ōkōchi Kazuo and others associated with "productive forces theory" were also discussing the need for autonomous, self-disciplined participation on the part of workers during a time of mobilization for total war.[57] A recent study of Ōkōchi notes, apropos of Ōtsuka's views, that

> Ōkōchi certainly discusses the importance of subjective [*shutaiteki*]
> human activity, and says that in the absence of autonomous, self-disci-
> plined participation on the part of workers, the long-term management
> of the wartime economy would have been impossible. . . . This kind of
> *shutaisei* and self-discipline was the essential psychological
> element in wartime economic mobilization. . . . Ōkōchi's conception
> was that in the historical era of wartime mobilization, the moment
> of democratic participation had to be activated to the highest possible
> level. However, for Ōkōchi the moment of democratic participation
> was certainly not at odds with state mobilization; on the contrary, he
> sought to encompass *shutaisei* and self-discipline within the war frame-
> work.[58]

It is interesting that because of their rejection of blind obedience, Ōtsuka's wartime works are often treated as acts of resistance, a judgment that is not without some persuasiveness. Even more interesting is Ōtsuka's reputation for having bridged the transition from wartime to postwar without having to make any changes in his views. Ōtsuka was able to continue full speed ahead from total war through democratic revolution. What this continuity enables us to see, therefore, is simply the complicity between totalitarianism and liberalism with regard to how subject-formation is related to the nation-state.[59] Although the state as "totality" is less prominent in his postwar writing, the *shutaisei* Ōtsuka advocates in the context of the postwar democratic revolution appears to be directly continuous with the proposals he made in 1943–44: Centered on the quality of self-discipline, his conception of *shutaisei* immediately calls to mind Michel Foucault's demonstration of the relationship between self-discipline and modernity. Modern subjectivity—whether liberal or authoritarian—appears to be pervaded by the form of self-surveillance that results when people internalize the gaze of state authority.

We are left, therefore, with the question of whether Ōtsuka's construction of subjectivity was adequate to the process of democratic revolution in early postwar Japan, and whether it still has relevance today. Ethnic groups, feminists, environmentalists, and others persist in their efforts to extend politics beyond the state and beyond the notion of a unitary society whose needs—whether for productivity or for leisure—are capable of claiming precedence over private wants. As they politicize new spaces in the interstices of the society, these forces also challenge the applicability of supposedly universal ethical paradigms such as "modern subjectivity."

The Democratic Subject and the State

[T]he political, ethical, social, philosophical problem of our days is not to try to liberate the individual from the state and from the state's institutions but to liberate us both from the state and from the type of individualization which is linked to the state.
—Michel Foucault[60]

Ōtsuka's major contribution was to relate an authoritative analysis of the subject of European capitalism not only to the situation of capitalist development in postwar Japan but to the question of how an economically based ethic could serve as the basis for democratic revolution. The task of developing a more thoroughly political analysis of subjectivity in its relationship to democratic practice and the state was left in part to the intellectual historian and political scientist Maruyama Masao.

Maruyama was born in 1914, the second son of a well-known journalist who was often critical of the prewar government. The younger Maruyama attended First Higher School from 1931 to 1934, graduated from the Law Faculty of the University of Tokyo in 1937, and after a few years became a professor in that same faculty.[61] He had begun as a student of European history and thought, but was persuaded by his mentor, Nanbara Shigeru, to delve instead into the texts of Japan's own past. Maruyama's sustained engagement with the thought of Japan's Tokugawa period (1603–1868) in the late 1930s and early 1940s led to the series of essays later published as *Nihon seiji shisōshi kenkyū* (in English translation as *Studies in the Intellectual History of Tokugawa Japan*). As he was still struggling to finish the last of these in July 1944, he was drafted into the army and sent to Pyongyang, Korea. Later he was posted to Hiroshima and was near that city when American forces dropped the atomic bomb there on August 6, 1945.

Maruyama resumed his position at the University of Tokyo soon after he was demobilized, and almost immediately set himself the task of critically interpreting Japan's recent past. His publication in May 1946 of "Chōkokkashugi no ronri to shinri" (The Logic and Psychology of Ultranationalism) created a sensation, as did several other essays he published during the years of Occupation.

Some were collected in *Gendai seiji no shisō to kōdō* (in English as *Thought and Behavior in Modern Japanese Politics*) and *Senchū to sengo no aida* (From wartime to postwar). Maruyama continues an active intellectual life and is one of the postwar Japanese intellectuals best known in Europe and America.

Democratic Subjectivity

Maruyama's concern with the development of modern political subjects in the context of the nation-state led him in the postwar era to reread the classical European liberal theorists. His conception of political subjectivity seems to have been strongly affected by a reading of John Locke, especially Locke's interpretation of freedom. In early postwar essays on that topic, Maruyama contrasted Locke's definition of freedom against those advanced by Sir Robert Filmer and Thomas Hobbes. Whereas Filmer and Hobbes defined freedom in a minimalist fashion as the absence of external constraint, Locke included in its meaning "a more positive, rational capacity for self-determination."[62]

In interpreting the content of Locke's concept of freedom, Maruyama begins with the aspect most directly related to the question of political subjectivity: Locke's view that freedom had to be understood as a form of self-limitation, especially as self-legislation: "By raising the concept of 'freedom' from a passive prescription of the 'absence of restraint' to a positive, constructive concept of self-legislation—the subjective freedom by which people impose norms upon themselves—Locke's was the first philosophy to establish systematically the principles of political liberalism."[63] Maruyama's account proceeds as follows. For Hobbes as for Locke, "the function of rationality was to calculate and make inferences with respect to pleasure and pain." However, in contrast to Locke, Hobbes understood freedom as "the absence of any external impediment which interferes with movement." Therefore, from Hobbes's standpoint, as people exercised rationality in making choices and thus decided upon laws to regulate their behavior, they subjected themselves to constraints and therefore lost freedom. In Hobbes's paradigm, "law as encumbrance and freedom as right were destined to be perpetual opposites." Put another way, the "deliberation" by which people determined their will was to be understood as a "de-liberation"— a subtraction of freedom. Therefore, in evolutionary terms the passage from the state of nature to the social state necessarily involved the abandonment of freedom.

Locke had written, on the other hand, that "nothing determined through our own judgment is a constraint on our freedom." Indeed, "man . . . has no freedom where there is no law." Freedom could exist only in society, where people "were governed or restrained by no will other than that of the laws promulgated by that government in accord with the purposes entrusted to it" by the people themselves. Therefore, freedom for John Locke was "none other than *the people's self-discipline*," which they exercised through parliamentary politics.[64]

But Maruyama does not stop there. In contrast to Hobbes, Locke also believed that the "state of nature" prior to the formation of political society was itself orderly, not an anarchy of desire. According to Locke, Maruyama writes, "man's natural existence itself is governed by essentially normative constraints. In fact, in Locke the unity of law and freedom in political society is guaranteed by the individual's *original sociality*." Individuals are social *by nature*, so the potential for concordance between self-interest and public interest is in place from the beginning.[65]

Maruyama was careful to contextualize political theory, Locke's included, by situating it in relation to the political and economic struggles of its time. Accordingly, he was concerned to show that in seventeenth-century England, the Filmer/Hobbes view of freedom was consistent with "royal (state) sovereignty and absolutism," while Locke's "was connected to popular sovereignty and democracy." He also clearly endorsed the Lockeian formulation as a crucial stage in the development of representative government: "If we may be permitted a rather expansive generalization, in modern intellectual history it was only when freedom as the absence of constraint converted itself actively into freedom as rational self-determination that its inner energy developed sufficiently to enable it to struggle mightily against feudal reaction and to form a new order."[66]

Accordingly, in the context of the postwar Japanese democratic revolution, Maruyama was led to ask whether a view of freedom as self-discipline comparable to Locke's could be said to have developed in the course of modern Japanese intellectual and political history. His answer was negative. During the Tokugawa period (1603–1868), the development of the ideals of freedom and equality had been inhibited by Confucianism, which postulated that the Five Relationships comprised an order intrinsic not only to the cosmos but to the inner nature of human beings as well. So long as Confucian norms were considered inherent to human nature, radical individuality would be suppressed and there could be no inner autonomy or freedom. "For a member of feudal society, obedience to the Five Relationships was a behavior pattern acquired at birth and deviations from it could only be conceived as a temporary clouding over caused by *kishitsu no sei* (material nature)."[67]

With that as the starting point, he concludes that "Tokugawa thought can be said to have been the process by which these Confucian norms became alienated from human internality and began to take on the character of external constraints." The eighteenth-century Confucian, Ogyū Sorai, especially, made public norms external, thereby liberating the person's private, inner life:[68] "On the one hand, Confucian norms were raised to the level of purely public, political entities, while on the other the private internality of human beings became separated from all normative constraints and filled with irrational sensuousness." Finally, in Kokugaku thought, this process was taken to the point where "human desire itself was elevated to the status of 'principle of Heaven.'"[69]

Maruyama's problem became, then, a matter of whether or not the externalization of Confucian norms in Tokugawa Japan, which had created "an opportunity for sensuous freedom *as the absence of constraint*" in something like the Hobbesian sense, ever led to the emergence of freedom as disciplined *self-determination*, similar to that conceptualized by Locke. Maruyama's answer is no, it did not: "Merely to set sensuous freedom in opposition to external, normative constraints does not necessarily direct the human spirit to the task of forming new norms."[70] Not only the Kokugaku thinkers but other so-called Tokugawa "liberals," as well, had maintained a largely passive social stance, betraying no inner-directed urge for political self-determination.

Was the ideal of self-legislation that Tokugawa thought had left unfulfilled finally brought to fruition after the Meiji Restoration of 1868? On the contrary, even the early Meiji "Enlightenment," whose intellectual outpouring included several examples of an active, self-limiting view of freedom, had the ultimate effect only of further "releasing the people's sensuous nature." It provided the people at large with no internal standards capable of restraining and guiding their behavior or of leading them to self-determination.

In a 1946 lecture on the Meiji period, Maruyama provided a more detailed analysis of the "etatism from above" that followed Japan's victory in the Sino-Japanese War of 1894–95. As a result of this increased authoritarianism, the people became estranged and isolated.

> It is usually said that national consciousness rose in the era following the Sino-Japanese War. However, in content, that national consciousness had the character of a liberation of sensuous impulses. It is extremely interesting that the era following the Sino-Japanese War saw the rapid spread of a phenomenon that differed from modern individualism, an *un*-political individualism, an individualism that fled from politics, or at least fled from everything connected to the state. Not political individualism, it was an individualism imbued with "decadence."[71]

In other words, by Maruyama's Lockeian standards, the growth of individual freedom was stunted at what he considered to be a centrifugal, unpolitical level. Once the Meiji absolutist state began to "stretch its brawny wings," the Japanese people's purely reactive form of freedom was pushed in two directions: domestically, it provided the basis for a "dwarfish petty bourgeois lifestyle cut off from everything social," while externally it "found a vehicle for its expansive urges in the external aggression of the Japanese state."[72]

But a caveat is in order. That he found it inadequate should not be taken to mean that Maruyama entirely rejected this centripetal, nonpolitical form of individuation and the purely private, hedonistic form of "freedom" he believed that it encouraged. In his study of Tokugawa thought, for example, Maruyama had evaluated Kokugaku highly for its insistence on the "inviolability of the world of inner sentiments." He wrote, "[I]f this resistance of inner nature to external standards is taken positively to its logical conclusions, it must lead to a denial of the limitations inherent in the feudal estates."[73]

Maruyama also showed in his famous indictment of Japanese fascism how vital he considered to be even the privatized, "negative" freedom achieved in the Meiji period. In his 1946 essay, "Theory and Psychology of Ultranationalism," he argued that the ultranationalism of twentieth-century Japan had attempted again to obliterate the distinction between the public and private worlds. In contrast to the modern European state, which "adopts a *neutral* position on internal values," the Japanese state "strove consistently to base its control on internal values rather than on authority deriving from external laws."[74] As a result, under Japanese ultranationalism "the personal, internal quality of private affairs could never be openly recognized," and no one, not even the emperor, could claim "free, subjective awareness."[75]

Therefore, it was precisely the construction of such an awareness, in the form of a "modern personality,"[76] that had to be the first step in the postwar process of democratic revolution. In a postscript to the short essay on freedom discussed above, he says, "We are again forced to confront the task of democratic revolution which the Meiji Restoration failed to complete. We must again grapple with the problem of human freedom." However, using terminology that echoes the early postwar Marxist conception of a democratic revolution to be led not by the middle class but by the proletariat, Maruyama cautions that "[t]he bearer of 'freedom' is no longer the 'citizen' as conceived by liberals since Locke, but rather the broad laboring masses centering on the workers and peasants." Now the workers and farmers would have to achieve "a new normative consciousness" and thus carry freedom beyond the centrifugal to a centripetal, responsibly self-disciplined level. If they failed to achieve that, an authentic democratic revolution could never occur.

In these early postwar reviews of the historical trajectory of political subjectivity in Japan, Maruyama implied that the development of an independent, democratic subject should be viewed as a two-stage process. First, it was necessary to construct a private, inner realm of "negative freedom," disencumbered of excessive political or moral constraints. This might be called the liberal, Hobbesian moment. Symbolically, at least, this moment was represented historically by Ogyū Sorai and the Kokugaku writers. However, in Maruyama's view, this Hobbesian "freedom *from*" was insufficient; national independence also required a democratic, Lockeian moment of "freedom *for*": Without fully abandoning the inviolate realm of privacy already secured, the free (male) "individual subject" was now obliged to discipline his hedonistic impulses and to assume responsibility for affairs of state in the public realm.

Postwar Nationalism

In light of the above, it should be clear that Maruyama's early postwar works offer an excellent opportunity to reassess the powerful relationship in modern thought between subjectivity and subjection to the state. Such a reassessment is especially important inasmuch as, since the 1960s, political theorists have increasingly questioned the liberal tendency to limit "politics" to activity oriented to a reified conception of the liberal-democratic state. Often influenced by Michel Foucault, these theorists have argued that too narrow an identification of politics with the state tends to inhibit rather than promote democratic revolution because it fails to address those political claims—increasingly prevalent in the 1990s, but clearly apparent in early postwar Japan as well—that "cannot be neatly contained either within the juridical boundaries of national states or within the modernist identification of political agency with national citizenship."[77]

In addition to dismantling a whole range of existing state institutions and ideological state apparatuses, the Allied Occupation of Japan also, in effect, reestablished the Japanese state in broadly liberal-democratic form. Therefore, at least hypothetically, Japanese intellectuals were confronted not only with the question of how to respond to the particular state system that the Occupation authorized, but also with the more fundamental question of whether the state should continue in postwar Japan to enjoy its former status as the single, privileged locus of political activity. It is true, of course, that Japanese intellectuals could in no way determine the form or extent of the postwar state itself. That prerogative was monopolized by the Occupation forces under the SCAP. And despite the theoretical possibility of reconceiving democratic revolution as the achievement of hegemony through an open-ended, unpredictable process of subject-formation and articulation that was capable of overflowing the confines and the control of the state-subject system as such, Maruyama Masao and other intellectuals were constrained by their most basic assumptions to limit democratic revolution to the construction of a liberal-democratic state and a modal subject for that state.

Maruyama's unusual willingness to advocate nationalism in the early postwar period when that sentiment was clearly out of favor might give us an initial clue to the centrality of the nation-state in his postwar thought.[78] In a 1947 essay on the Meiji journalist Kuga Katsunan, Maruyama observed that Kuga "correctly grasped the historical logic which necessitates a connection between democracy and nationalism." In other words, Kuga had proposed that "[n]ational politics means national independence externally and national unity within. . . . What is called national politics is in this sense tantamount to what is popularly known as public-opinion politics." Kuga also held that "to advocate onesidedly a kind of centrifugal freedom from the state was tantamount to mere empty formalism." Therefore, he wanted to see the Japanese state develop through a "correct balance between centrifugal (individual freedom) and centripetal (state power) elements."[79]

Maruyama points out that Kuga distinguished his "nationalism" clearly from chauvinism and militarism, and so often criticized the autocratic government through his editorials and articles that his newspaper, *Nihon*, was prevented from publishing thirty-one times between 1889 and 1905.[80] According to Maruyama, Kuga also firmly believed in the power of the people. He quotes Kuga: "The people are the water and the politicians the boat. Water is able to hold up a boat but is also quite capable of capsizing it, so the politicians must interpret its overall direction and act accordingly."[81]

At the same time, Maruyama points to what he feels are the inadequacies in Kuga's political analysis. For example, the latter's sense of the nation was tied intimately to a vision of the throne:

> For [Kuga], Japan's imperial throne was the point at which the centripetal principle was concentrated. Thus, through a thought process similar to Hegel's, he considered a constitutional monarchy to be the best political system through which to achieve national unification.
>
> For that reason, he demanded that "state, throne, cabinet and parliament all be made national in name and reality," and insisted that the

throne especially be liberated from domination by any faction or class, arguing that it was "desirable that the throne be above and in close proximity to the people of society, and that barriers between the two be reduced to a minimum."[82]

Although Maruyama admires Kuga for his perceptive understanding of modern nationalism, his stubborn criticism of the governments of the time, and his fidelity to principle, he also criticizes Kuga's totalistic, overly inclusive conception of the nation:

> The concept of "nation" on which the modern state, and especially the modern citizen revolution, are based does not just refer haphazardly to the whole body of members of the state, but rather designates particularly the social stratum that actively supports the modern state. Therefore, in principle, it excludes the ruling stratum of the old regime. . . . [However,] Katsunan says, "The basis of the modern state is not simply the nobility, nor simply the people, nor monarchical authority, but precisely the 'nation' which means the union of monarch and people." Here the nation is simply a collective name for the monarch and people, without any concrete limitation. . . . If one probes persistently all the confusion and compromise that beset his theory, one will find that it all originates in this trans-historical concept of the nation.[83]

Yet, overall, the analysis of Kuga suggests the degree to which Maruyama believed that democracy and freedom required the nation-state. In a concluding reference to the democratic revolution in postwar Japan, he proposes that the unity between nationalism and democracy Katsunan sought in the Meiji period was still a valid objective for postwar reform. "Precisely now, after having just ended a long period of *ultra*nationalist rule, we must combine nationalism in the true sense—a correct nationalist movement—with democratic revolution."[84]

The emphasis here on the need for modern nationalism suggests that in the postwar era of democratic revolution Maruyama was committed to the modern, liberal-democratic state as the "privileged expression of political community, and . . . site of political action."[85] Indeed, some of his other early postwar work suggests a broadly Hegelian conception. In a creatively written review of a work in European intellectual history by Bertrand Russell, for example, Maruyama has one of his two notional conversationalists (A and B) criticize English and American scholars for being "insufficiently aware that modern freedom is a structural principle of the nation-state itself."[86] Also significant is Sasakura Hideo's conclusion, based on a consideration of the entire corpus of

Maruyama's works, that Maruyama's conception of democratic consciousness parallels that of Hegel in making "an effort to mediate internally the autonomous individual with society (especially the modern state)."[87]

If the state required the support and participation of independent individuals, would Maruyama also argue, conversely, that people could only become independent individuals within the purview of the modern state? In fact, he had once written precisely that, in an essay he completed while still a student in 1936: "The individual is posited concretely as a thesis only when mediated by the state."[88] In other words, in at least one dimension of Maruyama's political philosophy, the nation/state and the individual are bound by necessity and perhaps even form a kind of dialectical whole. That is, "the state is mediated through the inner freedom of the individual."[89] Here Maruyama's Hegelian conception of the state places him in the same camp as Tanabe Hajime, as quoted at the beginning of chapter 3.

Maruyama's postwar analyses sometimes indicated that a certain necessity resides in the relationship between individuals and the nation-state. At the same time, the essay on Kuga suggests Maruyama's reluctance to accept any notion of nation or state as a transhistorical or mystical totality. He seems to be caught in a situation of ambivalence in which he accepts a conception of the close interconnection—what Sasakura calls "inner mediation" (*naizaiteki baikai*) but glosses as "Identität"[90]—between the individual and the state as a kind of totality, while remaining suspicious of any overly inclusive conception of the state or nation.

The Problem of the State

Maruyama found another model for relations between people and the state in the work of the Meiji-period Enlightenment thinker Fukuzawa Yukichi, to which he would return frequently in the postwar period. Indeed, just as in Ōtsuka's case, we get perhaps the clearest indication of Maruyama's underlying conception of political subjectivity from an essay on Fukuzawa published in the midst of World War II (1943), where Maruyama argues that Fukuzawa's "nationalism" and his "individualism" were not, as had often been assumed, contradictory but were rather complementary aspects of a coherent political approach.[91]

In this short essay, Maruyama calls into question both the nature of the Japanese state and the degree of autonomy displayed by the people. He says that "unless the state is such that each member of the nation feels in close touch with it, makes it his own, and is conscious of its course as his own destiny, how will the state be able to maintain sturdy independence under trying international circumstances." That is, he clearly calls for political self-determination: "Fukuzawa saw that what was missing above all from Japan's traditional national consciousness was the spirit of autonomous personality. . . . [H]e could never conceive of national independence in the absence of individual autonomy."

The wartime essay on Fukuzawa laid out the essentials of a close connection between state and individual that to some extent would remain paradigmatic for Maruyama's work throughout the early postwar period. This relationship is summed up from one angle in his statement that "[Fukuzawa] could never conceive of national independence in the absence of individual autonomy." That is, for Fukuzawa there was never any doubt that the independence and autonomy of the state (*kokkateki jishusei*) were the final goal, and that national autonomy had to be "mediated through the inner independence of personalities." More specifically: "Fukuzawa would have the nation (*kokumin*) make its approach to the state through the spontaneous decisions of each individual." The people found it easier to be "irresponsible" and to depend on the state, in part because they lacked a tradition of "independence and self-respect." Nevertheless, Fukuzawa believed that the Japanese people "had ample strength to comply with the strict, ethical demands" of modern citizenship. Independence, self-discipline, and a sense of responsibility for and to the state—these were the qualities Fukuzawa and, by extension, Maruyama prescribed for the Japanese people.[92]

It would appear that Maruyama's 1943 concept of political subjectivity, proposed in an environment of mass mobilization for total war under the aegis of the state, survived more or less intact to become the informing principle of his postwar concept as well, despite (or perhaps because of) the transformation the state went through in the same period. Maruyama apparently believed that the postwar process of democratic revolution had to entail the formation of a disciplined, responsible subject of the sort that had also been acceptable to the wartime authorities (despite their apparent preference for blind obedience)—that is, an "individual subject" actively committed to and involved in the nation-state. Yet this should hardly be cause for surprise. Michel Foucault argued that the liberal-democratic state emerged historically in parallel with a whole network of disciplinary mechanisms whose ultimate effect was to induce self-discipline as an integral dimension of subject-formation. To symbolize those mechanisms, Foucault referred to the Panopticon, a model prison designed in the early nineteenth century, each of whose inmates "becomes to himself his own jailer." Indeed, "In the perpetual self-surveillance of the inmate lies the genesis of the celebrated 'individualism' and heightened self-consciousness that are hallmarks of modern times."[93]

The question arises, therefore, as to whether modern political subjectivity (*shutaisei*) can only be constructed as a process of *subjection* to the state and its institutions—that is, as a process of *self-discipline* by which the gaze of state authority is internalized. Political philosophers since the 1980s have sought to show that a deepening of democratic revolution must involve a dissolution of the distinction between public and private and an increasing politicization of social relations so as to eliminate "the idea and the reality itself of a unique space of constitution of the political."[94] In a manner broadly commensurate with the women's movement slogan that "the personal is political," feminist theorists, especially, have sought conceptually and practically to expand the purview of the political beyond the channels, procedures, and institutions of the modern state. For some, this has made it necessary to reinterpret classical European political thought so as to clarify the logic by which the classical liberal thinkers tended to treat the political as "something abstracted from . . . the social relationships of everyday life." Indeed, Carole Pateman has argued that John Locke himself played an important role in this reification of the political. In Locke, she argues, as throughout liberal-democratic theory, "The political sphere appears as a 'thing'—'the state'—objectified and external to the members of society."[95] This interpretation is intriguing in view of Maruyama's well-known aversion to reification and inertia (*wakudeki*) in politics. Pateman's analysis makes Maruyama's insistence on distinguishing between public and private look like a form of the very reification he has tried so hard to discredit.[96]

Other theorists argue that the fixation in modern political theory on the "sovereign subject as a privileged political agent" and on the "sovereign state as a primary site of political struggle" always creates an excess composed of the multiple and at times fragmentary processes of identification and subject-formation that occur within the plurality of the social itself. That is, the belief that only an independent individual can be a proper political subject has the effect of excluding "all sectors of the population as were conventionally coded as 'dependent' or 'other' by the dominant cultural frame: women, children, labourers, aliens, the mad, and criminals, etc." Moreover, the assertion of rights by those defined as different in terms of gender, ethnicity, race, or class, for instance, may "imply potential solidarities not only within but beyond the domestic context or territorial confines of the national state."[97]

As Hidaka Rokurō among others has argued, Maruyama's wartime essay on Fukuzawa can legitimately be interpreted as an act of resistance.[98] Considering that in contemporary ultranationalist tracts, such as *Kokutai no hongi* (Fundamentals of Our National Polity), "individualism" was presented as the root of all evil, Maruyama's call by way of Fukuzawa for individual autonomy clearly went against the grain. Moreover, in a context in which militaristic forces might have preferred that Japanese subjects should display an attitude of unquestioning obedience, Maruyama's implied call for "individual autonomy" was bound to create anxiety in some quarters. In that sense, Maruyama's essay can perhaps be compared to Ōtsuka Hisao's 1944 essay, about which Ueno Masaji writes that "by urging individual awareness, through terms such as 'instrumental (methodical) rationality' and 'inner spontaneity' . . . Ōtsuka was able to take a posture of resistance against a 'totality' (state) that led people into blind cooperation with the war."[99]

The problem is not, therefore, located at the level of Maruyama's intentions, or in the immediate impact of his essay in 1943. Rather, what must be called into question is the effect of a particular liberal tradition, perhaps founded in part by John Locke but contributed to importantly by Kant, Hegel, and others, in which freedom is sought through a process of self-discipline, or self-legislation, focused on the nation-state. In this tradition, the exercise of self-discipline differentiates the private world of desire from the public world of reason; family and civil society from the state; and also, significantly, the realm of the female from that of the male.[100] Politics, moreover, tends to be limited to a narrow sphere of activity centered on the state. This is the tradition that seems to have informed both Maruyama's 1943 essay and his postwar political theory, and therefore to have undergirded his notion of how political subjectivity could be formed in the context of the postwar democratic revolution.

That is not to say that Maruyama's conception of politics focused myopically on the state. One of the distinguishing features of his early postwar work was his careful attention to the behavioral and psychological rather than just institutional levels of political phenomena.[101] Perhaps we are justified in concluding, overall, that in Maruyama's work the state structure is by no means a sufficient condition for the construction of democratic *shutaisei* but is nonetheless a necessary one. This suggests that in 1946, when he proposed the "establishment of a modern personality" (*kindaiteki seikaku no kakuritsu*) as the overriding task for the postwar period, he was referring to an individual possessed of the kind of discipline that qualifies a person for participation in the public realm dominated by the state.[102]

At the same time, to say that a centripetal orientation toward the state constitutes the major criterion of the political in Maruyama's scheme does not need to mean that for him private life and desire must be completely suppressed. Indeed, it is characteristic of political self-discipline as Maruyama envisions it to be not only voluntary but always in more or less tense equilibrium with centrifugal desire. The private is preserved and constantly reanimated even as it is subordinated to an overriding priority placed on public involvement. This subtle, inner dimension of the formation of political subjectivity was explored by Maruyama in a postwar study of the philosophical dimensions of Fukuzawa's writing.

Play and Subjectivity

Maruyama's attempt to glean a "philosophy" from Fukuzawa's late-nineteenth-century commentary can be taken to reveal central dimensions of Maruyama's own conception of political subjectivity, especially with respect to what he later called "an overlap between a certain kind of relativism in Fukuzawa's and my own [thought]."[103]

In focusing initially on Fukuzawa's commitment to the relativity of value judgments, Maruyama quotes Fukuzawa's own articulations, one of which comes near the beginning of that writer's only philosophical work, *Bunmeiron no gairyaku* (Outline of a Theory of Civilization, 1875): "Light and heavy, long and short, good and bad, right and wrong are all relative terms. . . . Therefore, one cannot discuss the right and wrong, the merits and demerits of an issue without first establishing a *basis of argumentation*."[104] According to Maruyama, Fukuzawa virtually never makes a value judgment in the abstract and never treats value as an entity fixed a priori. His perceptions, therefore, must always be understood to be conditional. Maruyama expresses this by saying that Fukuzawa's statements always need to be taken as if they were "in brackets" (*kakkotsuki*).[105] That is, they are valid only within the limits of a particular situation or point of view, and should not be taken as universally applicable or absolute.

At the same time, Maruyama argues that Fukuzawa was never merely a thoroughgoing relativist. Fukuzawa emphasized that one should always establish a "basis of argumentation"—take an autonomous position toward the world in order to grasp its significance. Maruyama says that Fukuzawa was saved from "aimless opportunism" by an inner "truth principle" that provided the degree of detachment sufficient to allow an independent judgment. Yet, according to Maruyama, Fukuzawa never grounded this principle in any metaphysical system. He "certainly did not reject the notion of objective truth; however, he denied that this 'truth principle' confronts us as an already fixed and stationary existence. Rather, his basic way of thinking was that it assumed specific form only within a particular situation."

Fukuzawa's orientation was similar to the pragmatism of James and Dewey in that he "argued for the determination of all perceptions by the practical goal (the 'basis of argumentation')." Value was never already there objectively; it

emerged only as the function of an encounter between subjective purposeful-
ness and a set of objective conditions. In order to make his point, Maruyama
contrasts Fukuzawa's approach to nature with that of his contemporary, the social Darwinist Katō Hiroyuki. Where Katō viewed objective nature pessimi-
stically, as an iron determinism, Fukuzawa saw it as raw material that was
constantly being worked, and thus rendered technological, through the practical
(*shutaiteki*) manipulations and experimentation of human beings.[106] Rather
than the results of science, Fukuzawa emphasized the scientific spirit: that is,
the experimental method. For him, knowledge was always linked to action:
people had to intervene subjectively (*shutaiteki ni*) from a position of relative
autonomy in order to render the world comprehensible.

According to Maruyama, "emphasis on the relativity of value judgments
correlated with respect for the autonomous activism (*shutaiteki nōdōsei*) of the
human spirit," and here Maruyama's emphasis shifts from the relativity of value
judgments to the quality of the subjectivity that is capable of making such judgments.

> [For Fukuzawa] only a tough, subjective spirit can resist treating
> values as fixed a priori, and instead constantly allow them to be fluid
> and relative to the concrete situation. While assessing each particular
> circumstance, and establishing an approach and a standard for action
> according to that assessment, it is also necessary to avoid becoming
> caught in a single perspective; one constantly has to maintain the spiri-
> tual composure necessary to rise above the existing conditions, and to
> adjust to the formation of a new situation. In contrast, a spirit poor in
> such subjectivity becomes firmly rooted in a particular situation and
> set in one view, and as a result abstractly absolutizes a single value
> standard that is actually bound to a particular context [*ba*].[107]

Here Maruyama's conception of a practical, nonmetaphysical subjectivity
begins to emerge clearly. As the capacity to make judgments according to
standards that arise in relation to lived, historical situations, it implies tireless
engagement with a historically changing environment. Modern subjectivity
requires the flexibility and composure necessary to make appropriate value
choices in practical situations. Its opposites are passive adaptation and rigid formalism, both of which are aspects of what Fukuzawa called *wakudeki* (irrational attachment, fetishism).[108]

Having delineated in a preliminary way the kind of subjective autonomy
Fukuzawa espoused, Maruyama moves to the level of society as a whole to
show how this quality relates to what Fukuzawa termed the social atmosphere
(*kifū*). Not surprisingly, he finds that in a closed, fixed society consciousness

tends toward fetishism, while in an open society a more active, flexible subjectivity prevails. Not only do autonomous individuals act in ways that disrupt rigid social norms but, conversely, free and open social institutions play a crucial role in enabling and encouraging autonomous action; on the other hand, "absolutism in judgment goes along with absolutism in politics." That is, "there is a correlation between rigidity in social relations and centralization of power, and between centralization of power and turgidity in human thought and judgment." In an open society,

> [o]ne cannot facilely depend today on the value standard that was appropriate yesterday. . . . so one must constantly investigate the current situation in order to distinguish those elements that are *more* beneficial or *more* true. . . . Human judgment progresses only under the pressure of constant activity and tension. At the same time, since this progress demands from the subject the sort of spiritual preparation that will allow it always to transcend the contemporary situation, this judgment continuously *renders its own perspective fluid*. Because it is impossible, therefore, for political power to dominate standards of value, that power itself becomes relativistic and recognizes the plurality of values [in society]. Then, the spirit is freed from all forms of "superstition" [*wakudeki*].[109]

Maruyama's argument here has important implications for democratic revolution. He affirms that modern subjectivity is not merely an epistemological mechanism but also entails an antiauthoritarian form of praxis. When the subject "renders its own perspective fluid"—and thus undergoes a continuous process of self-transformation—those in power lose control of values and have to recognize the legitimacy of pluralism. Maruyama illustrates this point by discussing Fukuzawa's view of freedom. That is, freedom that rules uniformly is no longer freedom at all: "freedom is born amidst unfreedom."[110]

Maruyama also discusses Fukuzawa's philosophy of history, which posits that progress consists in things becoming more numerous (*hanta*) and complex (*menmitsu*). He goes on to analyze in considerable detail Fukuzawa's conception of how "spirit" and society develop in parallel historically. In the realm of spirit, the vector of progress moves overall from "fetishism" to "subjective independence," encompassing such minor moments as those from rigidity to fluidity, from extremism (adherence to a single value) to tolerance (a logic of pluralism in values), from a preoccupation with custom and morality to a focus on intelligence and knowledge, and from the reproduction of habitual behavior to progress based on trial and error. In the realm of society, the movement of civilization is from power-orientation to freedom, with such elements as the transition from uniformity to complexity in social relations, from concentration of values in the state to the dispersion of values among various forces in civil society, from self-justifying institutions to instrumental ones, from ideological uniformity to coexistence of various ideologies, and from control based on homogeneity to unity through conflict.[111]

It should be noted that no aspect of this conception of progress or, indeed, of the "antiauthoritarianism" Maruyama's study implicitly places at the foundation of modern subjectivity is ever taken to suggest a reduction in the importance of the state. On the contrary, society retains its unity despite functional differentiation and increased fluidity, and the state continues to govern in the mode of "unity through conflict."

A fundamentally optimistic philosophy of history underlies Fukuzawa's belief in the promise of human emancipation through ever-increasing freedom and pluralism. Yet alongside Fukuzawa's optimism was an *almost* equally strong sense of modesty and awe. According to Maruyama, he "never forgot how powerless people were in the face of overwhelming domination by that part of nature which they had not yet explored and made into tools."[112] However, Maruyama argues that Fukuzawa's optimistic view of human potential always ultimately prevailed over his realization of human impotence. In a fascinating passage, in which he introduced play as the behavior appropriate to man's powerless state, Fukuzawa wrote:

> Once born into the world, a human being is indeed a small fry [*ujimushi*];
> but, on the other hand, he [or she] is not without a certain preparedness.
> What is that? While knowing that human life is but play [*tawamure*], it
> is in the nature of small fry to apply themselves to this playing as if it
> were not play at all but serious . . . work. Indeed, this is not really the
> way of small fry at all, but the pride of human beings alone as the very
> spirit of all things.

Fukuzawa paradoxically portrayed humankind as powerless "small fry" even while urging them to act as if they were omnipotent. But he went on to turn this very paradox into a "method of securing tranquility" (*anshinhō*):

> Take the fleeting world lightly and consider people and all things as so
> much play. Throw yourself into that play with all your energy, without
> respite; indeed, you should not only strive tirelessly, but push yourself
> to the limits of truth and enthusiasm. Then, at a certain moment, you
> will again remember that all is mere play in a fleeting world. Your ardor

will cool and you will turn about. Now, you must again just let play be
play. This is what I call the great, self-evident method of securing human tranquility.[113]

Of course, the effect of this willingness to play—the ludic dimension of practical action—is to free the human spirit from fetishism. Play provides the composure and open-mindedness that enable the individual to see beyond the
immediate situation. Maruyama says that "Fukuzawa's humanism is so surprisingly tough that he is undaunted by the dwarfishness of human existence in
the universe, and not only does he face it head on, but he converts the resulting
sense of powerlessness into an opportunity for a stronger spiritual subjectivity
[*shutaisei*]."

Maruyama argues that if one were to adhere single-mindedly to the viewpoint that life is play, he or she would most likely turn eventually to religious
escapism or nihilistic hedonism; if, on the other hand, one absolutized the serious dimension, the result would be fetishism and loss of autonomy. "It is only
when the seriousness of life and the frivolity of life augment and functionalize
each other that there can truly be an autonomous and independent spirit." A
functionally productive alternation between these dimensions is possible only
when one is able to act "as if"—*as if* life were play in order not to become im-
mobilized by the gravity of it all, and *as if* life were serious in order to resist the
temptations of escapism or opportunism. Only thus, Maruyama seems to suggest, can one conceive of a socialized but independent, democratic subject without resorting to theological guarantees.

In the conclusion to his essay, Maruyama both summarizes his overall
analysis of Fukuzawa's philosophy and, in a fascinating reference to a 1910
piece by the German sociologist Georg Simmel, opens that analysis to new interpretive possibilities:

> We have found that in Fukuzawa's work the main propositions are *con-
> ditional* and should be understood as in brackets. In that tendency, we
> see the characteristic of his thought, which is to shift perspective
> constantly. Moreover, his most inclusive "brackets" are around the
> proposition that life is play. As Simmel points out, play suspends all
> that is substantial in human activity and comes into being where that
> activity has become entirely formalized. It is, therefore, *fiction* in the
> purest sense, and fiction, above all, is entirely the product of humanity,
> borrowing nothing from either god or nature. By placing all of life in
> the brackets of "as if," and viewing it as fiction, Fukuzawa . . . pressed
> the logic of humanism to its furthest extreme.[114]

Maruyama refers to Georg Simmel's "The Sociology of Sociability."[115] His evocation of Simmel's essay is not accompanied by further explanation, but its contents obviously influenced him and are therefore worth a brief recounting. Simmel discusses play as a pure form, which draws its themes from real life but suspends their seriousness. But Simmel's main emphasis is rather on *sociability*, which he defines as the social counterpart of play, as well as of art. Just as play and art "draw their form from . . . realities but . . . leave . . . reality behind them," sociability "makes up its substance from numerous fundamental forms of serious relationships among men, a substance, however, spared the frictional relations of real life."[116] It is particularly significant that sociability, as the "sociological play-form,"[117] has no purpose outside its own fulfillment. It is self-sufficient, an end in itself. Simmel says that "sociability distils, as it were, out of the realities of social life the pure essence of association, of the associative process as a value and a satisfaction."[118]

Sociability provides, moreover, *an artificial space* in which both objective interests and personal egos are suspended, and each participant acts "as if " all were equal, and "as though he especially esteemed everyone." To pretend in this way is not duplicitous: "This is just as far from being a lie as is play or art in all their departures from reality. But the instant the intentions and events of practical reality enter into the speech and behavior of sociability, it does become a lie—just as a painting does when it attempts, panorama fashion, to be taken for reality."[119]

Sociability "lies," therefore, when realities are allowed to penetrate its space too directly and obtrusively—when they violate the autonomy of its world of forms: "as soon as the discussion gets business-like, it is no longer sociable; it turns its compass point around as soon as the verification of a truth becomes its purpose."[120] However, the play of sociability also lies when it attempts to separate itself entirely from seriousness. Simmel says, "If sociability cuts off completely the threads which bind it to real life and out of which it spins its admittedly stylized web, it turns from play to empty farce, to a lifeless schematization proud of its woodenness."[121]

Maruyama's evocation of Simmel's concepts of play, art, and sociability contributes a great deal to his portrayal of Fukuzawa's philosophy, primarily by augmenting the weight and significance of the ludic dimension. As noted above, for Simmel, play in the form of sociability is the quintessence of the social—a symbolically rich and productive activity that relates to material interests and drives in the manner of form to content but is nevertheless relatively autonomous from those forces and virtually their equivalent in value. By introducing

Simmel's analysis of play, Maruyama seems to be implying that we need to take
Fukuzawa fully at his word when he says "life is but play," and we need also to
realize that play in this sense is hardly trivial—certainly no mere derivative, or
ephemeral effluent, of material interests or hard realities but rather their necessary counterpart.

How, then, should one sum up the approach to subjectivity that is suggested
by the seminal essay on Fukuzawa's philosophy? On one hand, the insistence on
the relativity of value judgments that Maruyama inherits from Fukuzawa, and
the ludic turn in his philosophy of life, might be interpreted as weakening the
tendency to reify subjectivity in modern thought. In order to understand the
world, Fukuzawa's active subject must constantly transcend the secure refuge
of inertia and attachment, and "render its own perspective fluid." That is, subjectivity must repeatedly establish itself on a new basis of argumentation, which
provides the modicum of autonomy necessary to make judgments. Moreover,
its judgments are always enclosed in the bracketing of conditionality, since they
can rely on no metaphysical grounding equivalent to the Cartesian guarantee.
Indeed, serious subjectivity is unable to sustain itself indefinitely because the
very condition of its existence is an interlude that periodically replaces the logic
of domination (content) with the self-absorbed ecstasy of play (form). Seriousness is always becoming play, and vice versa, just as the human being, lord of
the universe, is always already the "small fry," dethroned by the irresistible
forces of nature.

On the other hand, Maruyama's Fukuzawa remains anthropocentrically
humanistic, devoted to the metanarrative of growth and progress through the
domination of nature, and convinced of the need for a "tough and resilient"
(male) subjectivity. Despite what seems to be its unstable ontological basis, this
subjectivity always recuperates and grows stronger as, according to Maruyama,
Fukuzawa "converts the . . . sense of powerlessness into an opportunity for a
stronger spiritual autonomy."

In a sympathetically critical study of Maruyama's work that covers some of
the same ground as the present one, Umemoto Katsumi concluded that the final
telos of Maruyama's philosophy lay in "commitment" rather than "relativism."
He says that "the words of Max Weber would serve most appropriately as
Maruyama's final 'brackets.'" He then quotes "Politics as a Vocation" where
Weber says,

> [I]n nine out of ten cases . . . [those who espouse the ethic of ultimate
> ends] . . . intoxicate themselves with romantic sensations. From a hu-
> man point of view this is not very interesting to me, nor does it move

me profoundly. However, it is immensely moving when a mature
man—no matter whether old or young in years—is aware of a responsibility for the consequences of his conduct and really feels such
responsibility with heart and soul. He then acts by following an ethic
of responsibility and somewhere he reaches the point where he says:
"Here I stand; I can do no other." That is something genuinely human
and moving.[122]

Umemoto's point is that, in the final instance, Maruyama would find it necessary
to depart from the attitude of fluid relativity in favor of a firm stand—indeed, a
"heroic" one, as suggested by Weber's paraphrase of Martin Luther—on a matter of principle.[123] His ultimate preference would be more "ascetic" than "self-
intoxicating," less involved in playful communion with nature and with others
than removed from them in a stance of ethical autonomy. Umemoto's intuition is
to some degree borne out by Maruyama's own retrospective self-reading in
which he labels his position in the debate on *shutaisei* as "neo-Kantian" in the
sense that it strenuously resisted any attempt to merge "value" with "existence."[124]

In sum, despite Maruyama's implication that they are equal and equivalent,
the instrumentalist dimension of serious subjectivity ultimately prevails over
the ludic dimension. Fukuzawa's deprecation of humanity is merely a temporary moment in the recuperation and strengthening of a human presence that
remains the privileged subject of consciousness, history, and politics concentrated on the state. Despite the constant reproduction and valorization among
Fukuzawa's human beings of private desire and play, these are always transcended and sublimated (i.e., disciplined) in the formation of a serious subjectivity
oriented to public power and principle.

Democracy as Sublimation

The concept of sociability, which Maruyama drew from Simmel, again plays a
central role in a consideration of the relationship between politics and literature,
and thus public and private, which Maruyama published in 1949 in the form of
an informal dialogue between "A" and "B." As a way of approaching the issue
of how pornographic description differs from proper fiction, "B" contrasts the
weakness of sociability in Japan with its presumptive vitality in Europe. He
says, "To put it in exaggerated terms, I should almost say that [in Europe] everyday life as such is already to a certain extent a 'literary creation,' that subject
matter itself has already been given form."[125] This hypothetical difference in
the quality of sociability is paralleled by a contrast in dominant literary form. In

Japan, "the minds of our writers cling like leeches to natural, sensual phenomena, and lack a really free flight of the imagination, so in one sense all of our
literature is 'carnal.'" This is because "the mediating force of the spirit is weak.
It fails to preserve the internal unity of fiction itself and in the end it's dragged
off in all directions by separate, disjointed sensual experiences."[126] Just as, for
Simmel, sociability turns false when egocentric desires and interests intrude,
for Maruyama's interlocutor the fictional integrity of a literary work is destroyed when the author injects his or her real life into the narrative.

As the conversation proceeds, Maruyama converts the notion of fiction, as
reality mediated by subjective spirit, into a model for modern society and politics. "B" asks, "Why does the modern spirit believe in the value and use of fiction, and why does this spirit keep turning out fiction?" He pursues an answer
initially through etymology:

> Look up the word [fiction] in the dictionary and you'll see it comes
> from the Latin word *fingere*.[127] I'll tell you that it originally meant "to
> fashion" or "to invent." Then the connotation of the word changed, and
> it came to mean "to imagine" or "to pretend." In other words, it origi-
> nally referred, in a broad sense, to a human being having some purpose
> in mind, and *producing* something in line with his idea.

Accordingly, the truly modern spirit "rates the product of intellectual activity
much higher than natural realities." It also "sees 'mediated' reality as being on a
higher level than 'immediate' reality."[128]

"B" then sketches a brief history of modern attitudes toward society, focusing on the emergence of "an awareness that the public order, institutions, *mores*,
in short the whole social environment that encompasses mankind, is man-made,
and can be changed by the force of man's intellect." He also contrasts Western
humanism against Asian "humanism," arguing that in the latter, the human being is "not thought of as an independent entity, but as part and parcel of a concrete environment," and "every act . . . is bound up in social proprieties and
customs."[129]

"B" goes on to explain, in a manner vividly reminiscent of Fukuzawa, that
institutions are also "fictions." They are always made by human beings "for the
sake of some convenience or to carry out some kind of function," yet tend over
time to become hypostatized as part of the natural environment. Therefore, "we
have to keep on re-examining institutions and organizations in the light of their
objectives and functions. If we don't keep re-examining them they solidify, so
to speak, and end up simply as conventions." When that happens, "there's
no mediation going on between ends and means, and so means quickly turn

into ends in themselves." Fukuzawa would characterize this as fetishism (*wakudeki*).

For example, even the postwar parliamentary system could "turn into nothing but a body with enormous autocratic power."[130] Indeed, the premodern nature of Japanese social relations is such that

> in this country we have more to worry about than just the danger of modern organizations or institutions becoming hypostatized and no longer performing their original function.
>
> We've always had a vast arena in Japan where social coordination takes place without ever going through the channel of organizations. The things that go on in this arena are everything from naked violence, terror, and intimidation, down to the subtler pressures exerted by *oyabun* and other kinds of bosses. I suppose we can say that these are methods of solving the problem by means of *direct* human relations.[131]

"B" 's discourse, which we can take to represent Maruyama's views, implies that a democratic system ought to be fictional in the sense that it is produced and reproduced by human beings in accord with the purpose or idea (the fiction) of democracy itself. In contrast to the premodern form of social determinism he detects in Japan, where behavior is coerced by and through tradition and communal habit masquerading as natural forces, democracy as an idea and as a constructive process would require that individuals continuously strive to estabish their relative autonomy in a basis of argumentation and then make the value judgments that can be effective in bringing reality ever closer to an ideal state. Their attempts are always directed toward concrete situations, and thus are in brackets; nevertheless, they flow from a firmly (if always conditionally) established position of modern autonomy, and thus are always more than mere passive adaptation.

Like sociability, a democratic political system should be relatively free of the *direct* clash of interests and drives, and especially of violence. Within its realm, interests and desires should be introduced systematically and then mediated and adjusted in a manner that preserves a high degree of integrity and autonomy: if the realm of the political is directly penetrated by raw economic interests, social obligations, and personal desires—or, conversely, completely cut off from the social world of interests and desires—then democratic politics will be a lie rather than a fiction.

By situating such expressive modes as "play," "sociability," and the production of "fiction" in the space between unsocialized desire and politics, Maruyama is able to show how the process of modern self-discipline operates.

Political subjectivity is formed only when the individual is propelled toward participation in the public sphere by a practical, creative impulse that, through the gradual mediation of structured "play" and "sociality," is conditioned toward "responsible" self-discipline. The "individual subject" must bridge the divide between private life and politics (the state), although by doing so he (masculine pronoun intentional) by no means eliminates it. As Hegel put it, "The individuals have to make themselves into a universal through negation of themselves, through externalization and education (*Entäusserung und Bildung*)."[132]

This consideration of some of Maruyama's postwar works reveals a certain conception of political subjectivity. A submerged but pervasive theme is the need for an internal bifurcation between the subject of desire and the subject of politics. This bifurcation, or dualism, has taken different forms in the various essays we have considered, having been represented variously as the tension in such oppositions as unrestrained will vs. rational self-determination, raw desire or objective interest vs. sociability (play), and "carnality" vs. fiction. That is, for Maruyama the formation of political subjectivity consists in negotiating the modern separation of life into two realms: the private, where people follow personal desires, and the public, where they are required to suppress private desire to pursue the common good. This form of political modernity, so well described by Hegel, was attacked by the young Marx:

> Where the political state has achieved its full development, man leads a double life, a heavenly and an earthly life, not only in thought or consciousness but in *actuality*. In the *political community* he regards himself as a *communal being*; but in *civil society* he is active as a *private individual*, treats other men as means, reduces himself to a means, and becomes the plaything of alien powers. The political state is as spiritual in relation to civil society as heaven is in relation to earth. . . . The contradiction between the religious and the political man is the same as that between *bourgeois* and *citoyen*, between the member of civil society and his *political lion skin*.[133]

In sum, Maruyama's postwar political theory, like liberal-democratic theory in general, "continues to present the political as something abstracted from, as autonomous or separate from, the social relationships of everyday life."[134] His construction of political subjectivity in a disciplinary role vis-à-vis private desire can be seen to parallel his conception of the state in relation to civil society. Political subjectivity and the state reflect and require each other in response to the demands of liberal-democratic government.

His understanding of politics in relation to the state raises questions about the implications of Maruyama's work in the early postwar period. Were there not, during the Occupation as well as in the 1980s, cases in which the process of democratic revolution transgressed the bounds of the liberal-democratic state, leading to the contingent formation of political subjectivity entirely within the social milieu? Of course, one thinks immediately of the production control movements, which, by mid-1946, are said to have involved more than a million Japanese workers.[135] Yet, in search of cases outside the boundaries of the state in which power is implicated in subject-formation, one could just as well look beyond production control to more mundane acts such as dealing on the black market or securing a divorce from one's husband. Such choices are typical of the quotidian acts that continue to form subjects potentially capable, not necessarily of resisting the state but, perhaps more importantly, of resisting self-discipline. Yet their full politicality seems to be difficult to grasp in terms of the modernist approach to democratic revolution.

The Positivist Challenge

The modernist conceptions of *shutaisei* advanced by Maruyama and Ōtsuka Hisao ran into opposition from other non-Marxist (or semi-Marxist) behavioral scientists, among them the psychologist Miyagi Otoya and the sociologist Shimizu Ikutarō. The perspectives advanced by critics such as Miyagi were very similar in some aspects to Maruyama's. They had in common an appreciation for pragmatism (although, compared to Miyagi and Shimizu, Maruyama was more deeply schooled in the European—especially German—intellectual tradition than the American), a desire to promote scientific method, and a tendency to base arguments on the presumption of a developmental scale from premodernity to modernity.

Yet there were also differences, which in some ways paralleled the division in nineteenth- and twentieth-century social science between the positivism of Auguste Comte, J. S. Mill, and Emile Durkheim on the one hand, and the stream of "moral science" (*Geisteswissenschaft*) contributed to by the historians J. G. Droysen and W. Dilthey, the philosophers H. Rickert and W. Windelband, and the sociologists Simmel and Weber. Typical of the positivists were strong confidence in the unity of scientific method as the single legitimate epistemology for social and behavioral as well as natural sciences, and a preference for causal as opposed to teleological or other forms of explanation. Adherents to the antipositivist, or hermeneutic, approach tended to differentiate the study of human history and society from the natural sciences, insisting that whereas natural scientists aimed at explanation (*Erklären*), the human sciences should seek a form of understanding (*Verstehen*), which should rely in part on empathy, encompass teleological models, and concentrate on recreating the "mental atmosphere" and intentionality of human actors.[136] Whereas Ōtsuka and Maruyama, along with Marxists such as Mashita Shin'ichi, adhered in one degree or other to major assumptions of the hermeneutic tradition, they were challenged in the early postwar period not only by positivist Marxists such as Matsumura Kazuto but by non-Marxist, or semi-Marxist, behavioral scientists of a positivist bent such as Shimizu and Miyagi, and the historian Hayashi Kentarō.

Shimizu argued in late 1947 that the controversy over *shutaisei* reflected something fundamental about postwar intellectual culture in that "the main focus of intellectual reflection in Japan in the wake of World War II has been the relationship between science and action." This was because, first, Japan's defeat led to collapse of the authoritative, prewar value system that had "provided the standards for action and had been able to unify the inner and outer dimensions of life," leaving in its place uncertainty and anxiety. Second, the iconoclastic impact of defeat had been especially serious in Japan because the prewar value system had "permeated the very flesh" of those who lived under it and had effectively excluded all "freedom, reflection and criticism." Therefore, defeat had left people entirely unaccustomed to autonomous decision-making. Third, in the confusion and uncertainty of defeat, people lost confidence in scientific method and instead sought finalistic authority.

Despite the special conditions he listed, Shimizu did not claim that a tendency to appeal to authority was peculiar to Japan. Indeed, he quotes the American philosopher Irwin Edman to the effect that Americans also felt the "uneasiness of freedom." Thus, concludes Shimizu, "If we can take Edman at face value, this means that we are on the threshold of a universal problem which Japan suffers to a grotesque extreme."[137]

Shimizu graduated in sociology from Tokyo Imperial University in 1931 and in 1932 became a member of the Marxist Materialism Study Group with Tosaka Jun and others. In 1938 he took charge of the scholarly-oriented liberal arts column (*gakugei-ran*) of the prestigious daily *Asahi shinbun* and also, with Miki Kiyoshi and a number of other former Marxists, became a member of the cultural section of Prime Minister Konoe's brain trust, the Shōwa Research Association. In 1941, while lecturing first at Tokyo's Sophia University and then at Meiji Gakuin, he joined the editorial board of another major daily, *Yomiuri shinbun*, where he remained throughout the war. After Japan's defeat, he wrote prolifically and also organized and led the influential Nijusseiki Kenkyūjo (Twentieth-Century Research Institute), whose leadership included Miyagi Otoya, along with the labor specialist Ōkōchi Kazuo, the literary critics Fukuda

Tsuneari and Nakano Yoshio, the historian Hayashi Kentarō, the sociologist of law Kawashima Takeyoshi, the political scientist Maruyama Masao, and the philosopher Mashita Shin'ichi. In 1949 Shimizu joined the faculty of Gakushūin University, where he taught sociology until his retirement.

According to Shimizu, postwar intellectuals were anxious to possess a fetish that would give them final, comprehensive truth, and this desire, in turn, resulted in a widespread "desire for philosophy and . . . hunger for *shutaisei*" at the expense of adherence to scientific method. The search for *shutaisei* was particularly widespread among social scientists, and paradoxically Shimizu partially attributes its prevalence to advances in the application of scientific method. Apparently referring to the resurgence of positivism between the world wars, he wrote:

> [A]s social science transcended hermeneutic historiography (*Geistesgeschichte*) through increased use of the objective methods of modern science, the desire that had always been satisfied in ambiguous form through *Geistesgeschichte* emerged more clearly as the desire for *shutaisei*. . . . It appears that the establishment of objectivity in social science combined with a powerful demand for practice led to a split in which the desire for *shutaisei* as the basis for practice was separated off from the objective analysis of social phenomena. . . . it seems to me that the desire for *shutaisei* is based on the sense that independent of objective social science, and supplementing it, there is a need for a philosophy that can undergird subjective activism.

Once scientific method and *shutaisei* had come to be thought of as contending positions, *shutaisei* was considered exempt from scientific objectification and analysis. This was dangerous because "whenever it appears that something refuses objectification, we are in danger of being drawn in spite of ourselves into a mystical realm. And when this dark, mystical world is described through the use of objective, social-science terminology, the inevitable result will be obscure reasoning."[138]

Shimizu then proceeds to rephrase his argument in the temporal framework of social evolution. On the one hand, he posits a premodern circumstance, in which desires are satisfied within a single communal group. In such a situation, "the meaning and value of each thing is predetermined so that attitudes and behavior follow as a matter of course." He then juxtaposes against this a modern society, where groups are multiple and objects are severed from all intrinsic value and implications for action. Citing George Herbert Mead's *The Philosophy of the Act*, Shimizu concludes that in the modern milieu the things of the world are neutral: they contain neither metaphysical essence nor vitalistic entelechy. This development is to be welcomed because only value neutrality "satisfies the fundamental condition for scientific method" and for freedom of action. That is, "it is by extracting all entelechy from objects that people secures their own freedom of action."

Scientific method relied directly on the processes of externalization and objectification, which also led incrementally to increases in human control over the natural and, analogously, the social environment. However, modernity understood in this sense also created "new problems for action and ethics." In other words, "so long as things were understood to contain a metaphysical essence or entelechy . . . human action was in fact limited by the intrinsic meanings and telos of things." However, once things took on "different values in different contexts" and eventually became entirely neutral, they lost their ability to determine action and instead fell increasingly under human control. Yet this very control raised urgent and difficult questions related to ethics, instrumentality, and values.[139]

Indeed, many postwar intellectuals wanted to sidestep those difficult issues, and in order to do so they implicitly sought to reinstate entelechy in the human realm. Shimizu argued, in sum, that the postwar "desire for *shutaisei*" was little more than a nostalgic urge to return to a premodern situation or, in other words, a desire to "recognize a certain entelechy in human beings" that is immune from externalization and objectification. According to Shimizu, the argument for *shutaisei* amounted to a demand that scientific method be supplemented by a norm of "immediate sincerity." By "immediate sincerity" he seems to mean honest but irrational commitment to a goal or ideal of a sort similar, perhaps, to Umemoto's theory of selfless commitment to the destiny of the proletariat. To Shimizu, however, such a norm implied that all the important choices would be between black or white, good or bad, whereas, in fact, "real-life conflict takes place among multiple values." As Dewey had written, "Only dogmatism can suppose that serious moral conflict is between something clearly bad and something known to be good, and that uncertainty lies wholly in the will of the one choosing."[140] In the modern world, ethical choices had to be made among competing values that were all colored in shades of gray. Ethicality, therefore, required rational scientific assessment rather than wholehearted commitment.

According to Shimizu, in Japan, especially, there was "a tendency to view the social as something substantial that transcends the individual," and at times this was reflected in a propensity to "ignore and suppress the human dimension."[141] Moreover, paralleling this reification of "social nature" was a tendency to treat science not as a method but as a set of substantive truths that were beyond dispute. An overly rigid reification of "social nature" as a determining force was counterpart in the postwar milieu to the *shutaisei*-theorists' appeal to "direct sincerity" and entelechy. In other words, "the inclination to turn science into an authoritative doctrine reinforces and legitimizes a tendency to seek the source of behavior in a mystical realm of *shutaisei*, making it impossible to dismantle either reification."[142] The only solution was to promote science as a practical method rather than as substantialized truth, and to apply scientific method to the human dimension as well as the social. If that were done, there would be no need for a separate theory of *shutaisei*.

Shimizu was especially concerned to establish the relevance of scientific method to problems of human intention and choice. Did the inability of science to produce value judgments mean that it was entirely incapable of providing a fuller understanding of subjective action? Shimizu answers that, according to Max Weber, scientific method could contribute to value judgments in at least four ways: First, it could help clarify what means were the most suitable to the attainment of an end or ideal. Second, scientific method could give an account of what *results* would be likely to follow from the application of a certain means, irrespective of the ends sought; that is, it could "reveal not only the results an actor would find desirable but those he or she would find undesirable." Third, science could provide knowledge regarding the "significance" of an end and its connections with other ends and results. Fourth, it could help clarify ultimate standards for value choices.[143]

In a later interpretation of Shimizu's essay as an attempt to reconceptualize *shutaisei* in an "objective" manner, his fellow sociologist Sakuta Keiichi synthesized the above tenets as aiming at either self-determination, by which he meant the modern individual's capacity to choose among competing demands, or value consistency, which he defined as the "individual's faculty for resisting the impact of change in the external environment and instead maintaining a consistent pattern of action in conformity with internalized values."[144]

Shimizu's essay did not go without criticism in the postwar milieu, of course. Among those who responded was the philosopher Takakuwa Sumio, who argued that Shimizu failed to distinguish among the different kinds of *shutaisei* that were being proposed, lumping together those that were relatively solipsistic and egocentric (e.g., Ara Masato's) and others that sought *shutaisei* in social theory (e.g., Umemoto's). Takakuwa also took issue with Shimizu's attribution of the "desire for *shutaisei*" to a kind of nostalgia for the certainty of life in premodern community or, alternatively, the fascist era, preferring to see in the increased interest in philosophy that accompanied the debate on subjectivity an encouraging sign for the future. In sum, Takakuwa argued that rather than rejected out of hand as unscientific, demands for *shutaisei* ought to be granted basic recognition and channeled away from solipsism into direct engagement with the social-historical situation.[145]

Miyagi Otoya was another important proponent of the positivist position. A 1931 graduate in psychology and philosophy of Kyoto University who studied at the University of Paris and then taught from 1934 at Keio University, Miyagi was a tireless critic of theories of *shutaisei* in the early postwar period. He argued ironically that the intellectuals' preoccupation with *shutaisei* could be attributed largely to the concept's vagueness and imprecision, but in part it also resulted from overemphasis within Marxism on historical necessity. Therefore, he proposed that the notion of necessity be abandoned in favor of a more scientific concept of probability. If this were done, the desire among intellectuals for something like *shutaisei* would disappear.[146]

Miyagi was also a pivotal participant in a now-famous roundtable discussion organized by editors of the intellectual monthly *Sekai*. Other participants were Matsumura Kazuto, Hayashi Kentarō, Maruyama Masao, Mashita Shin'ichi, and the Communist philosopher Kozai Yoshishige. The occasion for the roundtable, entitled "Yuibutsuron to shutaisei" (Materialism and Subjectivity), was the publication in *The American Scholar* of an essay by James Marshall, entitled "Freud and Marx at UNESCO." Marshall argued that in assessing the causes of war it was necessary to take into account both the materialistic explanations inspired by Marx and the psychological ones inspired by Freud.[147] Although the discussion focused initially on questions raised directly by the Marshall article, it quickly moved on to grapple with the more general issue of how to reconcile historical materialism with subjective action. Major issues included the scope and nature of economic determinism and, more broadly, of scientific method, the origin of class consciousness, the relationship between values and praxis, and whether historical materialism could be best characterized as a science, a worldview, or some combination of these.

Marxism for Miyagi was to be defined as scientific socialism, and historical materialism was its methodology. Therefore, Marxism could never be static so long as science continued to develop. While it was no doubt true that Marx and Engels had, as Engels admitted in a letter to Mehring, overemphasized the "economic side," there was no need to bring in a mystical conception of subjective commitment. Any lacuna in Marxist theory regarding individual intentionality and action (or the "superstructure" in general) could be filled through the application of personality theories developed by Freud and elaborated by a generation of personality and social psychologists. Psychology offered a science of human behavior in relation to the environment, and according to that science all intentionality should be understood as arising from drives and desires grounded in biology and the material conditions of existence.[148]

From Miyagi's viewpoint, practice was to be reduced to behavior (kōdō) and subjectivity to adjustment. Indeed, scientific method was to be understood as little more than a systematization of the "praxis" of response and experimentation applied by an individual or group in solving day-to-day problems of adjustment in order to secure optimum satisfaction of desires.[149] Of course, it was possible for people to sacrifice short-term satisfaction, but only as a more intelligent assessment of how to maximize their satisfaction over a longer period of time, not because of devotion to a worldview or ideal. Therefore, science—including Marxism—was to be seen as encompassing both epistemology and practice, in that it not only guided perception but also provided strategy and tactics for action. Marxism was not, according to Miyagi, a worldview except insofar as science was itself a worldview.[150] Indeed, worldviews could be shown always to change in accordance with developments in science, not the other way around.[151]

Finally, for Miyagi the dialectic was primarily a "law of movement of objective things"[152] and did not significantly involve the subject. To have argued otherwise would have implied that the object of perception was not independent of the subject, suggesting, therefore, that the subject to some extent *constituted* its object in the course of practical activity. This would have called into question the positivistic view of perception as a "copy" of external reality.

In opposition to Miyagi, Mashita Shin'ichi argued that the problems of subjectivity and practice were properly within the purview of philosophy rather than science. To attempt to analyze the subject from the perspective of psychology was to "objectify" it and therefore to eliminate any subjectivity in the true sense of the word. Moreover, as Umemoto had suggested, Marxism had to be seen as a worldview in addition to a science; indeed, its status as a worldview was even more fundamental than its function as a science. If it had been mere methodology, where would its goals come from? What possible meaning could it have? Mashita observed at one point that *shutaisei* could be seen as the equivalent of "meaning" in the sense that practice and method always had to be guided by a particular goal or purpose.[153]

In response to Miyagi's proposition that scientific knowledge was prior to and the proper basis of all worldviews, Mashita posed the question of those who had employed their Marxist "scientific methodology" in the service of fascism during the war. Surely it had been their failure to premise "science" on a prior commitment to a Marxist worldview that had been responsible for such a distortion of perspective.[154] Mashita also insisted that dialectics had to be understood as involving both subject and object.

In the final analysis, Mashita proposed that subjectivity be defined in terms of class partisanship (*tōhasei*). Commitment to the cause and destiny of the proletariat could provide a basis for value judgments and a criterion for committed action that would ensure that scientific method and technology would always be employed as means toward a worthy end.[155] Here, particularly, Mashita's view mirrored that of Umemoto.

More orthodox Marxist participants such as Matsumura Kazuto and Kozai Yoshishige attempted to maintain their independence from the positions of both Miyagi and Mashita but unquestionably leaned more toward the former than the latter. Matsumura accepted the applicability of dialectic method both to natural processes in the external world and to relations between subject and object, thereby softening Miyagi's objectivist position. Kozai even admitted that Marxism is at once "a science, a worldview, and also a scientific worldview."[156] Predictably, Matsumura warned that to try to borrow a conception of subjectivity from the Kyoto School philosophers would invite dire consequences:

> There are, of course, many problems Marxism has yet to solve. . . .
> Matters such as new scientific developments, incorporation of wartime
> experiences, and so on, should provide the basis for incremental aug-
> mentation and a contribution to overall development. However, at the
> level of fundamental principle, there is absolutely no need to incorpo-
> rate existential philosophy, the philosophy of Nishida Kitarō, or other
> fashions. To do so would be a serious mistake. Mr. Mashita has said
> that the problems addressed by existential philosophy must be taken up
> by Marxists or else the young people will lose interest. Yet even if they
> were to approach Marxism from such a perspective, insofar as they did
> so primarily out of an attraction to existentialism or Nishida's philoso-
> phy, they would never become truly Marxist. In that sense, I think Mr.
> Mashita's interpretation of Marxism is dangerous.[157]

A fourth position in the debate, in addition to the scientific materialism of Miyagi, the existential Marxism of Mashita, and the orthodox Marxism of Matsumura and Kozai, was Ōtsuka's liberal-modernist definition of subjectivity in terms of values, or ethos, put forward here by Maruyama Masao. Maruyama supported Mashita's stand with regard to Marxism as a worldview,[158] but sought to go beyond it by speaking more broadly about the importance of values and value judgments in revolutionary change.

In relation to Mashita's equation of *shutaisei* with class partisanship, Maruyama raised the question of whether practice founded on partisanship was to be understood as actually "in being *(Dasein)*"—in other words, presently tangible—or merely as a conception of what *should* be. Was so-called class consciousness actually the consciousness of real proletarians, or only the consciousness they ought to possess if they could more fully and accurately perceive their situation? How could Marxists speak of "high" class consciousness as opposed to "low" without some value-criterion by which to judge? Marxist science, he concluded, must in fact be premised upon a value orientation—a sense of what *should* be—which would serve as a basis for evaluating what *is*. Moreover, it was precisely the ideals or values implied by that "should"—and for Marxism that meant "total human liberation, free development to the fullest extent of human potential and the construction of a society conducive to that development"[159]—that would be capable of eliciting commitment at the expense of personal happiness and perhaps of one's life. Such values could, therefore, serve as the foundation for subjective engagement.

Of course, for Maruyama, the possible range of values was not limited to the sort of "partisanship" that attracted the existential Marxists. A major aspect of his perception of the need for Japanese Marxists to clarify and emphasize their value premises was his conviction that non-Marxists—such as Christians—who shared the value of human liberation should be encouraged to join with Marxists in a democratic front.[160]

Although Maruyama tacitly admitted the logical possibility of adhering to a thoroughgoing scientific materialist position, he cautioned that such an emphasis would be politically fatal to progressive forces in the early postwar political milieu:

> There would be no problem if the sort of scientism espoused by Mr. Miyagi were followed entirely and the worldview of scientism were generally accepted. Unfortunately, however, it fails to attract many people. In order to fill the gap [left by the absence of an adequate scientific worldview], the majority of people turn to religion, existential philosophy, or something else. That might be because they are weak in spirit. Perhaps tough-minded people can get along on scientism, but tender-minded folks like me find it difficult to deal with all the problems of humanity through science alone. If, in the real world, and not only in Japan, the majority of people are on the tender-minded side, surely it is not "scientific" to ignore them.[161]

Maruyama's position in relation to the Marxists and scientific materialists was summarized aptly in an epigrammatic exchange toward the conclusion of the discussion. To add emphasis, the discussants expressed their formulas partially in English:

Miyagi: [speaking of the future of Marxism,] Symbolically, it will be a
matter of Marx plus Freud.
Maruyama: You should rather say, Marx plus Freud plus Ethos.[162]

Although it did not include any of the literary figures who had contributed to
discussions of subjectivity, or even such central participants on the philosophical side as Umemoto Katsumi, the roundtable discussion was timed in such a
way as to mark a kind of watershed in the discourse on *shutaisei*. Already in
statements such as Matsumura's to the effect that "Mr. Mashita's interpretation
of Marxism is dangerous," one gets a foretaste of the Communist party's official
denunciations of the subjectivist position that were issued only half a year later
in the context of a party-led campaign to criticize "modernism" (*kindaishugi*).
Moreover, by mid-1948 a sea change was beginning that would bring into increasing salience various dimensions of the national unit. These tendencies will
be discussed in the following chapter.

F I V E

Nationalism

> The term *shutaisei* is now outdated. Nevertheless, it would be a great mistake to con-
> clude that the problem it referred to has been solved. It would be more correct to imag-
> ine it as an open construction site left exposed to the rain.
>
> —Takakuwa Sumio[1]

In the September 1951 issue of the journal *Bungaku* (Literature), the specialist
in modern Chinese literature Takeuchi Yoshimi observed that the problem of
minzoku (Volk, race, nation) had again "risen to the surface of consciousness" in
Japan, and that this event marked "the development of a new stage in the postwar era." He noted that new attention to *minzoku* was evident not only in political rhetoric but in scholarly discourse. According to Takeuchi, this new Volk-
consciousness was noteworthy because since defeat in August 1945 the term
minzoku had been taboo in scholarly circles, where "the very existence of the
Volk was thought inevitably to be evil."[2] That is, "in order to forget the blood-
drenched bad dream of nationalism, there had been a tendency to exclude the
Volk entirely from consciousness."[3]

> From one angle, one can say that the psychology of avoiding con-
> frontation with nationalism reveals insufficient consciousness of war
> responsibility—in other words, a lack of conscience, originating in a
> failure of courage. People are afraid of getting hurt, so they try to forget
> their blood-spattered Volk. They are reluctant to call themselves Japa-
> nese. But the blood cannot be washed away through forgetfulness.[4]

In Takeuchi's view, the "abnormal psychological state"[5] of repression that
prevailed in the early postwar period was the fault especially of modernism
(*kindaishugi*), which, as an ideology, was defined by its "failure, indeed, active
refusal, to include the Volk in the realm of discourse."[6] Marxism had participated in a repressive strategy as well, in that even before the war proletarian
writers had employed the category of class "in order to suppress the nation,"
leading to a "highly extended posture" that crumbled under the onslaught of
fascism. Moreover, in their attachment to such abstractions as the individual,
class, and humanity, they had fundamentally distorted the "whole human being," an essential part of which was volkish identity. Their "sense of self-impor-
tance" had led them to "sever all relations with concrete, whole human beings
and to treat those abstract or class-bound concepts as if they were perfect entities in themselves."[7] As they attempted to "make a part encompass the whole,"
it was not surprising that "out of the dark corners that had been neglected there

arose anguished voices crying for a restoration of the whole human being." It was self-evident that "consciousness of the Volk grows as a result of suppression." Conversely, so long as it was not repressed, it would remain below the surface as mere latent potential. However, in Takeuchi's view, it was only by confronting volkish nationalism that Japanese intellectuals and writers could pacify it and prevent it from again bursting forth to link up with imperialism to become ultranationalism. Moreover, nationalism would provide an essential mediation in Japan's attempts to reestablish relations with the former targets of its aggression in Asia.

On the basis of Takeuchi's version of postwar thought one would gather that in the period from 1945 down to 1950–51, when in his view the "return to *minzoku*" began, prominent Japanese intellectuals—especially those of a modernist bent—had thoroughly ignored the question of nationalism. As revealed in our readings of Maruyama and Ōtsuka, this is hardly the case. Takeuchi's ambiguous relationship to modernist varieties of nationalism seems to reflect his propensity to reduce nationalism to what he considered to be authentic *minzoku*-consciousness, a variant of nationalism that usually mobilizes ethnic and racial as well as cultural and political criteria and is especially tied to the romantic notion of a unique historical ethnos. He seems to be correct in observing that "nationalism" in that racial/ethnic sense was not yet a prominent feature of postwar discourse. As we have seen, that does not mean that the works of early postwar thinkers—and especially the modernists—were not themselves implicated in other forms of nationalism that relied somewhat less explicitly on racial or ethnic identity. Indeed, I have argued that for the most part their concepts and theories of historical subjectivity cannot be understood properly apart from nationalism in its various guises.

In the early postwar modernist milieu, one of the progressive writers most explicitly committed to a variety of nationalism was Maruyama Masao. It is important to recognize that even in his wartime essays on Tokugawa thought, Maruyama had taken pains to distinguish among the various terms that are used to translate "nationalism" into Japanese, including *minzokushugi, kokuminshugi*, and *kokkashugi*. Remarking that "*kokuminshugi* (modern nationalism, or the principle of nationality)" is the "demand for national unification and national independence that develops against the background of . . . national consciousness," he explains, regarding the more racial/ethnic variety of nationalism, that

> [n]ationalism has also been translated into Japanese as *minzokushugi* (sense of racial identity), but this term is appropriate to a people with

the status of a minority race in another nation-state, or a colonized people, that gains its independence, or when a race that has been split into several groups under different nation-states unites to constitute an independent nation. But its use is questionable in the case of Japan.[8]

He goes on:

Of course, ever since the foundation of the country, the minds of the people had always contained the idea of Japan as the Land of the Gods and a sense of racial (*minzoku*) self-confidence based on the uniqueness of the Japanese state system. But this did not automatically rise to the level where the nation possessed a sense of political solidarity, nor did it lead directly to national unity. The internal social conditions necessary for this were still undeveloped.[9]

According to Maruyama, legitimate nationalism can only be *kokuminshugi*, which he believes to be consistent with democracy; indeed, "the formation of the nation-state must be expressed in an active commitment by every individual." Moreover, this "nationalism seeks above all to eliminate the force or structure that intervenes between the nation and the state, preventing the direct union of the two."[10] In sum, modern nationalism must involve, at a minimum, both an inner commitment on the part of each participant and unity between the nation and the state structure. As Naoki Sakai has pointed out, Maruyama's *Nihon seiji shisōshi kenkyū* (Studies in the Intellectual History of Tokugawa Japan) found its central problem in the analysis of historical development from "the Japanese *minzoku*" to "the Japanese *kokumin*."[11] Maruyama situated *minzokushugi* as a less modern and less mediated form of nationalism.

Takeuchi did not distinguish so clearly between the two terms, emphasizing *minzokushugi* but referring often to *kokuminshugi* as well. Indeed, one of the fundamental questions begged by a focus on the broad trend toward "nationalism," which by 1951–52 was transforming and recontaining the problematic of *shutaisei*, is whether nationalism as *minzokushugi* remained distinct from nationalism as *kokuminshugi*. In Takeuchi's interventions, especially, the two concepts tended ultimately to merge.

The Communist Critique of Modernism

As we have seen, the Occupation had begun to turn against the organized Left as early as May 20, 1946, when MacArthur issued a stern warning against "the growing tendency toward mass violence" he perceived in the Food May Day demonstrations. This turn continued in the broader "reverse course" that got under way following SCAP's cancellation of the February 1, 1947, general strike. Sensitive to this changing atmosphere, the Japan Communist party had begun to edge away from its earlier policies of support for the American reforms.

Following the roundtable discussion that was published on the problem of *shutaisei* in February 1948 (see chapter 4), the party's theoreticians launched a campaign against "modernism," which the party took to refer to any argument that shifted emphasis away from class structure and proletarian leadership toward issues of subjectivity or values. Included in the party's modernist category were not only liberals such as Maruyama Masao but existential Marxists such as Umemoto Katsumi and Mashita Shin'ichi. The party's critique included an attack on the historical school inspired by Ōtsuka Hisao.[12]

The reaction against modernism seems to have revealed the party's nascent antagonism toward American imperialism and any intellectual tendencies that seemed capable of bolstering the Occupation's bourgeois-liberal approach to democratic revolution and emerging Cold War hostility to Soviet and Asian Communism. Accordingly, the critique of modernism was related to a new nationalism that became increasingly manifest in Japanese Communist terminology and posture.

Communist strategists devoted the entire August 1948 issue of the party's theoretical journal, *Zen'ei* (Vanguard), to the critique of "modernism" in its various manifestations. Defining modernism as "one of the corrupt tendencies that appeared in bourgeois culture in the final stage of capitalism, especially in the imperialist era," Kurahara Korehito noted that this tendency was a vital issue insofar as the culture of the intelligentsia, in which modernism flourished, interacted with mass culture and in the process interfered with the "healthy democratic tendencies" that were rooted among the "working masses" (*kinrō taishū*).[13] Although Kurahara admits that modernism was evident not only in the arts but in science, philosophy, and quotidian culture, he chooses to focus on graphic art, literature, and music.

In Kurahara's view, modernism was born in France in the 1870s, manifesting itself initially in symbolism and impressionism, then in neo-romanticism, primitivism, cubism, futurism, and expressionism, and finally in surrealism and existentialism. Throughout, the most important assumption underlying the modern aesthetic was individualism,[14] and this dimension provided a major link between modern art and modern social thought and philosophy. Kurahara says that at the historical stage of the bourgeoisie's battle against the feudal ruling class, individualism had "advocated the primacy of the individual in relation to society" but never negated society as such. By the mid-nineteenth century, however, "the self (*jiga*) had been made the sole substantial entity"; not only was society considered "illusory" but there emerged forms of thought which opposed every social constraint that threatened to impinge on the individual. Thus, individualism went from being asocial to antisocial, and this antisocial tendency remained characteristic of postwar Japanese modernism. It is interesting to note the convergence between Kurahara's interpretation of modernism and Takakuwa's analysis of "anti-social" tendencies in postwar Japanese society (see chapter 3).

Modernism granted supreme importance to the individuality of the artist, and thus, "the more a work of art is deprived of sociality and becomes unique, the more value it is thought to have." Similarly, in philosophy Jean Paul Sartre's focus on individual responsibility might appear to be moral, but in fact it ignored "objective laws and universal morality," denied "social duty and responsibility," and supported a willfully antisocial brand of individualism.[15] Despite Sartre's contention that "existentialism is a humanism,"[16] individualism and humanism were in fact diametrically opposed. That was because in the individualism of the existentialists, characteristics such as selfishness were viewed "not as if they were socially and historically conditioned but rather as eternal dimensions of humanity."[17]

Even the antirealism of modern art, with its tendency toward conceptual idealism, contributed to modernism's politically reactionary stance: "Because of their fear and antipathy toward the democratic mass movement, the bourgeois artists tend to express only the insubstantial surface of phenomena while at the same time they actually flee reality to become closed up in their own little world."[18]

Kurahara realizes that modernism in itself was easily alienated from capitalism and was not necessarily actively supportive of the imperialist bourgeoisie. That was why, as agents of the bourgeoisie, "the Nazis rejected as decadent all modernistic tendencies in art." Nevertheless, "in the absence of effective ideological weapons of its own, the reactionary bourgeoisie of the postwar era is actively using modernism against the revolutionary forces and their art." In sum, modernism in art served reactionary purposes,

> first, by disseminating a pessimistic view of the future of humans and society and making the working masses relinquish their characteristically rational confidence in the construction of a new society; second, by propagating individualism and thereby weakening the spirit of solidarity among the masses and between them and the intelligentsia, and denying the social and moral responsibility of artists; third, by diverting, through antirealistic works, the attention of the people from the realities of class conflict in society toward sensual interests and idealis-

tic issues related to the subject; and fourth, by denying the objectivity
of perceptions of reality, demanding revision of Marxism-Leninism,
and fostering ambiguity in the guise of progressivism in place of partisanship in culture and the arts.[19]

The only way to overcome the baneful effects of modernism was to propagate a
healthy alternative that reflected the masses' hopes for the future.

Directed more specifically to the postwar Japanese scene and to the type of
modernism that was involved in the *shutaisei* debate was an essay by Amakasu
Sekisuke, which focused on "one of the most powerful and influential sources
of contemporary theory regarding *shutaisei*," the *Kindai bungaku* writer Ara
Masato. In this essay, Amakasu, who had earlier been in some degree sympathetic to the problematic of *shutaisei*, asserts critically that Ara's approach is
reducible to two major premises: that postwar Japan is a backward, premodern
society, and that postwar Japanese should affirm the ego and thereby establish
shutaisei. These two premises reinforced each other.[20]

Ara's propositions also entailed a certain approach to revolutionary strategy.
That is, in Ara's view, Japan's backwardness—equivalent to that of France
before the Revolution—and the Japanese failure to foster an internalized self,
implied that Japan was immediately in need of a thorough bourgeois revolution,
while socialist revolution could only be a long-term objective. This perception
left it very ambiguous whether in Ara's scheme the proletariat was to lead the
popular masses in the bourgeois revolution.

Ara and the *shutaisei* theorists were lacking not only in theory but in practice:

> The masses' feudalistic attitudes and lack of *shutaisei* could be tran-
> scended, not simply through a movement for popular enlightenment,
> but by means of struggle against the actual feudal relations that con-
> strain them. In that sense, the significance of the current, proletariat-led
> struggle in giving the masses confidence and self-awareness and in
> "consolidating *shutaisei*" is incalculable. Nevertheless, it appears that
> those who verbally advocate the consolidation of *shutaisei* have no in-
> tention of connecting up with that movement.[21]

Ara and the others had found backwardness even in the proletarian movement itself, and in its organization and leadership. Not that the proletarian
movement was without defects, but the *shutaisei* theorists had portrayed those
defects out of context, and their attempts to introduce individualism and liberalism into the movement weakened its organization and discipline. Despite their
best intentions, they were serving the purposes of the bourgeoisie.[22]

For his part, Katsube Hajime posited three dimensions of *shutaisei* as it was promoted in the postwar milieu: (1) The notion of *shutaisei* as ego-formation, which evoked the historical context of nascent capitalist opposition to feudal absolutism, when the bourgeoisie had originally formed its individualistic ideology; (2) the notion of *shutaisei* in existentialist philosophy, which, rather than militant and active like the spirit of the rising bourgeoisie, was an "anxious," resigned form of "escapist quietism infected by powerlessness" (according to Katsube, in Japan this angst had spread rapidly among petty bourgeois intellectuals in the interwar period); and (3) *shutaisei* as contribution to Marxism.[23] In postwar Japan these three approaches had been combined in various ways in different arguments and had attracted a considerable following. However, to Katsube they functioned overall as a theoretical stumbling block in the path of youths who should have been devoting themselves wholeheartedly to democratic revolution. His conclusion is blunt:

> Instead of showing the true means of individual liberation to those in their twenties, who are drifting around amidst the nihilism and disenchantment that accompanied defeat and the loss of faith in emperor-system absolutism, [the *shutaisei* theorists] expound upon the ego and the subjectivity of Gide and Kierkegaard. What is the objective function of this [effort]? . . . [In sum], despite the rationalistic fables and rhetoric of the intellectuals, the advanced stratum of worker sees clearly that "*shutaisei*" is an anticommunist term, and anticommunist is synonymous with anti-people (*jinmin*).

For Katsube, there was no need to become preoccupied with the question of subjectivity because "true science, and especially Marxism, is [already] extremely practical in nature." For workers, "the perception of objective truth is in itself practice, and no gap intervenes."[24]

Matsumura Kazuto also participated in the critique of modernism, as it was now defined by the party. It will be recalled that Matsumura had stigmatized Umemoto's *shutaisei* as fundamentally separate from the practical standpoint of the proletariat, which he believed was always already engaged subjectively in struggle through class consciousness. Thus, Matsumura's critique of Umemoto clearly paralleled Nakano's attack on Ara Masato and Hirano Ken. From the perspective of the guardians of party orthodoxy, Umemoto had erred on the same side as the *Kindai bungaku* writers in the sense that he had failed to situate his perspective squarely in the standpoint of the masses, led by the proletariat. Umemoto's analysis of revolutionary *shutaisei* was designed to solve his own problem—the problem of how a petty bourgeois intellectual would be able to make a commitment to revolutionary action—not the problems faced by the masses in their struggle against capitalists, landlords, and state bureaucrats. Therefore, although Umemoto's conceptualizations might be useful in the struggle against feudalistic autocracy, they were as potentially damaging to the cause of democratic revolution as were Ara's argument for "egoism" and Hirano's attempt to separate politics and literature. As Nakano had said of Ara and Hirano, in their espousal of such views they functioned as "spokesmen for the political forces seeking to transfer from the proletariat to the petty bour- geoisie the power to lead Japan's . . . democratic revolution." Of course, as we have seen, the *Kindai bungaku* writers were encouraged to believe that they could contribute to democratic revolution as petty bourgeois intellectuals by the party's own political program, which, as enunciated by Nosaka, had provided a leading role for not only intellectuals but even small and medium-scale capital- ists. Umemoto was less conscious of his own standpoint as a petty bourgeois intellectual than were Ara and his compatriots, but from the perspective of the party's cultural arbiters his thought was equally distant from the approved standpoint of the masses.

In the context of the critique of modernism of 1948, Matsumura made much more explicit this parallel between the *Kindai bungaku* position in the realm of literature, on the one hand, and that of Umemoto and others (such as Mashita Shin'ichi) in philosophy on the other. Taken together, these literary and philo- sophical ploys represented to Matsumura complementary aspects of bourgeois humanism, "a new ideological offensive arising in opposition to people's de- mocracy."[25] By definition, this bourgeois mode of thought "seeks the essence of humanity in the individual grasped as an independent entity."[26] A classical spokesman for this mode of thought had been Rousseau, "who believed in a 'human nature' separate from social life, and thought that independent human beings pursued their happiness by forming society through a social contract." Rousseau had "attributed to this human nature a content which typified that of actual members of the bourgeoisie, and through that content projected a hope for new principles of social organization." This viewpoint had played a progres- sive role in social development at the time.[27]

Bourgeois humanism, in turn, was the source of two complementary streams of thought, individualism and idealism. An ideology of individualism, which virtually denied the legitimacy of the social, resulted when the bourgeois hu- manist notion of the independent human being was carried to an extreme. At the same time, since "the human being always has certain abilities, and adheres to norms, ideals, and so on, which could not be explained on the basis of his or her independent existence," and since bourgeois individualism is incapable of understanding the social origins of these phenomena, it tends to "idealize or mystify them" in some variety of idealism: "Kant is typical of this way of thinking. Kant cannot accept the selfish origin of morals, nor can he find their social origin. So he has morality develop within the individual as a human ability a priori—as the capacity for practical reason. Moreover, for Kant this ability is entirely different from, and contradictory to, other human abilities; eventually, he connects this human intelligence to God."[28]

Matsumura then employs these two manifestations of bourgeois humanism as the basis for a comparison—ultimately an equation—between the *Kindai bungaku* viewpoint on the one hand and Umemoto's philosophical theory of *shutaisei* on the other:

> Individualism and social idealism are two inseparable facets of the bourgeois way of thought, and the bourgeois view of man appears in the complex interweaving of these two aspects. . . . However, this does not mean that they always coexist. Among present-day Japan's literary writers and philosophers, those in literature strongly manifest the individualistic dimension while those experimenting with "*shutaisei*"-oriented revisionism in Marxist philosophy exemplify the idealistic dimension.

Moreover, these views share a common affinity to European varieties of idealistic socialism and revisionism.

> The broad, overall direction of "*shutaisei*"-oriented revisionism is the same as utopian socialism, True Socialism, and the neo-Kantian revisionism of the Second International. The overall content of utopian socialism [for example] is that while it heads in a socialist direction, its way of thinking does not ultimately escape the basic attitude of bourgeois thought. That is, it is not clearly conscious that the demand for socialism is a class demand, but rather thinks of it as arising from humanity in general. . . . The fundamental ideology that runs through all these is that what ought to be seen as originating in concrete history, society, and class are cut off from the concrete and postulated a priori as abstract standards.[29]

For Matsumura, the appropriate historical-materialist viewpoint on problems of action and *shutaisei* was enunciated by Marx in "The Holy Family":

> It is not a matter of what this or that proletarian or even the proletariat as a whole pictures at present as its goal. It is a matter of what the proletariat is in actuality and what, in accordance with this being, it will historically be compelled to do. Its goal and its historical action are pre-

figured in the most clear and ineluctable way in its own life-situation as well as in the whole organization of contemporary bourgeois society.[30]

Proletarians act because they have to, not because they are able beforehand to appreciate the "meaning" of an action and on that basis to make a decision for partisanship: "Of course, individual consciousness is necessary. But what should the individual be conscious of? It is social self-consciousness that is necessary. And this class consciousness means being aware of the major enemy and knowing who one's friends are. This self-consciousness has nothing to do with individualistic self-consciousness. Indeed, it is the opposite."[31]

But was not Japan in the midst of a democratic revolution, in which to some degree even bourgeois individualism would be able to play a progressive role? Matsumura echoes Nakano Shigeharu's view that bourgeois individualism would be destructive because the contemporary democratic revolution differed from the one that had occurred a century or two before in Europe. The contemporary revolution could be led only by the proletariat and the philosophy of Marxism, not by the bourgeoisie or the ideology of individualism.

> Ever since Lenin's "Two Tactics of Social Democracy in the Democratic Revolution" (1905) it has been clear to true Marxists that it is possible, and necessary, for the proletariat to lead the bourgeois democratic revolution. It is the proletariat whose interests are decisively at stake in this revolution, and the revolutionary subject consists in all the working people whose leader is the proletariat. This also indicates what kind of thought will have the leading role in the pursuit of this revolution. Needless to say, it must be the thought of the working class—that class's own self-consciousness, Marxism-Leninism. Ara wants to pose the question of, "How can we establish individualism while gazing toward socialism on the far horizon?" But it is not the case that the bourgeois revolution must be carried out with bourgeois thought and then socialism achieved with the thought of the working class. In the democratic revolution as well as the socialist revolution the leading subject and the leading thought are the same.[32]

So, at the end of the debate, the question of how to define the subject of democratic revolution in social and class terms remained the key question for Marxists who stood firm on the mainstream materialist standpoint. The primary bulwark against any attempt to raise the question of subjectivity even in a purely qualitative sense remained the need to keep a practical commitment to proletarian leadership, and thus defend against any definition of the subject that might grant legitimacy to a petty bourgeois "individual subject," or even participation by bourgeois intellectuals *as such* without renouncing their bourgeois class position. In other words, the Leninist second narrative of proletarian leadership, which began as a hegemonic adaptation to particular historical circumstances, had long since become a matter of rigid doctrine in Japan.

In the context of revolutionary Communist victories in China and a heating up of the Cold War on a global scale, the critique of modernism—whose provenance and current sway were associated with modernity in Western Europe and the U.S.—was paralleled and reinforced by a gradual turn toward nationalism on the Communist Left. Moreover, as detailed below, this nationalism was to become increasingly Asian, especially Chinese, in orientation. Before pursuing further the question of nationalism on the left, let us look at shifts in modernist discourse that occurred in response to international events and the new issue of a peace treaty between the U.S. and Japan.

Peace and Democracy: Modernist Nationalism

In 1949 Occupied Japan was on the brink of major political transition. In February of that year American Secretary of the Army Kenneth Royall visited Japan to reopen the question of a Japanese peace treaty on terms, favored by the Joint Chiefs of Staff, that would make Japan into a forward military base against the Soviet Union.[33] Of course, the Japanese government favored an early peace but was anxious to avoid the sort of settlement that would be unacceptable to the Soviet Union and the Communists in China.[34] Japanese intellectuals, moreover, were in general set much more firmly than was their government against a "partial peace"—one that would leave out some of Japan's former enemies—and the exclusive alignment with the West such a peace would entail; many were also committed to an international position of unarmed neutrality for Japan. In January 1949 the prestigious monthly *Sekai* reprinted a UNESCO document on the causes of war. In March, soon after Royall's visit, it followed up with a pacifist statement signed by sixty or so of Japan's leading intellectuals, and in April published a special collection of essays on "World Peace and the Treaty Issue." From this point on, the magazine pursued an editorial policy vigorously opposing any peace settlement that would exclude the Soviet Union, and the centerpiece of that policy was a December 1950 article signed by thirty-five members of the Peace Problems Discussion Circle (Heiwa Mondai Danwakai), entitled "On Peace: Our Third Statement." The latter essay, drafted by Maruyama Masao, was so well received by the Japanese public that it is said to have been responsible for doubling *Sekai*'s circulation.[35] Between the two statements, of course, Mao Zedong had proclaimed establishment of the People's Republic of

China in October 1949, and in June 1950 the Korean War broke out, contributing urgency and immediacy to confrontation between left and right in Japan.

The third statement clearly reflects the pragmatic approach to politics that Maruyama had developed out of the Fukuzawa study. Fukuzawa's commitment to the relativity of value judgments, and the notion that therefore one can only understand the world after first establishing a basis for argumentation, are clearly evident. The statement says: "[A]s any view of international politics contains volitional elements, it is impossible to achieve any objective understanding which is unrelated to a subjective position. . . . if we believe it possible to adjust relations without resort to arms, we will greatly increase such a likelihood."[36] Also apparent is resistance against fixed viewpoints established a priori, in this case represented by the rigid preconception that the two Cold War blocs are irreconcilably opposed: "We further believe that there is no one single 'ism' or view which is adequate for an understanding of present day antagonisms. . . . [No] state exists as the perfect implementation of an ideology."[37]

However, the statement did more than just outline a point of view on the problem of world peace. It also reflected and further sharpened a political and intellectual opposition that had emerged in the domestic Japanese context between "progressives," who militantly opposed a one-sided peace treaty, and those calling themselves "realists," who accepted global confrontation as inevitable and supported Japan's alignment with the West in the Cold War. Indeed, a vigorous struggle against this kind of realism was the self-consistent political expression of the intellectual attitude Maruyama had first articulated in his work on Fukuzawa and later politicized in the dialogue on carnal politics and other essays. From this point of view, Japanese "realism" was an inflexibly deductive form of infatuation that was blind to the particularities of the Japanese and other situations.

Maruyama had, in fact, already elaborated his objections to so-called realism in the domestic political arena—with particular attention to the problem of Japanese "democracy"—in an essay entitled "Aru 'jiyūshugi'sha e no tegami" (Letter to a Certain Liberal). The essay took the form of a reply to a certain "K," whose identity was confirmed when the increasingly conservative Hayashi Kentarō published a rebuttal of Maruyama's position the following month.[38]

Hayashi's original letter, which is answered in Maruyama's published essay, had apparently criticized Maruyama for not being vigorous enough in opposing communism, which Hayashi and other realists now believed to constitute a clear and present threat to Japanese democracy. In his reply, Maruyama continues to draw out the political implications of the intellectual position he had developed in the course of his study of Fukuzawa: "At least in the world of political judgment, I intend to be the consummate pragmatist. Therefore, regardless of political ideology, and no matter what the political or social forces involved, I will admit to no assumption of intrinsic or absolute truth, but will make a judgment in each concrete political situation, according to each concrete function."[39]

Accordingly, he argues that the starting point must be the situation rather than a schematic framework prescribed a priori:

> I would like to emphasize first of all that, when we discuss our own society and politics, it is very dangerous to begin by viewing reality from above [*amakudariteki ni*], in terms of an abstract ideology or scheme. In my view, real social relations always must be taken to mean the concrete relations that go on between human beings, and one must grasp the behavioral principles that actually govern those concrete relations through an empirical investigation of the whole pattern of behavior in the total environment of those people, including home, workplace, associations, travel, place of entertainment, etc. [Those principles] cannot necessarily be deduced from the "ideology" ["*shugi*"] that these people consciously are trying to follow.[40]

Although there are self-appointed Communists, Socialists, and Liberal Democrats in the Japanese environment, according to Maruyama one cannot assume that the pattern and implications of their behavior will be the same there as elsewhere. In order to make his point, he focuses on what he considers to be the actual characteristics of Japanese "democracy," which he explains in terms very similar to those he employed in the dialogue on carnality, and contrasts them against a Western democratic ideal. The effect of his argument is to contest the substantial reality of democracy in the Japanese context. "Where," Maruyama asks, "in Japanese society does there already exist a democracy worth 'defending'? . . . Western-style civil democracy is for us still a goal [*kadai*], not a reality."[41] Moreover, cries to "defend" British and American-style democracy were in fact encouraging the revival and strengthening of "premodern elements."

It should not be forgotten, Maruyama says, in a manner that echoes not only Fukuzawa but John Dewey as quoted earlier by Shimizu Ikutarō, that "in practice, social and political problems are never a matter of a choice between the best and the worst, but always a matter of choosing what is better."[42] By this criterion, the left-wing parties were relatively progressive:

> It seems to me that the modernization of Japanese society . . . is a task that can be carried out only by actually determining, in concrete histori-

cal situations, where among the various classes, movements and social
organizations there reside, in relative terms, the most forces that are actually promoting modernization; by opposing any tendency that seems
likely to weaken them even slightly; and then supporting tendencies
that promise to strengthen them. . . .

You say I am championing left-wing absolutism, defending fanati-
cal revolutionaries. . . . However, in a society like Japan's, under
present conditions, the Communist Party, and the Socialist Party as
well, are playing a role in the establishment of European-style democracy. Therefore, any effort to suppress or weaken them harbors in itself
the danger of a movement toward virtual absolutism.[43]

In sum, Maruyama's critique of "realism" affirmed the importance of a subjectively (*shutaiteki ni*) constructive—i.e., "fictional"—position in both the international and the domestic political environments. In the international context, it was important to take note of the differences among elements within both
the Eastern and Western blocs, and also the situational possibilities for accom-
modation between those blocs; and then, based on these hopeful signs, to act
flexibly and open-mindedly *as if* peace rather than war were a real possibility.
Similarly, in the domestic arena, it was necessary to view democracy as a constructive process of "a human being having some purpose in mind, and producing something in line with his idea," and therefore to evaluate institutions and
political parties such as the Communists or the Socialists "in brackets" according to how directly and adequately they functioned as means toward the realization of that idea.

Maruyama expanded his ideas concerning Japanese nationalism in an essay
that influenced Takeuchi and formed an important part of what the latter believed to be the new discourse on nationalism in the early 1950s.[44] Maruyama
employed his by then familiar strategy of contrast, by which he shows that
supposedly modern or transmodern Japanese ideas and institutions were in
fact pervaded by premodern patterns. Most important as a manifestation of
Maruyama's own evaluation of nationalism is the way he describes the European variant of that process, which provides the model for the "new nationalism" he believes Japan must cultivate in the postwar period. This nationalism
presumes an international order governed by law in which plural nation-states
accept the constraints of the general principles that govern their interaction; it
also is not limited to the government or the elite but is capable of penetrating
individual life, where it reinforces and is reinforced by personal independence
and autonomy. In Europe at its origin, and in postwar Japan, this "new nationalism" must be consistent with popular sovereignty and "united with the demo-

cratic revolution."[45] Rather than originating in irrational ethnocentrism, it must
be rational, premised as in Europe on a "common normative consciousness."[46]
In fine, as Maruyama argued in his studies of Fukuzawa Yukichi, it must rely on
the "supreme principle of a valid nationalism: popular independence."[47]

Maruyama's work demonstrates again the central importance of nationalism
in postwar modernism. Takeuchi claimed to agree with Maruyama's 1951 essay, but continued in his own work to associate modernism with the repression
of nationalism. For Takeuchi, it seems that Maruyama's modern nationalism,
mediated through both state and citizen, failed to address the raw emotions connected to the image of *minzoku*, which Takeuchi felt had to be expressed in
thought and literature.

Shimizu Ikutarō was among the positivistically-oriented modernists who
took up questions related to nationalism in the early postwar period. As early as
September 1948, in an essay advocating the more thorough injection of a scientific mode of analysis into the people's consciousness, Shimizu put forward a
conception of the kind of thought he believed was "subscribed to by most of the
nation in their daily lives." He calls it "anonymous thought" and locates it at a
"deep level" where it "determines human behavior and moves people." It "lives
on as a certain feeling pervading the behavior of the people of the nation."[48]
This thought had been to some degree unified with state ideology before and
during the war, but defeat had caused a crisis. Now, in the wake of that crisis,
events would determine whether or not it would result in a major transformation
toward a scientific worldview consistent with the objective change that had occurred in society. A possible means of hastening that process was to "use" anonymous thought in order to change it, but this would require "a kind of wager,"
especially because in the early postwar period anonymous thought (as opposed
to the thought articulated by the intellectuals) was shot through with *minzoku*-
consciousness:

> Are there not likely to be cases in which we think we have succeeded
> in using anonymous thought to defeat it when in fact we ourselves are
> defeated by it? The problem of *minzoku* that has recently been dis-
> cussed from a number of angles is an example of an extremely effective
> and at the same time dangerous mechanism. To the extent that it takes
> the form of a call to *minzoku*-consciousness, it will naturally penetrate
> people's minds quickly and deeply. This idea belongs to a lineage of
> organic, substantial group life that allowed one to set aside the differen-
> tiation and splitting of actual society and project into that group life the
> totality of one's being. It is able to accommodate all the desires that
> are dormant within each of us. As is well known, the fascists were very

skillful in using this mechanism. Across most of the nation the concept
of *minzoku* was a mainstay of anonymous thought, and at present it is
taking on different meanings from those of wartime. Nevertheless,
there remains a question of how far these new meanings will penetrate
and how much the concept will change.[49]

Shimizu's own position with respect to volkish nationalism appears to have
been ambiguous at this juncture. He advocates the imposition of scientific consciousness in place of the existing variety of anonymous thought but seems
himself to be drawn powerfully by the force of popular nationalism he has identified. No doubt, others in the late 1940s and early 1950s also considered the
potential homeopathic benefits of Volk-consciousness for purposes of rational
enlightenment. In any case, contra Takeuchi, it is necessary to conclude that
postwar modernism and positivism were hardly averse to various forms of nationalism.

Shimizu continued to grapple with the question of nationalism, arguing in
January 1950 for a new concept of the Japanese "people." In an essay in the
journal *Tenbō*, he pointed out that several different terms had in the past been
used to refer to the Japanese people as a whole, the most colorless and formal of
which was *kokumin* (nation), which referred to all members of the modern state.
Prior to the end of the war, however, the same group had been referred to as
shinmin (subjects), with the implication of a people obedient to the emperor;
and since the war this group had been called the *jinmin* (people), implying that
the vast majority opposed the ruling class. Shimizu proposes that a third term,
shomin (common people), be applied to the same group. In Shimizu's conception, this term "differentiates those it designates not only from the emperor and
the ruling class but also from the intelligentsia and leaders in general." They
were entirely "cut off from the public and the realm of the state."[50] This group
had several characteristics:

First, the *shomin* were "clearly a certain group, but a group that entirely
lacks organization." By way of contrast, the *kokumin* were organized in the
sense of being members of the state, while "the *shinmin* and *jinmin* exist as entities that [by definition] should be organized through their service and devotion
to the emperor in the former case and their struggle against the ruling class in the
latter."[51] The *shomin*, however, were unorganized both ideally and actually.

Second, rather than public and ceremonial, the *shomin* were private and quotidian. Whereas the *kokumin*, *shinmin*, and *jinmin* all implicitly presumed that
"human desires should be either completely excluded or ignored, . . . the
shomin are those who, in order to live, actually take responsibility for satisfying

those supposedly denied or ignored desires."[52] This coming to grips with the need to satisfy desires was a corollary of the absence of organization.

Third, the *shomin* did not seek advancement in professions or fame in the world, but were epitomized in the "man on the street," who was loath to put on airs. *Kokumin, shimmin*, and *jinmin* all tried in one way or another to transcend their everyday existence. The *shomin*, however, were dominated not by will or ambition but by feelings (*kanjō*).[53]

Fourth, the *shomin* were "the bearers of Japanese history and lived in the shadows along Japan's mountains and rivers." Their lineage was ancient.

> The colorless *kokumin* were born concurrent with the formation of the state via the Meiji Restoration, and it was in the era following that event that the *shinmin*, who stand in a relationship of obedience to the emperor, were formed. If the *jinmin* appeared more recently through consciousness of a destiny of struggle against the ruling class, then the *shomin* are especially noteworthy for their age. Despite the series of incidents that separate them, the *shomin* who appeared in Tokugawa period documents and the *shomin* of today have a surprising amount in common.[54]

In Shimizu's view, democracy had inaugurated the age of the *shomin*, and the Japanese people could progress to a new plane only "when we discover the *shomin* within and among ourselves, and discover our values in their desires and our method in their experiences."[55]

In a short book on patriotism published in the same year, Shimizu argued that in contrast to nationalism in modern Europe, the patriotism of Japanese prior to World War II had been unrelated to democracy. Moreover, he argued that the world-historical transformation that occurred after the war, caused by the advent of nuclear weapons, called urgently for the "completion of democracy." Therefore, "peace" and "democracy" had to be intimately connected to any rebirth of patriotism that might occur in postwar Japan.[56]

That modernism and positivism should have been linked securely with nationalism in early postwar Japan is hardly surprising, in that nationalism has always been a fundamental element of modernization. Nor is it surprising on the face of it that the Communist party should have criticized modernism. What is noteworthy is that the Communist attack on modernism should have been paralleled by a clear turn toward nationalism by the party itself.

The Communist Shift to National Liberation

The Communist party itself took up the rhetoric of *minzoku* as early as February 1948 by calling for a *Minshu minzoku sensen* (Democratic National Front).[57]

This new party line was linked clearly to the issue of *shutaisei* by Amakasu Sekisuke in a short note following his contribution (discussed above) to the August 1948 critique of modernism.

> In Japan's present crisis, those who belong to the so-called "postwar" group of writers should unstintingly cooperate in the Democratic Ethnic-National [*minzoku*] Front called for by the party. The recent arguments for *shutaisei* came principally from this group of theorists, but the consolidation of *shutaisei* becomes meaningless in the absence of popular [*jinmin no*] autonomy and ethnic-national [*minzoku no*] independence. Therefore, in the interest of correctly developing the argument for *shutaisei*, it would be most fortunate if these writers would join the Front.[58]

According to Amakasu, that is, left-wing subjectivity had now to be linked explicitly to the achievement of national independence through a peace treaty.

The party's new appeal to the Volk was rationalized at more length by the Communist philosopher Kozai Yoshishige in a 1948 speech. Kozai criticized the early postwar, conservative strategies of "Japanizing" democracy, charging that they sought to retain elements of the emperor system. He then argued that, properly speaking, the term "Japanese" (*Nihonteki*) ought to refer only to something produced historically and communally by the Japanese Volk, and which exuded the peculiar quality of that Volk. Indeed, "Volk" in this sense could refer properly only to the workers (*kinrōsha*) and people (*jinmin*) who formed the nucleus of communal Japanese life. However, because in Japan the bourgeois revolution had been incomplete, Japan was "poor in volkish culture," and it was up to the postwar "cultural revolution" to augment that culture "from the standpoint of a new internationalism."

In general, therefore, "A truly revolutionary spirit must take a serious interest in Volk, tradition and history," while striving to overcome their weaknesses. Kozai admitted that in the past, "materialism—Marxism-Leninism—tended to enter [political discourse] laterally like a power saw, cutting right through tradition," but argued that now it must show new respect for "things Japanese."[59]

It was more or less as a result of the party's new nationalism that in 1951 the Marxist Historical Research Association also took a new look at the issue of *minzoku*. In essays gathered in the two-volume work *Rekishi to minzoku no hakken* (History and the Discovery of the Japanese Nation) (1952–53), Ishimoda Shō argued that discussions of the issue of *minzoku* should be traced back to a premodern milieu where they had been connected to the lives and feelings of ordinary people engaged in resistance against domination—resistance that was not unrelated to the sort of spirit that was necessary in the modern era if socialist revolution were ever to be achieved. Previous historiography had neglected the lives of the masses, so Ishimoda urged young researchers to commit themselves to illuminating this dimension of the Volk.

Similarly, Tōyama Shigeki argued that researchers should be aware of the confrontation between progressive and reactionary nationalisms in Japanese history, and should try to bring out the revolutionary tradition that sprang from the grass roots. This "revolutionary tradition of the people" was from the same underground stream that was feeding postwar nationalism elsewhere in Asia. Thus, in the early 1950s some members of the Historical Research Association complemented Takeuchi's effort to draw a relationship between submerged, potentially progressive tendencies in the Japanese Volk and the forms of nationalism apparent in the Chinese revolution and comparable Asian movements.[60]

It is important to keep in mind that the years between 1948 and 1951 brought a series of national and world events that were to lead the Communist party toward a drastic change of direction. The Communist victory in China in 1949 had hardened the Occupation's anticommunist stance, and when the JCP was implicated in some violent incidents in May 1950, the Occupation authorities initiated a Red Purge that focused first on the Central Committee and the party organ paper, *Akahata* (Red Flag), but eventually was expanded to affect some twelve thousand party members and sympathizers.

However, the decisive event that changed the orientation of the JCP, away from peaceful democratic revolution under the Occupation toward militantly nationalistic anti-imperialism, occurred on January 6, 1950, in the form of a blistering attack on the JCP line launched by the Cominform in Moscow. Appearing as an article in the Cominform organ, *For a Lasting Peace, For a People's Democracy!*, the critique targeted Nosaka Sanzō specifically. It charged him with adopting "a Japanese variation of the anti-Marxist and anti-Socialist 'theory' of the peaceful growing over of reaction to democracy, of imperialism into Socialism, a 'theory' which was exposed long ago and which is alien to the working class." According to the Cominform, this theory "misleads the Japanese people and helps the foreign imperialists to turn Japan into a colonial appendage of foreign imperialism, into a new center of war in the East."[61] Then, on January 17, an article appeared in the Chinese Communist organ, *People's Daily*, substantially supporting the Cominform's position. Since, as noted above, Nosaka had been close to the Chinese, this very much enhanced the shock to the party and to Nosaka himself. After a damaging split in the party between Mainstream and International factions, Nosaka eventually engaged in self-criticism and by initiating a fundamental transformation of the JCP program was miraculously able to retain his leadership position. Eventually, responding to the purge, the JCP put into effect plans to move the party underground. Top leaders, including Nosaka, Tokuda Kyūichi, Itō Ritsu, and others, secretly made their way to Beijing.

The new JCP policy of armed struggle seems to have been articulated initially in the pages of the Mainstream faction's underground journal, *Naigai hyōron* (Internal-External Review), which first discussed violent revolution in the autumn of 1950. However, *Naigai hyōron* was sent only to party leaders at various levels and was disguised by such titles as "The Way to Health" and "Guide to Bulb Cultivation."[62] The line of armed struggle was not officially ratified until the Fourth Party Congress of February 1951.

According to early explanations and discussions of the party's new line, Japan had to be considered similar to China in some respects. Mao had argued that China was half colonial and half feudal, internally beset by feudal oppression, externally besieged by imperialism; it had no parliamentary system and no workers' right to organize unions or to strike. In such a country, Mao pointed out, the Communist party could not follow the usual program of beginning in the cities and then taking the countryside. It had, in fact, to do just the opposite. There could be no legal struggle for power, and it was necessary to begin by consolidating rural base areas. This was the analysis that formed the starting point for the new JCP program. A JCP document of October 1950 concludes:

Not only are political conditions of the sort Mao points to as colonial rapidly becoming dominant in Japan, but the rural population is considerable, and to some extent conditions favor base areas and guerrilla warfare. Accordingly, although not adopting a strategy of "from the countryside to the cities," we naturally have to pay attention to the organization of armed struggle in agrarian villages, even as we devote major attention to workers' struggles in the cities under the leadership of the proletariat. Thus, rather than (as in China) comprising the main force of the revolution, armed struggle in farming villages will perform the important secondary roles of aiding and augmenting that revolution by dispersing and exhausting the enemy's military forces and, at times, dealing them a decisive blow.

In sum, a foundation in a people's national front centered on proletarian leadership in firm alliance with the farmers, a movement toward armed struggle in the agrarian sector, and preparation of the masses for revolution through economic and political struggle in both cities and countryside—these are the elements of the new line for Communists in accord with the new postwar situation.[63]

The 1951 Program of armed struggle was to be executed through two types of organizations. In urban areas, the Kōdō Chūkakutai (Action Nucleus Units) were directed to work through labor unions and mass organizations to precipitate strikes, demonstrations, and other types of political action, and to form spearhead forces when such events occurred. The term Chūkaku Jieitai (Nucleus Self-Defense Units) was sometimes used for corps that were intended to engage more directly in violent activities. These units were to "organize and prepare the people in factories and farms to take up weapons to defend themselves and attack the enemy." They were responsible for producing and/or obtaining weapons that could be stockpiled and distributed, and for studying military technology, adapting it to existing conditions, and disseminating it among the people. In industrial plants, they were to "organize heroic action" against police and other oppressive elements and disrupt the production and shipping of military weapons; in rural areas their mission was, in part, to liberate forest and mountain areas (from large landowners) and prevent the requisitioning of land for military bases. Ultimately, by expanding and deepening such struggles, they were to "create the conditions for arming the nation."[64]

Of course, the formation of such units was easier said than done. One secret party communication of March 21, 1951, ordering the development of what it called military organizations (*gunji soshiki*), noted:

> The tendency for these to be merely concepts or topics for discussion rather than the objects of practice is very strong. Accordingly, it is fair to say that there has been virtually no organizational activity directed toward the actual composition and arming of even a few Nucleus Self-Defense Units as self-conscious people's militia within broad-based, ardent mass struggles. . . . It is necessary to promote activities that will lead to the arming of these units through the seizure of weapons from the enemy. Only the active preparation of armed force will cause these to escalate into struggles of the entire nation and be decisive in insuring their victory.[65]

As a result of actions in compliance with party policy, such as the Bloody May Day Incident of May 1, 1952, and the Suita Incident of June 24–25, 1952, some 4,050 arrests were made and the antirioting provisions of the penal code were invoked six times between 1948 and 1952.[66] At the same time, Sanson Kōsakutai (Mountain Village Operations Units), composed of workers and students, were sent to rural areas to lead struggles against landlords and, eventually, to create liberated zones that could serve as base areas for a people's war. Mao's influence was especially evident in this rural strategy, which proved to be woefully inadequate to postwar Japanese conditions. Although the party attempted to concentrate its rural activism in mountainous and forested regions that had been exempt from the Occupation's land reform and therefore were still dominated by large landowners, it appears that the Operations Units failed utterly to establish productive contact with Japanese farmers.

Clearly, the overall orientation of the JCP between 1951 and 1955 was to a significant degree inspired by Mao and the Chinese revolution. This is evident not only in the fact that the Japanese party leaders led from Beijing throughout this period but also in other factors, such as the close parallel between the JCP's theoretical rationale for its policy and the contemporary Chinese Communist party (CCP) line, and also the degree of seriousness with which the Japanese party took demands for a rural strategy despite the obvious differences between Chinese and Japanese conditions.[67]

Yet even beyond the JCP and, indeed, for some writers despite it, the early 1950s marked the high point of post–World War II influence of Mao Zedong's thought. Building upon the foundation for understanding laid by the early essays of Takeuchi Yoshimi and a few others, and often in dialogue with their later writings, Japanese intellectuals (especially students) read and were inspired by Mao. A six-volume set of his selected works was made available in translation between February 1952 and June 1953 by the publisher San'ichi Shobō. In addition to the early philosophical works, "On Practice" and "On Contradiction," Japanese attention focused especially on what in Japan were called the "Seifū bunken," that is, the party reform documents authored by Mao and others that were related to the *zhengfeng* reform movement that had been carried out in Yan'an, 1942–44.[68] The popularity of these works is to some degree understandable in relation to the postwar Japanese intellectual climate, which, on the revolutionary Left at least, was dominated by questions concerning the subjective dimension of Marxism, ethics, and the national question. Concerned that Japanese Marxism had "forgotten the human being," and anxious to cultivate an ethically committed revolutionary subject in the Japanese environment, left-wing intellectuals and activists discovered in the *zhengfeng* reform movement a guide to the process of educating themselves and others to form and, indeed, to become that subject. They also found exemplified there a flexible emphasis on practice through which Mao "used Marxism rather than being used by it" and thus seemed able to adapt theory to dynamic Chinese conditions.

Umemoto Katsumi was among those who by the early 1950s were in some ways attracted to the thought of Mao Zedong. As a professor at Mito Higher School—which, in accord with directives from SCAP and the Ministry of Education, was to become the liberal arts faculty of the newly created Ibaraki

National University—Umemoto was slated for a position in the university's philosophy department. However, on July 9, 1949, he was told by the president of the new university that Occupation representatives had directed him that as a Communist party member Umemoto should be excluded from the university's faculty; at the end of March 1950, Umemoto received final word that he would not be appointed. As if that were not enough, Umemoto was especially vexed by the split in the party because although he was affiliated with the Mainstream faction, the Mito branch of the party was a stronghold of the new International faction.[69]

In any case, jobless and exploring a new interest in classical poetry as a partial escape from the stressful world, Umemoto continued to write. His work in the early 1950s was pervaded by a new interest in the works of Mao, especially the essays "On Practice" and "On Contradiction." Umemoto wrote directly on the former work, which was translated into Japanese in June 1951, in an essay in the party journal *Riron* in December 1951, and on both works in his 1953 book, *Ningenron* (A Philosophical Anthropology). Indeed, Mao's notions of practice and the mass line seem to have provided Umemoto with a route out of his earlier concern with *shutaisei* to a new problematic centering on organization.

Takeuchi on China

Takeuchi Yoshimi, a straightforward critic of the Communist party's change in direction, was not only the most articulate Japanese observer of the new trend toward nationalism and ethnic self-consciousness. He was also most instrumental in forming the post–World War II Japanese intellectuals' image of modern China, the Chinese Communist party (CCP), and Mao Zedong. Born in 1910, Takeuchi visited China for two months on a government grant while still a student in the Chinese literature department of Tokyo Imperial University, and later wrote that the trip caused him to fall in love with China and changed his life. The only student out of thirty-four in the department who focused on modern literature, in 1934 he submitted a graduation thesis on the Chinese writer Yu Dafu. He then started a study group and began editing a monthly journal on Chinese literature. In 1937, right after the Marco Polo Bridge incident, he again went to China on a Japanese government research project, living for two years with a Chinese family in Beijing. When Japan attacked Pearl Harbor he became a supporter of the war, writing that "we need have no moral doubts about routing the invader from East Asia."[70] Nevertheless, his journal was put on a suspect list, and in 1943 he voluntarily suspended publication. In the same year, he was drafted and sent to central China as a railway guard, where he remained until war's end; in the meantime, his book on the Chinese writer Lu Xun was published in December 1944. Once back in Japan, he began to make a living by translation and writing.

In a November 1948 essay, Takeuchi argued that of all Asian nations on whom modernity had been forcibly imposed by Europe, Japan had put up the least resistance. The Japanese elite had responded to imperialism in the manner of eager "honor students" who were willing do anything for good marks, industriously throwing out all the old principles and mastering the new. By conventional measures, the strategy had worked, of course, and Japan's modernization had "succeeded." Indeed, in the era of Allied Occupation in which Takeuchi wrote, Japan was again responding industriously to modernization imposed from above. Yet part of what was iconoclastic about Takeuchi's essay, written at a time when modernity was as securely identified with the "West" and "America" as ever before, was his charge that Japan's Westernizing strategy had in fact been a failure. The crucial, missing ingredient was resistance, the absence of which had given Japan's leaders superficial success at the expense of an authentic transformation.

According to Takeuchi, the Meiji Restoration had amounted to a counter-revolutionary revolution in that the leading elements themselves imposed an authoritarian order from above. Moreover, the Japanese leaders' devotion to Europe combined with an imperialist posture toward Asia showed that "their progress is that of slaves, and their industriousness merely slave-like industriousness."[71] Indeed, Japan "sought to escape from slavery by becoming a slave-master" and from this new superordinate position had then sought to awaken Asia. But as Takeuchi points out, in an implicit gloss on Hegel's master-slave dialectic, the slavemaster is as dependent and unfree as the slave: each lacks the autonomous subjectivity (*shutaisei*) that can come only through a process of becoming truly "oneself" through resistance.[72] By abandoning all resistance to the West, Japan had gained power, wealth, and prestige but could never gain freedom and autonomy.

However, what distinguished Takeuchi's argument from those of the other Japanese intellectuals who in the past had also pointed to the superficiality of Japan's modernity was his argument that Japan's neighbor China, then in the throes of civil war, was in full possession of the revolutionary selfhood and authenticity Japan lacked. In contrast to the "success" of the Meiji Restoration, the 1911 Revolution in China had "failed" by conventional standards. Yet, significantly, it had been recognized to be a failure even by its would-be leaders, such as Sun Yat-sen. Precisely because it did not easily "succeed," the revolution had continued, setting itself first against the Qing, then against the warlords, and

finally against the Japanese invaders and the Nationalists. Because of this negative element of resistance that constantly regenerated to animate not only elites
but peasants and workers at the base of society, the revolution renewed itself
constantly from below in opposition to powerful reactionary forces. By virtue
of the resistance they confronted, Chinese revolutionary forces formed and reformed themselves as an autonomous, historical subject that embodied not only
a class but ethnic identity. Rather than abandoning its own identity in search of
high marks from European tutors, therefore, China was succeeding in the much
more difficult process of incessantly reconstituting itself through struggle.[73]
The clear implication of Takeuchi's essay at the time was that Japanese intellectuals should look to China in place of Western Europe and the U.S. as their
model as they sought to affect Japan's postwar revolutionary change.[74]

Takeuchi's intervention was extremely influential against an early postwar
background in which, among intellectuals at least, the image of revolutionary
China was just beginning to be reconstructed in rudimentary but sympathetic
terms. One important event in this process had been the translation and informal
distribution (because of Occupation censorship) of Edgar Snow's *Red Star
Over China*. This work provided basic information on the Chinese revolution
and presented its principals, especially Mao Zedong, in a positive light.[75]

A second factor was the connection in people's minds between the Chinese
Communists and the popular Japanese Communist leader Nosaka Sanzō, who,
as noted in chapter 1, spent the war years with the Chinese Communists in
Yan'an, where he was strongly influenced by Mao Zedong's thought, especially
the program of New Democracy. Nosaka's "lovable" party caught the imagination of a broad segment of the Japanese population in the early postwar period,
and his connection with China's Communists helped convey a positive image of
their struggle.[76]

Third, Takeuchi's arguments with respect to China resonated with the critique of objectivism in Marxism that had formed such an important dimension
of the *shutaisei* debate. In a 1949 essay, Takeuchi himself contrasted the objectivism of Japanese Marxism against the subjective practicality he perceived in
Chinese revolutionary theory. Japanese Marxism was "the kind of determinism
that measures all value and analyzes all history with reference only to the single
material standard of the productive forces." The effect of such objectivist determinism was to call attention to China's economic backwardness and thus provide a "scientific" basis for Japanese contempt of China.[77] It led to other errors
as well: It caused Japanese Marxists to ignore the national (*minzoku* = Volk)
dimension of China's revolutionary struggle; it also led them to underestimate
the degree to which the CCP was heir to a historically continuous stream of

Chinese morality, exemplified in the party's attitude toward opium dealing and treatment of the peasantry. To be sure, this continuity was paradoxical, since it arose from the Chinese party's "complete denial of tradition." Nevertheless, "even as the CCP is the most radical critic of tradition, it is also the embodiment of the Chinese people's highest morality."[78]

Of course, Takeuchi was far from claiming that Mao's revolutionary Marxism was so dominated by subjective factors like morality as to pay no attention to the role of production. Takeuchi cites Mao's "On Protracted War" in order to show that Mao "did not view the war [against Japan] in a moralistic frame . . . but rather grasped its essence through the fundamental condition of modern warfare which is productive power." Since the development of Japan's productive forces far exceeded China's, a simple quantitative measure would have suggested that China could never resist successfully. However, Mao's dialectical turn of mind, which included a strongly subjective dimension, caused him to believe that it would be possible to use the enemy's own power against him: "the factories provisioning the CCP were not in Yan'an but in Tokyo and Osaka." Takeuchi concludes that "[h]ad Mao been a vulgar Marxist, a slavish formalist" like the Japanese, "he could never have grasped productive forces in such a dynamic manner." His judgment "relied upon the subjective condition that an autonomous war of resistance was possible." That is, in the course of its long struggle the CCP had indeed formed itself into a revolutionary subject capable of using Marxism rather than being used by it. As a result of this long experience, Marxism had been adapted to Chinese conditions even as those conditions had been gradually transformed: "The CCP contained a form of subjectivity (*shutaisei*) that was penetrated by an elevated sense of ethics."[79]

As Takeuchi's work suggests, in the early 1950s Chinese Communism and Mao Zedong's thought were associated in Japan with a process of subject-formation through praxis.[80] Important moments in this revolutionary process were an active epistemology along with a strong ethical dimension and an indigenous ethnic identity that was evident to Takeuchi in the sinicization of Marxism and Mao's prototypical "Chineseness."[81] As noted above, the emphasis on subject-formation in the Chinese revolution resonated powerfully with the domestic debate on subjectivity in the context of the postwar democratic revolution. The Japanese perception of a strong element of ethnic particularity in China's revolution can also be contextualized in relation to rising nationalism among intellectuals in Japan. In his early essays, Takeuchi in fact often used the Chinese revolutionary model as one way of trying to convince his intellectual peers that the Eurocentric approach to social change, i.e., "modern-

ism," had to be replaced by a strategy based on the historical identity of the
Japanese Volk.

From Modern Literature to National Literature

As demonstrated at the beginning of this chapter, in the early postwar period
Takeuchi did not expend all of his very considerable energies writing about
China; indeed, his primary concern was still Japanese literature. His September
1951 essay on "modernism," mentioned at the beginning of this chapter, had
included a plea for the kind of "immanent, internal critique" of nationalism—
manifested primarily in the wartime "Romantic faction" of writers—that
would eventually allow for reconstruction of a truly "national literature" (*kokumin bungaku*). Such an immanent, dialectical critique had been shunned by
postwar modernist critics, and their reticence had given rise to the "pathological" suppression of nationalism and Volk-consciousness in the postwar era. Required now was a new "self-assertion" in literature, one that could be attained
only by "salvaging the totality" of the Volk and in the process "actualizing the
whole human being" and making true social revolution possible.[82]

In May 1952 Takeuchi published a letter to the literary critic Itō Sei, in which
he argued that the problematic of a truly "national" Japanese literature had
for some time formed a critical undercurrent in the postwar era. Moreover,
the question was premised upon a certain historical trajectory. It had been implicit in literary perspectives adopted in the early stage of modern literature in
Japan, extending from Futabatei Shimei through Kitamura Tōkoku and Ishikawa
Takuboku, and had been maintained during the Pacific War through the contentions of the Japan Romantic faction. Beginning in 1951, however, "voices
calling for national literature" had become public and insistent, so Takeuchi
concluded by asking Itō's opinion regarding its prospects.[83]

Itō professed basically to agree with Takeuchi regarding the importance of
the issue, but objected to the view that "literature for the nation [*minzoku*]" and
"literature to establish the modern ego" were necessarily at odds. Second, he
said he had some difficulty taking the call for "national literature" entirely at
face value because it was related to a political party program—implicitly that of
the JCP—that was currently emphasizing "national independence." That is, it
seemed that literary priorities were being dictated by politics. Third, regarding
the split between pure and mass literatures, he argued that such a division was
inevitable under the system of commercialism.[84]

In his response, Takeuchi broadened the issue by observing that in fact the
stunted growth of national literature had to be viewed as a manifestation of

the failure of modern literature as a whole, a failure that was symptomized in the estrangement of pure from mass literature. That is, in Takeuchi's view, it was not only commercialism that was ultimately responsible for that estrangement, but—in Japan's case, at least—also a premodern social structure that had given rise to the elite literary guild, the *bundan*, whose members were the custodians of "pure" literature. The *Kindai bungaku* faction had also criticized the premodernity of *bundan* literature but had not extended that critique to the "structural base" on which *bundan* literature was founded: "Mass literature shares common roots with *bundan* literature, and a national literature can only emerge from the destruction of both."[85]

Throughout, Takeuchi emphasized that the construction of national literature had to be intimately related to the formation of a *modern* nation (here, using the term *kokumin*). Indeed, "national liberation" did not consist *merely* in "the independence of the *minzoku*" but also in the "independence of the individual." That is, he argued for clearer recognition of the links between nationalism and liberal democracy: "In the absence of an attitude of national solidarity, individual independence will never be achieved, and the obverse is also the case."[86]

It is important to note that, despite Takeuchi's vitriolic attack on modernism and his affection for the Volk, his argument here about the relationship between individual and national independence is virtually indistinguishable from Maruyama's wartime and early postwar nationalism. Clearly, from a broader perspective, Takeuchi shared Maruyama's modernist understanding of nationalism.

> The term national literature does not refer to a specific literary form or genre but rather to literature's mode of existence *as* the totality of the country. As such, it is a historical category. Like democracy, it is a goal in search of realization, and like the perfect civil society, it is difficult to achieve. It is an ideal goal that one strives toward in daily practice. It can never be adequately captured in a preformed model.[87]

We are reminded again of Maruyama's characterization of democracy as a "fiction," with only virtual existence: "national literature," like "democracy," could never be fully actualized and therefore could never lose its critical function in relation to reality.

In combination, the tendencies recounted above brought the debate on *shutaisei* to a premature close: it was indeed, as Takakuwa remarked, left as an "open construction site." It is indicative, perhaps, that *Kindai bungaku* suspended publication for four months in 1950 and when it reappeared was a less ambitious periodical without its former luster. It might be said that the "postwar period" was ending.

Conclusion: The Subject of Modernity

We believe that an anti-essentialist theoretical stand is the sine qua non of a new vision
for the Left conceived in terms of a radical and plural democracy.

—Phronesis[1]

It is now possible to attempt a provisional assessment of the major approaches
to *shutaisei* that vied in the early postwar years. The above chapters attempt to
think along with the postwar theorists, while at the same time trying to maintain
a critical perspective conditioned by certain late-twentieth-century conceptions
of political subjectivity and democratic revolution. Inasmuch as such an effort
inaugurates a political as well as academic dialogue with the historical materials
and contexts selected, it must transcend this or any other work. Therefore, this
book is best viewed as a kind of interim report.

I have presented the legacy of early postwar Japanese discourse on democracy and subjectivity in a broadly positive light. Despite the presence of the Occupation, which in the short term at least severely limited the available choices,
the early postwar was in some ways a crucial moment in that the postwar crisis
of authority, values, and priorities for reform presented opportunities for political action of a sort that had not been possible before and during the war. One
need not go so far as some contemporaries, who have characterized the early
postwar as a virtual utopia of freedom, in order to see that it was a time not only
of extreme material hardship and military occupation but also of cultural and
political optimism, especially for intellectuals.[2] The debate on subjectivity and
the discourse on democratic revolution were to an extent reflections of this optimism and revealed a radical political impulse.

The *shutaisei* theorists established subjective engagement as opposed to
contemplation as the fundamental criterion of productive political discussion in
the postwar era. Although their specific arguments varied, they all insisted that
political thought had to respond to not only epistemological but existential and
practical demands: it had to abandon all purely observational roles to become
(in Marx's expression) actively "sensuous" and historically engaged. Despite
the validity in some cases of the charge of elitism, their discourse was generally
oriented directly or indirectly toward a milieu of social action. They also challenged the essentialist forms of determinism that were being advanced by both
the JCP and conservative forces—determinism that underwrote claims to authority and hegemony—and encouraged a view of democracy *as a revolution*
that had to produce more than just formal institutions.

Postwar Constructions of Subjectivity and Democratic Revolution

Although contemporaries often criticized them for egoism, apoliticality, and hyperindividualism, *Kindai bungaku* writers like Ara Masato were very aware of connections between the models of authorial subjectivity they sought to promote and the ongoing processes of democratic revolution. Indeed, Ara focused more explicitly than any other *shutaisei* writer on the social identity and political engagement of the subject of democratic revolution. The model of subjectivity—never given unified definition—that Ara and the others put forward was weighted toward individuality and the primacy of artistic expression over more direct forms of social engagement. Yet their argument—as advanced especially by Honda and Hirano—that art had to be cleanly separated from "politics" could never adequately account for the genuinely political implications of "art" as the *Kindai bungaku* critics themselves practiced and criticized it.

The *Kindai bungaku* writers' prewar experiences with the vanguard party's stifling domination of artistic production had etched into their minds a conception of "politics" as both separate from art and imperiously interventionist in relation to it. In other words, for Hirano "politics" under the prewar state amounted to the same thing as the "politics" practiced by the Communist party: both state and party presented themselves as "public," transcendent authorities entitled to intrude coercively into "private" matters such as artistic expression, family, and love. According to these writers, neither the emperor-centered state nor the party ever respected the distinction between public and private, and in that sense they were not yet truly modern. At the same, they were apparently so preoccupied with their own and other writers' victimization at the hands of the party and the prewar state that they seem only rarely to have confronted the potential for oppression latent in the "democratic" institutions being constructed around them at the time they wrote.

In a postwar era of "Enlightenment," when Japan was often believed to be completing its modernization, it is not surprising that separation between public and private should have been considered the hallmark of modernity. Yet, as argued above, the politics of democratic revolution took place at many levels, and democratic subjectivity appeared in the midst of civil society in a variety of local contexts, including schools, workshops, universities, and rural cooperatives. It is instructive to remember that recent conceptions of democratic revolution tend to define as political the very process of subject-formation itself, as it takes place through and within the social realm. In addition to encouraging us to apprehend the dynamic of democratic revolution in all its diverse, local contexts, such a definition also subverts normative conceptions of political subjec-tivity that emphasize "self-discipline" in conformity to the requirements of a circumscribed, "public" realm of (male) power.

Ara's conviction of the need to place egoism at the foundation of humanism directly challenged the autonomy-based conceptions of humanism put forward by Katō Shūichi, Ōtsuka Hisao, and Maruyama Masao. To a large extent, the ego was merely another name for the priority of private needs over public re-sponsibilities, and in that respect it paralleled the postwar fascination with the body and carnality. As such, it also directly challenged Umemoto's conviction of the need for selfless, sacrificial struggle—the aspect of Umemoto's thought that Matsumura Kazuto called the "spirit of the suicide pilots"—and the sup-pression of desire that was called for by Otsuka and Maruyama.

Despite their baleful view of "politics" as symbolized in coercive party prac-tices, the *Kindai bungaku* writers were themselves part of the broader demo-cratic process by which political subjects were formed in what conventionally were thought to be unpolitical contexts. As evidenced in the concentrated criti-cism they received from Nakano Shigeharu and, eventually, from the party as a whole, their arguments—even for the unpoliticality of art!—had considerable political force at a time when Communists were contending with Socialists and others for the privilege of defining the meaning and implications of democratic revolution, and when the immediate question had to do with how to recognize and/or construct the subject of that revolution.

At the same time, Ara and his comrades challenged the party from a position that had not fully renounced the metahistorical system upon which, ultimately, the party's own claim to dominance was based, and they therefore were vulner-able to rejoinders from Nakano and his allies. Moreover, this very inability to conceive of history as structured any differently from the way it is explicated in the canonical texts of dialectical materialism ensnared the *Kindai bungaku* writers in a vicious circle of supplementarity. The ego (or body), which they essentialized as an irreducible ground, competed for ontological primacy against historically determined social structure, leading to a dualistic system in which ego and structure not only depended on but duplicated and contested each other, leading always to the generation of an anomalous surplus.

The logic of supplementarity also plagued the philosophers who sought to provide a Marxist theory of political subjectivity. Some, like Matsumura and in a somewhat different way Taketani, tried to avoid supplementarity and essen-tialism by denying the externality of *shutaisei*, insisting that it was always already encompassed in and guaranteed by metahistory. For Umemoto, however, it was clear that, despite the indisputable truth of historical materialism, subjective action did not follow logically or inevitably from maturation of the forces of production or their contradiction with productive relations. In other words, *shutaisei* could not be entirely internal to metahistorical essence.

Umemoto's sensitivity to the logical lacuna in historical materialism led him away from normative reification of the subject toward a nondualistic politics, that is, a politics in which creative agency occurs as the result of a constitutive lack, and where subjectivity itself is conditional. By such a view, subjectivity occurs only as the result, or product, of history's failure to totalize, that is, its failure to become a fully autonomous, objective process. Umemoto came close to such a conception in his awareness of the lacuna in historical-materialist explanation and in his conviction that Marxist subjectivity was generated as a result of that lacuna.

Yet, for Umemoto as well as the *Kindai bungaku* writers, the subject of decisive action was always ultimately reducible to an individual; more specifically, an individual that (following Watsuji) had to be conceived as a tense relationship between (social) production and (individual) rebellion. For most purposes, despite Umemoto's sophistication with respect to the relationship between structure and agency, he still insisted that an individual *becomes* the subject through self-negation (negation of the negation); that is, he held that by negating themselves individuals are able to "regain their original nature and secure true freedom" in an "absolutely negative unity of individual and totality."[3] The impetus toward self-negation arises from the individual's conviction of the metahistorical destiny of the proletariat, a destiny that can be secured only through commitment to a closed, repetitive system. The result, as with the *Kindai bungaku* writers, was a dualistic structure in which each pole (subject/history, individual/society) is reputedly independent and yet ultimately dependent upon the other as supplement.

Most other Marxist philosophers who advocated *shutaisei* also located it, implicitly or explicitly, in the individual in opposition to a historical or social totality. Takakuwa made this quite explicit in essays where he juxtaposed the individual to what he called "socialization," or the priority of the social, in postwar reform. However, in his discussion of death and the subjectivity of Christians, he approximated an Althusserian analysis of ideology in showing how the Christians' identification with Christ as Subject transforms their own subjectivity. His conception of the individual's self-denying commitment to a group of believers as the necessary mediation in the formation of active subjectivity also seems to have much in common with Umemoto's analysis. One who clearly avoided the postwar preoccupation with individuals, positing *shutaisei* as intrinsically collective, was Taketani Mitsuo. For Taketani, *shutaisei* was immersed in technology as social praxis, and to that extent his approach is heir to the prewar work of Miki Kiyoshi.

Ōtsuka adhered in the early postwar period to a version of the historical-materialist metanarrative that was believed to prescribe sequential stages, each equipped with the historical subject proper to it. It was only in relation to such a narrative that one could speak of the two "roads" from feudalism to capitalism, one or the other of which had to prevail in each specific historical context. And yet, in the bulk of Ōtsuka's early postwar writing in which he dealt directly or indirectly with *shutaisei*, he allowed metahistorical essence to recede to the far horizon, leaving maximum scope for historical agency motivated by the modern ethos. In the process, Ōtsuka relocated the binary that for the *Kindai bungaku* partisans and the Marxist philosophers had produced ambivalent forms of supplementarity: where they had encountered it as a bifurcation between essentialized history and subjectivity, Ōtsuka constructed it in the partially dehistoricized form of a juxtaposition between subject and the social whole (totality), which is ultimately internalized as self-discipline *for* the totality. Put another way, Ōtsuka's conviction of the historical importance of the modern ethos leads him to the task of reforming mentality and values. However, rather than as "politics," he envisions that reform as a prepolitical process of education throughout society. Ōtsuka's subject of democratic revolution had to be constructed by instilling the modern ethos uniformly throughout a unified social whole (nation or, during the Pacific War, the state as "totality"); indeed, Ōtsuka's subject always produces *for* this social whole and is thoroughly subjected to it as an individual who works "by himself." Here, of course, the continuity between Ōtsuka's wartime and postwar stances is most clear. While the vast expansion of the productive forces that is expected from the reform of values is ultimately to be revolutionary in effect, it apparently does not necessarily result in class warfare and the overthrow of the capitalist order but rather in a gradual transition to a kind of socialism.

Maruyama Masao also constructed *shutaisei* as a normative process of self-discipline. However, that construction took place in the course of his research on the history of politics and political thought rather than economic history, and as a result he was concerned more explicitly with the state and citizenship than with the forces of production. In the course of his studies of European political and intellectual history he did not fail to notice the close relationship historically between the modern individual and the nation-state and, as we have noted, much of his early postwar conceptualization suggests that he considers this relationship to be not only historically contingent but for most purposes necessary and intrinsic. Therefore, his notion of *shutaisei* presumes the state as the sovereign adjudicator of rights and reifies the public realm as the privileged site for political action.

For Maruyama, accordingly, the public realm as the site of the political is distinct from the private world. Because democracy is participatory and integrative, and requires that private needs and desires be given political expression, the political individual must negotiate the distance between the private and public realms. Yet the public realm of power, legitimacy, and responsibility can accommodate only certain kinds of demands and representations. Therefore, rather than transmitted directly into the political arena, "raw desires" must be mediated and transformed. Indeed, subjectivity itself must be refined and moderated; it must be disciplined to become properly "political." The realm of publicity—like Simmel's place of "sociability"—demands that political individuals assume a certain attitude, or approach, whose central quality is suggested in Maruyama's metaphor of the "fiction." That is, figuratively speaking, the materiality of the body and its insistent needs must be transcended in a spirit of imagination and creativity that constructs interests in a manner appropriate to the disinterested neutrality of the state. Subjectivity infused by such a spirit is free, flexible, and pragmatic in relation to context; yet it is also centripetally focused and self-disciplined. Maruyama does not reify or take as given any of the specific forms of government institutionalization, but rather treats them all as "fictions" in constant need of subjective reevaluation and intervention. Indeed, his view of democracy as a "fiction" that is never entirely realized implies a kind of permanent revolution, albeit always securely within the framework of the state. He does take for granted the state's existence as the privileged locus of political demands and the need that it be approached only in accordance with certain protocols. For Maruyama, political *shutaisei* is always a process of self-discipline as well as mobilization.

Takeuchi Yoshimi's conception of *shutaisei* included a form of self-discipline that was to some degree cognate with that of the modernists, that is, the Chinese Communists' revolutionary self-discipline he found so woefully absent from Japan's modernization. Yet Takeuchi's most noteworthy innovation was his reintroduction of the "blood-spattered Volk" as the vehicle for *shutaisei*, in tense competition with such units as class, humanity, or individual. Takeuchi clearly believed that ethnic/national identity was capable of providing a far more immediate, visceral experience of historical agency than class ever could. Moreover, he seems at least to have matched Maruyama in the degree to which he took the nation for granted as an encompassing whole. At the same time, Takeuchi was unusually sensitive to the performative dimension of subject-formation and was often radically constructivist in his understanding of wholes such as "Japan" and "Asia." Moreover, Takeuchi found in Lu Xun a form of resistance that reactively reified neither subject nor object. As Lu Xun once wrote, "[T]he earth had no roads to begin with, but when many men pass one way, a road is made."[4] Takeuchi was unusual in this respect among the early postwar theorists.

Democratic Revolution as Modernization

Despite the cogency and passion of many of their interventions, the weaknesses of early postwar theories of *shutaisei* are equally apparent. Participants in the debate often failed adequately to recognize, theorize, and engage actively with the processes of democratic revolution that were already occurring at various levels of Japanese society. Of course, this inadequacy can to some extent be explained by calling attention to the elitism, egocentrism, or lack of political commitment of the writers themselves.[5] Yet revolutionary theory is as integral to revolutionary action as the idea of a building is to the process of its construction. That is why we have paid particular attention to how postwar theorists envisioned, framed, and defined democratic revolution; how they expressed the need for *shutaisei*; and what they believed *shutaisei* to be. In order to begin to synthesize some of the specific problems that have been noted, it is useful to refer to a characterization of early postwar discourse on democracy offered by a leading intellectual historian, Matsumoto Sannosuke:

> An extremely valuable lesson of our defeat was that superficial modernization is impotent and meaningless. As a result of this lesson many Japanese came to realize that the essential task of modernization is to "democratize" the way people think and act in their everyday affairs. It was on the basis of this lesson that many leading Japanese intellectuals . . . felt it was an absolute necessity immediately after the war to plant the seeds of democracy in the people's hearts and minds.
>
> In fact, the more the outward forms of postwar society were democratized, the more intellectuals felt it necessary to stress the human aspects of political modernization.[6]

Matsumoto's persuasive account of the nature and significance of the early postwar discourse on democratic revolution provides insight into the major constitutive weakness of that discourse, which was to conflate the democratic construction of *shutaisei* with a process of modernization. Modernization in the postwar Japanese context implied not only a metahistorical framework of progress—including but not limited to historical-materialist-stage theory—but commitment to the cultivation of a particular type of human subject that would enact and promote that modernity. In Japan as in Europe, more often than not, it implied the hypostatization of the modern subject as a concrete individual in possession of autonomous subjectivity.

Derek Sayer has argued that the modern subject is typically conceived in the form of an individual "self" whose actions are to be understood as "symptoms and expressions of an underlying ethical . . . personality," internally coherent and detached from society. In this conception, agency, subjectivity, morality, etc., are all understood to be properties or effects of the autonomous individual: morality, for example, "is . . . abstracted from all particularistic contexts, becoming an ontological attribute of the *subject* rather than of his or her discrete *actions*, and it provides the basis upon which this new subjectivity is unified."[7] Here the autonomous personality is taken as an essence, the origin of productivity and democratic revolution, and the foundation on which a modern, democratic society must be built. Moreover, this personality "becomes the object of 'ethical rigorism'" and "the moral ground upon which modern forms of power are constructed."[8]

Sayer encapsulates for us the type of subject that was envisioned by most of the early postwar *shutaisei* theorists, regardless of the degree of their allegiance to Marxism. Of course, those theorists were also fully capable of transcending essentialism, and they succeeded in effectively criticizing the least productive conceptions of democratic revolution that were offered at the time, such as mechanistic Marxism and positivism. Moreover, they moved closer to the kind of revolutionary theory and subjectivity that would have been capable of interacting productively with ongoing movements for equality and participation. Thus, they went a long way toward developing a conception of democratic revolution adequate to the times.

However, as we have seen, despite the subtlety of particular arguments and the ways in which they threatened to burst discursive limits, the postwar theorists were for the most part encouraged by the logic of the modern subject into one or another form of individualistic essentialism. Indeed, as was the case with *Kindai bungaku* theorists like Ara, and even Umemoto and some liberals as well, a preoccupation with the quality of one's own and others' subjectivity entailed serious risk of solipsism. Some of the postwar theorists, such as Mashita and Takakuwa, as well as such critics of *shutaisei* as Nakano Shigeharu and Kurahara Korehito, realized that historical agency could not be constructed through solitary introspection, but only in practice. They demanded choice and immediate social commitment, from themselves and others. Yet such rigor was not necessarily dominant, and reification of the notion of a modern individual led many toward introspection and contemplative retreat. Moreover, their essentialization of the "individual subject" threatened to impede the process of democratic revolution by directing attention only to certain types of subject and ignoring or excluding others; as a result, it led them into paternalistic versions of an Enlightenment program through which, it was hoped, modern subjects could be molded. This implied that, in the meantime, the political processes and priorities of democratic revolution, including a political confrontation with war responsibility that would go beyond Ara and Odagiri's introspective turn back to the "emperor system within," would have to be deferred. As democratic theorists have pointed out, a distinction between those who may be considered mature, modern individuals capable of making decisions and those who are still in one sense or another immature and thus must be spoken for rather than allowed to speak is intrinsic to modern European liberalism. John Stuart Mill once observed that "[d]espotism is a legitimate mode of government in dealing with barbarians, provided the end be their improvement."9 In the postwar Japanese context, this liberal tradition was manifested in the convictions of Ōtsuka Hisao and others that top priority should be granted to the construction of modern subjects through a broad-based system of education. It was also latent in the Communist theorists' insistence that only a process of education that included the liquidation of petty bourgeois attitudes could qualify writers for a progressive role in democratic revolution.

The crowning irony is that, as suggested in continuities between wartime and postwar conceptions of *shutaisei* that are evident in the work of Ōtsuka and Maruyama and reinforced by other studies of postwar film as well as social theory, the paternal, autonomous, responsible individual idealized as a model in the postwar era was, in fact, to a large extent already in place as a concomitant of developmental capitalism in the prewar and wartime eras.10 This suggests, of course, the bankruptcy of a modernist paradigm that insisted on explaining the supposed failure or unfeasibility of democratic revolution as the result of lingering premodernity.

As the corollary to their essentialization of *shutaisei* as a property of individuals, or of social entities such as the working class that were treated as single individuals, the early postwar theorists devoted themselves to the task of constructing a modern subject *for* democratic revolution. In doing so, they failed to recognize that democratic revolution *is* the very process of subject-formation itself. In other words, they often failed to credit sufficiently the constructive, performative dimension that was so well illustrated in some of Takeuchi's writing, favoring instead a normative stance focused on certain static attributes of an ahistorical model of the subject. *Shutaisei* came to imply "being" a certain way rather than "doing" something.

Several recent theorists, Marxist as well as non- or post-Marxist, have registered the insight that, rather than being self-defining essences, subjects of all sorts (including classes) are formed oppositionally. E. P. Thompson has argued that class is not a thing but rather an event that "happens" when people "feel and articulate the identity of their interests as between themselves, and as against other men [sic] whose interests are different from (and usually opposed to) theirs."[11] In other words, as Sayer points out, class conflict precedes and, indeed, gives rise to class subjectivity.[12] Similarly, it might be said that antagonism and thus agency (not *necessarily* in the form of class struggle) precedes the formation of a subject (not *necessarily* in the form of a class). Laclau makes the same point, arguing that "strategies create identities, not the opposite":[13] "It's not a question of 'someone' or 'something' producing an effect of transformation or articulation, as if its identity was somehow previous to this effect. Rather, the production of the effect is part of the construction of the identity of the agent producing it. . . . one cannot ask *who* the agent of hegemony is, but *how* someone becomes the subject through hegemonic articulation."[14] To envision the self-conscious subject as a free-standing entity that preexists and initiates agency is to essentialize and hypostatize as a thing what is better understood as a practice, or event.

Laclau argues further that subjectivity is constituted negatively rather than positively, out of lack rather than plenitude. Affirming that all social situations are to a large extent structured institutionally, Laclau argues nevertheless that sociality inevitably involves undecidability and antagonism, which prevent the formation of any fully "sutured," or securely closed, social space—that is, an institutional structure in which all behavior is determined. Decisions are always necessary in order to maintain institutions, and such decisions never *merely* maintain but inevitably change them over time. Decisions (agency) respond to the structure's need for maintenance—its "dislocation" or, to use Umemoto's term, its "lacuna" (*kūgeki*). Agency, in turn, occurs via the formation of a subject. Thus, "the location of the subject is that of dislocation." The subject is never a preexisting essence or object, but merely "the result of the impossibility of constituting the structure as such."[15] Here is an approach to the dynamics of *shutaisei* whose fundamental insights were anticipated at certain points by Ara, Umemoto, Mashita, Takakuwa, Shimizu, and Takeuchi, among others, but which was for the most part overwhelmed by the logic of modernization, which implied the need for a particular kind of modern subject as the precondition for revolutionary change.

In addition to an individualistic bias and a tendency to hypostatize the subject as an autonomous prime mover, a third major weakness of early postwar theories of *shutaisei* can be found in their nationalistic orientation. As we have seen, democratic revolution in early postwar Japan provided a site for the confirmation and (re)installation of the modern subject as the foundation of social order and productivity. Constitutive of this modern subject—as Max Weber and Marx no less than Michel Foucault have shown—is an ethic of self-discipline that is conducive to capitalism but also to the modern bureaucratic state. As we have seen, the modern subject constructed in the course of the Japanese debate was almost always intimately tied at least implicitly to the nation-state. The modern, "individual subject" performed not only as part of the enormous productive forces of the modern industrial economy but also as "the moral ground" for nationalism.[16] Marx, among others, expressed the insight that "it is only through the state that individualism is possible."[17]

Of course, that is not to say that all early postwar versions of this modern subject were equally nationalist. Despite the striking degree to which Umemoto Katsumi's self-sacrificing revolutionary subject mirrored in its duty of self-negation the subject of the fascist and, indeed, the liberal-capitalist state, one cannot but admire his scrupulous avoidance of explicit nationalism and his resolute attachment to class as the only viable revolutionary vehicle.

And yet, overall, it seems that few postwar thinkers could confidently argue against Takeuchi's view of class as an "abstraction" that, in his view, distorted the "whole human being" that was manifested in nationalism. Insight into the presumed artificiality of class compared to ethnic, national, or communal bonds is certainly not unique to Takeuchi. Sayer writes that "class appears to be less internal or essential a component of subjectivity than is caste, or servility, or slavery—in sum, those relations Max Weber analysed in terms of 'status.' It presents itself as a matter of mere 'accidental circumstance' rather than inherent being, as something which is extrinsic to the essence of personality."[18]

As we have seen, these insights were borne out in the postwar Japanese context, where national/ethnic identity proved to be too powerful to ignore, even on the far left. It is significant in this respect that the most influential theories of *shutaisei* or the related concept, *jiritsu* (independence), that reemerged in the 1960s certainly did not ignore class but larded it heavily with neonativist ethnonationalism.[19]

Democratic Revolution vs. "Democracy"

What has been the fate of democratic revolution in contemporary Japan? Assessments vary, of course, but probably the prevalent Japanese view since at least the 1970s is that, as once observed by the influential political-economist, commentator, and government adviser Murakami Yasusuke, "The postwar Japanese political system [is] one of the more satisfactorily working parliamentary democracies. In respect to freedom of expression and association, postwar Japan compares favorably to any society and is better than most."[20] Moreover, Japan has "achieved greater equality than almost any country in the West."[21] According to this view, the democratic revolution has in all important respects succeeded, and democracy is fait accompli.

Murakami's confident assertion is the culmination of a stream of political thought whose beginnings in the early postwar period might be traced to the exchange between Maruyama Masao and Hayashi Kentarō around 1950, recounted briefly in chapter 5. In the background, of course, was the increasingly anticommunist position taken by SCAP in the later years of the Occupation. An extended quotation from Matsumoto Sannosuke is warranted to illuminate the context of the Maruyama-Hayashi debate:

> One development was particularly disturbing to those concerned about the fate of democracy in Japan. This was the change in Occupation policies toward the end of the 1940s. It was, of course, inevitable that SCAP policies should respond to changes in the international situation, specifically to the rise of Soviet-American tensions, the cold war, and armed conflict in Korea. Unfortunately, however, this response took a reactionary, undemocratic course: tighter control of the labor movement; stronger legislation to preserve public order, a purge of communists from government positions, private industry and many professions; and preliminary moves toward rearmament. As these "reverse-course" policies progressed, the concept "democracy" became succeedingly formalized. Rather than develop into a functional idea used to effect democratization, the concept deviated from its original relation to internal renovation to become more and more fixed as a political doctrine related to the external forms of government. In substance, SCAP's "reverse-course" democracy became no more than a principle used to legitimize the established political order, a dogma employed to protect Japan's already "democratized" legal and political systems from progressive forces and revolutionary movements.
>
> At this point supporters of Japanese democracy split into two camps: those for the "new" principle of conserving what had already been accomplished, and those for the "old" principle of democratic revolution which had been pursued since the end of the war. The former camp felt that democratic principles are best exemplified by systems of governmental procedure or by institutions. Those of this opinion con-

cluded that the survival of democracy depends on its ability to combat any ideology or group which attempts to suppress political freedom or negate the principle of parliamentary government. In short, they came to equate democracy with anticommunism.

On the other hand, those who supported the "old" principle realized that true democracy could not exist as long as democracy is accepted only as a way of ruling rather than as a way of life. They held that a political idea must be evaluated in terms of how seriously it deals with the necessity of refurbishing society. Or, to put it in slightly different terms, those hoping for a democratic revolution felt that the significance of democracy as a political idea lay in how effective it might be, given the circumstances at any particular moment, in reforming entrenched social relationships in Japan.[22]

The Maruyama-Hayashi debate is therefore especially revealing as an early clarification of the issue that would divide the "progressive" view of democratic revolution from the emerging neoconservative one: is Japanese democracy a completed project or merely an unfulfilled promise? The schism between the "old" (early postwar) conception of thoroughgoing democratic revolution and the "new" conception of democracy as an anticommunist system that is "better than most" was further clarified in the early 1960s, when the Japanese publishing house Chikuma Shobō asked Hayashi to edit a volume on "neo-conservatism" for a widely read series concerned with contemporary Japanese thought. In his introduction to that volume, Hayashi described himself and other Japanese neoconservatives in relation to a number of criteria: they opposed postwar "progressivism" not because they rejected progress but because they believed so-called progressivism to be impeding rather than encouraging beneficial forms of advancement;[23] they inherited liberalism's emphasis on individual freedom and rallied to its defense when communism posed a threat to that freedom;[24] they supported the welfare state out of concern for the commonweal; they were independent enough to resist intellectual and political fashion, and sought to reform the weaknesses of conservative politics;[25] and they tempered their conservatism with flexibility and cautious appreciation for change.[26] Above all, however, they were united in a strong aversion to the postwar Left, and especially communism.[27]

Of course, from the beginning, neoconservatives sought to strengthen their position through historical reconstruction, focusing especially on the postwar era. One of many examples of what I would call a neoconservative perspective on postwar democracy appeared in early 1986.[28] The author, Seki Yoshihiko, was trained at Tokyo Imperial University in economics and spent his academic career as a professor in the history of social thought at Tokyo Metropolitan University. He has written widely on the Fabian movement and the British Labour Party, and was one of the drafters of the provisional platform of Japan's Democratic Socialist party.

In Seki's view, the most valuable contributions to political thought during the Occupation period were the essays on democracy published by the "old liberals," who had been "silenced" during the war—men such as Minobe Tatsukichi, Rōyama Masamichi, and Hasegawa Nyozekan.[29]

> The issues they dealt with included the ideals undergirding parliamentary democracy as a system, democracy's relation to the traditional Japanese modes of thought and the emperor system, the problems surrounding legislative bicameralism, and the issue of morality among politicians in light of the political scandals that began around that time. These were all issues that went to the heart of democracy.[30]

Note that when Seki reviews early postwar writing on democracy, he has in mind something quite different from democratic revolution as defined in the above chapters. Seki apparently conceives of democracy as a normative system of rule rather than as a revolutionary social movement to extend equality and liberty. Of course, the two are not unrelated. They differ primarily with regard to the sites where democratic action is located: democracy in the sense given it by Seki is primarily a system of government, centered in the public realm and especially in the state, and governed by a set of norms consistent with the main lines of the Western European and American liberal traditions; democratic revolution as used here, on the other hand, refers to processes, diffused throughout private as well as public spaces, by which relations of subordination are challenged, leading to the hegemonic extension of equality and liberty to new social contexts. Intrinsic to the latter processes is the construction of a subject as the adjunct to agency.

Seki argues, however, that despite the productive discourse on democracy that he found in early postwar discussions among the "old liberals," the dominant tendency later in the postwar era was quite contrary to that of the early discourse. He locates the turning point around 1950 in conjunction with a transition from the era of postwar Enlightenment to that of antiestablishment movements, a transition he finds to have been catalyzed by the emergence of the peace treaty issue, the formation of the Peace Problems Discussion Circle, and the emergence of a political situation in which pacifist democrats were under great pressure to form a united front with the Communists in order to protest the partial peace. Of course, 1950 is also precisely the moment of the Maruyama-

Hayashi debate and what might be called the inauguration of postwar neoconservatism. Faithful to the legacy of Hayashi's position, Seki finds lasting negative significance in Maruyama's contention that an anti–Communist party
posture should be avoided on the grounds that the Communist party was a major
vehicle of modernization. From this point forward, according to Seki, a view of
democracy as consisting primarily in the exercise of a "right to protest" gained
ascendancy, and the values connected with the parliamentary system were dis-
paraged.[31] This led to what Seki considers to be a distorted, impoverished view
of democracy in postwar discourse. What characterized this distorted view was,
first, its lack of any concern for moral philosophy. In language reminiscent of
Ōtsuka Hisao's early postwar position, Seki explains that

> [for] the Puritans and John Locke , , , civil liberty   [was] a means
> toward the realization of moral freedom, understood not as a matter of
> living in accord with one's desires but of controlling those desires and
> living in accord with God's will. . . . Civil liberties were means toward
> the end of moral freedom. Parliamentary democracy was merely the
> political system most capable of giving maximum protection to those
> civil liberties. Accordingly, to forget the goal and to exercise civil liber-
> ties to the utmost was considered to be nothing but self-indulgence.[32]

Although Seki is eager to criticize Maruyama's approach to democracy, his
conviction of the importance of the state and nationalism is paradoxically quite
consistent with central tendencies in Maruyama's early postwar thought:

> If one takes democracy as an antiestablishment ideology, then that is
> different, but if one wants to understand it as a political system . . .
> alongside monarchy and aristocracy, it is impossible to argue that such
> a system does not presume the existence of the state. I'm not so sure
> about other countries, but at least in England, which is considered the
> homeland of democracy, the classical texts on democracy take the state
> for granted and discuss how to reconcile state power with other demo-
> cratic values like freedom, equality and cooperation. That is what
> distinguishes democracy from anarchism.[33]

Because Seki is concerned to show that "nationalism and democracy are not
contradictory in the least," he is disturbed by what he believes to be the antina-
tionalistic tendency of postwar democracy: "Perhaps because of the spread of
democracy [since 1950] without any attention to the state, the spirit of nationalism in the sense of thought directed to the maintenance and perpetuation of Japan's national community . . . is very weak. Individuals' devotion to entities

higher than themselves stops at the family or corporation, rarely extending to the state as a national community."[34]

I have surveyed Seki's critique at some length because his perspective on postwar democracy is so radically contrary to that put forward in the above chapters. First, of course, he finds the early postwar discourse on democracy to have been dominated by the "old liberals," whereas the most influential as well as interesting voices on democratic revolution I have found in that era belong to the theorists of *shutaisei*.

Second, while Seki is committed to finding in postwar Japanese discourse a view of democracy as an institutional system of government, I have looked for evidence of democratic revolution as a decentralized process of subject-formation that takes place largely outside the formal bounds of institutionalized politics. To the extent that postwar theorists failed to develop an approach to subjectivity that was consistent with the democratic social imaginary, they also failed to understand thoroughly and engage with the kind of democratic revolution that was, in fact, already under way throughout society. Their understanding was impeded by practical preconceptions of revolution that either remained historicist or conformed to a normative framework that prevented them from engaging with actual processes of subject-formation (e.g., production control).

Third, whereas for Seki 1950 marks the turn in Japanese society toward an antistate, antinationalist discourse on democracy as embodied in social movements, in the narrative implicit in the above chapters 1950 also belongs to the moment when nationalism was openly and securely installed at the center of left-wing thought and practice. It marked the point, therefore, when democratic revolution as a vital drive for hegemony proceeding by way of an open articulation among different standpoints (subject positions) became increasingly distant.

Fourth, and ironically, Seki fails to recognize that it was precisely in the context of the early postwar debate on *shutaisei* that the elements of liberal, institutional democracy Seki himself idealizes—that is, the moral philosophy of self-discipline, reliance on the state, and modern nationalism—were given their earliest and most forceful expression. Indeed, some of what the above chapters identify as the all-too-evident and problematical dimensions of early postwar conceptions of democratic *shutaisei* are valorized by Seki as important tendencies that in his view eventually disappeared from the postwar Japanese discourse. Maruyama, Ōtsuka, and other early postwar "progressives" propounded the very values Seki finds so regrettably absent after the early postwar era. Therefore, his concerns about the post-1950 ascendancy of a protest-centered, "anti-nationalist" conception of democracy seem exaggerated, if not paranoic, despite protests against reactionary government moves in the 1950s and the Japan-U.S. Security Treaty in 1960, university student revolts in the late 1960s, and the rise of citizens' and residents' movements in the 1970s.[35]

Since the 1970s—and especially since the collapse of socialist economies everywhere but in East Asia—the view of postwar Japanese democracy that is propounded by Hayashi, Seki, Murakami, and others has become broadly hegemonic in contemporary Japan. Arrayed against it for a while was political modernism, manifested not only in the influential analyses of postwar political economy and culture published frequently by progressive intellectuals (*shinpoteki bunkajin*) in the *sōgō zasshi* (general interest monthlies for the intelligentsia),[36] but also in the progressive movements (*kakushin undō*) that emerged in the 1950s to defend "peace and democracy" from government leaders who for a time sought to reverse democratization measures instituted during the Occupation. Underlying the ideologies of these progressive intellectuals and movements was often one or another variety of *shutaisei* theory, especially the version premised on the assumption that a "modern ethos" must transform the values and behavior patterns of the Japanese population before truly revolutionary change could occur. Despite the optimism generated among progressives in the 1960s and 1970s as a result of widespread citizen's movements, the underlying premises of the modernist approach to *shutaisei* led its proponents to defer indefinitely the radical change they ostensibly favored. Modernist intellectuals were often most articulate and persuasive when describing—in the tradition of the *kōza-ha* Marxism espoused by the Communist party—the deep-rooted, feudal (or "Asiatic") qualities of Japanese political culture.[37] In sum, if meaningful change depended on a modern ethos and the ethos of the Japanese people was still pervasively premodern, there was little hope for such change.

In the late 1960s and 1970s, not only modernist approaches to *shutaisei* but Japan's entire postwar political economy of "Potsdam democracy" were vigorously challenged by anti–Communist party student radicals. Significantly, the psychohistorian Robert J. Lifton noted the great importance among even student radicals of "that much-discussed, elusive, sometimes near-mystical, but always highly-desirable entity known as *shutaisei*."[38] Indeed, it has been argued that the students' preoccupation with reified and sometimes solipsistic notions of *shutaisei* often detracted from hard situational and tactical analysis and contributed to their defeat.[39] The result was ultimately to reinforce right-wing dominance; significantly, some of present-day Japan's leading neoconservative ideologues were student leaders in the radical Zenkyōtō movement of the early 1970s.

It is tempting to see a more broadly applicable object-lesson in the apparently self-defeating political implications of the tendency among *shutaisei* theorists in early postwar Japan, and in the 1960s and 1970s as well, to give strategic priority to the cultivation of a certain kind of modern subject. That is not to say that the mechanistic Marxists or liberal positivists who opposed them were right all along, but rather that a new approach is called for—one that proceeds on the assumption that the revolutionary subject is produced in conjunction with revolutionary action rather than as its prerequisite. Also useful, perhaps, is a conception of democratic action that denies "the uniqueness of the national state both as a site and as an object of political struggle." Rather than always presenting rights claims to the state, and thus reinforcing its authority, such a conception of democratic revolution would imply "addressing such claims to each other, and to each 'other,' whoever and wherever they may be."[40] Of course, it is also likely (and desirable) that, if such processes were pervasive in society, it would have the indirect effect of disrupting the logic of state sovereignty and destabilizing existing power structures.

In the meantime, Japanese neoconservatism has been, and is, greatly reinforced by analogous forms of viciously complacent conservatism elsewhere in the world, especially in England and the U.S. Of course, it is difficult to sustain an argument that what passes for democracy in Japan is any less "democratic" than its counterparts in Europe or North America; indeed, the revival of radical notions of democratic revolution in Europe and the U.S. has been stimulated directly by the solidification of neoconservative hegemony there at a time when the full promise of "equality and liberty for all" is still grievously unfulfilled. It is not that the democratic revolution in Japan or the U.S. or England has failed, but rather that, as Jürgen Habermas has said of modernity, it remains an "incomplete project."

Notes

Introduction

1. Raymond Williams, *Keywords: A Vocabulary of Culture and Society*, rev. ed. (New York: Oxford University Press, 1983), 308.

2. Naoki Sakai, "Subject and/or Shutai and the Inscription of National Culture," Cornell University, May 13, 1993, 7.

3. Miyagi Otoya, "Shutaisei ni tsuite," *Riron* (January 1948).

4. SCAP released political prisoners only after a Reuters correspondent found out about them in the course of his investigation of the prison death on September 26, 1945, of philosopher and suspected Communist-sympathizer Miki Kiyoshi. See Rokurō Hidaka, *The Price of Affluence: Dilemmas of Contemporary Japan* (Tokyo: Kodansha International, 1984) 16–17; also Takemae Eiji, "Early Postwar Reformist Parties," in Robert E. Ward and Sakamoto Yoshikazu, eds., *Democratizing Japan: The Allied Occupation* (Honolulu: University of Hawaii Press, 1987), 346–8.

5. Ernesto Laclau and Chantal Mouffe, *Hegemony and Socialist Strategy: Towards a Radical Democratic Politics* (London: Verso, 1985), 156.

6. I use the expression here even though, as Mark Poster has pointed out, "The term *poststructuralist*, local to certain intellectual circles in the United States, draws a line of affinity around several French theorists who are rarely so grouped in France and who in many cases would reject the designation." Mark Poster, *Critical Theory and Poststructuralism: In Search of a Context* (Ithaca, NY: Cornell University Press, 1989), 4.

7. M. H. Abrams, "What Is a Humanistic Criticism?" *The Bookpress* 3/4 (May 1993): 1.

8. Jürgen Habermas, "Neoconservative Criticism in the United States and West Germany: An Intellectual Movement in Two Political Cultures," in Richard J. Bernstein, ed., *Habermas and Modernity* (Cambridge, MA: MIT Press, 1985), 78–94.

9. Perry Anderson, *In the Tracks of Historical Materialism* (Chicago: University of Chicago Press, 1984), 32.

10. Takeuchi Yoshirō, "Posto-modan ni okeru chi no kansei," *Sekai* (November 1986): 92–114.

11. Christine Di Stefano, "Dilemmas of Difference: Feminism, Modernity, and Postmodernism," in Linda J. Nicholson, ed., *Feminism/Postmodernism* (New York: Routledge, Chapman and Hall, Inc., 1990), 75.

12. Judith Butler, "Contingent Foundations: Feminism and the Question of 'Postmodernism,' " in Judith Butler and Joan W. Scott, eds., *Feminists Theorize the Political* (London and New York: Routledge, Chapman and Hall, Inc., 1992), 9. See also Gloria Anzaldua, *La Fontera/Borderlands* (San Francisco: Spinsters Ink, 1988), and Gayatry Spivak, "Can the Subaltern Speak?" in Cary Nelson and Lawrence Grossberg, eds., *Marxism and the Interpretation of Culture* (Urbana: University of Illinois Press, 1988).

13. Butler, 15.

14. Joseph McCarney, *Social Theory and the Crisis of Marxism* (London: Verso, 1990), 180.

15. Ibid., 192–3. For a Japanese equivalent, see Shirakawa Masumi, "Shutai no saisei: zentaisei no kakutoku," *Kuraishisu* 40 (winter 1990): 35–43.

16. Chantal Mouffe, "Hegemony and New Political Subjects: Toward a New Concept of

Democracy," trans. Stanley Gray, in Nelson and Grossberg, eds., *Marxism and the Interpretation of Culture*, 89–104.

17. Ernesto Laclau, *New Reflections on the Revolution of Our Time* (London: Verso, 1990), 30, 41, 61.

18. J. Victor Koschmann, "The Debate on Subjectivity in Postwar Japan: Foundations of Modernism as Political Critique," *Pacific Affairs* 54/4 (winter 1981–82): 609–31.

Chapter 1

1. Vladimir I. Lenin, "Two Tactics of Social-Democracy in the Democratic Revolution," in *Marx, Engels, Lenin: on Democracy—Bourgeois and Socialist* (Moscow: Progress Publishers, 1988), 67.

2. John B. Thompson has characterized the "social imaginary," as elaborated in the work of Cornelius Castoriadis and Claude Lefort, as "the creative and symbolic dimension of the social world, the dimension through which human beings create their ways of living together and their ways of representing their collective life." He further writes, "The social imaginary is expressed primarily through the constitution of a world of significations. By means of these significations—these symbols and myths in which a society represents its present and its past—a society is endowed with an identity and distinguished both from other societies and from an undifferentiated chaos." Thompson, *Studies in the Theory of Ideology* (Berkeley: University of California Press, 1984), 6, 24.

3. Claude Lefort, *Democracy and Political Theory*, trans. David Macey (Minneapolis: University of Minnesota Press, 1988), 18.

4. The concept of absolutism was central to the Comintern Theses on Japan, and also to Japanese Marxist analyses of the prewar Japanese state. This was especially true of the Kōza-ha, or Lectures Faction, of scholarly Marxism. See Germaine A. Hoston, *Marxism and the Crisis of Development in Prewar Japan* (Princeton, NJ: Princeton University Press, 1986), 208–21.

5. Claude Lefort, *The Political Forms of Modern Society: Bureaucracy, Democracy, Totalitarianism*, ed. John B. Thompson (Cambridge: The MIT Press, 1986), 302–3.

6. Robert E. Ward, "Presurrender Planning: Treatment of the Emperor and Constitutional Changes," in Ward and Sakamoto, eds., *Democratizing Japan*, 1–41. For more details, see Nakamura Masanori, *The Japanese Monarchy: Ambassador Joseph Grew and the Making of the 'Symbol Emperor System,' 1931–1991* (Armonk, NY: M. E. Sharpe, Inc., 1992), especially 87–106.

7. "Constitution of Japan," in Kyoko Inoue, *MacArthur's Japanese Constitution: A Linguistic and Cultural Study of Its Making* (Chicago: University of Chicago Press, 1991), 303.

8. Miyakawa Tōru, Nakamura Yūjirō, and Furuta Hikaru, *Kindai Nihon shisō ronsō* (Tokyo: Aoki Shoten, 1971), 147–51. On Watsuji's wartime and postwar philosophy in relation to the emperor system, see Sakai Naoki, "Seiyō e no kaiki/Tōyō e no kaiki," *Shisō* 797 (November 1990): 102–36. H. D. Harootunian also analyzes Tanabe Hajime's postwar views of the emperor; see Harootunian,"Ichiboku hitokusa ni yadoru tennōsei," *Shisō* 797: 85–101. For analysis of the American decision, see Nakamura, *Japanese Monarchy*; Ward, "Presurrender Planning;" and Takeda Kiyoko, *The Dual Image of the Japanese Emperor* (New York: New York University Press, 1988).

9. Yamaguchi Jirō, "Nihon kanryōsei to tennōsei," *Shisō* 797: 183–95.

10. Lefort, *Democracy and Political Theory*, 19.

11. Laclau andMouffe, *Hegemony and Socialist Strategy*, 115.

12. Mouffe, "Hegemony and New Political Subjects," 90. Ernesto Laclau and Chantal Mouffe characterize discourse as follows: "Let us suppose that I am building a wall with an-

other bricklayer. At a certain moment I ask my workmate to pass me a brick and then I add it to the wall. The first act—asking for the brick—is linguistic; the second—adding the brick to the wall—is extralinguistic. . . . This totality which includes within itself the linguistic and the non-linguistic, is what we call discourse. . . . [But] . . . what must be clear from the start is that by discourse we do not mean a combination of speech and writing, but rather that speech and writing are themselves but internal components of discursive totalities."

Not only subjects but objects are socially constructed through discourse in the sense that a spherical object "is a football only to the extent that it establishes a system of relations with other objects, and these relations are not given by the mere referential materiality of the objects, but are, rather, socially constructed. This systematic set of relations is what we call discourse. . . . The fact that a football is only a football as long as it is integrated within a system of socially constructed rules does not mean that it thereby ceases to be a physical object. A stone exists independently of any system of social relations, but it is, for instance, either a projectile or an object of aesthetic contemplation only within a specific discursive configuration." Laclau and Mouffe, "Post-Marxism without Apologies," in Laclau, *New Reflections* 100–3.

13. *Political Reorientation of Japan, September 1945 to September 1948* (Washington, DC: U.S. Government Printing Office, 1949), 78–79.

14. Moore, Joe Baldwin, "Production Control and the Postwar Crisis of Japanese Capitalism 1945–1946" (Ph.D. diss., University of Wisconsin-Madison, 1978; published by University Microfilms, Ann Arbor, MI, 1979), 18.

15. Mary Dietz, "Context Is All: Feminism and Theories of Citizenship," in Chantal Mouffe, ed., *Dimensions of Radical Democracy: Pluralism, Citizenship, Community* (London: Verso, 1992), 67.

16. Moore, 176.

17. Hata Ikuhiko, "Japan under the Occupation," *The Japan Interpreter* 10/3–4 (winter 1976): 378.

18. Kirstie McClure, "On the Subject of Rights: Pluralism and Political Identity," in Mouffe, ed., 116–17.

19. Susan Pharr, "The Politics of Women's Rights," in Ward and Sakamoto, eds., *Democratizing Japan*, 222.

20. Ibid., 238.

21. Ibid., 246.

22. Moore, 190.

23. McClure, 115, 117.

24. Robert E. Ward, "Reflections on the Allied Occupation and Planned Political Change in Japan," in Robert E. Ward, ed., *Political Development in Modern Japan* (Princeton: Princeton University Press, 1968), 485–6, 528.

25. For readable accounts including data on wartime destruction and early postwar hardship see, for example, Tatsurō Uchino, *Japan's Postwar Economy: An Insider's View of Its History and Its Future* (Tokyo: Kodansha International, 1983), 13–18, and Ōe Shinobu, *Sengo kaikaku* [Nihon no rekishi 31] (Tokyo: Shōgakukan, 1976), 118–35. Ōe reports that as soldiers and civilians were repatriated from overseas, some thirteen million were unemployed; the 1945 harvest was only 57 percent of the highest wartime figure, with the result that even middle-class families spent some 80 percent of their income on food in order to consume merely 1200–1500 calories per day, only half the necessary minimum. Wage workers and the unemployed hadn't the means to secure even that. Starvation was a regular occurrence in the large cities. Moreover, even three years after the war, one in four households had nowhere to live.

26. Ōe, 131.

27. Ibid., 134.

28. Moore, 391.

29. Ibid., 407–8.

30. Ōe, 122–3.

31. Joe Moore, "Production Control: Workers' Control in Early Postwar Japan," *Bulletin of Concerned Asian Scholars* 17/4 (1985): 9.

32. Ōe, 131.

33. Moore, "Production Control: Workers' Control in Early Postwar Japan," 17.

34. Kan Takayuki, *Sengo seishin: sono shinwa to jitsuzō* (Tokyo: Mineruva Shobō. 1981), 17.

35. Moore, "Production Control: Workers' Control in Early Postwar Japan," 14.

36. Takeuchi Shizuko, "Seisan kanri tōsō," *Ryūdō* (November 1978): 62.

37. Kan, *Sengo seishin*, 26–8.

38. Moore, "Production Control and the Postwar Crisis of Japanese Capitalism," 134.

39. Ibid., 417.

40. SCAP, GHQ Summation, quoted in ibid., 422.

41. Ibid., 424.

42. Ibid., 427.

43. Mark Gayn, "Food Demonstrations and MacArthur's Warning," and Miriam Farley, "SCAP Policy toward Labor Unions," in Jon Livingston, Joe Moore, and Felicia Oldfather, eds., *Postwar Japan: 1945 to the Present* (New York: Pantheon Books, 1973), 145–52.

44. Moore, "Production Control: Workers' Control in Early Postwar Japan," 23.

45. For opposing views on the extent and nature of "reverse course," see essays by Justin Williams, Sr., John W. Dower, and Howard Schonberger, "A Forum," *Pacific Historical Review* 7/2 (May 1988): 179–218.

46. Laclau and Mouffe, *Hegemony and Socialist Strategy*, 21.

47. Ibid., 24.

48. There was ample precedent for this logic of political intervention as an aid to necessity in the Second-International Marxism of the Austro-Marxists and Bernstein, especially. Ibid., 30.

49. Perry Anderson, "The Antinomies of Antonio Gramsci," *New Left Review* 100 (November 1976/January 1977): 15–16.

50. *Marx, Engels, Lenin: On Democracy—Bourgeois and Socialist*, 68.

51. Laclau and Mouffe, 49.

52. *Marx, Engels, Lenin*, 69.

53. Ibid., 66.

54. Laclau and Mouffe, 47–48.

55. Jacques Derrida, *Of Grammatology*, trans. Gayatri Chakravorty Spivak (Baltimore: Johns Hopkins University Press, 1974), 141–64.

56. Ibid., 144.

57. Ibid., 145.

58. Jacques Derrida, *Speech and Phenomena*, trans. David Allison (Evanston, IL: Northwestern University Press, 1973), 89.

59. Jonathan Culler, *On Deconstruction: Theory and Criticism after Structuralism* (Ithaca: Cornell University Press, 1982), 103.

60. Laclau and Mouffe, 54.

61. Anderson, 17–18.

62. Laclau and Mouffe, 61–65.

63. Ibid., 64.

64. George Beckmann and Okubo Genji, *The Japanese Communist Party, 1922–1945* (Stanford: Stanford University Press, 1969), 279–80.

65. "Appendix F: Theses on the Situation in Japan and the Tasks of the Communist Party, May 1932," in ibid., 338–40.

66. Joe Moore, "Production Control and the Postwar Crisis of Japanese Capitalism," 151.

67. Tokuda Kyūichi, "Gokuchū jūhachinen (shō)" (1947), in Haniya Yutaka, ed., *Kakumei no shisō* [Sengo Nihon shisō taikei 6] (Tokyo: Chikuma Shobō, 1969), 44.

68. See the biographical sketch in Rodger Swearingen and Paul Langer, *Red Flag in Japan: International Communism in Action 1919–1951* (Cambridge: Harvard University Press, 1952), 107–11.

69. Quoted in Masumi Junnosuke, *Postwar Politics in Japan, 1945–1955*, trans. Lonny E. Carlile (Berkeley: University of California, Institute of East Asian Studies Japan Research Monograph no. 6, 1985), 89.

70. Pointed out by Joe Moore, *Japanese Workers and the Struggle for Power, 1945–1947* (Madison: The University of Wisconsin Press, 1983), 113.

71. Nihon Kyōsantō Shutsugoku Dōshikai, "Jinmin ni uttau," in Hidaka Rokurō, ed., *Sengo shisō no shuppatsu* [Sengo Nihon shisō taikei 1] (Tokyo: Chikuma Shobō, 1968), 245–6.

72. Quoted in Moore, *Japanese Workers*, 117–18.

73. Tokuda, "Gokuchū jūhachinen (shō)," 44.

74. Moore, "Production Control and the Postwar Crisis of Japanese Capitalism," 152–4.

75. Ibid., 161.

76. Ibid., 162.

77. Kanda Fuhito, *Nihon no tōitsu sensen undō* (Tokyo: Aoki Shoten, 1979), 152–3.

78. Masumi, *Postwar Politics in Japan*, 87.

79. Tatsuo Morito, "The Democratic League for National Salvation: Its Prospects," *Journal of Social and Political Ideas in Japan* 3/1 (April 1965): 25.

80. Especially Nosaka, "Minshuteki Nihon no kensetsu," a speech at the Seventh National Congress of the Chinese Communist party, in *Nosaka Sanzō senshū*, vol. 1 (Tokyo: Nihon Kyōsantō Chūōiinkai Shuppanbu, 1964), 419–68. For background, see Swearingen and Langer, 73–83.

81. See biographical sketch in Swearingen and Langer, 111–15.

82. See Nosaka's criticism of Tokuda and Shiga during a SCAP interrogation, reported by Moore, *Japanese Workers*, 125.

83. "A Letter to the Japanese Communists from Okano [Nosaka Sanzō] and Tanaka [Yamamoto Kenzō], Moscow, February 1936," in Beckmann and Okubo, *Japanese Communist Party*, 254–60, 355.

84. Quoted in Masumi, 91.

85. Ibid., 92.

86. Mao Tse-tung, "On New Democracy," *Selected Works of Mao Tse-tung*, vol. 2 (Peking: Foreign Language Press, 1965), 339–84.

87. Nosaka Sanzō, "Minshu sensen ni yotte sokoku no kiki o sukue," *Sengo shisō no shuppatsu*, 247–58.

88. Translation from Moore, *Japanese Workers*, 124.

89. Nihon Kyōsantō, "Daigokai tōtaikai sengen," in Haniya, ed., *Kakumei no shisō*, 57–60.

90. Moore, *Japanese Workers*, 124.

91. Takemae Eiji, "Early Postwar Reformist Parties," in Ward and Sakamoto, eds., *Democratizing Japan*, 343.

92. Yamakawa Hitoshi, "Toward a Democratic Front," *Journal of Social and Political Ideas in Japan* 3/1 (April 1965): 23.

93. Masumi, 91.

94. Kanda, 183.

95. Ibid., 188.

96. Nihon Kyōsantō, "Daigokai tōtaikai sengen," 57.

97. Kanda calls attention to this, 195.

98. Nihon Kyōsantō, "Daigokai tōtaikai sengen," 57–60.

99. Ernesto Laclau has suggested that "any subject is a mythical subject": "The 'objective' condition for the emergence of myth . . . is a structural dislocation. The 'work' of myth is to suture that dislocated space through the constitution of a new space of representation. Thus, the effectiveness of myth is essentially hegemonic: it involves forming a new objectivity by means of the rearticulation of the dislocated elements. . . . The moment of myth's realization is consequently the moment of the subject's eclipse and its reabsorption by the structure—the moment at which the subject is reduced to 'subject position.'" Laclau, *New Reflections*, 61.

Chapter 2

1. Sakaguchi Ango, "Zoku-darakuron," *Sakaguchi Ango zenshū* 14 (Tokyo: Chikuma Shobō, 1991), 590.

2. Miyoshi Yukio, quoted in Amino Takeo et al., *Tenbō sengo zasshi* (Tokyo: Kawade Shobō Shinsha, 1977), 57.

3. These topics are listed in Tsurumi Shunsuke, "Chishikijin no hassō jiten: *Kindai bungaku* gurūpu," in Kuno Osamu, Tsurumi Shunsuke, and Fujita Shōzō, *Sengo Nihon no shisō* (Tokyo: Keisō Shobō, 1966), 9.

4. Honda Shūgo, "Geijutsu, rekishi, ningen," *Kindai bungaku* 1 (February 1946), 2.

5. Indeed, it is said that even in the postwar era, the Communist leader Tokuda Kyūichi would customarily inscribe "selfless devotion" in response to an admirer's request for an autograph. Hidaka Rokurō, *The Price of Affluence: Dilemmas of Contemporary Japan* (Tokyo: Kodansha International, Ltd., 1980), 68.

6. Honda, 2.

7. For a translation of one of Nakano's *tenkō shōsetsu*, "Mura no ie," see Brett de Bary, *Three Works by Nakano Shigeharu*, Cornell East Asia Papers 21 (Ithaca, NY: Cornell University East Asia Program, 1979).

8. For an account of different responses to *tenkō* by Nakano and Murayama, see Tsurumi Kazuko, *Social Change and the Individual: Japan Before and After World War II* (Princeton, NJ: Princeton University Press, 1970), 58–64.

9. Kōsaka Susumu, "Sengo 'shutai' no fūka kakusan to 'kindai bungaku'-ha," *Ryūdō* (April 1976): 52.

10. Yoshio Iwamoto, "Aspects of the Proletarian Literary Movement in Japan," in Bernard S. Silberman and H. D. Harootunian, eds., *Japan in Crisis: Essays on Taishō Democracy* (Princeton, NJ: Princeton University Press, 1974), 164.

11. Tatsuo Arima, *The Failure of Freedom* (Cambridge: Harvard University Press, 1969), 198–203.

12. Ibid., 212. See Furukawa Sōichirō (pseud.), "Proretaria geijutsu undō no soshiki mondai," and Tanimoto Kiyoshi (pseud.), "Geijutsuteki hōhō ni tsuite no kansō," I and II, in *Kurahara Korehito hyōronshū* 2 (Tokyo: Shin-Nihon Shuppansha, 1968), 109–36, 180–261.

13. Kurahara, "Geijutsu riron ni okeru rêninshugi no tame no tōsō;" quoted in Kōsaka,

48. For more on Kurahara's literary theory in this era, see Iwamoto, 163–70, and George T. Shea, *Leftwing Literature in Japan* (Tokyo: Hosei University Press, 1964), 233–74.

14. Kurahara Korehito, "Atarashii bungaku e no shuppatsu," *Kurahara Korehito hyōronshū* 3 (Tokyo: Shin Nihon Shuppansha, 1967), 3–7.

15. Ibid., 5.

16. Kurahara Korehito, "Shin Nihon bungaku no shakaiteki kiso," *Shin Nihon bungaku* 1 (March 1946): 2–3.

17. Ibid., 7–8.

18. Ibid., 7.

19. See Max Weber, "Science as a Vocation," in Hans Gerth and C. W. Mills, trans. and eds., *From Max Weber: Essays in Sociology* (New York: Oxford University Press, 1946), 138.

20. Arima, 212; for example, see Kurahara Korehito, "Geijutsuteki hōhō ni tsuite no kansō (zenpen)," *Kurahara Korehito hyōronshū* 2, 206.

21. Honda, 6.

22. Tsurumi, 2.

23. For an explanation of the Communist leaders' *tenkō*, see Matsuzawa Hiroaki, "'Theory' and 'Organization' in the Japan Communist Party," in J. Victor Koschmann, ed., *Authority and the Individual in Japan: Citizen Protest in Historical Perspective* (Tokyo: University of Tokyo Press, 1978), 108–27.

24. Honda, 9.

25. Ara Masato et al., "Bungaku to genjitsu: Kurahara Korehito o kakonde," *Kindai bungaku* 1 (February 1946): 18.

26. Ibid., 18–19.

27. Ibid., 22–23.

28. Ibid., 25–26.

29. Honda Shūgo, "Kaisetsu," *Ara Masato chosakushū* 1 (Tokyo: San'ichi Shobō, 1983), 33–34. Honda writes that the date was confirmed by Odagiri Hideo, and speculates that Ara joined the party when he learned that it would adopt a policy of peaceful revolution.

30. Ara Masato, "Daini no seishun," *Kindai bungaku* 2 (March 1946): 3.

31. Maire Kurrik observes that in Kant's notion of the sublime there is "a new consciousness of negativity, put in the service of subjectivity." See Kurrik, *Literature and Negation* (New York: Columbia University Press, 1979), 51.

32. Walter Kaufmann, ed., *Existentialism from Dostoevsky to Sartre* (New York: New American Library, 1975), 12.

33. Ara, "Daini no seishun," 5.

34. For a brief account, see Beckmann and Okubo, 242–5.

35. Ara, "Daini no seishun," 6–7.

36. Ibid., 4.

37. Ibid., 12.

38. Ibid., 14.

39. Tsurumi Shunsuke, "Nihon no jitsuzonshugi—sengo no sesō," in Kuno Osamu and Tsurumi Shunsuke, *Gendai Nihon no shisō* (Tokyo: Iwanami Shinsho, 1956), 198.

40. Tamura Taijirō, "Nikutai wa ningen de aru," *Gunzō* (May 1947): 11.

41. Ibid., 12.

42. Tamura Taijirō, "Nikutai no mon," in Itō Sei et al., eds., *Kitahara Takeo, Inoue Tomoichirō, Tamura Taijirō shū* [Nihon gendai bungaku zenshū, Kōdansha-ban 94] (Tokyo: Kōdansha, 1968), 318–19.

43. Ibid., 317.

44. Ibid., 318.

45. Osamu Dazai, *The Setting Sun*, trans. Donald Keene (New York: New Directions Publishing Corporation, 1956), 62.

46. Ibid., 124–5.

47. Ibid., 172.

48. Ara Masato, "Minshū to wa tare ka," *Kindai bungaku* 3 (April 1946): 8–9.

49. Ibid., 12.

50. Ibid., 8.

51. In December 1945, the newly formed Keisei Electric Railway Labor Union included among its demands a "five-times wage increase." Moore, "Production Control and the Postwar Crisis of Japanese Capitalism," 251.

52. Ara, "Minshū to wa tare ka," 17–18.

53. Ara, "Daini no seishun," 13.

54. On Kasai, see Edward Fowler, *The Rhetoric of Confession: Shishōsetsu in Early Twentieth-Century Japanese Fiction* (Berkeley: University of California Press, 1988), chapter 9.

55. Katō Shūichi, "IN EGOISTOS," *Kindai bungaku* (July 1947): 1–6.

56. Ara Masato et al., "Zadankai: bungakusha no sekimu," reprinted in Usui Yoshimi, ed., *Sengo bungaku ronsō* 1 (Tokyo: Banchō Shobō, 1972), 65–7.

57. Ara Masato, "Nakano Shigeharu-ron," *Ara Masato chosakushū* 1 (Tokyo: San'ichi Shobō, 1983), 187.

58. Ara Masato, "Tetsugakusha Q e no tegami," reprinted in Mashita Shin'ichi, ed., *Shutaisei ronsō* (Tokyo: Hakuyōsha, 1949), 122–3.

59. Ara Masato, "Sanjūdai no me," *Ara Masato chosakushū* 1, 122–3; also see Ara, "Hareta jikan," ibid., 135–6.

60. Nakano, "Hihyō no ningensei (3)," *Nakano Shigeharu zenshū* 12 (Tokyo: Chikuma Shobō, 1979), 109.

61. Immanuel Kant, *Critique of Practical Reason*, trans. Lewis White Beck (New York: Macmillan Publishing Company, 1956), 136.

62. Hirano Ken, "Hitotsu no hansotei," *Hirano Ken zenshū* 1 (Tokyo: Shinchōsha, 1975), 182–3.

63. See Nancy Tuana, *Woman and the History of Philosophy* (New York: Paragon House, 1992); on Hegel's view that "[w]oman is associated with the emotions, man with reason. Woman is passive, man, active," see 98–108. Also Seyla Ben Habib, "On Hegel, Women and Irony," in Mary Lyndon Shanley and Carole Pateman, eds., *Feminist Interpretations and Political Theory* (University Park: The Pennsylvania State University Press, 1991), 129–45.

64. Hirano, 183. Kurahara explains the actions of "I" (the protagonist) as follows: "Both 'I' and the author are criticizing (the woman) Kasahara's petty-bourgeois emotional life and conduct. True love never lies just in giving what one's companion wants, but lies in elevating one's companion. 'I' who is a Communist hopes that Kasahara will come to have Communist feelings, and works for the sake of that, but in the first part, at least, he did not succeed. Kasahara would not be induced to subordinate her individual life and interests to social class life and interests. . . . However, the Communist 'I' cannot accept that as such. While he understands that Kasahara has such feelings, and is sympathetic on that certain point, he cannot help but criticize that. Therein the gap between the two is produced. That is what the author has tried to describe." Quoted in Shea, p. 336.

65. Hirano,184–5.

66. Hirano, "Seiji to bungaku (1)," *Hirano Ken zenshū* 1, 190.

67. Ibid., 192.

68. On spying and lynching incidents in the JCP, see Elise Tipton, *Japanese Police State:*

Tokkō in Interwar Japan (Honolulu: University of Hawaii Press, 1990), 26–7. Also Richard H. Mitchell, *Janus-Faced Justice: Political Criminals in Imperial Japan* (Honolulu: University of Hawaii Press, 1992).

69. Hirano Ken, " 'Seiji no yūisei' to wa nani ka," *Hirano Ken zenshū* 1, 224.

70. On Kobayashi's murder, see Tipton, 26.

71. Hirano, " 'Seiji no yūisei' to wa nani ka," 223.

72. Tsurumi, *Social Change and the Individual*, 310.

73. Shea, 377.

74. Miriam Silverberg, *Changing Song: The Marxist Manifestos of Nakano Shigeharu* (Princeton, NJ: Princeton University Press, 1990), including the chronology, 230–4.

75. Brett de Bary, introduction to *Three Works by Nakano Shigeharu*, 1–6.

76. Nakano Shigeharu, "Hihyō no ningensei—Hirano Ken, Ara Masato ni tsuite," *Nakano Shigeharu zenshū* 12, 84.

77. Ibid., 91–93.

78. Ibid., 87.

79. Ibid., 94.

80. Ara Masato, "Hareta jikan," in *Ara Masato chosakushū* 1, 131.

81. Nakano Shigeharu, "Hihyō no ningensei (2)—bungaku handō no mondai nado," *Nakano Shigeharu zenshū* 12, 96.

82. Ibid., 96–97.

83. Ibid., 103.

84. Nakano Shigeharu, "Hihyō no ningensei (3)," *Nakano Shigeharu zenshū* 12, 107.

85. Ibid., 110–12.

86. Ibid., 115.

87. Ara Masato, "Yoko no tsunagari," *Kindai bungaku* (October 1947): 8.

88. Ernesto Laclau and Chantal Mouffe, "Recasting Marxism: Hegemony and New Political Movements," *Socialist Review* 12/6 (1982): 100.

89. Oda Makoto, *Ningen: aru kojinteki na kōsatsu* (Tokyo: Chikuma Shobō, 1968); translation and abridgement by J. Victor Koschmann, in Koschmann, ed., *Authority and the Individual in Japan*, 156.

90. To point to the oppressive dimensions of postwar censorship is not necessarily to agree with the extensive indictment against Occupation censorship leveled by the neoconservative critic Etō Jun, who seeks to vindicate the Japanese bureaucratic elite and a continuation of the prewar state in place of the process of democratic revolution. Yet he is not entirely mistaken in his charge that *Kindai bungaku*'s writers and critics somewhat opportunistically celebrated their postwar "liberation" amidst various forms of postwar oppression. See Etō Jun, "Sengo bungaku wa hasan no kiki," *Mainichi shinbun*, January 24, 1978. Also his *Ochiba no hakiyose* (Tokyo: Bungei Shunjū, 1981).

91. See Hidaka Rokurō, ed., *Sengo shisō no shuppatsu* [Sengo Nihon shisō taikei 1] (Tokyo: Chikuma Shobō, 1968), 3–7.

92. Kōsaka Susumu, "Sengo 'shutai' no fūka kakusan to 'kindai bungaku'ha," 39.

93. Ibid., 40.

94. Odagiri Hideo, "Shin bungaku sōzō no shutai—atarashii dankai no tame ni," *Shin-Nihon bungaku* (May–June 1946): 74.

95. Honda, "Geijutsu, rekishi, ningen," 9. Also quoted by Kajinoki Gō, who makes an argument similar to that advanced here. See Kajinoki, "Kindai bungaku: eikō to hisan," in Dentō to Gendai Hozonban, *Sengo shisō no genzai* (Tokyo: Dentō to Gendaisha, 1981), 35.

96. Ara Masato, "Hareta jikan," *Ara Masato chosakushū* 1, 135. Also quoted by Kajinoki, 40.

97. Kajinoki, 39.

98. Hirano Ken, "Seiji to bungaku (2)," *Hirano Ken zenshū* 1, 209.

Chapter 3

1. Karl Marx, "Theses on Feuerbach," in Robert C. Tucker, ed., *The Marx-Engels Reader* (New York: W. W. Norton and Co., 1972), 107.

2. Matsumura Kazuto, "Shūsengo no handō tetsugaku no shuryū," *Zen'ei* (October 1947): 49.

3. Kan Takayuki, *Sengo seishin*, 203–4.

4. Kuno, Tsurumi, and Fujita, *Sengo Nihon no shisō*, 36.

5. Tanabe, "Seiji tetsugaku no kyūmu" (originally published in *Tenbō*, March 1946), preface to the first edition, *Tanabe Hajime zenshū* 8 (Tokyo: Chikuma Shobō, 1963), 325.

6. Tanabe, "Shu no ronri no imi o akiraka ni su" (1937), quoted in Arakawa Ikuo, *Gendai Nihon shisōshi* 5 (Tokyo: Aoki Shoten, 1971), 200–1.

7. Tanabe, "Seiji tetsugaku no kyūmu," 334.

8. Ibid., 334–5.

9. Ibid., 325.

10. The role of the emperor in Tanabe's pre- and postwar work is assessed in H. D. Harootunian, "Ichiboku hitokusa ni yadoru tennōsei," 85–101.

11. Tanabe, "Seiji tetsugaku no kyūmu," 368.

12. Ibid., 369.

13. Ibid., 370.

14. Ibid., 371.

15. Masumi Junnosuke, *Postwar Politics in Japan, 1945–1955*, 96.

16. T. A. Bisson, "April 1946 Elections," in Livingston, Moore, and Oldfather, eds., *Postwar Japan: 1945 to the Present*, 61.

17. Ibid., 59, 61.

18. Tanabe, "Shakaitō to Kyōsantō no aida," *Tanabe Hajime zenshū* 8, 378.

19. Ibid., 388–92.

20. Ibid., 379.

21. For further biographical information, see Takei Kunio, *Umemoto Katsumi ron: henkyō ni okeru shutaisei no ronri* (Tokyo: Daisan Bunmeisha, 1977). Also see Umemoto Katsumi, "Yuibutsuron to dōtoku—Matsumura Kazuto to no taidan," *Umemoto Katsumi chosakushū* 1 (Tokyo: San'ichi Shobō, 1977), 239–41.

22. Umemoto, "Ningenteki jiyu no genkai," *Umemoto Katsumi chosakushū* 1, 9.

23. Takei Kunio, 56.

24. Umemoto Katsumi, "Daiichibu e no tsuiki" [1961], in Umemoto, *Yuibutsuron to shutaisei* (Tokyo: Gendai Shichōsha, new edition of 1974), 324–5.

25. Translation from Karl Marx, "On the Jewish Question," in Tucker, ed., 44.

26. Umemoto borrows language from Marx, *The German Ideology*; translation from Tucker, ed., 161.

27. Paul Smith characterizes Marx's view of the subject/individual's development as a "quasi-religious trajectory." See Smith, *Discerning the Subject* (Minneapolis: University of Minnesota Press, 1988), 10.

28. Friedrich Engels, "Socialism: Utopian and Scientific," in Tucker, ed., 637.

29. Umemoto takes another jab at Tanabe along the way: "Insofar as freedom's objective conditions of possibility are historical, political forms will naturally correspond to those conditions, so *idle speculation to the effect that property held in common will mean an alienation*

of freedom is utterly meaningless" (emphasis added). Umemoto, "Ningenteki jiyū no genkai," 11.

30. Ibid., 11–12.

31. English version of Engels from Roy Bhaskar, "Determinism," in Tom Bottomore, ed., *A Dictionary of Marxist Thought* (Cambridge: Harvard University Press, 1983), 118.

32. Here Umemoto places himself in a long line of Marxist critics who have contested scientistic, mechanistic readings of Marxism. For a recent example see Smith, especially 24–40.

33. Umemoto, "Ningenteki jiyū no genkai," 13–14.

34. Ibid.

35. Ibid., 18.

36. The Marxist critic Stanley Aronowitz defines the basics of "vulgar" Marxism as: "(1) the reflection theory of knowledge and (2) a correspondence theory of truth grounded in the distinction between base and superstructure in which the latter is determined by the former, not only in the *final* instance, but in each of them." Aronowitz, *The Crisis in Historical Materialism: Class, Politics and Culture in Marxist Theory* (New York: Praeger Publishers, 1981), 15.

37. See Georg Lukács, *History and Class Consciousness: Studies in Marxist Dialectics,* trans. Rodney Livingstone (Cambridge: MIT Press, 1968), 1–24.

38. Umemoto, "Ningenteki jiyū no genkai," 24.

39. Maruyama Masao, introduction to *Studies in the Intellectual History of Tokugawa Japan* (Tokyo: University of Tokyo Press, 1974), xxiv—xxv.

40. Umemoto, "Yuibutsuron to ningen," in *Umemoto Katsumi chosakushū* 1, 33–34.

41. Ibid., 34.

42. Wilhelm Reich, *Sex-Pol Essays* (New York: Vintage Books, 1972), 284; quoted in Smith, 5.

43. Umemoto, "Yuibutsuron to ningen," 34–35.

44. Marx and Engels, "The German Ideology, Part I," in Tucker, ed., 126.

45. Karl Marx, "Critique of Hegel's *Philosophy of Right*," in Tucker, ed., p. 22.

46. Marx, "On the Jewish Question," in Tucker, ed., 44.

47. Umemoto, "Yuibutsuron to ningen," 36.

48. Ibid., 37.

49. Watsuji Tetsurō, *Rinrigaku* 1 (Tokyo: Iwanami Shoten, 1937; rev. ed. 1949), 225.

50. Ibid., 12.

51. Ibid., 38.

52. Ibid., 24.

53. Umemoto, "Yuibutsuron to ningen," 39. English equivalent from Tucker, ed., 114.

54. Ibid., 39–40. English from Tucker, ed., 121. Watsuji quotes the same passage; see *Rinrigaku* 1, 47.

55. Umemoto, "Yuibutsuron to ningen," 40. English from Tucker, ed., 122.

56. Watsuji Tetsurō, *Ningen no gaku to shite no rinrigaku* (Tokyo: Iwanami Shoten, 1934; revised 1951, 1971), 175–6. Also quoted in Takei, 23.

57. Umemoto, "Yuibutsuron to ningen," 43–4.

58. Tucker, ed., 4.

59. Umemoto, "Yuibutsuron to ningen," 44.

60. Ibid., 45.

61. The same point has been made more recently by Ernesto Laclau and Chantal Mouffe in *Hegemony and Socialist Strategy*, 156.

62. Umemoto, "Yuibutsuron to ningen," 47.

63. Ibid., 48–49.

64. Ibid., 49.

65. Watsuji, *Rinrigaku* 1, 354.

66. Umemoto, "Yuibutsuron to ningen," 50–51.

67. Watsuji, *Rinrigaku* 1, 199.

68. Ibid., 193–4.

69. Naoki Sakai, "Return to the West/Return to the East: Watsuji Tetsurō's Anthropology and Discussions of Authenticity," in Masao Miyoshi and H. D. Harootunian, eds., *Japan in the World: A Special Issue of Boundary 2* (Durham, NC: Duke University Press, 1991), 237–70.

70. Watsuji, *Rinrigaku* 1, 174.

71. Sakai, "Return to the West," 255.

72. Smith, 17.

73. Umemoto, "Yuibutsuron to ningen," 34.

74. Kuno, Tsurumi, and Fujita, 41.

75. Matsumura Kazuto, "Tetsugaku ni okeru shūseishugi—Umemoto Katsumi no tachiba ni tsuite," in *Yuibutsuron to shutaiseiron* (Tokyo: Hyōronsha, 1949), 31, 37–38, 62.

76. Ibid., 31.

77. Ibid., 27.

78. Ibid., 28.

79. Ibid., 29.

80. Ibid., 34.

81. Ibid., 36–37.

82. Ibid., 42.

83. Ibid., 51.

84. Ibid., 54.

85. Shimizu Ikutarō, Matsumura Kazuto, Hayashi Kentarō, Kozai Yoshishige, Maruyama Masao, Mashita Shin'ichi, and Miyagi Otoya, "Yuibutsuron to shutaisei: zadankai," *Sekai* (February 1948): 24.

86. Matsumura, "Tetsugaku ni okeru shūseishugi," 53.

87. Ibid., 53, 61 (emphasis added).

88. Shimizu et al., 30. Also see Laclau, *New Reflections*, 15, 25.

89. Laclau, *New Reflections*, 126.

90. Shimizu et al., 30.

91. Ibid., 59.

92. Tanabe Hajime, "Kirisutokyō to marukushizumu to Nihon bukkyō: dainiji shūkyō kaikaku no yosō," (*Tenbō*, September 1947); *Tanabe Hajime zenshū* 10 (Tokyo: Chikuma Shobō, 1963), 271–324.

93. Umemoto Katsumi, "Mu no ronrisei to tōhasei: Tanabe tetsugaku hihan, tokuni dainiji shūkyō kaikaku no yosō no tame ni" (*Tenbō*, March 1948); *Umemoto Katsumi chosakushū* 1, 69, 73.

94. Ibid., 73–7.

95. Ibid., 78–9.

96. Ibid., 82–4.

97. Ibid., 85–6.

98. Tanabe Hajime, *Philosophy as Metanoetics*, trans. Takeuchi Yoshinori (Berkeley: University of California Press, 1986), i—ii.

99. Umemoto, "Mu no ronrisei to tōhasei," 85–7.

100. Ibid., 91–2.

101. Ibid., 93.

102. For a critique, see Joan W. Scott, "Experience," in Butler and Scott, eds., *Feminists Theorize the Political*, 22–40.

103. Friedrich Engels, "Ludwig Feuerbach and the End of Classical German Philosophy," *Marx and Engels Selected Works* II, 341; quoted in Umemoto Katsumi, "Yuibutsu benshōhō to mu no benshōhō" (*Risō*, March 1948), *Umemoto Katsumi chosakushū* 1, 95–6.

104. Umemoto, "Yuibutsu benshōhō to mu no benshōhō," 105–6.

105. Nishida Kitarō, *Fundamental Problems of Philosophy: The World of Action and the Dialectical World*, trans D. A. Dilworth (Tokyo: Sophia University Press, 1970).

106. Umemoto, "Yuibutsu benshōhō to mu no benshōhō," 114. Nishida had written, "Existence in time means existing in some kind of a determined present, so that it is always determined by such a present. But at the same time it destroys that present and is a process of changing it. Thus time becomes the form of the self-determination of being. . . . That the individual is . . . the ultimate determination of the universal would imply the destruction of the determined universal. But this would in turn imply the determination of a new universal." Nishida, *Fundamental Problems of Philosophy*, 27.

107. Matsumura Kazuto, " 'Tetsugakusha' no shutaiseiron ni tsuite" (*Riron*, June 1948), in Matsumura, *Yuibutsuron to shutaiseiron*, 68–72.

108. Ibid., 76.

109. Ibid., 79–80, quoting from Karl Marx, *The Poverty of Philosophy* [1847]; English from David Caute, ed., *Essential Writings of Karl Marx*, (New York: Collier Books, 1967), 193.

110. Ibid., 84–6.

111. Ibid., 87–90.

112. Umemoto Katsumi, "Shutaisei to kaikyūsei—Matsumura Kazuto no hihyō ni kotaete," *Risō* (July 1948); *Umemoto Katsumi chosakushū* 1, 153–4.

113. Ibid., 161.

114. Ibid., 161–3.

115. Ibid., 173.

116. Lukács, *History and Class Consciousness*, 149.

117. Ibid., 75.

118. Laclau and Mouffe, 156.

119. Ibid., 176.

120. Amakasu Sekisuke, "Yuibutsuron to ningen" (*Riron*, August 1948), in Mashita Shin'ichi, ed., *Shutaisei ronsō*, 4–7.

121. Ibid., 19–22.

122. Ibid., 10–12.

123. Ibid., 22–5.

124. Ibid., 39–43.

125. Funayama Shin'ichi, "Tetsugaku no shutaiteki taishōteki kōzō" (*Risō*, February 1948), in Mashita, ed., *Shutaisei ronsō*, 157.

126. Ibid., 162.

127. Ibid., 164–7.

128. Ibid., 170–1.

129. Mashita Shin'ichi, "Shutaiseiron: yuibutsuron no shutaiteki haaku to kanren shite" (speech at Meiji University, October 1947), in *Mashita Shin'ichi chosakushū* 1 (Tokyo: Aoki Shoten, 1979), 79–81.

130. Ibid., 87.

131. Ibid., 83–4.

132. Ibid., 85–7.

133. Ibid., 88.

134. Ibid., 89–90.

135. Komatsu Setsurō, "Jitsuzon tetsugaku to yuibutsu shikan" (*Risō*, 1948), in Mashita, ed., *Shutaisei ronsō*, 173–83.

136. Ibid., 189.

137. Ibid., 191–3.

138. Ibid., 192.

139. Ibid., 201–2.

140. Ibid., 204.

141. Umemoto Katsumi, "Hihan to kyōdō" (*Risō*, June 1948), in *Umemoto Katsumi chosakushū* 1, 122–3; quoting Umemoto, "Yuibutsuron to ningen," *Umemoto Katsumi chosakushū* 1, 34–5.

142. Umemoto, "Hihan to kyōdō," 128.

143. Takakuwa Sumio, "Gendai no seishin jōkyō: mu no tōhasei o chūshin to shite," *Shisō* (November 1948): 21–5.

144. Takakuwa Sumio, "Shi no haaku to shutaisei" (*Shakai*, April 1948), in Takakuwa, *Yuibutsuron to shutaisei* (Tokyo: Kokudosha, 1948), 154.

145. Ibid., 154.

146. Takakuwa Sumio, "Shutaiteki jiyū ni tsuite" (*Shisō*, December 1947), in Takakuwa, *Yuibutsuron to shutaisei*, 122–4.

147. Ibid., 129–30.

148. Ibid., 131–3.

149. Tanabe Hajime, *Tenbō* (September 1948): 10; quoted in Takakuwa, "Shutaiteki jiyū ni tsuite," 135.

150. Takakuwa Sumio, "'Mu' no setchūsei to hishakaisei" [1947], in Takakuwa, *Yuibutsuron to shutaisei*, 172.

151. Ibid., 137–8.

152. Takakuwa Sumio, "Shutaisei no tadashii haaku" (*Hyōron*, April 1948), in Takakuwa, *Yuibutsuron to shutaisei*, 72–4.

153. Takakuwa, "Shi no haaku to shutaisei," 157.

154. Takakuwa, "Shutaisei no tadashii haaku," 84–5.

155. Ibid., 86–7.

156. Takakuwa Sumio, "Yuibutsu shikan to shutaisei" (*Risō*, April 1948), in Takakuwa, *Yuibutsuron to shutaisei*, 23–4.

157. Ibid., 24–5.

158. Takakuwa, "Shutaisei no tadashii haaku," 91.

159. Miki Kiyoshi, "Principles of Thought for a New Japan," trans. Lewis E. Harrington, June 1993, 29.

160. Ibid., 33–6.

161. Ibid., 10.

162. Ibid., 37.

163. Kōsaka Masaaki, Suzuki Shigetaka, Kōyama Iwao, and Nishitani Keiji, "The Standpoint of World History and Japan" (*Chūō kōron*, January 1942), trans. Mark Anderson, Cornell University, 44–7.

164. Naoki Sakai, "Modernity and Its Critique: The Problem of Universalism and Particularism," in Masao Miyoshi and H. D. Harootunian, eds., *Postmodernism and Japan* (Durham, NC: Duke University Press, 1989), 108–10.

165. Hoshino Yoshirō and Taketani Mitsuo, "Kaisetsu," in *Taketani Mitsuo chosakushū* 1 (Tokyo: Keisō Shobō, 1968), 363–89.

166. Aikawa Haruki, "Gijutsu oyobi tekunorogii no gainen," *Yuibutsuron kenkyū* 8 (June 1933): 62.

167. In another postwar essay, Taketani criticized prewar, idealist philosophies of praxis for "locating praxis on the side of the subject (*shutai*)," and proposed instead that the structure of praxis be probed "on the objective side." Taketani Mitsuo, "Jissen no mondai ni tsuite," *Kikan riron* (July 1948); reprinted in Taketani, *Kagaku-tetsugaku-geijutsu* (Tokyo: Sōryūsha, 1949), 90–106.

168. Taketani, "Jissen no mondai ni tsuite," 96.

169. Taketani, "Hakugai to tatakaishi kagakusha ni sasagu," *Shinsei* (February 1946): 23. This essay is reprinted as "Gijutsuron: Hakugai to tatakaishi kagakusha ni sasagu" in *Taketani Mitsuo chosakushū* 1, 125–41.

170. Karl Marx, *Capital*, vol. 1 (Moscow: Foreign Languages Publishing House, n.d.), 180.

171. Taketani, "Hakugai," 23.

172. Ernesto Laclau makes the same point with regard to the work of G. A. Cohen. Laclau, *New Reflections*, 12.

173. On productive forces theory, see Takabatake Michitoshi, "Seisanryoku riron: Ōkōchi Kazuo, Kazahaya Yasoji," in Shisō no Kagaku Kenkyūkai, eds., *Kyōdō kenkyū: tenkō* II, revised and expanded (Tokyo: Heibonsha, 1978), 202–49.

174. Ōi Tadashi, *Gendai no yuibutsuron shisō* (Tokyo: Aoki Shoten, 1959), 69–70.

175. Taketani, "Hakugai," 19.

176. English version of Engels from Roy Bhaskar, "Determinism," in Bottomore, ed., 118.

177. V. I. Lenin, *Materialism and Empirio-Criticism* (Peking: Foreign Languages Press, 1972), 219.

178. Taketani, "Hakugai," 22.

179. Cornelius Castoriadis, *The Imaginary Institution of Society*, trans. Kathleen Blamey (Cambridge, MA: The MIT Press, 1987), 30.

180. Karl Marx and Friedrich Engels, "Manifesto of the Communist Party," in Tucker, ed., *The Marx-Engels Reader*, 340.

181. Jürgen Habermas, "Technology and Science as 'Ideology': For Herbert Marcuse on his seventieth birthday, July 19, 1968," in Habermas, *Toward a Rational Society: Student Protest, Science and Politics* (Boston: Beacon Press, 1968), 83.

182. Herbert Marcuse, *One-Dimensional Man*, quoted in Habermas, 84–5.

183. Taketani, "Hakugai," 19.

184. Taketani, "Zunō no kaizō" (February 5, 1946), in *Taketani Mitsuo chosakushū* 4 (Tokyo: Keisō Shobō, 1969), 35.

185. Lefort, *Democracy and Political Theory*, 19.

186. Laclau, *New Reflections*, 30, 50, 61–4.

Chapter 4

1. *Hegel's Philosophy of Right*, trans. T. M. Knox (London: Oxford University Press, 1967), 161.

2. On Marxism in relation to Japanese social science and modernism see Andrew E. Barshay, "Imagining Democracy in Postwar Japan: Reflections on Maruyama Masao and Modernism," *Journal of Japanese Studies* 18/2 (1992): 365–406.

3. Louis Althusser, "Ideology and Ideological State Apparatuses (Notes towards an In-

vestigation)," *Lenin and Philosophy and other essays by Louis Althusser*, trans. Ben Brewster (New York: Monthly Review Press, 1971), 182 (italics deleted).

4. Ōtsuka Hisao, "Seisanryoku ni okeru tōyō to seiyō: Nishi-Ō hōken nōmin no to-kushitsu" (May 1946); *Ōtsuka Hisao chosakushū* 7 (Tokyo: Iwanami Shoten, 1969), 246–7.

5. Ibid., 248.

6. Karl Marx, *Pre-Capitalist Economic Formations*, ed. Eric J. Hobsbawm and trans. Jack Cohen (New York: International Publishers, 1964), 109.

7. Ōtsuka, "Kindaika to wa nani ka: kindaika katei ni okeru futatsu no michi" (February 24, 1947), *Ōtsuka Hisao chosakushū* 3 (Tokyo: Iwanami Shoten, 1969), 182–3.

8. Maurice Dobb, *Studies in the Development of Capitalism* (New York: International Publishers, 1947), e.g., 125. Dobb writes that the sixteenth century saw "a considerable growth of independent peasant farming by tenants who rented land as enclosed holdings out-side the open-field system. Among these there developed . . . an important section of richer peasants or yeomen, who as they prospered added field to field, by lease or purchase, perhaps became usurers (along with squire and parson and local maltster and corn-dealer) to their poorer neighbours, and grew by the end of the century into considerable farmers who relied on the hire of wage-labour, recruited from the victims of enclosures or from the poorer cottagers." Also see Kohachiro Takahashi, "A Contribution to the Discussion," in Paul Sweezy et al., *The Transition from Feudalism to Capitalism* (London: NLB, 1976), 88.

9. See the discussion of Takahashi's viewpoint in Hoston, *Marxism and the Crisis of Development in Prewar Japan*, 287–91.

10. Sugiyama Mitsunobu, *Sengo keimō to shakai kagaku no shisō* (Tokyo: Shin'yōsha, 1983), 79.

11. Ōtsuka Hisao, "Makusu uēbā ni okeru shihonshugi no 'seishin,'" *Ōtsuka Hisao cho-sakushū* 8 (Tokyo: Iwanami Shoten, 1969), 24. English translation from *Max Weber on the Spirit of Capitalism*, trans. Kondō Masaomi [I.D.E. Occasional Papers Series no. 13] (Tokyo: Institute of Developing Economies, 1976), 17–18.

12. Ibid., 69; trans. 51–2.

13. Ibid., 27; trans., 21–2.

14. Ibid., 64; trans., 47.

15. Ibid., 95; trans., 72.

16. Ibid., 86; trans., 65.

17. Ibid., 93; trans., 71.

18. Ibid., 96; trans., 73.

19. Ibid., 98; trans., 74–5.

20. Ibid., 100; trans., 76.

21. Ueno Masaji, "Keizaishi-gaku," in Chō Yukio and Sumiya Kazuhiko, eds., *Kindai Nihon keizai shisōshi* 2 [Kindai Nihon shisōshi taikei 6] (Tokyo: Yūhikaku, 1971), 210. Kan Takayuki writes, "No matter how exploitative they were domestically, how aggressive over-seas, or how violent their colonial administrations, the true modernization and true capitalism of England and the U.S. were Ōtsuka's models. . . . [Moreover], according to Ōtsuka's logic, what was bad about Japan was its 'oldness,' not that it invaded and set up colonies, massacred colonial peoples and, domestically, mobilized the Japanese proletariat through state vio-lence." Kan Takayuki, *Sengo seishin*, 64.

22. On Hayashi in relation to neoconservatism, see *Shin-hoshushugi*, ed. Hayashi Ken-tarō [Gendai Nihon shisō taikei 35] (Tokyo: Chikuma Shobō, 1963).

23. Hayashi Kentarō, "Rekishi ni okeru shutai no mondai," *Sekai* (April 1947): 22.

24. Karl Marx, *Capital*, vol. 3 (Moscow: Foreign Languages Publishing House, 1962), 327.

25. Hayashi, "Rekishi ni okeru shutai no mondai," 23–4.

26. Ibid., 28.

27. Ibid., 24.

28. Ibid., 25.

29. Ibid., 26.

30. Ibid., 35.

31. Ōtsuka, "Jiyū to dokuritsu" (August 1946), in *Ōtsuka Hisao chosakushū* 8, 177.

32. Ibid., 179–80.

33. Ibid., 184.

34. Ibid.

35. Ōtsuka, "Jiyūshugi ni sakidatsu mono" (December 1946), in *Ōtsuka Hisao chosakushū* 8, 190.

36. Ibid., 193; also Ōtsuka, "Kindai ni okeru jiyū to jiyūshugi" (1946), in *Ōtsuka Hisao chosakushū* 8, 208–9.

37. Ōtsuka, "Jiyūshugi ni sakidatsu mono," 197–8.

38. For the "Renaissance" and "Puritan" distinction applied to freedom see Ōtsuka, "Kindai ni okeru jiyū to jiyushugi," 204–9.

39. Ōtsuka, "Jiyūshugi ni sakidatsu mono," 200.

40. Ōtsuka Hisao, "Robinson Kurūsō no ningen ruikei" (*Jidai*, August 1947), in *Ōtsuka Hisao chosakushū* 8, 216. Original English wording from *The Life and Strange Surprizing Adventures of Robinson Crusoe, of York, Mariner*, ed. J. Donald Crowley (London: Oxford University Press, 1972), 4.

41. Ōtsuka, "Robinson Kurūsō no ningen ruikei," 217.

42. Ibid., 215.

43. Ibid., 219–20.

44. Ibid., 219.

45. Ōtsuka Hisao, "Seisanryoku ni okeru tōyō to seiyō" (May 1946), in *Ōtsuka Hisao chosakushū* 7, 256.

46. Ōtsuka Hisao, "Kindaiteki ningen ruikei no sōshutsu: seijiteki shutai no minshūteki kiban no mondai" (*Daigaku shinbun*, April 21, 1946), in *Ōtsuka Hisao chosakushū* 8, 169.

47. Ōtsuka Hisao, "Jiyūshugi ni sakidatsu mono—kindaiteki ningen ruikei no sōshutsu" (*Kirisuto bunka*, December 1946), in *Ōtsuka Hisao chosakushū* 8, 200.

48. Ōtsuka, "Kindaiteki ningen ruikei no sōshutsu," 169.

49. Ibid., 172.

50. Georg Wilhelm Friedrich Hegel, *The Philosophy of History*, trans. J. Sibree (New York: Dover Publications, Inc., 1956), 105, 111.

51. Marx, *Pre-Capitalist Economic Formations*.

52. Max Weber, *The Religion of China*, trans. and ed. Hans H. Gerth (New York: The Free Press, 1951).

53. Ōtsuka, "Kindaiteki ningen ruikei no sōshutsu," 173–4.

54. Althusser, "Ideology and Ideological State Apparatuses (Notes towards an Investigation)," 180–1.

55. Asada Akira, "Infantile Capitalism and Japan's Postmodernism: A Fairy Tale," in Miyoshi and Harootunian, eds., *Postmodernism and Japan*, 274–5.

56. Ōtsuka Hisao, "Saikōdo 'jihatsusei' no hatsuyō" (1944), in *Ōtsuka Hisao chosakushū* 8, 341.

57. Ōkōchi Kazuo, *Sumisu to risuto* (1943), in *Ōkōchi Kazuo chosakushū* 3 (Tokyo: Seirin Shoin Shinsha, 1969), 408–26.

58. Yamanouchi Yasushi, "Senjiki no isan to sono ryōgisei," in Yamanouchi Yasushi et

al., eds., *Nihon shakai kagaku no shisō* [Shakai kagaku no hōhō 3] (Tokyo: Iwanami Shoten, 1993), 156–7. See Ōkōchi Kazuo, *Sumisu to risuto*.

59. Complicity between liberalism and fascism in the Japanese environment was first analyzed in depth by the prewar Marxist Tosaka Jun in his "Nippon ideorogii-ron" of 1936. However, rather than pointing to similarities in the models of *shutaisei* typical of each, he argued that affinities with "Japanist" fascism were latent in the hermeneutic epistemology typical of Japanese liberalism. See Tosaka Jun, "Nippon ideorogii-ron," in *Tosaka Jun zenshū* 5 (Tokyo: Keisō Shobō, 1967).

60. Michel Foucault, "The Subject and Power," *Critical Inquiry* 8/4 (summer 1982): 785.

61. Barshay, "Imagining Democracy," 378.

62. Maruyama Masao, "Nihon ni okeru jiyū ishiki no keisei to tokushitsu" (August 21, 1947), in Maruyama Masao *Senchū to sengo no aida, 1936–1957* (Tokyo: Misuzu Shobō, 1976), 297–8.

63. Maruyama Masao, "Jyon Rokku to kindai seiji genri" (August 1949), in Maruyama, *Senchū to sengo no aida*, 404.

64. Ibid., 404–5 (emphasis added).

65. Ibid., 406–7.

66. Ibid., 300.

67. Maruyama, "Nihon ni okeru jiyū ishiki no keisei to tokushitsu," 298–9.

68. "The disintegration of the continuity between moral standards and nature . . . culminated in the Sorai school in the liberation of the private or inner life from all rigorism as a result of the sublimation of standards (the Way) in the political." Maruyama Masao, *Studies in the Intellectual History of Tokugawa Japan*, trans. Mikiso Hane (Princeton, NJ: Princeton University Press, 1974), 106.

69. Maruyama, "Nihon ni okeru jiyū ishiki no keisei to tokushitsu," 300. Also see Maruyama, *Studies in the Intellectual History of Tokugawa Japan*, 166.

70. Maruyama, "Nihon ni okeru jiyū ishiki no keisei to tokushitsu," 301.

71. Maruyama Masao, "Meiji kokka no shisō" (October 1946), in Maruyama, *Senchū to sengo no aida*, 232. Maruyama returned to this topic in the 1960s in his essay "Patterns of Individuation and the Case of Japan: A Conceptual Scheme," in Marius B. Jansen, ed., *Changing Japanese Attitudes Toward Modernization* (Princeton, NJ: Princeton University Press, 1965), 489–531. [Japanese version: Maruyama, "Kojin sekishutsu no samazama na patān— kindai Nihon o kēsu to shite," in Hosoya Chihiro, ed., *Nihon ni okeru kindaika no mondai* (Tokyo: Iwanami Shoten, 1968).]

72. Maruyama, "Nihon ni okeru jiyū ishiki no keisei to tokushitsu," 303–5.

73. Maruyama, *Studies in the Intellectual History of Tokugawa Japan*, 268.

74. Maruyama Masao, in *Thought and Behavior in Modern Japanese Politics*, expanded ed., ed. Ivan Morris (Oxford: Oxford University Press, 1979), 3–5.

75. Ibid., 17.

76. Maruyama Masao, "Kindaiteki shii" (January 1946), in Maruyama, *Senchū to sengo no aida*, 190.

77. McClure, 112. Also see Stuart Hall, "The Toad in the Garden: Thatcherism among the Theorists," in Nelson and Grossberg, eds., *Marxism and the Interpretation of Culture*, 35–57.

78. In an interview with Tsurumi Shunsuke, Maruyama Masao himself attributes his early postwar affirmation of nationalism to a certain "spirit of perversity" (*amanojaku seishin*). "Maruyama Masao: fuhen genri no tachiba," in Tsurumi Shunsuke, *Kataritsugu sengoshi* 1 (Tokyo: Shisō no Kagaku Sha, 1969), 85–6.

79. Maruyama Masao, "Kuga Katsunan: hito to shisō" (February 1947), in Maruyama, *Senchū to sengo no aida*, 284–5.

80. Ibid., 289.

81. Ibid., 287.

82. Ibid., 285.

83. Ibid., 291–2.

84. Ibid., 294.

85. McClure, 110.

86. Maruyama Masao, "Russeru 'Seiyō tetsugakushi (kinsei)'" (1946), in Maruyama, *Senchū to sengo no aida*, 260.

87. Sasakura Hideo, *Maruyama Masao-ron nōto* (Tokyo: Misuzu Shobō, 1988), 72.

88. Maruyama Masao, "Seijigaku ni okeru kokka no gainen" (1936), in Maruyama, *Senchū to sengo no aida*, 32. Quoted in Sasakura, 13.

89. Maruyama Masao, "Fukuzawa Yukichi ni okeru chitsujo to ningen" (November 25, 1943), in Maruyama, *Senchū to sengo no aida*, 144.

90. Sasakura, *Maruyama Masao-ron nōto*, 47.

91. Maruyama, "Fukuzawa Yukichi ni okeru chitsujo to ningen," 143.

92. Ibid., 144–5.

93. Sandra Lee Bartky, "Foucault, Femininity, and the Modernization of Patriarchal Power," in Irene Diamond and Lee Quinby, eds., *Feminism and Foucault* (Boston: Northeastern University Press, 1988), 61, 63. See Michel Foucault, *Discipline and Punish: The Birth of the Prison*, trans. Alan Sheridan (New York: Vintage Books, 1979), chap. 3, 195–228.

94. Laclau and Mouffe, *Hegemony and Socialist Strategy*, 181.

95. Carole Pateman, *The Disorder of Women* (Stanford: Stanford University Press, 1989), 104.

96. Maruyama Masao, "Fukuzawa Yukichi no tetsugaku—toku ni sono jiji hihan to no kanren," in Hidaka Rokurō, ed., *Kindaishugi* [Gendai Nihon shisō taikei 34] (Tokyo: Iwanami Shoten, 1964); and Maruyama Masao, "Fukuzawa ni okeru 'wakudeki,'" in *Fukuzawa Yukichi nenkan* 13 (1986): 25–86.

97. McClure, 110–11.

98. See Hidaka's brief introduction to "Fukuzawa Yukichi ni okeru chitsujo to ningen," in Hidaka Rokurō, ed., *Kindaishugi*, 55.

99. Ōtsuka Hisao, "Saikōdo 'jihatsusei' no hatsuyō" (1944), *Ōtsuka Hisao chosakushū* 8, 339–44. Ueno Masaji, "Keizai shigaku," 214.

100. Linda Nicholson, *Gender and History: The Limits of Social Theory in the Age of the Family* (New York: Columbia University Press, 1986), 162–3.

101. See Nakamura Akira, "Maruyama Masao and the Ontology of Politics," *The Japan Interpreter* 12/2 (spring 1978): 263.

102. Maruyama, "Kindaiteki shii," in *Senchū to sengo no aida*, 190.

103. Maruyama Masao and Andō Jinbei, "Umemoto Katsumi no omoide," in Maruyama Masao, Satō Noboru, and Umemoto Katsumi, *Sengo Nihon no kakushin shisō* (Tokyo: Gendai no Rironsha, 1983), 396–97.

104. Maruyama, "Fukuzawa Yukichi no tetsugaku," 60–2; English translation from Fukuzawa Yukichi's *Outline of a Theory of Civilization*, trans. David A. Dilworth and G. Cameron Hurst (Tokyo: Sophia University, 1973), 5–6 (emphasis added).

105. Maruyama, "Fukuzawa Yukichi no tetsugaku," 63.

106. Ibid., 67–9.

107. Ibid., 69.

108. Fukuzawa developed his use of this word in the course of his readings of the British

historian H. T. Buckle and other European writers, and sometimes meant it as the equivalent of their "prejudice," "superstition," or "credulity." For a detailed discussion of the various nuances of Fukuzawa's use of the term, see Maruyama Masao, "Fukuzawa ni okeru 'wakudeki,'" 25–56.

109. Maruyama, "Fukuzawa Yukichi no tetsugaku," 72 (emphasis added).

110. Ibid., 75.

111. Ibid., 80.

112. Ibid., 85.

113. Ibid., 86 (emphasis added).

114. Ibid., 87–8 (emphasis added).

115. Georg Simmel, "The Sociology of Sociability," in J. H. Abraham, ed., *Origins and Growth of Sociology* (New York: Harmondsworth, 1973).

116. Ibid., 290.

117. Ibid., 294.

118. Ibid., 290.

119. Ibid., 294.

120. Ibid., 296.

121. Ibid., 298.

122. Max Weber, "Politics as a Vocation," in H. H. Gerth and C. Wright Mills, trans. and eds., 127.

123. Umemoto Katsumi, "Marukusushugi to kindai seijigaku," *Gendai ideorogii* 5 (1962); reprinted in Umemoto, *Marukusushugi ni okeru shisō to kagaku* (Tokyo: San'ichi Shobō, 1969), 214–5.

124. Maruyama Masao and Andō Jinbei, "Umemoto Katsumi no omoide," 386.

125. Maruyama Masao, "From Carnal Literature to Carnal Politics," trans. Barbara Ruch, in Maruyama, *Thought and Behavior in Modern Japanese Politics*, 249.

126. Ibid., 251.

127. The word *fingere* seems to be the contribution of Maruyama's translator, Barbara Ruch. In the original Japanese text, Maruyama uses the term *fictio*. The point in both cases, of course, is to show an etymological root that means to fashion or invent.

128. Maruyama, "Carnal Literature," 253–4.

129. Ibid., 255–8.

130. Ibid., 260.

131. Ibid., 264.

132. G. W. F. Hegel, *Jenaer Realphilosophie II: Die Vorlesungen von 1805/6*, 244–5; quoted in Shlomo Avineri, *Hegel's Theory of the Modern State* (London: Cambridge University Press, 1972), 102.

133. Marx, "On the Jewish Question," quoted in Pateman, *The Disorder of Women*, 91–2.

134. Pateman, 92.

135. Kan Takayuki, *Sengo seishin*, 17.

136. Georg Henrik von Wright, *Explanation and Understanding* (Ithaca, NY: Cornell University Press, 1971), 1–8.

137. Shimizu Ikutarō, "Shutaisei no kyakkanteki kōsatsu" (*Tetsugaku*, winter 1947), reprinted in *Shimizu Ikutarō chosakushū* 8 (Tokyo: Kōdansha, 1992), 148–50.

138. Ibid., 151–2.

139. Ibid., 152–9.

140. Ibid., 162–3; citing John Dewey, *The Quest for Certainty: A Study of the Relation of Knowledge and Action* (New York: Minton, Balch, 1929), 266.

141. Shimizu, 169.
142. Ibid., 175.
143. Ibid., 171.
144. Sakuta Keiichi, "The Controversy over Community and Autonomy," in Koschmann, ed., *Authority and the Individual in Japan*, 233.
145. Takakuwa Sumio, "Shakaiteki shutai no mondai" (1948), in Takakuwa, *Yuibutsuron to shutaisei*, 31–58.
146. Miyagi Otoya, "Shutaisei ni tsuite," 160.
147. James Marshall, "Freud and Marx at UNESCO," *The American Scholar* 16/3 (summer 1947): 304–11.
148. Shimizu Ikutarō et al., "Yuibutsuron to shutaisei: zadankai," 24.
149. Ibid., 20.
150. Ibid., 37.
151. Ibid., 24.
152. Ibid., 23.
153. Ibid., 27.
154. Ibid., 24.
155. Ibid., 27.
156. Ibid., 41.
157. Ibid., 29.
158. Ibid., 41.
159. Ibid., 29.
160. Ibid., 35.
161. Ibid., 40.
162. Ibid., 42.

Chapter 5

1. Quoted in Umemoto Katsumi, "Shutaiseiron no gendankai: sono keika to kongo no tenbō," in Umemoto, *Katoki no ishiki* (Tokyo: Gendai Shichōsha, 1975), 173.
2. Takeuchi Yoshimi, "Kindaishugi to minzoku no mondai" (*Bungaku*, September 1951), in *Takeuchi Yoshimi zenshū* 7 (Tokyo: Chikuma Shobō, 1981), 28–9.
3. Ibid., 30–1.
4. Ibid., 36.
5. Ibid., 29.
6. Ibid., 32.
7. Ibid., 33. One Communist-party Marxist who did not hesitate to use the term *minzoku*, even in the first year or two after the war, was Nakano Shigeharu.
8. Maruyama, *Studies in the Intellectual History of Tokugawa Japan*, 324, n. 2.
9. Ibid., 327.
10. Ibid., 325–6.
11. Sakai Naoki, "Nihon shakai kagaku hōhō josetsu: Nihon shisō to iu mondai," in Yamanouchi Yasushi et al., eds., *Nihon shakai kagaku no shisō*, 28.
12. Daigaku Shinbun Renmei, ed., *Ōtsuka shigaku hihan* (1948); see Furuta Hikaru, "Shutaisei ronsō III: ronsō no tenkai to mondaiten," *Gendai to shisō* 15 (March 1974): 254.
13. Kurahara Korehito, "Kindaishugi to sono kokufuku," *Zen'ei* (August 1948): 41.
14. Ibid., 44.
15. Ibid., 45.

16. Jean Paul Sartre, "L'existentialisme est un humanisme" (1946); see "Existentialism Is a Humanism," in Kaufmann, ed., *Existentialism from Dostoevsky to Sartre*, 345–69.

17. Kurahara, "Kindaishugi to sono kokufuku," 47.

18. Ibid., 49.

19. Ibid., 52.

20. Amakasu Sekisuke, "Kindaishugi no shutaiseiron," *Zen'ei* (August 1948): 55.

21. Ibid., 57.

22. Ibid., 58–9.

23. Katsube Hajime, "Iwayuru 'shutaisei' no mondai ni tsuite," *Zen'ei* (August 1948): 61.

24. Ibid., 63–4.

25. Matsumura, "Burujyoateki ningenkan ni tsuite," in Matsumura, *Yuibutsuron to shutaiseiron*, 3.

26. Ibid., 7.

27. Ibid., 4–5.

28. Ibid., 8.

29. Ibid., 10–11.

30. Ibid., 12; English equivalent from Tucker, ed., 105–6.

31. Matsumura, 15.

32. Ibid., 20.

33. See Michael Schaller, *The American Occupation of Japan: The Origins of the Cold War in Asia* (New York: Oxford University Press, 1985), 164–5.

34. Ibid., 166.

35. See Seki Yoshihiko, "Part I: World Tension and the Cold War: Notes by the Editor," *Journal of Social and Political Ideas in Japan* 1, no. 1 (April 1963): 11.

36. Heiwa Mondai Danwakai, "Mitabi heiwa ni tsuite," *Sekai*, December 1950, 21–52. Page references are to a summary translation of the first part of the statement: Peace Problems Discussion Circle, "On Peace: Our Third Statement," *Journal of Social and Political Ideas in Japan* 1, no. 1 (April 1963), 14. Also see "Statement by the Peace Study Group on Peace Settlement for Japan," in Livingston, Moore, and Oldfather, eds., *Postwar Japan: 1945 to the Present*, 250–3.

37. Peace Problems Discussion Circle, 15.

38. Hayashi Kentarō, "Gendai chishikijin no ryōshiki: Maruyama Masao-shi ni taisuru hi-hihanteki hihan," *Sekai*, October 1950, 97–103.

39. Maruyama, "Aru 'jiyūshugi'sha e no tegami," *Sekai*, September 1950, 37.

40. Ibid., 30.

41. Ibid., 32–5.

42. Ibid., 36.

43. Ibid., 37.

44. Maruyama Masao, "Nihon ni okeru nashonarizumu: sono shisōteki haikei to tenbō," *Chūō kōron* (January 1951), reprinted in Maruyama, *Zōhoban: Gendai seiji no shisō to kōdō* (Tokyo: Miraisha, 1964), 152–70; in English as "Nationalism in Japan: Its Background and Prospects," trans. David Titus, in Maruyama, *Thought and Behavior in Modern Japanese Politics*. Page numbers refer to the English version.

45. Maruyama, "Nationalism in Japan," 152.

46. Ibid., 140.

47. Ibid., 153.

48. Shimizu Ikutarō, "Tokumei no shisō" (*Sekai*, September 1948), in *Shimizu Ikutarō chosakushū* 8, 208–9.

49. Ibid., 218.

50. Shimizu Ikutarō, "Shomin" (*Tenbō*, January 1950), in *Shimizu Ikutarō chosakushū* 8, 286–7.

51. Ibid., 288.

52. Ibid., 288–9.

53. Ibid., 289–90.

54. Ibid., 290.

55. Ibid., 298, 302.

56. Shimizu Ikutarō, "Aikokushin" (Tokyo: Iwanami Shinsho, 1950), in *Shimizu Ikutarō chosakushū* 8, 3–125.

57. Furuta Hikaru, Sakuta Keiichi, and Ikimatsu Keizō, eds., *Kindai Nihon shakai shisōshi* 2 [Kindai Nihon shisōshi taikei 2] (Tokyo: Yūhikaku, 1971), 296.

58. (no title), *Sekai*, August 1948, 59.

59. Kozai Yoshishige, "Yuibutsuron to Nihonteki no mono," in Nijusseiki Kenkyūjo, ed., *Tetsugaku kyōshitsu* (1948); discussed by Furuta Hikaru in "Nashonaru na mono no saihyōka o meguru shoronsō," in Miyakawa, Nakamura, and Furuta, eds., *Kindai Nihon shisō ronsō*, 214–16.

60. Arase Yutaka, "Sengo shisō to sono tenkai," in Ienaga Saburō, ed., *Kindai Nihon shisōshi kōza* 1 (Tokyo: Chikuma Shobō, 1959), 372; and Furuta Hikaru et al., eds., 297.

61. Quoted in Robert A. Scalapino, *The Japanese Communist Movement, 1920–1966* (Berkeley: University of California Press, 1967), 61.

62. Takazawa Kōji, Sanaga Shirō, and Matsumura Ryōichi, eds., *Sengo kakumei undō jiten* (Tokyo: Shinsensha, 1989), 199.

63. "Naze buryoku kakumei ga mondai ni naranakatta ka" (October 20, 1950), reprinted in Nihon Kyōsantō (Kakumei saha) Kanagawa-ken Jōnin Iinkai, ed., *Teppō kara kokka kenryoku ga umareru: busō junbi to kōdō no tame ni* (July 1970), 23–24 [Takazawa Collection, Sinclair Library, University of Hawaii, File 316].

64. "Nihon Kyōsantō gozenkyō hōkokusho: shinkōryō no seishiki kettei" (*Kyūkon saibaihō*, October 1951), in Nihon Kyōsantō (Kakumei saha) Kanagawa-ken Jōnin Iinkai, ed., 39.

65. "Gozenkyō ikō no busō kōryō jitsugen ni kan suru," in Nihon Kyōsantō (Kakumei saha) Kanagawa-ken Jōnin Iinkai, ed., 137–8.

66. Peter J. Katzenstein and Yutaka Tsujinaka, *Defending the Japanese State*, Cornell East Asia Series 53 (Ithaca, NY: East Asia Program, 1991), 9–10.

67. Scalapino, 79–86.

68. Matsuzawa Hiroaki, personal communication, November 1993. English translations of these works are provided in *Mao's China: Party Reform Documents, 1942–44*, translation and introduction by Boyd Compton (Seattle: University of Washington Press, 1952). Compton explains the term Cheng Feng (*zhengfeng*) as follows: "*Cheng tun*: to correct. *Tso feng*: style of work, spirit. The contraction is *Cheng Feng*" (p. xvi).

69. Takei Kunio, *Umemoto Katsumi ron: henkyō ni okeru shutaisei no ronri*, 81ff.

70. Lawrence Olson, *Ambivalent Moderns: Portraits of Japanese Cultural Identity* (Savage, MD: Rowman and Littlefield Publishers, Inc., 1992), 52.

71. Takeuchi Yoshimi, "Kindai to wa nani ka? (Nihon to Chūgoku no baai) (Chūgoku no kindai to Nihon no kindai)" (November 1948), in *Takeuchi Yoshimi zenshū* 4 (Tokyo: Chikuma Shobō, 1980), 147–8.

72. Ibid., 158.

73. Ibid., 164.

74. Matsuzawa Hiroaki, personal communication, November 1993.

75. Ibid.
76. Ibid.
77. Takeuchi Yoshimi, "Nihonjin no Chūgokukan" (*Tenbō*, September 1949), in *Takeuchi Yoshimi zenshū* 4, 9.
78. Ibid., 10–11.
79. Takeuchi Yoshimi, "Chūgoku no rejisutansu" (*Chisei*, May 1949), in *Takeuchi Yoshimi zenshū* 4, 36–8.
80. Matsuzawa Hiroaki, personal communication, November 1993.
81. Takeuchi Yoshimi, "Shin-Chūgoku no seishin" (*Shisaku*, December 1949), in *Takeuchi Yoshimi zenshū* 4, 96.
82. Takeuchi, "Kindaishugi to minzoku no mondai," 28–37.
83. Takeuchi Yoshimi, "Kokumin bungaku no teishō: Itō Sei-shi e no tegami" (*Nihon dokusho shinbun*, May 14, 1952), in *Takeuchi Yoshimi zenshū* 7, 38–42.
84. Furuta Hikaru, "Nashonaru na mono no saihyōka o meguru shoronsō," in Miyakawa, Nakamura, and Furuta, eds., *Kindai Nihon shisō ronsō*, 224–5.
85. Takeuchi Yoshimi, "Kokumin bungaku no mondaiten" (*Kaizō*, August 1952), in *Takeuchi Yoshimi zenshū* 7, 48.
86. Ibid., 49.
87. Ibid., 47.

Conclusion

1. Conclusion to the manifesto of a new book series from Verso entitled Phronesis, in Mouffe, ed., *Dimensions of Radical Democracy*, frontispiece.
2. See Kan Takayuki, *Sengo seishin*, 10–19.
3. Umemoto, "Yuibutsuron to ningen," 50.
4. Naoki Sakai, "Modernity and Its Critique: The Problem of Universalism and Particularism," in Miyoshi and Harootunian, eds., *Postmodernism and Japan*, 118–21.
5. For example, see Masao Miyoshi, *Off Center: Power and Culture Relations between Japan and the United States* (Cambridge: Harvard University Press, 1991), 97–125.
6. Matsumoto Sannosuke, introduction to *Journal of Social and Political Ideas in Japan* 4/2 (August 1966): 5–7.
7. Derek Sayer, *Capitalism and Modernity: An Excursus on Marx and Weber* (London: Routledge, 1991), 121.
8. Ibid., 121, 128.
9. John Stuart Mill, quoted in Samuel Bowles and Herbert Gintis, *Democracy and Capitalism: Property, Community, and the Contradictions of Modern Social Thought* (New York: Basic Books, 1986), 124.
10. See Joanne Izbicki's analysis of the paternal policeman in Kurosawa Akira's 1949 film *Stray Dog* for an argument along these lines. Joanne Izbicki, "Scorched Cityscapes and Silver Screens: Negotiating Defeat and Democracy in Occupied Japan" (Ph.D. diss., Cornell University, 1996). Conversely, Maruyama Masao's argument regarding the lack of *shutaisei* among Japanese Class-A war criminals emphasizes the "premodern" dimensions of their personalities. See Maruyama Masao, "Gunkoku shihaisha no seishin keitai" (1949), in Maruyama, *Zōhoban: Gendai seiji no shisō to kōdō* (Tokyo: Miraisha, 1964), 88–130; English translation in Maruyama, *Thought and Behavior in Modern Japanese Politics*, chap. 3.
11. E. P. Thompson, *The Making of the English Working Class* (New York: Vintage Books, 1963), 9.
12. Sayer, 71.

13. Laclau, *New Reflections*, 233.

14. Ibid., 211.

15. Ibid., 41.

16. Sayer, 128.

17. Ibid., 80.

18. Ibid., 69.

19. E.g., Yoshimoto Takaaki and Tanigawa Gan, whom Sakuta Keiichi has tagged the "folk-nativist faction" (*minzoku-dochakuha*). See Wesley Sasaki-Uemura, "Citizen and Community in the 1960 Anpo Protests" (Ph.D. diss., Cornell University, 1993), chaps. 4 and 5; also Sakuta, "The Controversy over Community and Autonomy," in Koschmann, ed., *Authority and the Individual in Japan*, 238–49.

20. Yasusuke Murakami, "The Japanese Model of Political Economy," *The Political Economy of Japan,* vol. 1: *The Domestic Transformation*, ed. Kozo Yamamura and Yasukichi Yasuba (Stanford: Stanford University Press, 1987), 61.

21. Yasusuke Murakami, "The Debt Comes Due for Mass Higher Education," *Japan Echo* 15/3 (autumn 1988): 78.

22. Matsumoto, 11–12.

23. Hayashi Kentarō, "Kaisetsu," in Hayashi, ed., *Shin-hoshushugi*, 7.

24. Ibid., 20.

25. Ibid., 30–1.

26. Ibid., 22.

27. A more recent characterization of Japanese neoconservatism and "liberal nationalism" in the 1980s is offered by Kenneth B. Pyle, *The Japanese Question: Power and Purpose in a New Era* (Washington, DC: The AEI Press, 1992), 71ff.

28. An influential commentator on and critic of matters related to democracy, Seki had earlier written "Sengo Nihon no minshushugi," *Jiyū* (February 1967) and "Sengo minshushugi no mondai jōkyō," in Minshushakaishugi Kenkyūkai, ed., *Gensō no kokufuku* (Tokyo, 1971).

29. On Rōyama's role in conceiving the prewar Greater East Asia Coprosperity Sphere, see Miles Fletcher, *The Search for a New Order: Intellectuals and Fascism in Prewar Japan* (Chapel Hill: University of North Carolina Press, 1982), and Kimitada Miwa, "Japanese Policies and Concepts for a Regional Order in Asia, 1938–1940," in James W. White, Michio Umegaki, and Thomas R. H. Havens, eds., *The Ambivalence of Nationalism: Modern Japan between East and West* (Lanham, MD: University Press of America, Inc., 1990). On Hasegawa, see Andrew E. Barshay, *State and Intellectual in Imperial Japan: The Public Man in Crisis* (Berkeley: University of California Press, 1988); on Minobe, Frank O. Miller, *Minobe Tatsukichi: Interpreter of Constitutionalism in Japan* (Berkeley: University of California Press, 1965).

30. Seki Yoshihiko, "'Sengo minshushugi' o saikentō suru," *Shokun* (January 1986): 149–50.

31. Ibid., 150–1.

32. Ibid., 158.

33. Ibid., 162.

34. Ibid., 166–7.

35. On the issue of postwar democracy and protest, see Koschmann, ed., *Authority and the Individual in Japan*; Ellis S. Krauss, *Japanese Radicals Revisited: Student Protest in Postwar Japan* (Berkeley: University of California Press, 1974); Kurt Steiner, Ellis S. Krauss, and Scott C. Flanagan, eds., *Political Opposition and Local Politics in Japan* (Princeton, NJ: Princeton University Press, 1980); Margaret A. McKean, *Environmental Protest and Citizen*

Politics in Japan (Berkeley: University of California Press, 1981); and Gavan McCormack and Yoshio Sugimoto, eds., *Democracy in Contemporary Japan* (Armonk, NY: M. E. Sharpe, Inc., 1986).

36. For a brief description of the intellectual monthlies, see the introduction to *Journal of Social and Political Ideas in Japan* 1/1 (April 1963): 2–3.

37. For example, Maruyama Masao, "Rekishi ishiki no 'kosō,'" in Maruyama, ed., *Rekishi shisō shū* [Nihon no shisō 6] (Tokyo: Chikuma Shobō, 1972), 3–46; also Matsushita Keiichi, "Citizen Participation in Historical Perspective," in Koschmann, ed., *Authority and the Individual in Japan*, 171–88.

38. Robert J. Lifton, "Youth and History: Individual Changes in Postwar Japan," *Asian Cultural Series* 3 (Tokyo: International Christian University, 1962), 124. Also see Kazuko Tsurumi, "Student Movements in 1960 and 1969: Continuity and Change," *Research Papers*, series A-5 (Tokyo: Institute of International Relations, Sophia University, n.d.), 30.

39. Guy Yasko, "Beyond the Denial of the Self: The Zenkyōtō Interpretation of Yoshimoto Takaaki," and "Zenkyōtō and the Communist Party: Towards a Materialist Critique of Postwar Democracy," Cornell University, 1994–95.

40. McClure, 122–3.

Works Cited

"A Letter to the Japanese Communists from Okano [Nosaka Sanzō] and Tanaka [Yamamoto Kenzō], Moscow, February 1936." In *The Japanese Communist Party, 1922–1945*, edited by George Beckmann and Okubo Genji. Stanford: Stanford University Press, 1969.

Abrams, M. H. "What Is a Humanistic Criticism?" *The Bookpress* 3, no. 4 (May 1993).

Aikawa Haruki. "Gijutsu oyobi tekunorogii no gainen." *Yuibutsuron kenkyū* 8 (June 1933).

Althusser, Louis. "Ideology and Ideological State Apparatuses (Notes towards an Investigation)." In *Lenin and Philosophy and other essays by Louis Althusser*, translated by Ben Brewster. New York: Monthly Review Press, 1971.

Amakasu Sekisuke. "Kindaishugi no shutaiseiron." *Zen'ei* 30 (August 1948).

———. "Yuibutsuron to ningen." In *Shutaisei ronsō*, edited by Mashita Shin'ichi. Tokyo: Hakuyōsha, 1949.

AMc. See Ara Masato, *Ara Masato chosakushū.*

Amino Takeo et al. *Tenbō sengo zasshi.* Tokyo: Kawade Shobō Shinsha, 1977.

Anderson, Perry. *In the Tracks of Historical Materialism.* Chicago: University of Chicago Press, 1984.

———. "The Antinomies of Antonio Gramsci." *New Left Review* 100 (November 1976/January 1977).

Anzaldua, Gloria. *La Frontera/Borderlands.* San Francisco: Spinsters Ink, 1988.

"Appendix F: Theses on the Situation in Japan and the Tasks of the Communist Party, May 1932." In *The Japanese Communist Party, 1922–1945*, edited by George Beckmann and Okubo Genji. Stanford: Stanford University Press, 1969.

Ara Masato. *Ara Masato chosakushū.* 5 vols. Tokyo: San'ichi Shobō, 1983 (*AMc*).

———. "Daini no seishun." *Kindai bungaku* (March 1946).

———. "Hareta jikan." In *AMc* 1.

———. "Minshū to wa tare ka." *Kindai bungaku* (April 1946).

———. "Nakano Shigeharu-ron." In *AMc* 1.

———. "Sanjūdai no me." In *AMc* 1.

———. "Tetsugakusha Q e no tegami." In *Shutaisei ronsō*, edited by Mashita Shin'ichi. Tokyo: Hakuyōsha, 1949.

———. "Yoko no tsunagari." *Kindai bungaku* 14 (October 1947).

Ara Masato et al. "Bungaku to genjitsu: Kurahara Korehito o kakonde." *Kindai bungaku* (February 1946).

Ara Masato, Odagiri Hideo, Sasaki Kiichi, Haniya Yutaka, Hirano Ken, and Honda Shūgo. "Zadankai: bungakusha no sekimu." In *Sengo bungaku ronsō*, vol. 1, edited by Usui Yoshimi. Tokyo: Banchō Shobō, 1972.

Arakawa Ikuo. *Gendai Nihon shisōshi 5.* Tokyo: Aoki Shoten, 1971.

Arase Yutaka. "Sengo shisō to sono tenkai." In *Kindai Nihon shisōshi kōza*, vol. 1, edited by Ienaga Saburō. Tokyo: Chikuma Shobō, 1959.

Arima, Tatsuo. *The Failure of Freedom.* Cambridge: Harvard University Press, 1969.

Aronowitz, Stanley. *The Crisis in Historical Materialism: Class, Politics and Culture in Marxist Theory.* New York: Praeger Publishers, 1981.

Asada Akira. "Infantile Capitalism and Japan's Postmodernism: A Fairy Tale." In *Post-*

modernism and Japan, edited by Masao Miyoshi and H. D. Harootunian. Durham, NC: Duke University Press, 1989.

Avineri, Shlomo. *Hegel's Theory of the Modern State*. London: Cambridge University Press, 1972.

Barshay, Andrew E. "Imagining Democracy in Postwar Japan: Reflections on Maruyama Masao and Modernism." *Journal of Japanese Studies* 18, vol. 2 (1992).

———. *State and Intellectual in Imperial Japan: The Public Man in Crisis*. Berkeley: University of California Press, 1988.

Bartky, Sandra Lee. "Foucault, Femininity, and the Modernization of Patriarchal Power." In *Feminism and Foucault*, edited by Irene Diamond and Lee Quinby. Boston: Northeastern University Press, 1988.

Beckmann, George, and Okubo Genji. *The Japanese Communist Party, 1922–1945*. Stanford: Stanford University Press, 1969.

Ben Habib, Seyla. "On Hegel, Women and Irony." In *Feminist Interpretations and Political Theory*, edited by Mary Lyndon Shanley and Carole Pateman. University Park: Pennsylvania State University Press, 1991.

Bhaskar, Roy. "Determinism." In *A Dictionary of Marxist Thought*, edited by Tom Bottomore. Cambridge: Harvard University Press, 1983.

Bisson, T. A. "April 1946 Elections." In *Postwar Japan: 1945 to the Present*, edited by Jon Livingston, Joe Moore, and Felicia Oldfather. New York: Pantheon Books, 1973.

Bowles, Samuel, and Herbert Gintis. *Democracy and Capitalism: Property, Community, and the Contradictions of Modern Social Thought*. New York: Basic Books, 1986.

Butler, Judith. "Contingent Foundations: Feminism and the Question of 'Postmodernism.'" In *Feminists Theorize the Political*, edited by Judith Butler and Joan W. Scott. London and New York: Routledge, Chapman and Hall, Inc., 1990.

Castoriadis, Cornelius. *The Imaginary Institution of Society*. Translated by Kathleen Blamey. Cambridge: MIT Press, 1987.

Caute, David. *Essential Writings of Karl Marx*. New York: Collier Books, 1967.

Culler, Jonathan. *On Deconstruction: Theory and Criticism after Structuralism*. Ithaca, NY: Cornell University Press, 1982.

Dazai, Osamu. *The Setting Sun*. Translated by Donald Keene. New York: New Directions Publishing Corporation, 1956.

De Bary, Brett. *Three Works by Nakano Shigeharu*. Cornell East Asia Papers, no. 21. Cornell University East Asia Program, 1979.

Defoe, Daniel. *The Life and Strange Surprizing Adventures of Robinson Crusoe, of York, Mariner*. Edited by J. Donald Crowley. London: Oxford University Press, 1972.

Derrida, Jacques. *Of Grammatology*. Translated by Gayatri Chakravorty Spivak. Baltimore: Johns Hopkins University Press, 1974.

———. *Speech and Phenomena*. Translated by David Allison. Evanston, IL: Northwestern University Press, 1973.

Dewey, John. *The Quest for Certainty: A Study of the Relation of Knowledge and Action*. New York: Minton, Balch, 1929.

Di Stefano, Christine. "Dilemmas of Difference: Feminism, Modernity, and Postmodernism." In *Feminism/Postmodernism*, edited by Linda J. Nicholson. New York: Routledge, Chapman and Hall, Inc., 1990.

Dietz, Mary. "Context Is All: Feminism and Theories of Citizenship." In *Dimensions of*

Radical Democracy: Pluralism, Citizenship, Community, edited by Chantal Mouffe. London: Verso Editions, 1992.

Dobb, Maurice. *Studies in the Development of Capitalism*. New York: International Publishers, 1947.

Engels, Friedrich. "Socialism: Utopian and Scientific." In *MER*.

Etō Jun. *Ochiba no hakiyose*. Tokyo: Bungei Shunjū, 1981.

―――. "Sengo bungaku wa hasan no kiki." *Mainichi shinbun*, January 24, 1978.

Farley, Miriam. "SCAP Policy toward Labor Unions." In *Postwar Japan; 1945 to the Present*, edited by Jon Livingston, Joe Moore, and Felicia Oldfather. New York: Pantheon Books, 1973.

Fletcher, Miles. *The Search for a New Order: Intellectuals and Fascism in Prewar Japan*. Chapel Hill: University of North Carolina Press, 1982.

Foucault, Michel. *Birth of the Prison*. Translated by Alan Sheridan. New York: Vintage Books, 1979.

―――. "The Subject and Power." *Critical Inquiry* 8, no. 4 (summer 1982).

Fowler, Edward. *The Rhetoric of Confession. Shishōsetsu in Early Twentieth-Century Japanese Fiction*. Berkeley: University of California Press, 1988.

Fukuzawa Yukichi's Outline of a Theory of Civilization. Translated by David A. Dilworth and G. Cameron Hurst. Tokyo: Sophia University, 1973.

Funayama Shin'ichi. "Tetsugaku no shutaiteki taishōteki kōzō." In *Shutaisei ronsō*, edited by Mashita Shin'ichi. Tokyo: Hakuyōsha, 1949.

Furukawa Sōichirō [Kurahara Korehito], "Proretaria geijutsu undō no soshiki mondai." In *KKh* 2.

Furuta Hikaru. "Shutaisei ronsō III: ronsō no tenkai to mondaiten." *Gendai to shisō* (March 1974).

―――. "Nashonaru na mono no saihyōka o meguru shoronsō." In *Kindai Nihon shiso ronsō*, edited by Miyakawa Tōru, Nakamura Yūjirō, and Furuta Hikaru. Tokyo: Aoki Shoten, 1971.

Furuta Hikaru, Sakuta Keiichi, and Ikimatsu Keizō, eds. *Kindai Nihon shakai shisōshi*, vol. 2. Kindai Nihon shisōshi taikei 2. Tokyo: Yūhikaku, 1971.

Gayn, Mark. "Food Demonstrations and MacArthur's Warning." In *Postwar Japan: 1945 to the Present*, edited by Jon Livingston, Joe Moore, and Felicia Oldfather. New York: Pantheon Books, 1973.

"Gozenkyō ikō no busō kōyō jitsugen ni kansuru." In *Teppō kara kokka kenryoku ga umareru: busō junbi to kōdō no tame ni*, edited by Nihon Kyōsantō (Kakumei saha) Kanagawa-ken Jōnin Iinkai. Tokyo, July 1970. In the Takazawa Collection, Sinclair Library, University of Hawaii, File 316.

Habermas, Jürgen. "Neoconservative Criticism in the United States and West Germany: An Intellectual Movement in Two Political Cultures." In *Habermas and Modernity*, edited by Richard J. Bernstein. Cambridge, MA:MIT Press, 1985.

―――. "Technology and Science as 'Ideology': For Herbert Marcuse on his seventieth birthday, July 19, 1968." In *Toward a Rational Society: Student Protest, Science and Politics*. Boston: Beacon Press, 1968.

Hall, Stuart. "The Toad in the Garden: Thatcherism among the Theorists." In *Marxism and the Interpretation of Culture*, edited by Lawrence Grossberg and Cary Nelson. Urbana: University of Illinois Press, 1988.

Harootunian, H. D. "Ichiboku hitokusa ni yadoru tennōsei." *Shisō* 797 (November 1990).

Hata Ikuhiko. "Japan under the Occupation." *The Japan Interpreter* 10/3–4 (winter 1976).

Hayashi Kentarō. "Gendai chishikijin no ryōshiki: Maruyama Masao-shi ni taisuru hihihanteki hihan." *Sekai* 58 (October 1950).

―――. "Rekishi ni okeru shutai no mondai." *Sekai* 16 (April 1947).

―――, ed. *Shin-hoshushugi*. Gendai Nihon shisō taikei 35. Tokyo: Chikuma Shobō, 1963.

Hegel, Georg Wilhelm Friedrich. *The Philosophy of History*. Translated by J. Sibree. New York: Dover Publications, Inc., 1956.

Hegel's Philosophy of Right. Translated by T. M. Knox. London: Oxford University Press, 1967.

Heiwa Mondai Danwakai. "Mitabi heiwa ni tsuite." *Sekai* 60 (December 1950).

Hidaka Rokurō, ed. *Sengo shisō no shuppatsu*. Sengo Nihon shisō taikei 1. Tokyo: Chikuma Shobō, 1968.

―――. *The Price of Affluence: Dilemmas of Contemporary Japan*. Tokyo: Kodansha International, 1948.

Hirano Ken. *Hirano Ken zenshū*. 13 vols. Tokyo: Shinchōsha, 1975 (*HKz*).

―――. "Hitotsu no hansotei." In *HKz* 1.

―――. "'Seiji no yūisei' to wa nani ka." In *HKz* 1.

―――. "Seiji to bungaku (1)." In *HKz* 1.

―――. "Seiji to bungaku (2)." In *HKz* 1.

HKz. See Hirano Ken, *Hirano Ken zenshū*.

Honda Shūgo. "Kaisetsu." In *AMc* 1.

―――. "Geijutsu, rekishi, ningen." *Kindai bungaku* 1 (February 1946).

Hoshino Yoshirō and Taketani Mitsuo. "Kaisetsu." In *TMc* 1.

Hoston, Germaine A. *Marxism and the Crisis of Development in Prewar Japan*. Princeton, NJ: Princeton University Press, 1986.

Inoue, Kyoko. *MacArthur's Japanese Constitution: A Linguistic and Cultural Study of Its Making*. Chicago: University of Chicago Press, 1991.

Iwamoto, Yoshio. "Aspects of the Proletarian Literary Movement in Japan." In *Japan in Crisis: Essays on Taishō Democracy*, edited by Bernard S. Silberman and H. D. Harootunian. Princeton, NJ: Princeton University Press, 1974.

Izbicki, Joanne. "Scorched Cityscapes and Silver Screens: Negotiating Defeat and Democracy in Occupied Japan." Ph.D. diss., Cornell University, 1996.

Kajinoki Gō. "Kindai bungaku: eikō to hisan." In *Sengo shisō no genzai*. Tokyo: Dentō to Gendaisha, 1981.

Kan Takayuki. *Sengo seishin: sono shinwa to jitsuzō*. Tokyo: Mineruva Shobō, 1981.

Kanda Fuhito. *Nihon no tōitsu sensen undō*. Tokyo: Aoki Shoten, 1979.

Kant, Immanuel. *Critique of Practical Reason*. Translated by Lewis White Beck. New York: Macmillan Publishing Company, 1956.

Katō Shūichi. "IN EGOISTOS." *Kindai bungaku* 12 (July 1947).

Katsube Hajime. "Iwayuru 'shutaisei' no mondai ni tsuite." *Zen'ei* 30 (August 1948).

Katzenstein, Peter J., and Yutaka Tsujinaka. *Defending the Japanese State*. Cornell East Asia Series, no. 53. Cornell University East Asia Program, 1991.

KKh. See Kurahara Korehito, *Kurahara Korehito hyōronshū*.

Komatsu Setsurō. "Jitsuzon tetsugaku to yuibutsu shikan." In *Shutaisei ronsō*, edited by Mashita Shin'ichi. Tokyo: Hakuyōsha, 1949.

Kōsaka Masaaki, Suzuki Shigetaka, Kōyama Iwao, and Nishitani Keiji. "Sekaishiteki tachiba to Nihon." *Chūō kōron* 653 (January 1942).

Kōsaka Masaaki, Suzuki Shigetaka, Kōyama Iwao, and Nishitani Keiji. "The Standpoint of World History and Japan." Translated by Mark Anderson. Cornell University, 1994.

Kōsaka Susumu. "Sengo 'shutai' no fūka kakusan to 'kindai bungaku'-ha." *Ryūdō,* (April 1976).

Koschmann, J. Victor. "The Debate on Subjectivity in Postwar Japan: Foundations of Modernism as Political Critique." *Pacific Affairs* 54, no. 4 (winter 1981–82).

Krauss, Ellis S. *Japanese Radicals Revisited: Student Protest in Postwar Japan*. Berkeley: University of California Press, 1974.

Kuno Osamu, Tsurumi Shunsuke, and Fujita Shōzō. *Sengo Nihon no shisō*. Tokyo: Keisō Shobō, 1966.

Kurahara Korehito. "Kindaishugi to sono kokufuku." *Zen'ei* 30 (August 1948).

———. *Kurahara Korehito hyōronshu*. 8 vols. Tokyo: Shin-Nihon Shuppansha, 1968 (*KKh*).

———. "Atarashi bungaku e no shuppatsu." In *KKh* 3.

———. "Geijutsuteki hōho ni tsuite no kansō (zenpen)." In *KKh* 2.

———. "Shin Nihon bungaku no shakaiteki kiso." *Shin-Nihon bungaku* 1 (March 1946).

Kurrik, Maire. *Literature and Negation*. New York: Columbia University Press, 1979.

Laclau, Ernesto. *New Reflections on the Revolution of Our Time*. London: Verso Editions, 1990.

Laclau, Ernesto, and Chantal Mouffe. *Hegemony and Socialist Strategy: Towards a Radical Democratic Politics*. London: Verso Editions, 1985.

———. "Recasting Marxism: Hegemony and New Political Movements." *Socialist Review* 12, no. 6 (1982).

———. "Post-Marxism without Apologies." In Ernesto Laclau, *New Reflections on the Revolution of Our Time*. London: Verso Editions, 1990.

Lefort, Claude. *Democracy and Political Theory*. Translated by David Macey. Minneapolis: University of Minnesota Press, 1988.

———. *The Political Forms of Modern Society: Bureaucracy, Democracy, Totalitarianism*. Edited by John B. Thompson. Cambridge: MIT Press, 1986.

Lenin, Vladimir I. *Materialism and Empirio-Criticism*. Peking: Foreign Languages Press, 1972.

———. "Two Tactics of Social-Democracy in the Democratic Revolution." In *Marx, Engels, Lenin: on Democracy—Bourgeois and Socialist*. Moscow: Progress Publishers, 1988.

Lifton, Robert J. "Youth and History: Individual Changes in Postwar Japan." *Asian Cultural Series,* no. 3. Tokyo: International Christian University, 1962.

Lukács, Georg. *History and Class Consciousness: Studies in Marxist Dialectics*. Translated by Rodney Livingstone. Cambridge: MIT Press, 1968.

Mao Tse-tung. "On New Democracy." *Selected Works of Mao Tse-tung*. Vol 2. Peking: Foreign Language Press, 1965.

Mao's China: Party Reform Documents, 1942–44. Translated by Boyd Compton. Seattle: University of Washington Press, 1952.

Marshall, James. "Freud and Marx at UNESCO." *The American Scholar* 16, no. 3 (summer 1947).

Maruyama Masao. "Aru 'jiyūshugi'sha e no tegami." *Sekai* 57 (September 1950).

———. "From Carnal Literature to Carnal Politics." Translated by Barbara Ruch. In *Thought and Behavior in Modern Japanese Politics*, expanded ed., edited by Ivan Morris. Oxford: Oxford University Press, 1979.

———. "Fukuzawa Yukichi ni okeru chitsujo to ningen." In *Ssa*.

———. "Fukuzawa ni okeru 'wakudeki.'" *Fukuzawa Yukichi nenkan* 13 (1986).

———. "Fukuzawa Yukichi no tetsugaku—toku ni sono jiji hihan to no kanren." In *Kindaishugi*, edited by Hidaka Rokurō. Gendai Nihon shisō taikei 34. Tokyo: Iwanami Shoten, 1964.

———. "Gunkoku shihaisha no seishin keitai." In *Zōhoban: Gendai seiji no shisō to kōdō*. Tokyo: Miraisha, 1964.

———. "Jyon Rokku to kindai seiji genri." In *Ssa*.

———. "Kindaiteki shii." In *Ssa*.

———. "Kojin sekishutsu no samazama na patân—kindai Nihon o kêsu to shite." In *Nihon ni okeru kindaika no mondai*, edited by Hosoya Chihiro. Tokyo: Iwanami Shoten, 1968.

———. "Kuga Katsunan: hito to shisō." In *Ssa*.

———. "Meiji kokka no shisō." In *Ssa*.

———. "Nationalism in Japan: Its Background and Prospects." Translated by David Titus. In *Thought and Behavior in Modern Japanese Politics*, expanded ed., edited by Ivan Morris. Oxford: Oxford University Press, 1979.

———. "Nihon ni okeru jiyū ishiki no keisei to tokushitsu." In *Ssa*.

———. "Nihon ni okeru nashonarizumu: sono shisō teki haikei to tenbō." *Chūō kōron* 743 (January 1951).

———. "Patterns of Individuation and the Case of Japan: A Conceptual Scheme." In *Changing Japanese Attitudes toward Modernization*, edited by Marius B. Jansen. Princeton, NJ: Princeton University Press, 1965.

———. "Rekishi ishiki no 'kosō." In *Rekishi shisō shū*, edited by Maruyama Masao. Nihon no shisō 6. Tokyo: Chikuma Shobō, 1972.

———. "Russeru 'seiyō tetsugakushi (kinsei)." In *Ssa*.

———. "Seijigaku ni okeru kokka no gainen." In *Ssa*.

———. *Senchū to sengo no aida, 1936–1957*. Tokyo: Misuzu Shobō, 1976 (*Ssa*).

———. *Studies in the Intellectual History of Tokugawa Japan*. Tokyo: University of Tokyo Press, 1974.

Maruyama Masao and Andō Jinbei. "Umemoto Katsumi no omoide." In Maruyama Masao, Satō Noboru, and Umemoto Katsumi, *Sengo Nihon no kakushin shisō*. Tokyo: Gendai no Rironsha, 1983.

Marx, Karl. *Capital*. 3 vols. Moscow: Foreign Languages Publishing House, n.d.

———. "Critique of Hegel's *Philosophy of Right*." In *MER*.

———. "On the Jewish Question." In *MER*.

———. *Pre-Capitalist Economic Formations*. Edited by Eric J. Hobsbawm and translated by Jack Cohen. New York: International Publishers, 1964.

———. "Theses on Feuerbach." In *MER*.

Marx, Karl, and Friedrich Engels. "Manifesto of the Communist Party." In *MER*.

————. "The German Ideology, Part I." In *MER*.

Mashita Shin'ichi. "Shutaiseiron: yuibutsuron no shutaiteki haaku to kanren shite." In *Mashita Shin'ichi chosakushū*, vol. 1. Tokyo: Aoki Shoten, 1979.

————, ed. *Shutaisei ronsō*. Tokyo: Hakuyōsha, 1949.

Masumi Junnosuke. *Postwar Politics in Japan, 1945–1955*. Translated by Lonny E. Carlile. Institute of East Asian Studies Japan Research Monograph no. 6. University of California-Berkeley, 1985.

Matsumoto Sannosuke. Introduction to *Journal of Social and Political Ideas in Japan* 4, no. 2 (August 1966).

Matsumura Kazuto. "Burujyoateki ningenkan ni tsuite." In *Yuibutsuron to shutaiseiron*. Tokyo: Hyōronsha, 1949.

————. "Shūsengo no handō tetsugaku no shuryū." *Zen'ei* 20 (October 1947).

————. "Tetsugaku ni okeru shūseishugi—Umemoto Katsumi no tachiba ni tsuite." In *Yuibutsuron to shutaiseiron*. Tokyo: Hyōronsha, 1949.

————. "'Tetsugakusha' no shutaiseiron ni tsuite." In *Yuibutsuron to shutaiseiron*. Tokyo: Hyōronsha, 1949.

Matsushita Keiichi. "Citizen Participation in Historical Perspective." In *Authority and the Individual in Japan: Citizen Protest in Historical Perspective*, edited by J. Victor Koschmann. Tokyo: University of Tokyo Press, 1978.

Matsuzawa Hiroaki. "'Theory' and 'Organization' in the Japan Communist Party." In *Authority and the Individual in Japan: Citizen Protest in Historical Perspective*, edited by J. Victor Koschmann. Tokyo: University of Tokyo Press, 1978.

McCarney, Joseph. *Social Theory and the Crisis of Marxism*. London: Verso Editions, 1990.

McClure, Kirstie. "On the Subject of Rights: Pluralism and Political Identity." In *Dimensions of Radical Democracy: Pluralism, Citizenship, Community*, edited by Chantal Mouffe. London: Verso Editions, 1992.

McCormack, Gavan, and Yoshio Sugimoto, eds. *Democracy in Contemporary Japan*. Armonk, NY: M. E. Sharpe, Inc., 1986.

McKean, Margaret A. *Environmental Protest and Citizen Politics in Japan*. Berkeley: University of California Press, 1981.

MER. See Tucker, Robert C., ed., *The Marx-Engels Reader*.

Miki Kiyoshi. "Principles of Thought for a New Japan." Translated by Lewis E. Harrington. Cornell University, 1993.

Miller, Frank O. *Minobe Tatsukichi: Interpreter of Constitutionalism in Japan*. Berkeley: University of California Press, 1965.

Mitchell, Richard H. *Janus-Faced Justice: Political Criminals in Imperial Japan*. Honolulu: University of Hawaii Press, 1992.

Miwa, Kimitada. "Japanese Policies and Concepts for a Regional Order in Asia, 1938–1940." In *The Ambivalence of Nationalism: Modern Japan between East and West*, edited by James W. White, Michio Umegaki, and Thomas R. H. Havens. Lanham, MD: University Press of America, Inc., 1990.

Miyagi Otoya. "Shutaisei ni tsuite." *Riron* (January 1948).

Miyakawa Tōru, Nakamura Yūjirō, and Furuta Hikaru. *Kindai Nihon shisō ronsō*. Tokyo: Aoki Shoten, 1971.

Miyoshi, Masao. *Off Center: Power and Culture Relations between Japan and the United States*. Cambridge: Harvard University Press, 1992.

Moore, Joe. *Japanese Workers and the Struggle for Power, 1945–1947.* Madison: University of Wisconsin Press, 1983.

———. *Production Control and the Postwar Crisis of Japanese Capitalism 1945–1946* (Ph.D. diss., University of Wisconsin-Madison, 1978). Ann Arbor, MI: University Microfilms, 1979.

———. "Production Control: Workers' Control in Early Postwar Japan." *Bulletin of Concerned Asian Scholars* 17, no. 4 (1985).

Morito, Tatsuo. "The Democratic League for National Salvation: Its Prospects." *Journal of Social and Political Ideas in Japan* 3, no. 1 (April 1965).

Mouffe, Chantal. "Hegemony and New Political Subjects: Toward a New Concept of Democracy." Translated by Stanley Gray. In *Marxism and the Interpretation of Culture*, edited by Cary Nelson and Lawrence Grossberg. Urbana: University of Illinois Press, 1988.

Murakami, Yasusuke. "The Japanese Model of Political Economy." In *The Political Economy of Japan*, vol. 1., edited by Kozo Yamamura and Yasukichi Yasuba. Stanford: Stanford University Press, 1987.

———. "The Debt Comes Due for Mass Higher Education." *Japan Echo* 15, no. 3 (autumn 1988).

Nakamura Masanori. *The Japanese Monarchy: Ambassador Joseph Grew and the Making of the "Symbol Emperor System," 1931–1991.* Armonk, NY: M. E. Sharpe, Inc., 1992.

Nakamura Akira. "Maruyama Masao and the Ontology of Politics." *The Japan Interpreter* 12, no. 2 (spring 1978).

Nakano Shigeharu. "Hihyō no ningensei (1)—Hirano Ken, Ara Masato ni tsuite." In *NSz* 12.

———. "Hihyō no ningensei (2)—bungaku handō no mondai nado." In *NSz* 12.

———. "Hihyō no ningensei (3)." In *NSz* 12.

———. *Nakano Shigeharu zenshū.* 28 vols. Tokyo: Chikuma Shobō, 1979 (*NSz*).

"Naze buryoku kakumei ga mondai ni naranakatta ka." In *Teppō kara kokka kenryoku ga umareru: busō junbi to kōdō no tame ni*, edited by Nihon Kyōsantō (Kakumei saha) Kanagawa-ken Jōnin Iinkai. Tokyo, July 1970. Takazawa Collection, Sinclair Library, University of Hawaii, File 316.

Nicholson, Linda. *Gender and History: The Limits of Social Theory in the Age of the Family.* New York: Columbia University Press, 1986.

Nihon Kyōsantō. "Daigokai tōtaikai sengen." In *Kakumei no shisō*, edited by Haniya Yutaka. Sengo Nihon shisō taikei 6. Tokyo: Chikuma Shobō, 1969.

"Nihon Kyōsantō gozenkyō hōkokusho: shinkōryō no seishiki kettei." In *Teppō kara kokka kenryoku ga umareru: busō junbi to kōdō no tame ni*, edited by Nihon Kyōsantō (Kakumei saha) Kanagawa-ken Jōnin Iinkai. Tokyo, July 1970. Takazawa Collection, Sinclair Library, University of Hawaii, File 316.

Nihon Kyōsantō Shutsugoku Dōshikai. "Jinmin ni uttau." In *Sengo shisō no shuppatsu*, edited by Hidaka Rokurō. Sengo Nihon shisō taikei 1. Tokyo: Chikuma Shobō, 1968.

Nishida Kitarō. *Fundamental Problems of Philosophy: The World of Action and the Dialectical World.* Translated by D. A. Dilworth. Tokyo: Sophia University Press, 1970.

Nosaka Sanzō. "Minshū sensen ni yotte sokoku no kiki o sukue." In *Sengo shisō no shuppatsu*, edited by Hidaka Rokurō. Sengo Nihon shisō taikei 1. Tokyo: Chikuma Shobō, 1968.

————. "Minshuteki Nihon no kensetsu." In *Nosaka Sanzō senshū*. Vol. 1. Tokyo: Nihon Kyōsantō Chūōiinkai Shuppanbu, 1964, 419–68.

NSz. See Nakano Shigeharu, *Nakano Shigeharu zenshū*.

Oda Makoto. *"Ningen: aru kojinteki na kōsatsu*. Tokyo: Chikuma Shobō, 1968.

Odagiri Hideo. "Shin bungaku sōzō no shutai: atarashii dankai no tame ni." *Shin-Nihon bungaku* 3 (May–June 1946).

Ōe Shinobu. *Sengo kaikaku*. Nihon no rekishi 31. Tokyo: Shōgakukan, 1976.

OHc. See Ōtsuka Hisao, *Ōtsuka Hisao chosakushū*.

Ōi Tadashi. *Gendai no yuibutsuron shisō*. Tokyo: Aoki Shoten, 1959.

Ōkōchi Kazuo. *Ōkōchi Kazuo chosakushū*. Vol. 3. Tokyo: Seirin Shoin Shinsha, 1969.

Olson, Lawrence. *Ambivalent Moderns: Portraits of Japanese Cultural Identity*. Savage, MD: Rowman and Littlefield Publishers, Inc., 1992.

Ōtsuka Hisao. "Jiyū to dokuritsu." In *OHc* 8.

————. "Jiyūshugi ni sakidatsu mono." In *OHc* 8.

————. "Kindaika to wa nani ka: kindaika katei ni okeru futatsu no michi." In *OHc* 3.

————. "Kindaiteki ningen ruikei no sōshutsu: seijiteki shutai no minshūteki kiban no mondai." In *OHc* 8.

————. "Makusu uēba ni okeru shihonshugi no 'seishin.'" In *OHc* 8.

————. *Max Weber on the Spirit of Capitalism*. Translated by Kondō Masaomi. Occasional Papers Series, no. 13. Tokyo: Institute of Developing Economies, 1976.

————. *Ōtsuka Hisao chosakushū*. 10 vols. Tokyo: Iwanami Shoten, 1969 (*OHc*).

————. "Robinson Kurūsō no ningen ruikei." In *OHc* 8.

————. "Saikōdo 'jihatsusei' no hatsuyō." In *OHc* 8.

————. "Seisanryoku ni okeru tōyō to seiyō: Nishi Ō hōken nōmin no tokushitsu." In *OHc* 7.

Pateman, Carole. *The Disorder of Women*. Stanford: Stanford University Press, 1989.

Peace Problems Discussion Circle. "On Peace: Our Third Statement." *Journal of Social and Political Ideas in Japan* 1, no. 1 (April 1963).

Pharr, Susan. "The Politics of Women's Rights." In *Democratizing Japan: The Allied Occupation*, edited by Robert E. Ward and Sakamoto Yoshikazu. Honolulu: University of Hawaii Press, 1987.

Political Reorientation of Japan, September 1945 to September 1948. Washington, D C: U.S. Government Printing Office, 1949.

Poster, Mark. *Critical Theory and Poststructuralism: In Search of a Context*. Ithaca, NY: Cornell University Press, 1989.

Pyle, Kenneth B. *The Japanese Question: Power and Purpose in a New Era*. Washington, DC: The AEI Press, 1992.

Sakaguchi Ango. "Zoku darakuron. "In *Sakaguchi Ango zenshū* 14. Tokyo: Chikuma Shobō, 1991.

Sakai, Naoki. "Modernity and Its Critique: The Problem of Universalism and Particularism." In *Postmodernism and Japan*, edited by Masao Miyoshi and H. D. Harootunian. Durham, NC: Duke University Press, 1989.

————. "Nihon shakai kagaku hōhō josetsu: Nihon shisō to iu mondai." In *Nihon shakai kagaku no shisō*. Iwanami kōza: shakai kagaku no hōhō 3, edited by Yamanouchi Yasushi. Tokyo: Iwanami Shoten, 1993.

————. "Return to the West/Return to the East: Watsuji Tetsurō's Anthropology and Discussions of Authenticity." In *Japan in the World: A Special Issue of Boundary 2*, edited by Masao Miyoshi and H. D. Harootunian. Durham, NC: Duke University Press, 1991.

————. "Seiyō e no kaiki/Tōyō e no kaiki." *Shisō* 797 (November 1990).

————. "Subject and/or Shutai and the Inscription of National Culture." 1993.

Sakuta Keiichi. "The Controversy over Community and Autonomy." In *Authority and the Individual in Japan: Citizen Protest in Historical Perspective*, edited by J. Victor Koschmann. Tokyo: University of Tokyo Press, 1978.

Sartre, Jean Paul. "Existentialism Is a Humanism." In *Existentialism from Dostoevsky to Sartre*, rev. and expanded ed., edited by Walter Kaufmann. New York: New American Library, 1975.

Sasaki-Uemura, Wesley. "Citizen and Community in the 1960 Anpo Protests." Ph.D. diss., Cornell University, 1993.

Sasakura Hideo. *Maruyama Masao-ron nōto*. Tokyo: Misuzu Shobō, 1988.

Sayer, Derek. *Capitalism and Modernity: An Excursus on Marx and Weber*. New York: Routledge, Chapman and Hall, Inc., 1991.

Scalapino, Robert A. *The Japanese Communist Movement, 1920–1966*. Berkeley: University of California Press, 1967.

Schaller, Michael. *The American Occupation of Japan: The Origins of the Cold War in Asia*. New York: Oxford University Press, 1985.

Scott, Joan W. "Experience." In *Feminists Theorize the Political*, edited by Judith Butler and Joan W. Scott. New York: Routledge, Chapman and Hall, Inc., 1992.

Seki Yoshihiko. "Part I: World Tension and the Cold War: Notes by the Editor." *Journal of Social and Political Ideas in Japan* 1, no. 1 (April 1963).

————. "Sengo minshushugi no mondai jōkyō." In *Gensō no kokufuku*, edited by Minshushakaishugi Kenkyūkai. Tokyo: Minshushakaishugi Kenkyūkai, 1971.

————. "'Sengo minshushugi' o saikentō suru." *Shokun* 18 (January 1986).

————. "Sengo Nihon no minshushugi." *Jiyū* 9 (February 1967).

Shea, George T. *Leftwing Literature in Japan*. Tokyo: Hōsei University Press, 1964.

Shimizu Ikutarō. "Aikokushin." In *SIc* 8.

————. *Shimizu Ikutarō chosakushū*. 18 vols. Tokyo: Kōdansha, 1992 (*SIc*).

————. "Shomin." In *SIc* 8.

————. "Shutaisei no kyakkanteki kōsatsu." In *SIc* 8.

————. "Tokumei no shisō." In *SIc* 8.

Shimizu Ikutarō, Matsumura Kazuto, Hayashi Kentarō, Kozai Yoshishige, Maruyama Masao, Mashita Shin'ichi, and Miyagi Otoya. "Yuibutsuron to shutaisei: zadankai." *Sekai* 26 (February 1948).

Shirakawa Masumi. "Shutai no saisei: zentaisei no kakutoku." *Kuraishisu* 40 (winter 1990).

SIc. See Shimizu Ikutarō, *Shimizu Ikutarō chosakushū*.

Silverberg, Miriam. *Changing Song: The Marxist Manifestos of Nakano Shigeharu*. Princeton, NJ: Princeton University Press, 1990.

Simmel, Georg. "The Sociology of Sociability." In *Origins and Growth of Sociology*, edited by J. H. Abraham. New York: Harmondsworth, 1973.

Smith, Paul. *Discerning the Subject*. Minneapolis: University of Minnesota Press, 1988.

Spivak, Gayatri. "Can the Subaltern Speak?" In *Marxism and the Interpretation of Culture*, edited by Cary Nelson and Lawrence Grossberg. Urbana: University of Illinois Press, 1988.

Ssa. See Maruyama Masao, *Senchū to sengo no aida*.

"Statement by the Peace Study Group on Peace Settlement for Japan." In *Postwar Japan: 1945 to the Present*, edited by Jon Livingston, Joe Moore, and Felicia Oldfather. New York: Pantheon Books, 1973.

Steiner, Kurt, Ellis S. Krauss, and Scott C. Flanagan, eds. *Political Opposition and Local Politics in Japan*. Princeton, NJ: Princeton University Press, 1980.

Sugiyama Mitsunobu. *Sengo keimō to shakai kagaku no shisō*. Tokyo: Shin'yōsha, 1983.

Swearingen, Rodger, and Paul Langer. *Red Flag in Japan: International Communism in Action 1919–1951*. Cambridge: Harvard University Press, 1952.

Takabatake Michitoshi. "Seisanryoku riron: Ōkōchi Kazuo, Kazahaya Yasoji." In *Kyōdō kenkyū: tenkō,* vol. 2, rev. and expanded ed., edited by Shisō no Kagaku Kenkyūkai. Tokyo: Heibonsha, 1978.

Takahashi Kohachiro. "A Contribution to the Discussion." In *The Transition from Feudalism to Capitalism*, edited by Paul Sweezy et al. London: NLB, 1976.

Takakuwa Sumio. "Gendai no seishin jōkyō: mu no tōhasei o chūshin to shite." *Shisō* 293 (November 1948).

———. "Shakaiteki shutai no mondai." In *Ys*.

———. "Shi no haaku to shutaisei." In *Ys*.

———. "Shutaisei no tadashii haaku." In *Ys*.

———. "Shutaiteki jiyū ni tsuite." In *Ys*.

———. "Yuibutsu shikan to shutaisei." In *Ys*.

———. *Yuibutsuron to shutaisei*. Tokyo: Kokudosha, 1948 (*Ys*).

Takazawa Kōji, Sanaga Shirō, and Matsumura Ryōichi, eds. *Sengo kakumei undō jiten*. Tokyo: Shinsensha, 1989.

Takeda, Kiyoko. *The Dual Image of the Japanese Emperor*. New York: New York University Press, 1988.

Takei Kunio. *Umemoto Katsumi-ron: henkyō ni okeru shutaisei no ronri*. Tokyo: Daisan Bunmeisha, 1977.

Takemae Eiji. "Early Postwar Reformist Parties." In *Democratizing Japan: The Allied Occupation*, edited by Robert E. Ward and Sakamoto Yoshikazu. Honolulu: University of Hawaii Press, 1987.

Taketani Mitsuo. "Gijutsuron: Hakugai to tatakaishi kagakusha ni sasagu." In *TMc* 1.

———. "Jissen no mondai ni tsuite." In *Kagaku-tetsugaku-geijutsu*. Tokyo: Sōryūsha, 1949.

———. *Taketani Mitsuo chosakushū*. 6 vols. Tokyo: Keisō Shobō, 1968 (*TMc*).

———. "Zunō no kaizō." In *TMc* 4.

Takeuchi Yoshimi. "Chūgoku no rejisutansu." In *TYz* 4.

———. "Kindai to wa nani ka? (Nihon to Chūgoku no baai) (Chūgoku no kindai to Nihon no kindai)." In *TYz* 4.

———. "Kindaishugi to minzoku no mondai." In *TYz* 7.

———. "Kokumin bungaku no mondaiten." In *TYz* 7.

———. "Kokumin bungaku no teishō: Itō Sei-shi e no tegami." In *TYz* 7.

———. "Nihonjin no Chūgokukan." In *TYz* 4.

———. "Shin-Chūgoku no seishin." In *TYz* 4.

————. *Takeuchi Yoshimi zenshū*. 17 vols. Tokyo: Chikuma Shobō, 1980 (*TYz*).

Takeuchi Yoshirō. "Posto-modan ni okeru chi no kansei." *Sekai* 494 (November 1986).

Tamura Taijirō. "Nikutai wa ningen de aru." *Gunzō*, May 1947.

————. "Nikutai no mon." In *Kitahara Takeo, Inoue Tomoichirō, Tamura Taijirō shū*. Nihon gendai bungaku zenshū, Kōdansha-ban 94. Tokyo: Kōdansha, 1968.

Tanabe Hajime. "Kirisutokyō to marukushizumu to Nihon bukkyō: dainiji shūkyō kaikaku no yosō." In *THz* 10.

————. *Philosophy as Metanoetics*. Translated by Takeuchi Yoshinori. Berkeley: University of California Press, 1986.

————. "Seiji tetsugaku no kyūmu." In *THz* 8.

————. "Shakaitō to Kyōsantō no aida." In *THz* 8.

————. *Tanabe Hajime zenshū*. 15 vols. Tokyo: Chikuma Shobō, 1963 (*THz*).

Tanimoto Kiyoshi [Kurahara Korehito], "Geijutsu hōhō ni tsuite no kansō" I, II. In *KKh* 2.

Thompson, E. P. *The Making of the English Working Class*. New York: Vintage Books, 1963.

Thompson, John B. *Studies in the Theory of Ideology*. Berkeley: University of California Press, 1984.

THz. See Tanabe Hajime, *Tanabe Hajime zenshū*.

Tipton, Elise. *Japanese Police State: Tokkō in Interwar Japan*. Honolulu: University of Hawaii Press, 1990.

TMc. See Taketani Mitsuo, *Taketani Mitsuo chosakushū*.

Tokuda Kyūichi. "Gokuchū jūhachinen (shō)." In *Kakumei no shisō*, edited by Haniya Yutaka. Sengo Nihon shisō taikei 6. Tokyo: Chikuma Shobō, 1969.

Tosaka Jun. "Nippon ideorogii-ron." In *Tosaka Jun zenshū*, vol. 5. Tokyo: Keisō Shobō, 1967.

Tsurumi, Kazuko. *Social Change and the Individual before and after World War II*. Princeton, NJ: Princeton University Press, 1976.

————. "Student Movements in 1960 and 1969: Continuity and Change." *Research Papers*. Series A-5. Tokyo: Institute of International Relations, Sophia University, n.d.

Tsurumi Shunsuke. "Chishikijin no hassō jiten: *Kindai bungaku* gurūpu." In Kuno Osamu, Tsurumi Shunsuke, and Fujita Shōzō, *Sengo Nihon no shisō*. Tokyo: Chikuma Shobō, 1966.

————."Nihon no jitsuzonshugi—sengo no sesō." In Kuno Osamu and Tsurumi Shunsuke, *Gendai Nihon no shisō*. Tokyo: Iwanami Shinsho, 1956.

Tsurumi Shunsuke and Maruyama Masao. "Maruyama Masao: fuhen genri no tachiba." In Tsurumi Shunsuke, *Kataritsugu sengoshi*, vol. 1. Tokyo: Shisō no Kagaku Sha, 1969.

Tuana, Nancy. *Women and the History of Philosophy*. New York: Paragon House, 1992.

Tucker, Robert C., ed. *The Marx-Engels Reader*. New York: W. W. Norton and Co., 1972 (*MER*).

TYz. See Takeuchi Yoshimi, *Takeuchi Yoshimi zenshū*.

Uchino, Tatsurō. *Japan's Postwar Economy: An Insider's View of Its History and Its Future*. Tokyo: Kodansha International, 1983.

Ueno Masaji. "Keizaishi-gaku." In *Kindai Nihon keizai shisōshi*, vol. 2, edited by Chō Yukio and Sumiya Kazuhiko. Kindai Nihon shisōshi taikei 6. Tokyo: Yūhikaku, 1971.

UKc. See Umemoto Katsumi, *Umemoto Katsumi chosakushū*.

Umemoto Katsumi. "Daiichibu e no tsuiki." In *Yuibutsuron to shutaisei*. Tokyo: Gendai Shichōsha, 1974.

————. "Hihan to kyōdō." In *UKc* 1.

————. "Marukusushugi to kindai seijigaku." In *Marukusushugi ni okeru shisō to kagaku.* Tokyo: Sani'ichi Shobō, 1969.

————. "Mu no ronrisei to tōhasei: Tanabe tetsugaku hihan, tokuni dainiji shūkyō kaikaku no yosō no tame ni." In *UKc* 1.

————. "Ningenteki jiyū no genkai." In *UKc* 1.

————. "Shutaisei to kaikyūsei—Matsumura Kazuto no hihyō ni kotaete." In *UKc* 1.

————. "Shutaiseiron no gendankai: sono keika to kongo no tenbō." In *Katoki no ishiki.* Tokyo: Gendai Shichōsha, 1975.

———— *Umemoto Katsumi chosakushū.* 10 vols. Tokyo: San'ichi Shobō, 1977 (*UKc*).

————. "Yuibutsu benshōhō to mu no benshōhō." *Risō* 179 (March 1948).

————. "Yuibutsuron to dōtoku—Matsumura Kazuto to no taidan." In *UKc* 1.

————. "Yuibutsuron to ningen." In *UKc* 1.

von Wright, Georg Henrik. *Explanation and Understanding.* Ithaca, NY: Cornell University Press, 1971.

Ward, Robert E. "Presurrender Planning: Treatment of the Emperor and Constitutional Changes." In *Democratizing Japan: The Allied Occupation,* edited by Robert E. Ward and Sakamoto Yoshikazu. Honolulu: University of Hawaii Press, 1987.

————. "Reflections on the Allied Occupation and Planned Political Change in Japan." In *Political Development in Modern Japan,* edited by Robert E. Ward. Princeton, NJ: Princeton University Press, 1968.

Watsuji Tetsurō. *Ningen no gaku to shite no rinrigaku.* Rev. ed. Tokyo: Iwanami Shoten, 1971.

————. *Rinrigaku.* Vol. 1, rev. ed. Tokyo: Iwanami Shoten, 1949.

Weber, Max. "Politics as a Vocation." In *From Max Weber: Essays in Sociology,* edited and translated by Hans H. Gerth and C. Wright Mills. New York: Oxford University Press, 1946.

————. "Science as a Vocation." In *From Max Weber: Essays in Sociology,* edited and translated by Hans H. Gerth and C. Wright Mills. New York: Oxford University Press, 1946.

————. *The Religion of China.* Edited and translated by Hans H. Gerth. New York: The Free Press, 1951.

Williams, Justin, Sr., John W. Dower, and Howard Schonberger. "A Forum." *Pacific Historical Review* 57, no. 2 (1988).

Williams, Raymond. *Keywords: A Vocabulary of Culture and Society.* Rev. ed. New York: Oxford University Press, 1983.

Yamaguchi Jirō. "Nihon kanryōsei to tennōsei." *Shisō* 797 (November 1990): 183–95.

Yamakawa Hitoshi. "Toward a Democratic Front." *Journal of Social and Political Ideas in Japan* 3, no. 1 (April 1965).

Yamanouchi Yasushi. "Senjiki no isan to sono ryōgisei." In *Nihon shakai kagaku no shisō.* Shakai kagaku no hōhō 3. Tokyo: Iwanami Shoten, 1993.

Yasko, Guy. "Zenkyōtō and the Communist Party: Towards a Materialist Critique of Postwar Democracy." Cornell University, 1994–95.

————. "Beyond the Denial of the Self: The Zenkyōtō Interpretation of Yoshimoto Takaaki." Cornell University, 1994–95.

Ys. See Takakuwa Sumio, *Yuibutsuron to shutaisei.*

Index